GENOCIDE, THE HOLOCAUST, AND ISRAEL-PALESTINE

GENOCIDE, THE HOLOCAUST, AND ISRAEL-PALESTINE

FIRST-PERSON HISTORY IN TIMES OF CRISIS

Omer Bartov

BLOOMSBURY ACADEMIC
LONDON • NEW YORK • OXFORD • NEW DELHI • SYDNEY

BLOOMSBURY ACADEMIC
Bloomsbury Publishing Plc, 50 Bedford Square, London, WC1B 3DP, UK
Bloomsbury Publishing Inc, 1385 Broadway, New York, NY 10018, USA
Bloomsbury Publishing Ireland, 29 Earlsfort Terrace, Dublin 2, D02 AY28, Ireland

BLOOMSBURY, BLOOMSBURY ACADEMIC and the Diana logo are trademarks of
Bloomsbury Publishing Plc

First published in Great Britain 2023
Reprinted 2024, 2025 (twice)

Copyright © Omer Bartov 2023

Omer Bartov has asserted his right under the Copyright, Designs and Patents Act, 1988,
to be identified as Author of this work.

For legal purposes the Acknowledgments on pp. vii–viii constitute an extension
of this copyright page.

Cover image: Photograph: Large vertical crack in the road. © DianaThomas / Stockimo / Alamy

All rights reserved. No part of this publication may be: i) reproduced or transmitted
in any form, electronic or mechanical, including photocopying, recording or by means of
any information storage or retrieval system without prior permission in writing from the
publishers; or ii) used or reproduced in any way for the training, development or operation
of artificial intelligence (AI) technologies, including generative AI technologies. The rights
holders expressly reserve this publication from the text and data mining exception as per
Article 4(3) of the Digital Single Market Directive (EU) 2019/790.

Bloomsbury Publishing Plc does not have any control over, or responsibility for,
any third-party websites referred to or in this book. All internet addresses given in this
book were correct at the time of going to press. The author and publisher regret any
inconvenience caused if addresses have changed or sites have ceased to exist, but can
accept no responsibility for any such changes.

Every effort has been made to trace the copyright holders and obtain permission to
reproduce the copyright material. Please do get in touch with any enquiries or any information
relating to such material or the rights holder. We would be pleased to rectify any omissions in
subsequent editions of this publication should they be drawn to our attention.

A catalogue record for this book is available from the British Library.

Library of Congress Cataloging-in-Publication Data
Names: Bartov, Omer, author.
Title: Genocide, the Holocaust and Israel-Palestine: first person history
in times of crisis / Omer Bartov.
Other titles: First person history in times of crisis
Description: London; New York: Bloomsbury Academic, 2023. |
Includes bibliographical references and index. | Summary: "A multifaceted
exploration of the Holocaust which connects its relationship with
genocide, the importance of first-person histories of atrocity, and links to the
1948 Palestinian Nakba together in unprecedented fashion"–Provided by publisher.
Identifiers: LCCN 2023014042 (print) | LCCN 2023014043 (ebook) |
ISBN 9781350332317 (PB) | ISBN 9781350332324 (HB) |
ISBN 9781350332348 (ebook) | ISBN 9781350332331 (epdf)
Subjects: LCSH: Holocaust, Jewish (1939-1945)–Historiography. | Holocaust,
Jewish (1939-1945)–Personal narratives–History and criticism. |
Genocide–Historiography. | Collective memory. | Collective
memory–Political aspects. | Local history.
Classification: LCC D804.348.B369 2023 (print) |
LCC D804.348 (ebook) | DDC 940.53/18–dc23/eng/20230330
LC record available at https://lccn.loc.gov/2023014042
LC ebook record available at https://lccn.loc.gov/2023014043

ISBN: HB: 978-1-3503-3232-4
PB: 978-1-3503-3231-7
ePDF: 978-1-3503-3233-1
eBook: 978-1-3503-3234-8

Typeset by Newgen KnowledgeWorks Pvt. Ltd., Chennai, India
Printed and bound in the Great Britain

For product safety related questions contact productsafety@bloomsbury.com.

To find out more about our authors and books visit www.bloomsbury.com
and sign up for our newsletters.

CONTENTS

Acknowledgments	vii
List of Abbreviations	ix

Introduction   1

PART I WRITING ATROCITY

1 Historical Uniqueness and Integrated History	11
2 Eastern Europe as the Site of Genocide	21

PART II LOCAL HISTORY

3 Reconstructing Genocide on the Local Level	47
4 Testimonies as Historical Documents	61

PART III JUSTICE AND DENIAL

5 The Holocaust in the Courtroom	83
6 Memory Laws as a Tool of Forgetting	105

PART IV FIRST-PERSON HISTORIES

7 H. G. Adler's (Un)Bildungsroman	123
8 Leaving the Shtetl to Change the World	135

PART V WHEN MEMORY COMES

9 Return and Displacement in Israel-Palestine	151

Contents

10 My Twisted Path to Auschwitz, and Back   **163**

11 Building the Future by Telling the Past   **173**

Notes   205
Select Bibliography   237
Index   239

ACKNOWLEDGMENTS

I would like to thank the following publishers and journals for allowing me to use updated, adapted, revised, or abridged versions of my own previously published book chapters, articles, and essays in this book. Chapter 1 was originally published as, and contains very minor updates to the contents and footnotes of, the chapter "The Holocaust as Genocide: Experiential Uniqueness and Integrated History," in *Probing the Ethics of Holocaust Culture*, edited by Claudio Fogu, Wulf Kansteiner, and Todd Presner (Cambridge, MA: Harvard University Press), 319–31, copyright © 2016 by the president and fellows of Harvard College, used by permission, all rights reserved. Chapter 2 is a revised, updated, and adapted version of "Eastern Europe as the Site of Genocide," *Journal of Modern European History* 80, no. 3 (2008): 557–93. Chapter 3 is a revised, updated, and adapted version of "The Voice of Your Brother's Blood: Reconstructing Genocide on the Local Level," in *Jewish Histories of the Holocaust: New Transnational Approaches*, edited by Norman J. W. Goda (New York: Berghahn Books, 2014), 105–34. Chapter 4 is a revised, updated, and adapted version of "Wartime Lies and Other Testimonies: Jewish-Christian Relationships in Buczacz, 1939–44," *East European Politics and Societies* 25, no. 3 (2011): 486–511. Chapter 5 is a revised and updated version of "Guilt and Accountability in the Postwar Courtroom: The Holocaust in Czortków and Buczacz, East Galicia, as Seen in West German Legal Discourse," *Historical Reflections* 39, no. 2 (2013): 96–123. Chapter 6 is an adapted version of "Criminalizing Denial as a Form of Erasure: The Polish-Ukrainian-Israeli Triangle," in *Memory Laws and Historical Justice*, edited by Ariella Lang and Elazar Barkan (New York: Palgrave, 2022), 195–221. Chapter 7 is a revised and adapted version of "H. G. Adler and First-Person History," in *H. G. Adler: Life, Literature, Legacy*, edited by Julia Creet, Sara R. Horowitz, and Amira Bojadzija-Dan (Evanston, IL: Northwestern University Press, 2016), 119–37, copyright © 2016 by Northwestern University Press, published 2016, all rights reserved. Chapter 8 is a revised and adapted version of "Tales from Half-Asia: Small Town Galicians Encounter the World," *Prooftexts* 37, no. 2 (2019): 469–96. Chapter 9 is a revised and adapted version of "The Return of the Displaced: Ironies of the Jewish-Palestinian Nexus, 1939–1949," *Jewish Social Studies* 24, no. 3 (2019): 26–50. Chapter 10 is composed of a revised, updated, and abridged version of the chapter "My Twisted Way to Buczacz," in *The Holocaust: Voices of Scholars*, edited by Jolanta Abrosewicz-Jacobs (Cracow: Centre for Holocaust Studies, Jagiellonian University, Auschwitz-Birkenau State Museum, 2009), 95–104, and of a revised and abridged version of the unpublished paper "Writing in the Diaspora." Chapter 11 is composed of parts of the essay "From Building a City to Demolishing Homes: Origins and Their Outcomes," *Tikkun—The Jewish, Interfaith and Secular Progressive Voice for Justice, Peace and Environmental*

Acknowledgments

Sanity 33, no. 4 (2018): 62–6; a revised, updated, and heavily abridged version of "From Buchach to Sheikh Muwannis: Building the Future and Erasing the Past," in *Dilemmas of Diversity After the Cold War: Analyses of "Cultural Difference" by U.S. and Russia-Based Scholars*, edited by Michele Rivkin-Fish and Elena Trubina (Washington, DC: Woodrow Wilson International Center for Scholars, 2010), 50–79; and a revised and abridged version of "National Narratives of Suffering and Victimhood: Methods and Ethics of Telling the Past as Personal Political History," originally published in and adapted from *The Holocaust and the Nakba*, edited by Bashir Bashir and Amos Goldberg (New York: Columbia University Press, 2019), 187–205, copyright © 2019 Columbia University Press, reprinted with permission of Columbia University Press.

ABBREVIATIONS

AAN	Archiwum Akt Nowych, Warsaw
AGAD	Archiwum Główne Akt Dawnych, Warsaw
AHR	*The American Historical Review*
AJS Review	*Association for Jewish Studies Review*
AP	*Australian Psychiatry*
AT-OeSt	Österreichisches Staatsarchiv, Vienna
AW	Archiwum Wschodnie, Warsaw
BArch	Bundesarchiv, Germany
BJ	Biblioteka Jagiellońska, Kraków
BR	*Boston Review*
CAW	Centralne Archiwum Wojskowe, Warsaw
CEC	*Cultures d'Europe Centrale*
CEH	*Contemporary European History*
CJ	*Contemporary Jewry*
CL	*College Literature*
CPCS	*Communist and Post-Communist Studies*
CSM	*Christian Science Monitor*
CSP	*Canadian Slavonic Papers*
DATO	State Archives of Lviv Oblast
EEJA	*East European Jewish Affairs*
EEPS	*East European Politics and Societies*
ESF	*European Studies Forum*
FO	Foreign Office, London
FPJ	*Foreign Policy Journal*
GARF	State Archives of the Russian Federation, Moscow
GJICL	*Georgia Journal of International and Comparative Law*
GLA	Generallandesarchiv, Karlsruhe
GLJ	*German Law Journal*
GSP	*Genocide Studies and Prevention*
H&M	*History & Memory*

Abbreviations

HDA SBU	State Archive of the Security Service of Ukraine
HI	Hoover Institution
HLS	Holy Land Studies
HUS	Harvard Ukrainian Studies
IA	Israel Affairs
IDF	Israeli Defense Forces
IS	Israel Studies
ISF	Israel Studies Forum
J.u.NS-V	Justiz und NS-Verbrechen
JAAP	Journal of the American Academy of Psychoanalysis
JGO	Jahrbücher für Geschichte Osteuropas
JGR	Journal of Genocide Research
JHE	Journal of Holocaust Education
JHR	Journal of Holocaust Research
JIH	Journal of Israeli History
JMEH	Journal of Modern European History
JMH	Journal of Modern History
JP	Jerusalem Post
JPS	Journal of Palestine Studies
JQR	Jewish Quarterly Review
JSI	Journal of Social Issues
JSMS	Journal of Slavic Military Studies
JSS	Jewish Social Studies
KA	Kriegsarchiv, Österreichisches Staatsarchiv, Vienna
KTB	Kriegstagebuch (war diary)
LEHR	Law and Ethics of Human Rights
LG	Landgericht
MfS	Ministerium für Staatssicherheit (*Ministry for State Security, GDR*)
MJ	Modern Judaism
MSW	Ministerstwo Spraw Wewnętrznych (Polish Ministry of the Interior)
MSZ	Ministerstwo Spraw Zagranicznych (Polish Ministry of Foreign Affairs)
MV	Mishpat Vetsava
NFA	Neue Feldakten, Österreichisches Staatsarchiv, Vienna
NGC	New German Critique
NJ	Nordisk Judaistik

NP	*Nationalities Papers*
NYREV	*New York Review*
NYT	*New York Times*
OUN	Orhanizatsiya ukrayinskykh natsionalistiv (Organization of Ukrainian Nationalists)
OW	*Ost und West*
P&P	*Past and Present*
PAAA	Politisches Archiv des Auswärtigen Amts, Berlin
POQ	*Public Opinion Quarterly*
PT	*Political Theory*
R.u.S.	Rasse und Siedlung Hauptamt
REES	*The Carl Beck Papers in Russian and East European Studies*
SA	*Strategic Assessment*
Schuma	*Schutzmannschaft* (auxiliary police)
SFV	Shoah Foundation Video collection, University of Southern California
SIPO	Sicherheitspolizei, Security Police
SR	*Slavic Review*
SZ	*Süddeutsche Zeitung*
TNA	The National Archives, Kew, London
TNR	*The New Republic*
TOI	*Times of Israel*
TsDIAK	Central State Historical Archives of Ukraine in Kyiv
TsDIAL	Central State Historical Archives of Ukraine in Lviv
UPA	Ukrainska povstanska armiya (Ukrainian Insurgent Army)
USHMM	United States Holocaust Memorial Museum Archives, Washington, DC
UVO	Ukrainska viiskova orhanizatsiya (Ukrainian Military Organization)
WSJ	*Wall Street Journal*
YFS	*Yale French Studies*
YVA	Yad Vashem Archives, Jerusalem
YVS	*Yad Vashem Studies*
ŻIH	Żydowski Instytut Historyczny

INTRODUCTION

In the past two decades several debates have consumed the attention of scholars writing on genocide, the Holocaust, and the relationship between them. These debates have inevitably and increasingly also spilled over to the case of Israel-Palestine, as well as to questions regarding the politics of memory in Germany and the utility of the genocide and Holocaust paradigms for understanding current international conflicts. At times, interventions in these controversies have been quite theoretical and limited to a community of specialists. There have also been more emotional and polemical interventions that reached the general public and received significant media coverage.

This was the case, for instance, with the so-called Catechism Debate in 2021, sparked by the genocide scholar Dirk Moses, who argued that the German intellectual and academic elite had created a memory cult around the Holocaust that made it impossible to have an open and critical discussion of Israeli policies of oppression against Palestinians. Whether the subsequent controversy of this "German catechism" succeeded in stirring up another *Historikerstreit*—the notorious German historians' debate of the mid-1980s over the uniqueness of the Holocaust—is doubtful, although this seems to have been the intention of Moses and some of his supporters. But it did revive the assertion concerning the malign impact of focusing too much on the "final solution." Whereas German conservatives had previously argued that the Holocaust was being used as a "moral cudgel" against Germany, the new opponents of the "German catechism" suggested that compulsive and self-serving preoccupation with the memory of the Holocaust played a role in perpetuating social injustice internally and distorting German foreign policy, especially vis-à-vis Israel.[1]

Another historical debate that garnered wide public attention was the trial of Polish historians Barbara Engelking and Jan Grabowski for infringing Polish memory laws in a book they coedited, *Night without End*, which contains detailed local studies of the Holocaust in Poland.[2] Often based on personal accounts and testimonies, these contributions by an array of Polish scholars exposed numerous cases of local complicity in denouncing, hunting down, and murdering Jews during Nazi Germany's occupation of Poland. Charged with defaming a particular individual and initially found guilty of "providing inaccurate information," the two scholars were ordered to issue an apology to the man's surviving niece. And although a higher court eventually dismissed the case, arguing that the "courtroom was not the right place for a historical debate," the entire episode had a chilling effect on historians engaged in excavating Poland's "difficult past," as it is often referred to.[3] Moreover, Poland's recent memory laws prohibiting, or at least limiting, discussion of local complicity in anti-Jewish violence also caused a rift with the Israeli government and public, since they appeared to constrain discussion of local Polish connivance, and thus grated against Israeli perceptions of Christian European indifference to or collaboration with the mass murder of the Jews.[4]

These recent debates over the study, commemoration, and politicization of the Holocaust exemplify the urgent issues taken up in this book, examined through five separate perspectives. First, the book assesses the tensions between Holocaust and genocide studies, which have repeatedly both enriched and clashed with each other. Second, it argues for the importance of local history and individual testimony in grasping the nature of mass murder. Third, it critically examines how legal discourse has served to both uncover and deny individual and national complicity. Fourth, it outlines how first-person histories provide a better understanding of events otherwise perceived as inexplicable. Finally, drawing on my own personal trajectory, the book outlines links between the fate of Jews in the Second World War and the plight of Palestinians on the eve and in the immediate aftermath of the establishment of the state of Israel. Put together, I hope to demonstrate that these five perspectives, rarely if ever previously discussed in a single volume, are inextricably linked, and shed much light on each other. Thus the Holocaust and other genocides must be seen as related catastrophes in the modern era; understanding such vast human tragedies necessitates scrutinizing them on the local and personal scale; this in turn calls for historical empathy, accomplished via personal–biographical introspection; finally, such truthful, open-minded, and rigorous introspection, without which historical understanding tends toward obfuscation, brings to light uncomfortable yet clarifying connections, such as that between the Holocaust and the Nakba—the mass flight and expulsion of the Palestinians in 1948.

The book is guided by two related concerns. The first is the attempt to understand the Holocaust both as part of the larger phenomenon of modern genocide and as an event of major impact on the history of Israel-Palestine. The second is the particular methodology of examining these links through the prism of local and first-person history. Indeed, throughout the book I am especially concerned with the relationship between History with a capital *H*—the narrative of events as seen from "above"—and history with a lowercase *h*—the way events are seen, experienced, and narrated from "below," by the protagonists upon whom it is enacted.[5] In this sense, what links the chapters in this book to each other is the focus on the individual in history, the voices of those who were both subjected to and the makers of the tumultuous twentieth century at its moments of greatest crisis. It is through their accounts that we can better understand what otherwise may seem unfathomable and ineffable. In other words, the book attempts to shed light on discrete events in history by presenting them as part of a larger, interconnected matrix, and insisting that such connections can become visible especially when perceived through the eyes of their protagonists. One such protagonist is the author, and in that sense the book also traces my own intellectual and scholarly journey over the past two decades, as I moved from the history of the Second World War to larger themes of comparative genocide, on the one hand, and to the microhistory of the Holocaust, on the other; from German history to interethnic relations in Eastern Europe, and from Jewish history to the ongoing conflict in Israel-Palestine.[6]

While the range of topics covered by this book is vast, its goal is to provide succinct and clear introductions to some of the most complex current debates over genocide and the Holocaust, memory laws, and the connections between the Holocaust and the Nakba, as well as to introduce readers to new approaches and methodologies, especially local history, the use of testimonies, and first-person history. What follows is a brief summary of the chapters, meant to help readers see how the topics they cover are linked to each other and progress from general and theoretical debates to the local and the personal.

Part I, "Writing Atrocity," consists of two chapters on the relationship between the Holocaust and genocide and on the geography of the Holocaust. Chapter 1 focuses on the emergence of the concept of genocide as a paradigm for Western colonialism and hegemony. This view arguably tends to either marginalize the Holocaust as an intra-European event—thereby asserting that its claim for universal significance is Eurocentric—or define it as a colonial genocide akin to many others perpetrated throughout Europe's far-flung empires—thereby dismissing its particular European roots, not least the continent's long anti-Semitic legacy. The chapter then proposes that rather than perceiving "uniqueness" and "integration" as competing concepts, they should in fact be understood as complementary. While each historical event contains unique characteristics, it can only be understood in relationship to others. Accepting that the Holocaust must be seen as part of several longer historical trajectories—of which the history of genocide is one, but not the only one—we must also study it on its own terms and not force it into contexts of limited explanatory value. Finally, the terms integration and uniqueness also refer to the fate of individuals in mass murder, whereby their unique stories must be integrated into the reconstruction of the event so as to undermine the logic of genocide, which seeks to obliterate individual human beings, the unique cultures of the groups they belong to, and their memory.

Chapter 2 scrutinizes the historical and geographical specificity of the Holocaust that is often ignored in comparative genocide studies. In a Europe awash with talk about memory, Eastern Europe retains innumerable sites from which the history of the Jews and of their genocide has been completely erased. The chapter suggests that until recently, this was reflected in a bifurcated Holocaust scholarship, written either from the perspective of the perpetrators or with a focus on the Jews only after their ghettoization, incarceration, and murder. The result has been that for many decades Eastern Europe—which contained the largest concentration of Jews in the world and was the primary site of their mass murder—remained uncharted territory for the most prominent historians of the Holocaust. The chapter further demonstrates that following the fall of communism, East European historiography and public discourse have been pulled between two poles of engagement with the reality of communal genocide hitherto silenced by the communist "anti-fascist" rhetoric, on the one hand, and the revival of local nationalisms that glorify those freedom fighters who had often collaborated with the Germans in the murder of the Jews, on the other. The chapter thus advocates more local studies that will explore the complex, often explosive interethnic relations in Eastern Europe, which largely determined the nature of the Holocaust there.

Part II, "Local History," thus focuses on researching the Holocaust on the local level, and using testimonies as historical documents in such local studies. Chapter 3 introduces my local study of the town of Buczacz in West Ukraine, formerly Eastern Galicia. The chapter argues that such local histories can help us better understand the intimate encounter between the perpetrators and the victims—previously largely ignored thanks to the historiographical focus on the main ghettos and extermination camps, which were specifically designed to minimize such encounters—and to grasp the impact of prewar interethnic relations on the way mass murder was implemented. The chapter shows that the twenty German Security Police personnel who murdered sixty thousand Jews in the Buczacz-Czortków region could have accomplished their task only with extensive local collaboration. It also demonstrates that in the many months prior to the commencement of mass killing, the Germans on the ground, who included whole families of administrators and other officials, had extensive contacts with the local Jews. Since over half of the victims were killed in their town or near it, the genocide was neither anonymous nor secret, but rather intimate and public, constituting a social event, in which the entire community participated in one way or another. This local study, in turn, provides an entirely different understanding of the Holocaust as a whole, since about half of the Jewish victims of the final solution were murdered under similar circumstances.

As Chapter 4 argues, such local studies must rely on extensive use of testimonies, defined here as all forms of evidence provided by individual protagonists in historical events. These include contemporary accounts and diaries, as well as postwar interviews; written, oral, audio, and videotaped testimonies; courtroom witness accounts; and memoirs. The chapter argues that such testimonies must be used as historical documents and were indeed often meant by those who provided them to serve as evidence for events that would have otherwise remained unrecorded, or only documented by the perpetrators. Additionally, the chapter suggests that to overcome the difficulties in using testimonies, they need to be integrated within a larger documentary context, using all available sources. While that is clearly impossible for the Holocaust as a whole, a local study makes it feasible to integrate testimonies in a manner that facilitates the production of a granular and nuanced, three-dimensional reconstruction of genocide at one site, as well as its perception and subsequent memory by the different protagonists and groups. This in turn greatly enhances our understanding of the Holocaust as a whole.

Part III, "Justice and Denial," introduces the fraught issues of legal retribution for genocide and attempts to legislate forms of remembrance that privilege one set of memories and marginalize or even criminalize others. As Chapter 5 demonstrates, genocide trials, especially those held in the Federal Republic of Germany from the late 1950s into the 1970s, also serve as an important source for reconstructing local events such as the mass murder of the Jews of Buczacz. But at the same time, such trials reveal the judicial difficulties of bringing the perpetrators of genocide to justice, as well as the psychological toll taken on survivor witnesses by the encounter with their former tormentors and the skepticism expressed by courts about the value of their testimonies. Ultimately, the chapter argues that these trials, while amassing invaluable documentation for future historians, also created a false picture of the Holocaust, by depicting even those defendants found guilty by the court as "victims of the circumstances of the time," and more often than not portraying survivors as unreliable witnesses. Moreover, because of the quirks of the German criminal code, which had to be used in these trials as a result of Germany's refusal to apply postwar genocide legislation ex post facto, as well as the fact that the courts were staffed by individuals who had lived as adults in Nazi Germany, justice was rarely done even in the few cases when suspects were indicted, years after returning to normal life at the end of the war, or in the even fewer instances of conviction.

If justice was often skewed in the case of genocide perpetrators, Chapter 6 highlights the extent to which the judicial system has also been used to determine which crimes must be remembered and which must not, to the extent that their invocation may be punishable by law. Examining how memory laws in Ukraine, Poland, and Israel are geared toward ensuring remembrance of their respective traumatic pasts, the chapter argues that these three states simultaneously engage in pushing back each other's attempts to claim the moral high ground as victims by legislating against exposure and commemoration of their own crimes. This triangular relationship also entails a balancing act between state-directed politics of memory on the one hand, and group or individual engagement with the past, on the other. What Jews, Ukrainians, and Poles—and, in the case of Israel, Jewish Israelis and Palestinian citizens—may remember as individuals or within their families often greatly differs from what their states legislate as legitimate or illegitimate memories. Historians who employ such personal and collective memories in reconstructing the past may consequently find themselves in direct confrontation with states engaged in memory suppression, even as they simultaneously denounce other states for criminalizing remembrance of their "difficult pasts."

Part IV, "First-Person Histories," examines more closely the effect of telling individual narratives on the reconstruction of the past, and the extent to which such first-person histories revise or undermine conventional perceptions of complex and traumatic pasts. This is hauntingly captured in historian and novelist H. G. Adler's quasi-biographical work *Panorama*, discussed in Chapter 7 as a powerful example of early postwar first-person history. Born in 1910 into an assimilated, German-speaking Jewish family in Prague, Adler peers back through the thick glass of time into his own making and unmaking. He asks, can one reassemble the fragments of a past life into a meaningful existence after the very notion of a shared humanity was dismantled in the camps? Instead of relating the process of coming to understand the world as in a conventional bildungsroman, Adler chronicles his protagonist's growing inability to decipher the world into which he was plunged, where both integration and a lack thereof threaten to strip him of his humanity. He thus remains mentally absent from it, peering at History as a detached observer, even as he watches his own self being mauled by History's fury. Ironically for a historian, Adler concludes that the only true memory of the event is that of those who had experienced it, a memory that will inevitably fade, whereas History, which remains always vivid and transparent, tells him little about himself. Yet from our own vantage point we can say that History provides far less clarity and transparency than Adler had hoped for in the immediate aftermath of the Holocaust, while memory has clung on, refusing to release its hold on the past.

As Chapter 8 illustrates, individual stories often go against the grain of state-imposed politics of memory and provide different, less uniform perspectives on the past that nation-states strive to homogenize. Examining the lives and works of several individuals from Buczacz and its environs—authors Ivan Franko, Karl Emil Franzos, and S. Y. Agnon, scholars David Heinrich Müller and his colleague Sigmund Freud, and socialists and anarchists Anselm Mosler, Max and Siegfried Nacht, and Adolf Langer, aka Ostap Dłuski—all born in the second half of the nineteenth century, this chapter argues that their biographies allow us to reconstitute the fabric of Europe's eastern borderlands on the eve of destruction. By witnessing the aspirations, experiences, and disillusionments of history's protagonists on the margins, we can lend the borderlands a human, experiential texture often missing from the simplified contours of national narratives. What links these figures—and many others of those last three pre-First World War generations—to each other is that in "stepping out into the world" they became heralds of modernity, often seeking to change the remote sites from which they came by transforming the entire universe. Some of them lived long enough to see the destruction that the brave new world—a world they had either sought to create or contemplated with growing horror—eventually wrought on their own communities of origin in what became the "shatterzone of empires."[7]

This brings us to the last part of the book, "When Memory Comes," dedicated to the effects of the reality and memory of collective and personal displacement on understanding the links between the Holocaust and the Nakba. Whereas Adler refused to draw any clear-cut conclusions from personal and collective catastrophe, Zionists perceived the Holocaust as proving the case they had been making since the late nineteenth century. Zionist historiography presents the 1948 "War of Independence" as the culmination of the long Jewish quest for rights and justice, reaching its climax in the immediate aftermath of the Second World War. But as Chapter 9 points out, from its very beginning, settlement in Palestine made for inextricable links between the fate of the Jews in Europe and the fate of Palestine's indigenous inhabitants. If the slaughter of European Jews demonstrated the urgent need for a Jewish nation-state, Jewish national hegemony was established in 1948 by mass expulsion of the Arab majority. Presenting the Nazi genocide of the Jews as an inevitable consequence of the Diaspora, Zionists saw the Palestinian expulsion as a necessary precondition for solving the "Jewish question." Yet once the displaced Jews displaced the Palestinians, they recreated a new version of the old "question." The land became theirs, and they became the majority, but their previously indisputable right to it has come to be increasingly questioned, as the Palestinians refuse to accept the logic of eviction or to forget their homes and their lands. This double displacement means that neither group can be truly at home until it is resolved.

Introduction

The complex links to the land that tie both Palestinians and Israeli Jews to it can best be understood through personal accounts, the sharing of which may perhaps be the only path toward reconciliation and a return to home. One indisputable success of Zionism was the emergence of a first generation of Jewish Israeli citizens born into the new state, a generation to which I belong. Chapter 10 traces my own trajectory from growing up in 1950s Israel, surrounded by Holocaust survivors and fed a steady diet of "negating the Diaspora" and denying the Nakba, through an early scholarly engagement with the myth of the Wehrmacht's "purity of arms," to a growing focus on the transformation of communities of interethnic coexistence in Europe's eastern borderlands into communities of genocide, to finally examining the history of my own generation. Put differently, this chapter follows my scholarly transition from writing a "history from below" on Germany's war in the east, to a local history of my mother's hometown of Buczacz, to a first-person history of my own first generation of Israelis. I argue that the links between these areas of research are just as much methodological and historical as they are personal, in that understanding the conduct of soldiers in war and the fraying of interethnic relations in Eastern Europe provides crucial clues to the study of 1948 and its aftermath.

In the final chapter I sketch out my ideas on writing the story of the first generation of Jewish Israelis and Palestinian citizens of the state as a personal political history, a project in which I am currently engaged. Setting out from Agnon's tale on the origins of his hometown and his notion of ending the Jews' transitory existence by coming to Jerusalem, and then contemplating my own encounter with the ruins of Agnon's hometown in Ukraine and the ruins of Palestinian civilization in my childhood, this chapter contemplates this generation's evolving relationship to the land as a process of overcoming two constitutive negations: that of the pre-Holocaust Diaspora and that of pre-Nakba Palestine. Yet, while the first generation of Israeli Jews emerged as the great "normalizer" of Jewish existence, the first generation of Palestinians born into the state was marginalized through the denial of its cultural and national identity, as well as of the very catastrophe that transformed it into a minority in its own land. These two generational groups are approximately as old as the state, and thus their personal biographies constitute the story of the state's own making. As this chapter argues, by listening to the stories of these generations, both Palestinians and Jews, especially of their gradual coming to terms with the past and overcoming these denials, we can better understand what ties them to the land and thereby also to each other. Moreover, listening to each other's stories and recognizing each other's evolving relationship to the place of their birth can become a first step on the long road to reconciliation. It is these first-person histories of Israel-Palestine that I still hope to write.

PART I
WRITING ATROCITY

CHAPTER 1
HISTORICAL UNIQUENESS AND INTEGRATED HISTORY

This chapter concerns the complex, and at times fraught, relationship between the study of the Holocaust and what has come to be known as genocide studies. In principle, there should not be any tension here. The so-called final solution was clearly a genocide. Indeed, the term "genocide" was coined by the exiled Jewish Polish lawyer Raphael Lemkin while the Holocaust was taking place, and he was obviously influenced in his thinking by this event. Subsequently, the Genocide Convention of 1948 was similarly agreed upon by the United Nations very much under the shadow of the recent genocide of the Jews. But at the same time, both Lemkin and the member states that agreed on the convention understood the Holocaust to be just one, albeit extreme, instance of genocide within the context of a series of such events.[1] The convention was meant to prevent the recurrence of genocide. Clearly it failed in accomplishing this task. And thus, we can say that genocide is a phenomenon that both preceded the Holocaust and has recurred many times since. Each genocide has its own unique characteristics. But they also have many features in common that make them part of the same phenomenon. The genocide of the Jews was one of them.[2]

All this would seem quite clear and obvious. But matters have been complicated both because of the evolving role of the Holocaust in our understanding of twentieth-century European history, and because of the emergence of the concept of genocide as a paradigm for Western colonialism and hegemony. In this chapter my intention is to point out that within the context of debates over the relationship between genocide and the Holocaust, the terms "uniqueness" and "integration," often seen as conflicting with each other, are better understood as complementary. While most historians will agree that unlike scientific experiments, historical events can never be precisely reenacted, the historical method is based on context and comparability. Hence the notion of a unique event that is both incomparable and may not be contextualized threatens to extract it from the very fabric of history and to catapult it into the spheres of metaphysics and myth. Conversely, recognition of the uniqueness of individual actors and experiences is crucial to the reconstruction of the past, especially when dealing with extreme events containing radically different perspectives, where one side attempts to eradicate another and thereby also to wipe out the record of its past existence and destruction—as in the case of genocide. Similarly, while the integration of events and perspectives into a larger matrix of the past is part and parcel of any historical reconstruction, by its very nature the historical method also necessitates making distinctions between these events and perspectives in order to maintain nuance, facilitate judgment, and avoid falling into false or facile parallels.

Over the years, I have become increasingly aware of what I now perceive as the productive tension between experiential uniqueness and historical integration. But clearly it has also produced blind spots, misunderstandings, and disputes. When I arrived at Oxford in 1980 to write a dissertation in modern German history, the Holocaust did not feature on the history curriculum there. At the time, it did not strike me as anomalous. In Israel, where I had my undergraduate training, the Holocaust was still largely taught in departments of Jewish studies rather than as a component of European history. This exclusion of the Holocaust from the history of Europe as a whole was common in most European and American universities as well, and was similarly reflected in historical monographs.[3] Personally, having grown up in Israel at a time when it was saturated with personal traumas and increasing state mobilization of the Shoah, I was, in any case, skeptical about the viability of studying it as an academic field of inquiry. Instead, I chose to research the indoctrination of German combat troops and its impact on their conduct on the Eastern Front of the Second World War, a topic that interested me in part also because of my own experience in the Israeli military.

For the next decade, I taught and wrote about the brutalization of Wehrmacht soldiers, the mass murder of Soviet prisoners of war and citizens, the visions of a demonic Judeo-Bolshevik enemy that permeated the minds of the troops, and the vigorous attempts by German veterans and historians to suppress the war of extermination on the Eastern Front and create a myth of the Wehrmacht's "purity of arms." My work focused on a "view from below," an attempt to understand the mentality and conduct of troops in a number of selected military formations. This entailed empathy—an effort to delve into the minds, grasp the daily experiences, and understand the motivation of those young German men who had internalized such views, committed these crimes, and themselves eventually died in large numbers on the battlefields of the Soviet Union.[4]

By the 1990s, I had become increasingly interested in the wider context of war crimes and genocide in the twentieth century. In particular, I explored the links between the industrial killing of the First World War and the industrial murder of the Second World War, especially as individual experience and representation. In part because of my focus on the origins and nature of modern violence, I grew progressively disenchanted with the common popular representations of the Holocaust, especially in the United State. It appeared to me, as I wrote at the time, that the "common tendency to view the Holocaust as a well-ordered plot, in which antisemitism led to Nazism, Nazism practiced genocide, and both were destroyed in a spectacular, 'happy' end," only "breeds complacency about our own world" and obscures the fact that "ultimately, the world we live in is the same that produced (and keeps producing) genocide."[5]

One reason why the Holocaust refused to recede into the historical past like most other events was that it became part of a fierce "competition of victimhood," in which past victimization was made into a central reference point for identity assertions and restitution claims, and the Holocaust came to be perceived as a measuring rod for all other cases of genocide and crimes against humanity.[6] As I argued in 1998, "in a century that produced more victims of war, genocide, and massacre than all of previous recorded history put together," the victim had become "both a trope and a reflection of reality." This, I thought, was "a dangerous prism through which to view the world, for victims are produced by enemies, and enemies eventually make for more victims."[7] It was for this reason, too, that I found assertions about the uniqueness of the Holocaust unhelpful, indeed harmful, not least because any ranking of victimhood is inherently pernicious and potentially provides license for a vicious cycle of endless retributive violence.[8]

In retrospect, it seems to me that over the years I had been trying to grapple with the phenomenon of modern violence from two distinct but related perspectives. One was that of the individual's experience, which was often obliterated by the vast forces put into play to wreak mass destruction; the other concerned the sociocultural context that bred and rationalized violence, and subsequently also determined the politics of memory.[9] I have come to view individual experience as both unique and representative of the fate of humanity in times of crisis; and I have conceptualized the larger context of violent events as a way of integrating cataclysmic moments of destruction into the historical record, thereby gaining a better understanding of them. Clearly, this double perspective was meant to counter the much-popularized notion that arose out of the First World War—and was subsequently, albeit belatedly, elaborated with even greater force after the Holocaust—of an event so extreme and unique that it defies historical explanation, becomes culturally unrepresentable, and remains perpetually incommunicable as individual experience and thus incomprehensible to humanity as a whole.

As I saw it, both the popular morality tales about the Holocaust, which essentially removed it from the general record of the past by representing it as unique and incomparable, and the more sophisticated arguments about the event as indecipherable and ineffable made it necessary to anchor the Shoah in a larger historical context. But what was the context of the Holocaust? Was it part of German, or Jewish, history? Did it belong to the history of modern genocide, or perhaps of colonial-imperialist war and war crimes? Was it merely a European event or one with universal meanings and implications? The latter was, of course, an old question, manifested by the long-held discomfort of accommodating the Holocaust into specific academic disciplines.[10] And any choice of context had clear implications for the interpretation of the event's place in modern history and its relationship to other cases of genocide. My own approach to it has again been twofold. During the first decade of this century, I directed a multiyear project on interethnic coexistence and violence in Europe's eastern borderlands, which spoke to the larger context of modern violence in that region specifically, and more generally to the relationship between interethnic communities and genocide.[11] During the following decade I wrote a monograph on communal violence in a single site with a focus on individual experience. By employing the method of "a view from below" that I had first used for my work on the Wehrmacht, I explored the collective "biography" of a multiethnic town over an extended period of time, seeking both what held it together and what eventually transformed it from a community of coexistence into a community of genocide. This study too has obvious ramifications for our understanding of numerous other cases of communal violence around the world.[12]

Especially as a consequence of working intensely with testimonies and other personal accounts by survivors of the Holocaust, in recent years I have become all the more aware of the missing dimension of the individual voice of the victim in many studies of genocide, including the Holocaust. Many early works on the final solution focused primarily on the organization of genocide by the perpetrators.[13] More recently, attempts to integrate the multiple perspectives of perpetrators, victims, and bystanders have naturally focused on a single genocide, most often the Holocaust.[14] Conversely, studies that have tried to integrate several genocides in a comparative framework have often felt unable to go beyond the perspective of the perpetrators.[15] This is primarily a methodological issue: even integrated studies of the Holocaust will often choose only certain types of victims' accounts, such as contemporary diaries, and leave out later testimonies and memoirs that are seen as tainted by time and external influences. And even comparative studies of genocide must choose some cases and omit others according to a more or less transparent set of categories.[16]

But here other arguments have also come into play. Some have averred that the Holocaust's claim to "uniqueness" casts a shadow on the study of other genocides and that it therefore must be properly contextualized. It has also been said that this uniqueness assertion emanates from a Western-centric view that perceives a European genocide as essentially different from other genocides; that this view originates in the kind of humanistic discourse that was at the root of colonial expansion, subjugation, and genocide; and that it continues to operate in our postcolonial world by relegating past and present genocides to a secondary position on the scale of inhumanity. Finally, it has been suggested that Israeli leaders and their supporters exploit the focus on the Holocaust to justify Zionist occupation policies of Palestinian lands.[17]

These are not arguments that can or should be easily dismissed. As I have remarked elsewhere, like any other historical event, the Holocaust had both unique features, such as the extermination camps, and features common to many other genocides, such as communal massacres; like any traumatic national event, it was and remains unique within its national context, particularly to the Jews and to some extent also to the Germans.[18] But while I continue to think that presenting the Holocaust as an entirely unique event sacrifices its status as a concrete episode in the annals of human history, that does not mean that its specific historical characteristics should be discarded in order to fit it into an interpretive framework to which it may not necessarily belong. The perceived shadow cast by the Holocaust on other genocides should not compel us to extract it from its own context of origins and circumstances simply so as to minimize its magnitude or to make it more easily comparable to other cases of genocide. Just as the long history of anti-Semitism is not a sufficient explanation for the final solution, so, too, the fact that colonialism predated the Holocaust does not mean that it originated it. This is not to say that the Holocaust was sui generis, but merely that, like all historical events, it had many origins, including imperialism and colonialism, anti-Semitism, and scientific racism, as well as the specific policies and circumstances of the Nazi regime. The very fact that Germany, which had the smallest and most short-lived colonial empire, conducted genocide in Europe, whereas France and Britain, with far larger and older empires, did not, indicates the limits of the colonial interpretation.

Western prejudices and racism certainly played a role in the differing perceptions by Europeans of crimes committed in the colonies and in Europe. That was why Europeans were more shocked by the First World War, in which white men industrially slaughtered other white men (although many colonial soldiers were also involved), than by colonial wars, where white men massacred non-whites in what appeared to many to be nothing more than a manifestation of Western superiority. Because the serial killing of Europeans by each other was more traumatizing to them than the killing of non-Europeans, the genocide of Jews in Europe by a perceived civilized European state in a modern, bureaucratic, and industrial manner was also shocking. And yet the responses of many Europeans to the "removal" of Jews from their midst also indicated that Jews were still seen by wide sectors of European society as alien, foreign, and potentially dangerous. It can also be argued that precisely because popular anti-Semitism had made the "disappearance" of the Jews more easily acceptable during the Holocaust, in the postwar period, the remnants of this sentiment, combined with the shame of complicity, contributed to the urge to universalize the Holocaust rather than viewing it as a specifically anti-Jewish undertaking in the heart of European civilization.

A rather different position contends that the Holocaust's "claim to uniqueness" relates it to "a long tradition of the West's attempts to universalize its own values," and that it was "those very claims to universalism" that "have themselves been at the heart of Europe's violent interaction with the rest of the world."[19] Indeed, it has also argued that this claim to uniqueness creates a "benign view" of "colonial and imperial wars" and conflicts, which "precludes the question of genocide by equating it with the Holocaust of European Jewry."[20] In other words, it is suggested that whether by evoking the universal (Western) implications of the Holocaust or by emphasizing its unique extremity, crimes committed by colonial and postcolonial powers are marginalized and minimized. At the same time, attempts have been made to both find a direct link between colonial genocides and the Holocaust, and to present the Holocaust itself as a colonial undertaking.[21]

As I noted above, there is little doubt that violence against or by non-Western groups had often been, and continues to be, marginalized in the West for reasons that date back to colonial times, and clearly have to do with a Western sense of innate superiority and deeply ingrained notions about the depravity, backwardness, and violent predilections of non-Westerners. Whether assertions about the uniqueness of the Holocaust have much to do with this is less clear. It is also not entirely obvious that presenting the Holocaust as a colonial genocide akin to such events elsewhere has much analytical value. I have argued elsewhere that "the differences between what happened in Poland in 1939–44 and, say, German Southwest Africa in 1904, are so vast that putting them both in the same explanatory framework of genocidal colonialism does not appear particularly useful."[22] This is, of course, not to deny that various connections might be traced between colonial genocides and the Holocaust, even though scholars have found it difficult to establish direct links.[23] Nor should one dismiss the importance of precedent and practice. Indeed, the genocide of 1904 had the distinction of being the first such case in the twentieth century, as well as of being carried out by a modern Western military organization that announced its intention to exterminate an African group. But a systematic comparison between colonial genocides and the Holocaust may well reveal more differences than similarities.

Jürgen Zimmerer, a German expert of Southwest Africa, has offered a judicious assessment of the relationship between the genocide of the Herero and the Holocaust. As he puts it, "there are no monocausal explanations for Nazi crimes, nor is there a linear progression from German colonialism to the murder of the European Jews." Rather, "the colonial example illustrates the genocidal potential already present in parts of the bureaucratic and military institutions of Germany." Furthermore, "colonialism produced a reservoir of cultural practices that the Nazi thugs could appropriate for themselves," or could at least "legitimize their actions by pointing to similarities with colonial time." Hence, "of the numerous routes that fed the criminal policies of National Socialism, one originated in the colonies, and that path was neither minor nor obscure."[24] Here, Zimmerer illustrates both the value and the limitations of seeking the colonial roots of the Holocaust. He rightly implies that earlier generations of Holocaust scholars had missed this important connection; and yet he also concedes that no direct links between one event and another can be established or, indeed, need to be, not least because the genocide of the Jews also had deep European roots that were either only marginally or not at all related to overseas colonialism.

But can one see the Holocaust itself as a colonial undertaking, or part of an even greater colonization project? This has certainly been argued by some scholars of Nazi Germany and the final solution, who have suggested that the genocide of the Jews was part of a vast plan to entirely alter the demographic structure of Eastern Europe by ethnically cleansing its mostly Slav populations and resettling it with ethnic Germans. The plan could not be implemented because of Germany's inability to win the war against the Soviet Union, and the only part of it that was fully carried out was the extermination of the Jews. This is not the place to discuss this interpretation, which has fruitfully contextualized the Holocaust within German wartime and colonization policy, yet has also been shown to have significant limitations as a comprehensive explanation of the Nazi genocidal dynamic against the Jews. But it is an important contribution to our understanding, adding a Nazi colonial dimension that was lacking from earlier interpretations.[25]

Some genocide scholars have pushed this interpretation further than most German scholars would go, suggesting that the Nazi occupation of Europe as a whole was a colonial undertaking akin to overseas colonialism, in which Europeans suddenly found themselves treated as colonial subjects by the Germans, leading them to revolt against oppression and exploitation. This view seems to elide the vast differences between the German occupation of such countries in Eastern Europe as Poland, which was completely devastated, and such Western European countries as France, which officially collaborated with the Nazi regime and experienced little relative damage by the Germans. It also suggests that Nazi policies toward European Jews were essentially the same as those practiced against non-Jews, in that all were treated as colonial subject, whereas in fact, Jews were targeted for genocide and suffered greater relative loss of life than any other European group with the possible exception of the much smaller Sinti and Roma population. As one genocide scholar writes, "many Europeans were prepared to participate in the Nazi anti-Bolshevik reconfiguration of the continent and were only pushed into non-cooperation or resistance by the Nazis' policies of plunder, which ... were experienced as colonial"; they were "only shocked by Nazism when it treated them—including Jews—as colonial subjects to be exploited, enslaved and murdered." But this equal treatment of all Europeans, it is claimed, "was screened out by depicting the Nazi genocide of the Jews as a massive hate crime." And it was this focus on the Jews that subsequently "promoted blindness to genocidal episodes around the world because they did not resemble the Holocaust."[26]

In his important study of the Nazi occupation of Europe, historian Mark Mazower has offered a useful distinction between the European overseas empires and Hitler's Europe. The former, he writes, "had generally grown up over long periods of time, in what were still largely rural societies." They "involved complex accommodations and compromises with local and native rulers, and ... were themselves coming under strain in the interwar period from emergent colonial nationalist movements." Conversely, the German occupiers of Europe "imposed their rule very suddenly in the midst of a war and ... chose to inflict this on urbanized societies which had powerfully shaped and already formed senses of their own national identity. What was striking," he stresses, "was not that Europeans resisted, but that they were mostly so hesitant to do so."[27]

Consequently, Mazower is critical of Aimé Césaire, whose own ideas have influenced some current genocide scholars. Césaire, he writes, argued that Europeans "had needed Nazism, in a sense, to bring home to them what racial prejudice produced. They had failed to grasp the true nature of colonialism because racism had prevented them sympathizing with the plight of those they oppressed. They tolerated 'Nazism before it was inflicted on them ... because, until then, it had been applied only to non-European peoples.'"[28] In fact, observes Mazower, "while Victorian international law legitimized colonial rule, it did so by holding out the promise of liberation," even if this was "a theory that was generally honoured only in the breach." Conversely, "it was this promise of eventual (if always tenuous) political redemption that Nazism decisively rejected," since it was "based upon the immutable truths of racial hierarchy," and "the only alternative it envisaged to domination was oppression and national death." In this sense, the Nazis were "tearing down the whole noble façade of nineteenth-century international law."[29]

This is an important distinction and, as Mazower also suggests, many Europeans, who were in fact treated by the Nazis neither as badly as certain colonial subjects nor, much more visibly, as their Jewish neighbors, eventually came to the conclusion that once the Jews were gone, they might be next.[30] But one should add that while this thinking applied to certain Slav populations, such as the Poles, who were from the beginning treated abysmally by the Germans—but not, for instance, to the Croats, who were allied with Germany—it did not quite apply to western and northern Europeans, who were never under any threat of extermination and, in many cases, would have been welcomed with open arms into the fold of an Aryan empire. Moreover, the growing resistance to collaboration with the final solution was largely fueled by rising fears of Allied retribution in view of an increasingly likely German defeat.

Alongside the view that the Holocaust can be related to past colonial genocides, and that it was itself part of a German colonial undertaking akin to other European colonial ventures, is the assertion that the genocide of the Jews, and especially insistence on its uniqueness, has served to justify the Zionist colonization of Palestine. This, too, is anything but a vacuous argument; there is little doubt that in Israeli political and educational rhetoric the slogan "never again" has been used both to legitimize the existence of the state as a haven for the Jews, and for giving it license to use any means needed to protect its existence. Parallels made by Israeli leaders and propagandists between such Palestinian organizations as the PLO and Hamas and the Nazis abound, just as Palestinian propaganda and anti-Israeli spokespeople and demonstrators in the West have a penchant for drawing parallels between Israeli and Nazi policies.

This kind of rhetoric is largely confined to the admittedly well-publicized realm of political demagogy, indoctrination, and ideological overkill. There are certainly colonial and racist undertones to right-wing and settler pronouncements and actions in Israel; and there are clear anti-Semitic undertones to radical Islamic and European right- and left-wing anti-Israel rhetoric. The shadow of Nazism and the Holocaust rests heavily on everyone, and true to its nature, Nazism has a poisoning effect on all who exploit it. But the question is to what extent this predilection has also affected Holocaust historiography. To be sure, since the nineteenth century, historians have been deeply complicit, indeed, have often played a major role in the creation of ethnocentric nationalism, and Israeli historians have been no exception. But it is clearly an exaggeration to suggest, as one scholar does, that Israeli Holocaust "historiography is as much an ethical discourse, indeed a political theology, as a secular investigation."[31]

One must also doubt that most Holocaust scholars would see themselves as belonging to either one of the "two rival narratives about the meaning of the Holocaust and the course of modern global history" that ostensibly dominate the discourse: one that "links Holocaust memory both to the universal values of human rights and the particular geopolitical agenda of Israel"; and another that "regards the Holocaust less as a racially-driven genocide against a helpless minority than the logical outcome of imperial-racial conquests that it holds Zionism to embody."[32] Instead, I would argue that this is a fatuous either–or view of Holocaust historiography, which reflects a tendency among some genocide scholars to perceive the Holocaust more as mobilized memory than as a historical event. In this sense, the call for the Holocaust to be "deprovincialized from its signification within an exclusively Jewish and western narrative about the triumphant achievement of human rights and genocide prevention" seems to reflect a frustration with the Holocaust as allegedly constituting an obstacle to fighting injustice in today's world.[33]

Much of this debate curiously boils down to a very specific historical question, namely, did the Nazis target the Jews for genocide in a manner that was essentially different from their treatment of any other group under their rule? This purely factual question appears to be important not only in analyzing Nazi policies but because different answers to it seem to affect the status of the Holocaust as unique. There can be little doubt that the Jews played a singular role in the Nazi *imaginaire* and that German Jewish policies distinguished them within the Nazi universe of murder and fantasy;[34] but other groups clearly have been similarly targeted in other genocides. Hence, in order to assert the comparability of the final solution with other genocidal undertakings, there is no need to speak of a "uniqueness myth that the Nazis intended the total destruction of the Jews,"[35] not least because most scholars of Nazism and the Holocaust would agree that the Nazi genocidal project was no myth.[36] Nor do all genocide scholars agree on this point. As one prominent genocide historian asserts, he had "always recognized the extremity of the Holocaust relative to other genocides ... the extreme fervor of the Nazi pursuit of Jews across national boundaries, and the totality of the desire ... to murder all Jews on whom hands could be laid." He thus rightly concludes that "the extent of the 'final solution' was ... shaped by an antisemitism that was colored by a different element over and above the racism and ethno-nationalism that explains the murder of other groups by Nazi Germany—that element being the view of 'the Jews' as an implacable, collective world enemy."[37]

To be sure, this makes the Holocaust unique only within the context of the Nazi empire—and even under Hitler's rule things might have transpired differently under different circumstances—but not a unique, albeit certainly a very extreme form of genocide, if one may apply such an adjective to the "crime of crimes." It certainly should not give license to create "a hierarchy that hinders the integrated study of genocides."[38] But while this warning by genocide scholars should be heeded, there does not seem to be much danger of such a hierarchy being maintained within the scholarly community (as opposed to political rhetoric). The difficult task is rather to create integrated histories of genocide—specific cases as well as comparative studies—that would do justice both to the perspectives of all protagonists and that would analytically sketch out differences and similarities between the variety of genocides that have plagued and keep plaguing our world.

The Holocaust was one of several major genocides in the twentieth century. As noted, it was particularly extreme, and aspects of it were and have remained unprecedented, most especially the extermination camps. Some aspects of it were remarkably similar to other genocides, and have repeatedly occurred, such as communal massacres. As an event, it was highly complex and transpired in a variety of very different contexts—the killing of Jews in a little town in Galicia, the transport of Jews from Paris to Auschwitz, the Romanian massacres of Jews in Transnistria, and the starvation of Jews in the ghettos of Poland were all part of the same genocide but also vastly different, as were the Jewish communities that experienced these atrocities.

To my mind, the history of the Holocaust, which was a European genocide in the middle of the twentieth century, is quite different from that of the Herero genocide in German Southwest Africa at the beginning of that century, or that of the Rwandan genocide toward its end. They were, of course, connected in various ways, although often these links are difficult to establish.[39] But they were also related to their own particular histories, and must be analyzed and understood within their specific historical and geographical contexts. For this purpose, they need to be studied not just by scholars of Holocaust studies or of genocide studies, but by area specialists who know the languages and histories of the perpetrators and victims. I still believe, as I did at the beginning of my own scholarly journey, that historians should not start off by specializing in an event but rather in a place and a time. Most important, they should be careful and meticulous with their facts, especially when these facts concern the mass murder of millions.

Having spent decades studying modern violence, I am still grappling with the complexities of writing an integrated history of genocide. Over the years, I have always sought to identify the individual human being upon whom history is enacted, but who, at the same time, is also its maker. I have never believed in unique events, but always highlighted the singular, personal experience that, collectively, makes up the fabric of human history. Perhaps because of my recent preoccupation with the history of communal violence in a single town, I have become increasingly aware, as I commented some time ago, that

> from the local perspective, it does not matter much which genocide one writes about; we will often encounter the same ethnically and religiously mixed communities, external forces triggering outbursts of communal massacres, and many instances of complicity and rescue, collaboration and resistance. But the witnesses of such events will also bring out the uniqueness of their experiences as individuals, as members of communities, of groups, of nations—a uniqueness that was denied them by the killers.[40]

As I see it, precisely because genocide is about the destruction of groups as such, it is the duty of the historian to rescue these groups from oblivion, even if only in history and memory. One way to oppose the will of the *génocidaires* to obliterate both the existence *and* the memory of their victims is to let the victims speak and to listen to their voices, not least because they demand to be heard, and then to write down their accounts and integrate them into the historical record for the sake of a fuller reconstruction of the event. It is not true that history is always the story of the powerful and victorious; but it is up to historians to collect and record, write and integrate the fates of those who were trampled upon and destroyed.[41]

CHAPTER 2
EASTERN EUROPE AS THE SITE OF GENOCIDE

Sites of Nonmemory—Memory without Sites

In many parts of contemporary Eastern Europe, one finds today innumerable sites from which vast chunks of history have been completely erased. The few who still remember, and others who know of this vanished past find very few physical traces on the ground. Crucial bits of evidence are missing—the sites of the killing, the houses and property of the deported, the bodies of the murdered. To be sure, the bodies, if not burned, are buried in mass graves, usually not far from where the murdered had lived; the property houses those who moved in after the murdered were taken away, and its condition has in many cases hardly changed; the sites of life and of death are generally if vaguely known. But these are not sites of memory, and never were. They are, in fact, sites of forgetting.

The memory of Jewish life and death in many towns and cities in Eastern Europe is therefore detached from the sites in which life was lived and murder perpetrated. Those who remember or know are not there; those who are there neither remember nor know (nor want to know). But the current inhabitants of these sites are hardly indifferent to memory. Indeed, they are engaged in creating their own sites of memory, sites from which the previous inhabitants and victims are blatantly absent, and must be absent, so as to facilitate the creation of a new memory, a new history, a new commemorative culture. Especially in such regions as West Ukraine, the vanished sites of Jewish life and death are being rapidly replaced by one-sided, invented, or expurgated histories of events that either never took place or took place in ways very different from those presently being commemorated.[1]

This is a somewhat unexpected condition in a Europe that is awash with talk about memory, commemoration, and representation. It is no less baffling because since the early 1990s enormous numbers of hitherto inaccessible documents have become available in archives freed from communist control and censorship. But freedom of information does not prevent its abuse, and liberation from communist dictatorship has also liberated nationalist sentiments, resentments, and prejudices. Moreover, the newly skewed nationalist narratives of the past have not only replaced the previous skewed narratives provided by the communists but have also at times chosen to conceal and forget precisely the same elements of that past. Many of those who erased then are erasing now, though with other rationalizations and goals, just as those who remembered then remember now, though their numbers are rapidly diminishing.

Meanwhile, the effects of biology and the erosion of nature, and a certain economic upswing in regions that preserved some remnants of the past simply because no one had the means to either build new edifices or to destroy the old, are all taking their toll.

Soon even the shadow of the shadow of these sites will vanish in concrete form and in the mind's eye. Yet, despite years of scholarship on memory and commemoration, and after literally millions of pages on the genocide of the Jews, the actual areas in which the murdered lived and in which they were murdered have received and are still receiving little attention both as historical sites and as sites of memory: so much for the cunning of history. Just as astonishing, until recently, the recorded voices of those who experienced firsthand the destruction of that world have all too often been treated with suspicion or ignored by many members of the historical profession, even as they privileged the ostensibly more objective documents emanating from Nazi files. This, to my mind, can only be seen as another version of the betrayal of the historians. In what follows I try, as briefly as possible, to outline some of the main issues entailed in this conundrum concerning the relationship between memory and site, documentation and forgetting, professional conventions and historical responsibility.

Bifurcated Scholarship

One of the more curious aspects of the historiography of the Holocaust is the relationship between the site on which the genocide of the Jews was perpetrated and the main focuses of historical research. For many decades, the most influential historical monographs written on the Holocaust focused on two types of protagonists: the perpetrators and the victims. The main perpetrators were of course the Germans, even if they were assisted by a variety of collaborators. Hence, research on the perpetrators linked them to the history of Germany and the evolution of Jewish policies by the Nazi regime.[2] Conversely, though the majority of the Jewish victims were in fact from Eastern Europe, scholars were more interested in their fate once they had been enclosed in ghettos and camps. From this perspective, it did not matter where the Jews came from, since they were supposedly cut off from the surrounding population.[3]

The result of this bifurcated Holocaust scholarship has been that Eastern Europe—even as it was recognized as both containing the largest concentration of Jews in the world and as the site of their mass murder—remained a largely uncharted territory for the most prominent historians of the Holocaust.[4] It was quite possible to study the bureaucracy and administration of the final solution with almost no knowledge of such crucial countries as Poland. The languages, history, politics, relations between different ethnic groups and denominations, as well as the prevalence and influence of anti-Semitism in the lands of Eastern Europe, received scant attention in such works. That there was in fact a growing mass of scholarship especially on Polish-Jewish relations before and during the Holocaust did not seem to have much of an effect on the grand narrative tradition of Holocaust historiography or on the major trends of interpretation and historical perspectives.[5] In some ways, this neglect of the peoples on whose territory genocide was enacted paralleled the inclination to write the history of the Holocaust with its victims left out. Thus many historians felt that while it was incumbent on them to reconstruct the decision-making process in the German leadership and possibly also to investigate the motivation of lower ranking killers, no knowledge of the exterminated Jewish populations was necessary in order to explain the event.[6] And, indeed, once the victims could be ignored, there was little reason to be interested in the relationship between the victims and their Gentile neighbors, since the latter seemed to matter even less than the Jews in explaining the process of implementing genocide.

Presented in this manner, the historiography of the Holocaust—often seen as richer, more innovative, sophisticated, and varied, than that of any other modern genocide—appears astonishingly narrow and constrained. The Holocaust, after all, was an international project, taking place as it did across an entire continent, involving the registration, systematic despoliation, transfer, incarceration, and murder of millions of citizens residing in the European countries occupied by or allied with Nazi Germany. Implementing this genocide thus entailed intricate negotiations between governments, complex bureaucratic and administrative arrangements, coordination between law enforcement agencies and military authorities, and the introduction of economic measures for looting and distributing property as well as for the exploitation of helpless forced labor. The material benefits of mass murder bought off the domestic German population, paid for the killing of those whose assets were robbed, financed much of the occupation of foreign lands, and bribed or silenced the occupied populations that resented foreign rule but enjoyed the profits of genocide.[7] Such exploitation and manipulation linked in myriad ways entire European populations that became exposed to, complicit in, or resistant to the systematic murder of a people. Add to this the obvious though for long underestimated fact that the Holocaust cannot be understood without tracing its imagery, fantasies, passions, and phobias, as well as practices and legislation, to medieval Europe and centuries of Christian anti-Jewish theology, incitement, and demagogy. The resulting powerful *imaginaire* was doubtlessly shared to a greater or lesser degree by the vast majority of Europeans.[8]

Hence the very idea that a historian could presume to write the history of the Holocaust without much knowledge of the cultures, languages, traditions, and politics of the people that was murdered, or of the peoples in whose midst the killing took place, or of the lands in which the majority of the victims had resided is truly remarkable. And yet, this has probably been the single most obvious characteristic, the most easily identifiable common denominator, of the scholarship on the Holocaust until quite recently. In a certain sense, this one-sided view of the event has revealed much more about the scholars involved in reconstructing it than about the nature of the event itself, although it is also related to the enormous geographical scale of this genocidal undertaking. Conversely, while those works that do focus on the victims often pay a great deal of attention to Jewish culture, traditions, responses to genocide, and the struggle to survive, they rarely examine in any detail the relationship between Jewish populations and their local Gentile surroundings. Generalizing assertions about Gentile anti-Semitism or rescue, collaboration or resistance can be found both in accusatory and in apologetic works; but systematic analyses of the triangular relationship between Jews, local Gentiles, and the German perpetrators are quite rare. Testimonies and other personal accounts are normally employed as anecdotal evidence rather than being subjected to a more rigorous examination and thus, unsurprisingly, tend to sustain otherwise contradictory interpretations.[9] The fact that the mass of the Gentile population was often hardly a unified block, but was divided into different and not seldom conflicting ethnic groups, religious affiliations, and classes (related in large part to the differences between the urban and rural populations), is again often missed in this literature.

This is not to say that there has been no East European scholarship on the Holocaust. Indeed, since the original version of this chapter was published in 2008, there has been a considerable increase in such works, especially as regards Poland, although the recent swing to the right in that country may have a deleterious impact on this development. But until quite recently, this literature has suffered from two related problems. First, for many years after the end of the Second World War the division of the continent into two blocks made it exceedingly difficult to do research in the archives of Eastern Europe. This limitation was felt both by West and East European scholars. Moreover, the communist narrative of the war left no room for the unique fate of the Jews during the Nazi occupation, instead folding it into the general narrative of "fascist" crimes and the victimization of the nation's citizens. In order to legitimize the establishment of alleged socialism—which became for all practical purposes nothing but communist dictatorships—in Eastern Europe, it was necessary to describe the majority of the population as innately anti-fascist. The very idea that there might have been any kind of popular complicity in the genocide of the Jews, let alone that anti-Semitic sentiments remained close to the surface in the postwar period, was anathema to the communist regimes established in Eastern Europe and unacceptable in the Soviet Union. Indeed, precisely because this heritage was not discussed and aired even as evidence of its reality was still visible for all to see, outbreaks of anti-Semitism in such countries as Poland continued after the war, both in the immediate aftermath of the Holocaust as in the cases of the pogroms in Kraków and Kielce, and decades later, when anti-Semitism was used as a political tool by the regime of Władysław Gomułka in 1968.[10]

Second, Eastern Europe, whether in its new guise as the communist part of the continent or in its previous image as the continent's more backward region—often seen by its neighbors to the west as at best only tenuously European—simply did not seem to merit any serious scholarly attention in discussions over the history and memory of the Holocaust.[11] Vehement scholarly controversies over this or that aspect of the Holocaust were peculiarly silent about Eastern Europe, exhibited a general indifference to the scholarship produced there, and remained reluctant to examine the role of East European countries in the complex matrix of continent-wide genocide. Conversely, even as such countries as Poland began looking into their past in a more critical manner, the often heated debates conducted there were hardly echoed in the West.[12] If we examine, for instance, the main proponents of the influential "intentionalist" and "functionalist" schools, as well as their primary research focuses, we find that neither the languages of Eastern Europe nor their histories and interethnic relations played any role in the articulation of these theories.[13] It was as if the Holocaust had happened on another planet, rather than in the heart of (Eastern) Europe.

It should be added that especially among Jewish historians the early postwar generation in fact included many scholars who had an intimate knowledge of the regions in which the Holocaust was perpetrated, not least because they often came from there, either shortly before the war or as survivors of the Shoah.[14] But the impact of the scholarship written by these historians on the contextualization of genocide within the social milieu of the victims is open to question. This has to do with several factors. First, some of these historians became associated with Yad Vashem in Jerusalem, an institution that especially in its early years perceived itself as committed to the pursuit of the political–ideological goals of Zionism even as it asserted that objective research on the Holocaust would inevitably serve to legitimize the Zionist worldview. Whatever one might think of this observation, it clearly established a very narrow prism through which to observe the Holocaust and its sociocultural context.[15]

Second, thanks to their background and their experiences, some of these scholars shared the prejudices of the regions from which they stemmed. In other words, intimate knowledge also brought with it shared views and biases. Whether it had to do with resentment against Polish Gentiles or against traditional Jews, such preconceptions imported from the "old world" could be detrimental to a more balanced and nuanced view of the social context of the Holocaust.[16] Third, for reasons that must be both objective and psychological, several scholars of this generation were greatly influenced by German historiography on Nazism and the Holocaust. This is all the more striking because these historians often disagreed with their German colleagues, not least because the latter offered a radically different view of the Holocaust and its interpretation and were openly suspicious of "Jewish" scholarship on the event in general and especially of its perceived focus on the experience of the victims.[17] Still, not unlike their German counterparts, Jewish scholars of the older generation rarely investigated the triangular relationship between Jews, local Gentiles, and Germans.

The focus of Yad Vashem on the Jewish experience led to the production of important works in Jewish history, and in that respect its historians distinguished themselves sharply from German scholars.[18] But the self-perception of German historians—belonging both to the older and younger generations—as providing a paradigm of objective and professional scholarship, and their reluctance to examine the distinct interethnic relations on the ground as an important factor in reconstructing and understanding the Holocaust, greatly influenced both the older and the younger generation of Jewish historians as well. And as the generation that traced its roots to the scene of the massacre slowly exited the scene, the younger men and women who took over were generally far less familiar with Eastern Europe and lacked the requisite linguistic skills, even as many of them maintained both strong biases against Eastern Europe, and especially Poland, and remained fascinated with Germany. The "land of the perpetrators" seemed much more interesting than the land in which genocide was perpetrated; and the scholarship produced there provided a much more attractive model. For a long time, then, the German perpetrators drew much more attention than the Eastern Jews or their Gentile neighbors.

Opening Pandora's Box

This situation has begun to change, especially after the fall of communism. The two conditions that worked against linking the history of the Holocaust with that of Eastern Europe (and, more generally, linking the history of West-Central Europe with that of East-Central Europe) no longer existed. First, access to East European and Russian archives became much more readily available, although in the latter case access has once more become increasingly restricted. Second, and related to the greater availability of sources, Western views of Eastern Europe as a place of little interest have been transformed. Many younger West European, American, and Israeli scholars have turned their attention to the "dark side" of the continent and discovered mountains of unexamined files, a long string of unanswered—and quite often also unasked—questions, and, not least, encountered a new generation of East European scholars eager to collaborate with them. Communist taboos over approaching the "Jewish question," researching the Holocaust as an event distinct from the war and discussing the fate of Jewish victims separately from that of other victims of Nazism were gradually lifted. Meanwhile a growing consensus in Western Europe on the centrality of the Holocaust culminated in a resolution by the European Parliament calling upon all member countries to commemorate and teach the event. This decision transformed the preoccupation with the Holocaust—already quite visible in much of West-Central Europe—into a precondition for entry into the European Union, a major political goal for most of the countries just emerging from decades of communist rule.[19]

All this would have been very good news for the historiography of the Holocaust had many of the old prejudices, biases, and constraints not been transferred more or less intact to this new era. Moreover, this all-too-smooth transition was accompanied by the resurfacing of a much older and deeper layer of images and memories that the previous communist regimes had suppressed for many decades. Here was the conundrum: as long as the communists ruled, they did not allow any open discussion of the fate of the Jews, even as they often pursued anti-Semitic policies. Once the communists were gone, the renewed public preoccupation with the Jews opened up the Pandora's Box that the communists had kept tightly sealed. In such countries as Germany and France, the eventual exposure of the myths and legends of the past largely discredited those myths; but Eastern Europe's stale old demons sought out a new, young constituency lacking personal memories of a murderous past and relying on sparse and often distorted historical knowledge. Streamlined and adjusted to contemporary circumstances, these indefatigable fabrications and conspiracy theories forged another link between the old and the new. This, too, has revealed the urgent necessity of including Eastern Europe in any new discussion of the Holocaust.

This need was of course most clearly demonstrated in the case of Jan Gross's study *Neighbors* and the debate that raged around it in Poland. Gross insisted on the Polish-Jewish aspect of the Holocaust, whereas scholarship in general had stressed the direct link between Germans and Jews as the only one worth pursuing. The scandal of revealing a massacre of Jews by their Polish neighbors was that it transformed innocent or at least indifferent bystanders into perpetrators, neighbors into killers, and Polish citizens—traditionally seen as both heroic resisters and innocent victims—into tools of Nazi genocidal policy.[20] The debate was also quite curious because the story of Jedwabne was hardly unknown, and instances of participation by local East European populations in the mass murder of the Jews were well documented and increasingly available to the public.[21] Beyond exposing the lies and obfuscations of generations of historians, intellectuals, politicians, and the media, Gross also struck a powerful blow at the very category of "bystander."[22] Indeed, it was precisely such regions as Eastern Europe—where Jewish populations were dense, killing was massive, and non-Jews were also both threatened and often brutalized by violence, prejudice, and poverty—that the slippage from bystander to perpetrator, from passivity to participation, from empathy to profit taking was too great to warrant the use of this term as anything more than an apologetic turn of phrase.

Here is another curious aspect of Eastern Europe's centrality as the site of the Holocaust. The late 1990s saw two important and painful debates: both focused on the Holocaust in Eastern Europe, and in both the dispute was between those who condemned the newly identified perpetrators for the mass murder of the Jews and those who blamed the Soviets and their alleged Jewish collaborators for bringing violence upon themselves in retaliation for their own brutalities during the Soviet occupation of 1939–41. The Jedwabne debate undermined the myth of Polish innocence, heroism, and martyrdom; the Wehrmacht debate shattered the legend of the German army's purity of arms and detachment from Nazi ideology and genocide.[23] The argument over the Wehrmacht's complicity in genocide concerned Eastern Europe only to the extent that the events on which it focused occurred in the east; it was very much a confrontation with German identity, guilt, and generational conflict. The fact that the atrocities carried out in those towns were also perpetrated by (mostly Ukrainian but also Polish) local citizens was merely an aspect of the German debate.

Conversely, the Jedwabne controversy was directly about the relationship between the site of genocide and those who carried it out and profited from it; it too was crucially about identity, self-image, and the sustaining but false narrative of the past. But the new narrative introduced Poles—and by extension other East Europeans—into the Holocaust as active protagonists rather than as passive bystanders, victims, or resisters. From this perspective, the Jedwabne debate was far more important to rewriting the Holocaust than the Wehrmacht controversy.

Finally, just as the Jedwabne debate seems to have had little effect on the German historiography of the Holocaust, so the debate on the Wehrmacht exhibition, discussed in more detail in Chapters 10 and 11, seems to have had little effect on the scholarship of the Holocaust in Ukraine. Indeed, in the town of Złoczów (Zolochiv), where one of the massacres shown at the exhibition occurred, the historical exhibit remains unchanged, portraying Ukrainians as victims of the Bolsheviks and not mentioning anywhere the massacre of the Jewish population of the town by their own neighbors—a massacre whose scale was in fact much larger than that of Jedwabne.[24]

Communal Massacre

How then can we bring Eastern Europe into the historiography of the Holocaust in a manner that will both contribute to our knowledge and understanding of the event and at the same time link together several historiographies that for long have been either entirely separated from each other or have only intersected at moments of dispute and controversy? Can we understand the relationship between the Holocaust and Eastern Europe not merely from the geographical perspective of a region that happened to be the site of genocide but by investigating the local circumstances and specific nature of mass killing in a territory where the majority of Europe's Jews had lived for centuries in mixed ethnic and religious communities? Finally, to what extent is our understanding of this explosion of violence influenced by the fact that it brought about a drastic transformation of the region through extermination, ethnic cleansing, and deportations, recreating it as an ethnically homogeneous space with little notion of its own rich heritage, while catapulting the survivors of other ethnic and religious groups to virtually all corners of the earth?

In this context it bears repeating that the vast majority of European Jewry was murdered in Poland, and that the vast majority of those killed were East European and Soviet Jews. Furthermore, approximately half of those murdered did not die in extermination camps. Over six hundred thousand Jews died in large and small ghettos scattered throughout German-occupied Eastern Europe. Many of the rest, however, were killed in mass executions at or near their places of residence. These were open-air events, often watched by the Gentile population. Even when the shootings were conducted at some distance from the towns—in forests, or cemeteries, or quarries—the brutal roundups (*Aktionen* or *akcje*), in which the old and the sick were dragged, humiliated, beaten, and shot; girls and women were raped; and babies were thrown out of balconies and windows, had their skulls smashed against walls, or were torn apart, all took place in public view. Nor was everyone simply watching as the Security Police and SS, along with numerous collaborationist auxiliary and local police detachments, did their work. For here was an opportunity to rob the corpses of the murdered, loot their homes or shelters, or take over their businesses.

Despite the increasingly common—and disturbingly comforting—image of the Holocaust as an event of impersonal, "clean" and distant industrial murder, hundreds upon hundreds of thousands of Jews, the majority of whom were children, women, the sick, and the elderly, were murdered in full view of the populations in whose midst they had lived: in Poland, the Baltic states, Belarus, Ukraine, Romania, and Western Russia. The Holocaust in these regions was therefore very much a communal genocide that left its imprint on all surviving inhabitants of these localities (much more so, it seems, than on the Germans). The impact of these extraordinarily savage massacres carried over both to people's daily existence and to their memories. This was a very different situation from that of Germany or occupied Western Europe since there the Jews were "simply" transported to the "East." Most of the deportees never came back, and the few who did often could not or would not tell what the "East" had been like, and in any case rarely found anyone willing to listen.[25] Conversely, the people of Eastern Europe, Jews and Gentiles alike, were direct witnesses to a genocide that was so much part of routine daily life as to appear almost "normal." Genocide was part of their war, their reality, their survival, whether it targeted or spared them. Here large numbers of Jewish victims were not taken away to a foreign land whose language they did not speak and whose landscapes they did not recognize. They were slaughtered in front of family members, friends, and colleagues, in the cemeteries where their ancestors were buried, on the forested hills where they had dated their lovers or picnicked with their children, in the synagogues in which they had prayed, in their own homes and farms and cellars.[26]

Nor could many of the people who filled the void and moved into the homes of the murdered be described as strangers. Even sixty years later some elderly residents, when prompted, would still remember the names of those who had once lived in this or that house (although rarely identifying their own home as looted property). Some could recount the circumstances of their neighbors' murder in detail, and one could not but wonder about the original inhabitants of such witnesses' own houses and much of their contents—the down blankets covering their beds, the pots and dishes in their kitchens, even the pictures on the walls. What is the psychological effect of living in stolen property for generations, sitting on the chairs, sleeping in the beds, and eating from the dishes of the murdered, while all along retaining a vivid memory of their eviction and execution? For this is the nature of a communal massacre, which by definition constitutes the precise opposite of the Nazis' most notorious invention, industrial, impersonal genocide. One must assume that the ancient biblical question, "have you both murdered and inherited?" cannot have entirely escaped the minds of those who remained in the newly cleansed towns and villages of Eastern Europe, and that it would eventually come back to haunt them. For communal massacre may not only devastate the lives of the victims but also spoil and distort the spirits of all who witness it, precisely because in reality no one is a passive observer: one is either killed or survives, either hunter or prey, either lost or makes a profit. To the sheer, hardly imaginable horror of those years must be added the moral contamination, the guilt and the rage, the shame and the terror, the self-deception and denial that have seeped through the generations and are still infusing the way in which people remember, speak, and write about the past.

This perspective on the Holocaust in Eastern Europe reminds us how intimate genocide can be, how personal, and therefore also how traumatic and simultaneously how profitable it can be for those who come into contact with it. Indeed, such a view of genocide teaches us that the category of "bystander" that has become so common in recent years is basically meaningless in situations of communal genocide, just as such attitudes as indifference and passivity do not actually exist under these circumstances. For what does it mean to be indifferent to the murder of your classmates under your own windows? What does it imply to be passive when you hear the shots and screams from the nearby forest, or when you move into the apartment vacated by those you have just heard being executed? Is using your neighbor's silverware a sign of indifference? Does tearing out the floorboards to look for their hidden gold indicate passivity, complicity, or just greed?

That the murders were part of everyday life is evident from numerous testimonies. One witness reported six decades after the event: "I remember well how the Hitlerites committed crimes against the Jews, how they buried them alive on Fedir [Fedor] hill, and how those people dug their own graves. From the street where I live (which is situated opposite that hill) I could see how the ground was moving over the people who were still not dead."[27] Another witness recounted, at the same distance of time:

> One day ... something drew us to a window [in the school] that faced the town center, the municipal hall. And what did we see? In the middle of the main street a crowd was going around the municipal hall toward the bridge over the Strypa [River]. Gendarmes with dogs, Gestapo and militia with six-pointed stars surrounded the crowd, hurrying it toward Fedir hill. What a horrible sight it was! There were women, men, old people and young—our schoolmates and friends. They were beautiful and wise, well brought-up, and young; they might have lived, loved, and worked ... They were our neighbors and strangers, but they were people! And they were led with dogs so that nobody would fall behind the crowd! Even now my heart breaks when I recall that day![28]

The sheer horror and intimacy of the killings is vividly portrayed by this witness. While everyone was a victim of a brutal occupation, some went to school, while others went to their death:

> From about the fall of 1942 to the end of 1943 they [the Germans] would hold *akcja*-shootings, always on Fridays. But they would start on Tuesday: on Tuesday evening the Jewish militia would collect jewels and other valuable things ... [as bribes from people seeking to escape massacre]. On Thursday evening the [Germans] would come [from nearby Czortków, the local Security Police headquarters] ... They looked really horrible—they had a metal shield ... on their breasts ... [which] hung from a metal chain ... On their heads they had high black hats with a skull and crossed bones. By their appearance they really resembled demons from hell. They would "act" or "work" all night, and the next morning as we were running to school, we could see the results of their work: corpses of women, men and children lying on the road. As for infants, they would throw them from balconies onto the paved road. And they were lying in the mud with smashed heads and spattered brains ... It was not hard to guess what was happening on Fedir hill: we could hear machine-gun fire accompanied by the drone of engines. But this only intensified the sound of the shooting instead of drowning it.[29]

There is, however, another side to such an exploration of the Holocaust on the local level in Eastern Europe's mixed ethnic communities. For while the majority of the Jews living in such towns and villages perished, often denounced by the population and not infrequently murdered by local collaborators, the few who did survive were almost invariably helped by Gentiles. Indeed, it was virtually impossible to survive without being given shelter and food by the non-Jews. Only the most sturdy and courageous, mostly young men and women, who decided to live on their own in the forests and became partisans after a manner, could survive without such help from Gentiles, and instead often subsisted on supplies stolen or robbed from villagers. But most of these groups of partisans were also killed, whether by the Germans and their collaborators or by other non-Jewish partisans.[30]

Further complicating this view of the Holocaust from below is the fact that in many cases precisely the same people who sheltered Jews ended up also denouncing them, at times even murdering them with their own hands. The motivation for offering shelter in the first place was complex. Some did so out of sheer kindness and altruism; others out of greed. Others still felt some sense of loyalty or duty toward those they were helping or members of their family. But sheltering people was dangerous and feeding them was a great hardship. When those in hiding ran out of money, or when it seemed that they might be betrayed by someone else, the solution was often either to send them away or to denounce them, so as not to be accused of sheltering Jews and risk brutal punishment. In many cases, real or putative rescuers were much more afraid of their own neighbors than of the Germans. Unlike the Germans, who could rarely tell one local from another, the inhabitants of small farming communities or little towns immediately recognized strangers and could often also detect changes in their neighbors' behavior indicating that they might be hiding someone. Denunciations could be construed as revenge for some offense or perceived injury by the rescuers; they might be motivated by an expectation of payment from the Germans; they could be part of a bid intended to frighten those still in hiding into paying larger bribes to potential informers; or they could stem from envy of the perceived profits made by those courageous or greedy enough to risk sheltering Jews.

A testimony given by a seventeen-year-old Jewish lad in 1947 provides a vivid description of this dynamic:

> The [Jews] who were hiding with peasants paid high sums of money for their shelters, and the simple-minded peasants went to town and bought large amounts of whatever they wanted. The peasants became jealous of each other, and this made the work for the Ukrainian murderers all the easier. They followed those peasants, found where they lived, set out on searches, and found Jews in attics, cellars, and so forth. After they found these victims, they shot them on the spot in the peasants' courtyards. This set off large-scale denunciations. The peasants themselves started killing the Jews or expelling them, because there were various rumors that whoever was found sheltering a Jew would be executed along with his family and his house would be burned down. The peasants believed this and tried to get rid of their Jews by all means, and in this manner made the work of the murderers all the easier. The Jewish fighters [a partisan group in the forest] could do nothing against this. Their own lives became difficult, because at the time all kinds of gangs were established, such as the Ukrainian bands (the Bandera men ["*Banderowcy*" or "*Banderivtsy*"]) and the Polish units (A.K. [*Armia Krajowa*, or

Home Army]), and especially the German-Ukrainian police, which did all it could to destroy the fighting Jewish group.[31]

The Economy of Genocide

Recent research has shown the crucial role played by property and capital in the implementation of the Holocaust.[32] It has been suggested that to a large extent the mass looting of the Jews actually funded not only their mass murder but also Germany's occupation policies, by facilitating mass bribery of the occupied populations with stolen Jewish property and goods as the price of their submission to foreign rule. Not surprisingly, this vast plunder operation also constituted a major element of postwar policies and agreements. Various restitution agreements have also had to contend with compensation for stolen material goods.[33] But at the same time, the immense quantities of Jewish property which fell into the hands of the inhabitants of Eastern Europe also inhibited discussions on restitution. During the communist era, the issue was hardly even raised. But following the fall of communism, fears were expressed that demands for the return of looted property or compensation for its theft would cripple the countries and economies in question and destroy the lives of untold thousands of people living in stolen homes. Indeed, one cannot begin to understand attitudes toward Jews, the Holocaust, restitution, and reconciliation in Eastern Europe without taking into account the alarm caused by the imagined threat of material deprivation, combined as it often is with the insecurity produced by the vague notion of living in stolen property. It is only through the prism of Eastern Europe that we can realize how crucial both the reality and the fantasy of property were in the impoverished towns and villages of this region, where even at the height of prosperity before the First World War people's expectations of material wealth were on an entirely different scale from what we are used to in contemporary Western society.

Hence we need to recognize that property was an important cause of resentment and greed; it often determined how one would be treated in good times and bad. Under the Soviet occupation of 1939–41, one's property determined one's fate just as much as ethnicity or religion.[34] Under the Nazis the Jews were often targeted both by the Germans and by local Gentiles as a mythical source of goods and riches, even as their actual condition was reduced to utter destitution. This belief added a dimension of festive enrichment and socioeconomic improvement to the horror of the local mass killings.[35] Genocide thus served as a mechanism for social mobility, moving into the better stone houses, taking over businesses, giving clothes and jewelry to one's wife or mistress or fetching toys for one's children, all facilitated by the shedding of blood.[36] And the memory of slaughter at the root of individual betterment is more difficult to erase than the stains of blood quickly washed from the pavement or absorbed into the earth. Many of the thousands, nay, hundreds of thousands of East Europeans who are still living in stolen property, would rather not discuss or remember this fact; after all, most of them have not stolen this property themselves. Elsewhere we find a different phenomenon that can only be called a celebration of virtual Jews.[37] Thus one can walk today into a restaurant in the Kazimierz quarter of Cracow, which has undergone a "Jewish" revival, and find it decorated almost entirely with looted goods: oil lamps, candelabra, menorahs, torah pointers, all probably bought for pennies at the flea market, where they ended up after being carted off from the homes of those moved to the ghetto, then to the concentration camps, then to the gas chambers. But whether it is the Jewish revival in Poland or the suppression of Jewish traces in West Ukraine, the context is not only the unmarked mass graves but also the still usable and useful looted goods and property.

This suppressed or exoticized memory makes for discomfort and apologetics. That too is an integral part of excavating Eastern Europe as the site of the Holocaust, so different in this respect from the affluent West. Poverty rarely breeds compassion, despite what some novels would tell us. Ivan Bobyk, who served as mayor of Buczacz during the German occupation, wrote after the war from his enforced exile:

> [Pre-Habsburg Jews] had immunity from the city authorities; they were exempted from taxes, but profited from fairs and markets ... All this resulted in the impoverishment of our citizens, who were forced to move to the outskirts of town. ... [Nevertheless, the citizens] were well disposed toward the Jews and lived together in peace ... [The Jews] did not like to serve in the [Austrian] army ... [During the Soviet occupation of 1939–41, while the] Jewish merchants, intelligentsia and craftsmen were not delighted with Bolshevik rule ... everybody knew that the leadership of the Communist Party [in the town] was mainly Jewish ... [During the German occupation] the Ukrainian population sympathized with the grim fate of the Jews and tried to help them whenever they had an opportunity, exposing themselves to the worst consequences ... However, it is very strange that almost all Jewish publications on World War II accuse the Ukrainian population of having helped the Germans to exterminate the Jews. It is true that in some cases the local Ukrainian police took part in police actions as escorts. But in some other Galician cities there were Jewish police as well. Besides, Ukrainian policemen never took part in executions. There were also some individual cases when local policemen persecuted the Jews, but this is no reason to accuse the entire Ukrainian population, just as we cannot accuse all the Jewish population on the grounds that some of them collaborated with the NKVD and helped to arrest and exile to Siberia the most prominent citizens of [the town].[38]

Mayor Bobyk's massive 1972 volume of over a thousand pages on Buczacz and its vicinity devotes only a few pages to the Jewish majority that had lived there before the war, and much of what he writes there would have better been left unwritten.

Yet Bobyk was in fact a compassionate man considering the conditions at the time. In defense of a crime he does not entirely acknowledge, Bobyk cites a letter sent to him in 1969 by Isidor Gelbart, a Jewish friend who survived in hiding along with his family. Gelbart's letter, as well as the postwar testimony he gave, confirm Bobyk's claims that he had behaved as decently as circumstances had allowed. Furthermore, this well-educated Jewish witness also acknowledged the help given his family and other Jews by Ukrainians and Poles. But very much unlike Bobyk's account, Gelbart's testimony stressed the collaboration of Ukrainian policemen in the killings, and the desperate isolation of the bulk of the Jews caught between a murderous German–Ukrainian police apparatus and a hostile population. Thus Gelbart reported that when the Germans marched into Buczacz in early July 1941,

> A Ukrainian police force was formed and soon thereafter Jewish women were dragged out of Jewish homes for cleaning work and were abused. Whoever had connections with the Ukrainians could still be helped; the Ukrainian Ivan Bobyk was appointed mayor, and fortunately he was a good, decent, and unprejudiced man who did all he could to stand by the Jews.[39]

However, Gelbart also notes that Bobyk was present when the Jews were rounded up and sent to nearby sites where they were shot by the German Security Police and Ukrainian militias. Gelbart was saved from the previous roundup—where Jewish men were only used for forced labor—by Bobyk, who recognized him and told him to go back home. During the second roundup, in August 1941, Gelbart decided not to go, while his brother, along with several hundred other members of the Jewish intelligentsia of the town, were killed. In June 1943 Gelbart, his wife, and his two sons found shelter with the Ukrainian peasant Zacharczuk (Zakharchuk) and his Polish wife and two small children in the village of Ćwitowa (Tsvitova) near Buczacz. They hid in the peasant's attic until the first liberation of the region by the Red Army in March 1944. The area was soon thereafter recaptured by the Germans and most of the Jews who came out of hiding (estimated at one thousand five hundred by Gelbart and closer to eight hundred in other accounts) were seized and murdered. But Gelbart and his family managed to escape to Czernowitz (Chernivtsi) and were saved.[40]

The accounts by Bobyk and Gelbart reflect the complexity of the situation on the ground and the manner in which people belonging to different groups and slated for different treatment by the German occupiers responded to the new conditions and subsequently formed different memories of these events. The exiled Bobyk's combination of prejudice and compassion found no counterpart in Soviet historiography. Soviet accounts simply ignore the fate of the Jews altogether, speaking only of the Soviet citizens murdered by the Germans and conveniently forgetting that some of those citizens were actively killing their own neighbors. For instance, Ihor Duda's 1985 tourist guide to Buczacz briefly recounts that

> On July 7, 1941, the Hitlerites occupied Buczacz. During the time of the occupation they exterminated about 7,500 civilians from the city and the district villages; 1,839 young men and women were driven to forced labor in Germany. 137 buildings were destroyed, as well as a number of industrial enterprises and schools. Nevertheless the population did not submit to the fascists.[41]

Nowhere in this peculiarly communist-nationalist-Ukrainian narrative of the city's history is the word "Jew" even mentioned.

But following the fall of communism, accounts of the Second World War once more reflect the spirit of Bobyk's perception of events, although they are written from a greater distance of time by men and women who have no direct memory of the occupation and who have also been stamped by the decades-long Soviet view of history. For instance, an article published in a local West Ukrainian newspaper in 2000 presents a strange mixture of compassion for the Jewish victims of Nazism, Soviet-era pathos and fabrication, nationalist pride and apologetics, and a good measure of unconscious prejudice. The author, Tetiana Pavlyshyn, asserts that "people of Jewish nationality came [to Buczacz] from everywhere" because this "ancient city ... has always been a profitable place for commercial activity." Yet, as it turned out, "those people had an inborn ability for commerce," and while "they would generously lend to you," they "knew how get their money back with interest."[42]

The Jews are thus described as a foreign element that came to an already wealthy town from the outside and made a neat profit there on the backs of the local population. Once this historical "fact" is established, Pavlyshyn attempts to reconstruct what actually happened in Buczacz during the Holocaust. For this purpose, she turns to several Ukrainian eyewitnesses (it does not seem to have occurred to her to consult any historical accounts or to look for testimonies by Poles and Jews). One witness is Ivan Synenkyi, who was a sixteen-year-old lad during the war. Synenkyi remembers seeing regular roundups, during which masses of people were shot in the forest. There were so many bodies there, some still alive, that the thin layer of soil over the pit would heave. Other mass shootings took place at the Jewish cemetery, after which, Synenkyi notes, "people could see streams of reddish liquid with a peculiar smell flowing from the slope where the grave was situated—human bodies were intensively decomposing. Later that liquid seeped into a water reservoir that was situated nearby and used by the local population."[43]

Instead of offering her own opinion on the massacre of the local Jews, Pavlyshyn cites Synenkyi's explanation for what he perceived as their peculiar response to the annihilation of the community: "The Jews themselves behaved in a strange way. Rarely if ever did they try to escape. There was no fear in their eyes. Some of them explained their behavior by old prophecies that came true; others would turn to the local people and say: 'We are the first, but you will be the next.'"[44]

Thus Synenkyi, and by extension also the author of the article who makes no further comment on his assertion, presents two explanations for the massacre. According to the first, the Jews died because of some "old prophecy," obviously meaning the Crucifixion. This was the traditional anti-Semitic rationalization of the Holocaust that clearly infused the minds of many local Christians and was often encouraged by the clergy. The second explanation, however, can be interpreted in different ways. It could be read as a warning to the Ukrainians that once the genocide of the Jews is completed, the Germans would turn their wrath against the local Gentiles. This argument was common also among those Poles who insisted on reporting the genocide of the Jews to the rest of the world for fear that the same indifference would subsequently greet the anticipated extermination of the Polish people.⁴⁵ Yet the line "we are the first, but you will be the next" could easily be seen also as a condemnation by those who are going to the slaughter of their Gentile neighbors observing them as they pass through the town. Possibly the inclusion of this line in the article reflects an awareness, or at least a subconscious acknowledgment, of the sense of betrayal felt by the Jews abandoned to their fate by their own community.

The community in question might have felt various degrees of compassion for the Jews. But people also had other things on their minds, and the Jews were well aware of this. The townsfolk were making a profit from this butchery: as Synenkyi candidly reported, "there was also a shop in the city where the clothes of the murdered were sold cheaply."⁴⁶ Nor was profiteering limited to the war years. According to Synenkyi, when the only surviving member of a Jewish family who lost his parents and twelve sisters returned to town after the war and "wanted to get back his house … the price fixed by the new owners was too high, so he had to abandon his dream" and move to Israel. As for rescue, Synenkyi's version strikes a more realistic note than Mayor Bobyk's, noting that assistance to the victims was anything but conspicuous. "The local people," he remarks, "were very careful about associating with the Jews in any manner. Most were scared for their lives; others did help, but very cautiously." When "a Jewish man who had managed to get out of a [mass] grave" came to a local resident in the middle of the night, "the host gave him the necessary help but could not let him stay in his house. That same night that man went away to the forest."⁴⁷

Testimony and History

It can therefore not be stressed enough that the Holocaust—including its postwar memory (and erasure) and the new socioeconomic conditions it produced through extermination and deportation of populations as well as massive property transfer—has had an incomparably greater overall impact on Eastern Europe than on Western and Central European countries. Jewish populations in Western and Central Europe were much smaller; their killing occurred very far from their places of residence; their property transfer, though substantial, left less of an economic and psychological mark on the nations from which they were deported; and, in many cases, the Jewish populations in these countries revived (often by absorbing former displaced persons from Eastern Europe) and reintegrated. The Jews of France and Italy today are more numerous than in 1939.⁴⁸ Even German Jewry has seen a remarkable expansion since the fall of the Wall.⁴⁹ Conversely, the Jews of Poland went on diminishing, under the impact of communist anti-Semitic regimes, throughout the postwar period; the same can be said for Ukraine and other Jewish communities in the borderlands of Eastern Europe, with the partial exception of Hungary. It remains unclear whether the tentative revival of Jewish life in some parts of Eastern Europe, not least in Poland, is more a cultural matter and an issue of identity, or a concrete expansion of population and renewal of a living community.⁵⁰

But how do we gain access to the reality of the Holocaust in Eastern Europe? Some recent studies have employed the traditional tools of the historian, while making increasing use of previously neglected or inaccessible documents, to reconstruct Nazi extermination policies in Eastern Europe. Most of these studies, however, have taken a country-wide or regional overview, and have largely focused on the policies of the occupiers and perpetrators, or on the cooperation between the invaders and local collaborators.[51] Such works are helpful in providing the framework of the genocide but not very useful in depicting the reality on the ground for the populations involved— namely, the Jews targeted for extermination, on the one hand, and their neighbors, who not only suffered under foreign occupations but also, in part, profited from the killing of the Jews and the massacres and expulsions of other populations, on the other. Indeed, most of these studies do not make any use of testimonies or utilize them only in a sketchy and anecdotal manner; they also rarely demonstrate any knowledge of the Jewish experience or of the relations between Jews and Gentiles on the local level.[52] They are based largely on official documents by the occupiers and perpetrators and on secondary literature. Conversely, those studies that do examine the fate of the Jews have little to say about interethnic relations, tend to decontextualize the manner in which this community experienced the Holocaust, and at times are geared more toward commemoration than historical reconstruction. While such studies will rely more on testimonies, they will normally limit themselves to those provided by Jewish witnesses, whose perspective was obviously determined by the circumstances and prejudices of the time.[53]

The neglect of testimonies as historical documents has many roots. Professional historians generally tend to find such so-called subjective accounts, often reporting about events witnessed at a considerable remove from the time in which they were experienced, rather suspect. Historians are trained to prefer documents that carry an official stamp, were produced at the time of the event by competent and responsible officials, and that are accessible at well-organized archival collections.[54] Such documents facilitate the relatively accurate reconstruction of the manner in which a bureaucratic organization formed and implemented policy. But one gains very limited insight into the manner in which the implementation of this policy was experienced by those upon whom it was enacted. Moreover, the overtly objective nature of such documentation is highly misleading; the officials who write memoranda and hand down orders are hardly free of bias, prejudice, or an intentional desire to veil the actual meaning of the documents they produce in a web of bureaucratic euphemisms, whether out of habit or because they do not wish to be implicated in policies they know to be objectionable or criminal.

This difficulty with official documentation is particularly acute in the case of the Holocaust, and historians have been well aware of it.[55] And yet very few have concluded that one way to lift the veil of obfuscation and euphemism and penetrate the reality of the event is to question those who were at the receiving end. Due to the very different nature of judicial proceedings (and with the important exception of the Nuremberg Tribunal), postwar trials of Nazi perpetrators have made much greater use of testimonies.[56] In fact, the records of such trials provide a revealing picture of the vast gap between the depiction of genocide by its makers (both during the event and years later in their testimonies to the court) and the memory of these same events by the victims. But even when the records of police interrogations and trials have been used in the historical literature, they have not been linked to the vast array of other testimonial documentation that would help to recreate the experience of the victims and others present at the local site of genocide.[57] This is mainly because such literature is still concerned with the motivation of the killers, and while it expresses sympathy with and shows some empathy for the victims, it remains conventional in regarding them merely as targets of genocide and not as historical protagonists whose own thoughts, actions, and memories have a bearing on the event.

The reluctance to use Jewish testimonies in the reconstruction of the Holocaust goes back to the early postwar years. The Nuremberg Tribunal was loath to use victim testimonies and relied almost exclusively on official documentation (and testimonies by the defendants) for fear that allegedly biased evidence by the persecuted would further undermine the court's somewhat questionable legitimacy and expose it as meting out victors' justice.[58] This was done despite the fact that at the time there were many thousands of available witnesses whose memories were still fresh and whose depictions of the crimes would have provided a far more vivid description than the dry, detached, and euphemistic documentary evidence. Subsequent German trials, especially since the late 1950s and throughout the 1960s, made much more extensive use of victims' testimonies, although the witnesses, many of whom were eager to testify, often found the process humiliating and the resulting sentences, when handed down at all, almost always laughable.[59] It was the trial of Adolf Eichmann in Jerusalem in 1961 that established the survivors as the main voice of the indictment and put them right at the center of the judicial proceedings. While the Israeli judges and other observers—not least Hannah Arendt—criticized the state attorney's strategy of presenting evidence not directly related to the defendant, the trial for the first time made the record of the atrocity as told by its survivors internationally available.[60] The long-range consequence of the Eichmann Trial was the gradual realization of the centrality of the Holocaust to the Second World War specifically and to the twentieth century more generally.[61]

Similarly, the decision of German courts shortly before the Eichmann Trial to make use of victim testimonies, the vast amounts of records collected in preparations for these trials (however lamentable their outcomes eventually were), and the wide publicity they received in the media combined to have a powerful long-term impact on German perceptions of the Holocaust. The publication of Peter Weiss's *The Investigation*, which provided the gist of the Frankfurt Auschwitz Trial, was the beginning of a process that led a new generation of Germans to face up to the crimes of the past and tear away the pious euphemisms that obscured them in the first two postwar decades.[62] There can be no doubt that these trials played an important role in the growing interest in what Germans came to call "Auschwitz" as a euphemism for the Holocaust. Indeed, the preoccupation of the 1968 generation with the extermination camps would have been unthinkable without these trials and the manner in which they exposed publicly for the first time in Germany—and within the august spaces of Germans courts—the true horror of the Holocaust.[63]

Testimonies have therefore played a major role in bringing perpetrators to justice and in transforming public perceptions. Yet historians have been very cautious, at times openly hostile, to using them. One case that was revealed only at the beginning of the present century by the German scholar Nicolas Berg exemplifies the extent to which Jewish testimonies, and Jewish historians writing on the Holocaust, seemed positively threatening to the very scholars who were researching the Third Reich and its crimes in the early postwar decades. In 1960 the historian Martin Broszat, member and spokesman of the influential Institute for Contemporary History at Munich, which he subsequently directed, launched a campaign to discredit the study on the Warsaw Ghetto by the Jewish scholar Joseph Wulf.[64] In part, this had to do with Broszat's own forthcoming book, which provided a very different picture of German policies in Poland.[65] While Wulf presented the director of the health authorities in occupied Warsaw, Dr. Wilhelm Hagen, as a man who had betrayed his ethical obligation as a physician, Broszat described him as a resister to the murderous policies of the Nazis. To be sure, Broszat was thinking of Hagen as saving Poles from epidemics; Wulf described Hagen as complicit in the murder of the Jews. And because Hagen held a senior position in the Federal Republic at the time of the dispute, the media also showed a great deal of interest.

The main point of contention, however, had to do with the fact that Wulf was not only a Jew of Polish origins who had himself survived the camps and lost most of his family in the Holocaust, but that he had given equal weight to Jewish documentation and testimonies along with German evidence in his account of events in the Warsaw Ghetto. It was for this reason that Broszat, along with the majority of other German historians at the time, could not accept Wulf's writing as scholarly. Indeed, Wulf found himself isolated from the German scholarly community and eventually committed suicide in 1974. Ironically, many years after his own death in 1989, it was discovered that Broszat, who had always insisted on the greater objective and factual value of official documents, had actually been a member of the Nazi Party, a fact he had never conceded in his postwar lifetime. In a public exchange with the historian Saul Friedländer in the mid-1980s, Broszat had argued in defense of a detached and sober scholarly history of Nazism and dismissed what he saw as the mythic Jewish historiography of the Holocaust. He also presented himself as a member of the Hitler Youth generation who was "certainly stricken with but hardly burdened" (*zwar betroffen aber kaum belastet*) by Nazism. In fact, Broszat joined the NSDAP on April 4, 1944.[66]

All this seems to indicate the extent to which arguments of objectivity can merely serve as a cover for obfuscation and falsification of the historical record. They also have to do with ideology. In 1958, three years before the dispute between Wulf and Broszat, Raul Hilberg was informed in a letter from Yad Vashem that it would not provide any assistance for the publication of his monograph, eventually known as one of the most important studies of the Holocaust, because "the book rests almost exclusively on the authority of German sources" and because of "reservations concerning" his "appraisal of the Jewish resistance ... during the Nazi occupation."[67] Yad Vashem was concerned that Hilberg's account seemed to assign a degree of responsibility to the victims for their own fate. But here one can also discern the vast difference between Hilberg and Broszat. Whereas Hilberg wrote the first meticulously documented history of the manner in which the Germans organized the murder of the Jews, Broszat's most influential book on the "Hitler State" contained only one paragraph that dealt directly with the Holocaust.[68]

Thus the use of testimonies or the reluctance to do so does not necessarily make for good or bad, innovative or misleading history writing. But it does direct one's focus at certain aspects of the event while leaving others in the dark. Had Hilberg been more preoccupied with testimonies, he would have realized that some of his generalizations about Jewish behavior during the Holocaust (from which Hannah Arendt, who rejected his book for publication with Princeton University Press, freely borrowed in her own account of the Eichmann trial) were at best tenuous and probably largely wrong. He would have also shifted his focus from the Berlin-centered account of events (largely still repeated by his former student Christopher Browning in his 2004 coauthored study, *The Origins of the Final Solution*) to the place of the genocide.[69] And that site was Eastern Europe, from which the vast majority of the testimonies stem, providing a far richer and more complex picture of individual and communal responses to genocide than one can find in German documentation.

What is fascinating about this reluctance, or inability, to use testimony and the insistence on restricting oneself to German documentation, despite all the built-in constraints and biases that such a choice entails, is that there is a vast amount of testimony documentation, some of which has remained almost entirely untapped for decades. One major source is the Jewish Historical Institute in Warsaw (*Żydowski Instytut Historyczny* or ŻIH), which keeps close to seven thousand personal narratives by Holocaust survivors, adults and children.[70] Copies of these testimonies can be found at Yad Vashem in Jerusalem and the US Holocaust Memorial Museum (USHMM) in Washington, DC. These testimonies, some of which are very detailed and others very brief, were recorded in several languages and collected in large part right after the liberation of Polish territories from Nazi rule. Hence these are fresh recollections from the immediate aftermath of the Holocaust, often by people who did not even know that a continent-wide genocide had taken place but had a very precise knowledge of what happened in their own communities. There are also several much longer accounts written as personal diaries during the Holocaust or in its immediate aftermath. A second large collection is in Yad Vashem, where one can find written testimonies, witness accounts submitted to postwar German courts for trials of former Nazis, and audio and video testimonies, spanning the entire period from the end of the war to quite recently.[71] A third important source is the Fortunoff Video Archive at Yale University, a collection of 4,400 videotaped testimonies of Holocaust survivors, witnesses, and liberators.[72] To this one can add the rediscovered David Boder collection of 120 remarkable interviews with Holocaust survivors recorded on an early version of a tape recorder in 1946 in displaced persons camps in Europe, of which Boder later transcribed seventy and published only eight.[73] Another outstanding recent collection is the "Archive of Memory," in which interviews with seventy-eight survivors of the Holocaust from the Brandenburg-Berlin area conducted in 1995–7 are collected and analyzed.[74] Finally, a vast project was launched in 1994 by Steven Spielberg and the Survivors of the Shoah Foundation in Los Angeles, currently located at the Institute for Visual History and Education of the Shoah Foundation at the University of Southern California, which contains by now fifty five thousand testimonies collected in fifty-six countries.[75] The archives of the USHMM also include important collections of testimonies as well as many other documents microfilmed throughout Eastern Europe, Ukraine, and Russia, among others.[76]

Additionally, there are important collections of testimonies by Poles who were deported by the Soviets in 1939–41 or ethnically cleansed by Ukrainians in the last phase of the war and immediately thereafter.[77] These testimonies provide valuable insights into events in former Polish localities that complement, even if at times they also contradict, the Jewish accounts of the period. Such groups experienced events differently and were struck by fate and the various occupation authorities in a different manner. Using them together creates a more balanced and richer picture of what happened on the ground. To this should be added also accounts by other ethnic groups, which, in the case of Eastern Galicia, means primarily Ukrainians. Often oral and written accounts in such regions have not been carefully collected, and some collections seem to have been edited with a certain apologetic bent that may have biased the selection.[78] Yet it is crucial to make use of whatever material exists and, though by now rarely possible, to interview eyewitnesses on the ground. For instance, in the case of contemporary West Ukraine, with very few exceptions, in the last few decades it was only among Ukrainians that one could still find individuals who had been in the same site their entire lives and had vivid memories of the war, although many of the inhabitants also arrived there after the war.[79]

Until a few years ago, it was also still possible to interview some of those who survived genocide and ethnic cleansing—Jews and Poles in the case of Galicia—even though their numbers were already rapidly diminishing. Publications by émigré communities such as memorial books, periodicals, occasional papers, and memoirs—all intended to preserve the memory of prewar communities and the horrors that put an end to them—are quite abundant.[80] The emigrants may be found in relatively nearby locations such as Wrocław (Breslau), or in much more distant lands such as Israel and the United States, South Africa and Latin America, New Zealand and Australia, as well as Canada, Russia and France, Britain and Belgium, the Netherlands and Scandinavia.

Work with such testimonies provides access to a highly neglected aspect of the Holocaust specifically and of genocide more generally. As we saw in the 1990s, communal killings in interethnic communities are often an important, and at times a central aspect of modern genocide. This of course appears to be a contradiction in terms. We would like to believe that precisely interethnic communities can serve as an example that people of different ethnicities and religions can live together, and as a bulwark against the essentializing rhetoric and dehumanizing imagery propagated by bigots, racists, integral nationalists, and other promoters of homogenous ethnicities and racial segregation. In fact, however, interethnic communities often explode into horrific violence when they find themselves in the midst of war, ethnic cleansing, and genocide. Rather than a bulwark, they serve as focal points of the worst and most brutal—because intimate—violence. Hence the example they provide serves the goal of the perpetrators, namely, to argue that the only solution to such communal slaughters is the separation, segregation, and expulsion or murder of those populations that do not fit into the desired ethnic mold—that is, the creation of homogeneous populations precisely along the lines proposed by those who propagated communal violence in the first place.

Eastern Europe as *Lieu de Mémoire*

This does not have to be the case and in fact is not always so. But the examples of Cambodia, Rwanda, Bosnia—indeed, also the Middle East—seem to show that under conditions of extreme ideologies and essentialist nationalism these situations are hard to prevent and often impossible to avoid. As we see now also in Western Europe, the relatively rapid introduction of new populations is the cause of much tension vis-à-vis the policies of integration and assimilation. If we want to understand the mechanism of intercommunal relations, then, we have to look at communities that had lived side by side for generations and ended up under a combination of circumstances—not only those of Soviet and German occupation but also going back to nationalism in the late nineteenth century and to the violence of the First World War and its aftermath in Eastern Europe—as communities of genocide.

Linking research on the Holocaust in Eastern Europe to general work on this event, and at the same time linking the history of the Holocaust to local histories of East European countries, is the challenge to a new generation of historians. Some work has been and is currently being carried out on specific communities, but this field is still in its infancy. The use of testimonies in a sophisticated and comprehensive manner has only recently begun.[81] Testimonies have been used as anecdotal evidence by historians, and increasingly as part of educational programs geared to teaching against intolerance.[82] But whatever one might think of the use of atrocity to teach humanism, this is certainly not a scholarly but a pedagogical undertaking. As far as historical reconstruction is concerned, the moment one attempts to use testimony in specific cases, one immediately realizes how many of the generalizations and conventional theories about the origins, nature, and effects of genocidal violence, indeed, even about the nature of testimonies, have to be discarded or at least substantially revised.

Suffice it to consider such works as Jan Gross's *Neighbors*, Shimon Redlich's *Together and Apart in Brzeżany*, and my own *Anatomy of a Genocide* to realize how much more can be done by combining testimonies with a focus on a specific location. Indeed, in the case of the Holocaust, we would do well to return, in a modified form, to the historical methodology of the 1970s and 1980s of local studies by applying it to specific multiethnic communities in Eastern Europe. William Sheridan Allen's study of the Nazi "seizure of power" in a small German town taught us a great deal about the nature of the process in the country as a whole.[83] So, too, such focused but complex and nuanced local studies, combining the use of more traditional documentation with a variety of personal testimonies recorded over the decades that have passed since the event in a variety of very different contexts, will give us clues as to the manner in which the war and the Holocaust were experienced—not by the bureaucrats who rarely ventured out of their offices but by those who actually were on the ground to see and experience it all.

Here we will also find that the increasingly recognized link—in the Holocaust and in other genocides and cases of ethnic cleansing and "population policies"—between the higher and the lower levels can be grasped much more clearly from the local perspective. Thus, for instance, issues of motivation become more complex and yet more easily understandable when we bring in the urge for property, career advancement, access to political and professional positions, and subsequently the perceived need to erase the traces of what made for this trajectory to personal success through the path of mass murder. In fact, the local level provides particularly vivid examples of why the present is so reluctant to deal with the past, since the contemporary implications are clear to all but the very old, the very young, the ideologically driven, and the simpleminded. The urge to suppress the compromising tales of the past is based on the perceived need to legitimize the present. But a present founded on an acknowledged—though rarely articulated—necessity to erase and suppress the past is and will always remain tenuous and under siege, since there is no telling when some revelation might crack the crust of denial and forgetting. The only way to build a self-assured and confident present is to return to the past and reveal its secrets.[84] And the only way to do that within small communities with long, and long-suppressed memories is through the words of the members of these communities, mostly in exile and dead by now, but still capable of telling their stories by means of the words they wrote, dictated, or uttered into an audiotape or video camera.

Eastern Europe is thus not merely the site of the Holocaust in the physical sense that most of Europe's Jews lived there and were murdered there. It was and remains the heart of the Holocaust in that it was where Jewish and Christian civilizations formed a long, though troubled, tradition of living side by side, and where that social and cultural fabric was ultimately shattered in the Second World War and the Holocaust. Eastern Europe was not "only" the site of industrial, impersonal, production-line mass murder but also where the Holocaust occurred in its most intimate, personal, and thus also vicious form, multiplied thousands upon thousands of times as endless communities were transformed into killing fields. Here the Holocaust has also remained so close to the surface precisely because its memory has been neglected and suppressed so thoroughly that it reemerges unscathed and undiminished. When one travels in Galicia today and sees the now rapidly disappearing ruined synagogues and overgrown cemeteries, one can still glimpse the last artifacts of a civilization that is determined to remind us of its past as a live and creative entity, whose memory can still regenerate and enrich the lives of those in whose midst its ruins jut out of the black earth. If there is any true *lieu de mémoire* in Europe (and one that Pierre Nora and his collaborators never seem to have contemplated), it is in the fields and hills, the riverbanks and towns of Eastern Europe.[85]

PART II
LOCAL HISTORY

CHAPTER 3
RECONSTRUCTING GENOCIDE ON THE LOCAL LEVEL

And God said to Cain: Where is Abel your brother? And he said: I don't know; am I my brother's keeper?

And He said: What have you done? The voice of your brother's blood is crying to me from the ground.

Genesis 4:9-10

Most people think of the Holocaust as an event of industrial killing, symbolized by Auschwitz: a vast undertaking of streamlined, anonymous mass murder. In fact, half of the total victims of what the Nazis called the "Final Solution of the Jewish question" did not die in extermination camps; they were killed in their own homes and streets, cemeteries and synagogues, in nearby hills, forests, and ravines. The killing was neither anonymous nor streamlined: the murderers often knew their victims by name and saw them face-to-face just before they shot them; their deaths were bloody, gruesome, and accompanied by many instances of gratuitous cruelty. The killers were not only German police and SS, or only Germans of any description, but also members of other ethnic groups from the victims' own regions and towns, often people they had known for years as classmates and colleagues and neighbors. There was nothing secret about these events: they were public, routine spectacles in which everyone played one role or another.[1]

Perpetrator behavior is often explained as the consequence of dehumanization: the obstacle to the killing of innocents is removed by perceiving them as nonhuman.[2] This view of mass murder allows us to avoid any discussion of the ghastly encounter between the killers and the killed, clearing the way for detached analyses of decision-making and the logistics of genocide. I have never bought into this argument. But in order to examine its veracity, I decided to investigate the Holocaust in an entirely different way—not from the prism of Berlin, and not strictly through the eyes of either one side or another. Instead, I chose to reconstruct the event in its entirety as it occurred in a single site.

Selecting the site had to do with its representative value and the availability of sources. Eventually I picked a town whose name was familiar to me but about which I knew very little. Buczacz, located in interwar eastern Poland and now in West Ukraine, was the birthplace of Nobel Prize Laureate Shmuel Yosef Agnon, whose stories I had studied in school in Israel.[3] It was also, as it happens, my mother's hometown, although

I had no intention of writing a family history. I was intrigued, however, by the notion of writing a biography of a town, a history through the eyes of the protagonists; in this sense my personal link to Buczacz clearly motivated me. The tension between analytical detachment and empathetic understanding was therefore built into my research project from its very origins.

No fewer than sixty thousand Jews were murdered in the area of Buczacz and Czortków, a nearby town in which the Security Police (*Sicherheitspolizei* or Sipo) outpost charged with this task was based. Accompanied by mistresses and wives, children and parents, who came to enjoy the rural surroundings, these twenty policemen led a comfortable existence, captured in hundreds of photographs kept in West German court archives. They were ably assisted by up to 350 Ukrainian auxiliary policemen (organized as a *Schutzmannschaft* or *Schuma* unit), along with local German and Ukrainian gendarmes, as well as Jewish policemen recruited into the so-called Ordnungsdienst and paid by the Jewish council (*Judenrat*).

From the local perspective, the Holocaust in Buczacz was a series of extremely violent roundups, assuming at times the character of communal massacres. Somewhat under half of the approximately ten thousand victims were transported by train to the Bełżec extermination camp, where they were gassed; the rest were killed in situ. This reflected the fate of the five hundred thousand Jews who were living in the entire region, known as Eastern Galicia before the First World War and designated as Distrikt Galizien by the occupying Germans in 1941: about two hundred fifty thousand Jews were gassed in Bełżec, while the rest were shot next to where they lived. Most of this massive bloodletting was accomplished within eighteen months in an area measuring less than half the size of the state of New York.[4]

For the Jews, Buczacz was a *shtetl*, as were many other similar towns in Eastern Europe. But the notion of a *shtetl* as a purely Jewish town was in truth a figment of Jewish lore rather than a reflection of historical reality. The quaint *shtetl* featured in Marc Chagall's paintings and the stories of Sholem Aleichem never actually existed.[5] The highest ratio of Jewish inhabitants in Buczacz during the modern era was reached in the second part of the nineteenth century, when Jews constituted over two-thirds of the town's population, the rest being Poles and Ukrainians. By the eve of the First World War, massive emigration caused by growing poverty, as well as increasing numbers of Christian town dwellers, had diminished the ratio of Jewish inhabitants to just over half of the total.[6] This was a characteristic pattern throughout Eastern Galicia, where rural Ukrainians constituted the majority of the population, while Poles and—especially in the smaller and mid-sized urban settlements—Jews dominated the towns and cities.[7]

This mix of populations meant that the German genocide of the Jews took place within a complex and increasingly volatile web of ethnic, religious, political, and national affiliations. In implementing the final solution throughout Europe, the Germans adapted with terrifying agility to vastly different local circumstances. Yet these circumstances largely determined the manner, speed, and scope of the killing, as well as its effects on the rest of the population.[8] As noted above, in studying the Holocaust on the local level, we discover that the category of bystanders becomes meaningless.

When an invading power joins forces with local elements to murder a segment of the population, there are only degrees of engagement, ranging from full cooperation to utter rejection. Within that context we can identify a prevalent gray zone: some who hide the persecuted also denounce them; some of the killers also shelter potential victims; some of the collaborators turn to resistance. Claims of indifference or passivity appear absurd, unless they encompass watching one's neighbors being shot, and then taking over their property.

The Germans marched into lands with a long history of both coexistence and conflict. That history had little to do with the occupiers, yet by necessity it played a part in the implementation of genocide. Even before the First World War, Galicia had been a site of contestation between Poles and Ukrainians, whose origins can be traced back to the 1600s. Four centuries of Jewish settlement in the area also left a legacy of often uneasy relations and occasional outbursts of violence. The conduct of all local protagonists during the Second World War was therefore in some measure governed by collective memories and acquired perceptions and norms of behavior.

Buczacz allows exploration into the deep roots of local genocide. We can reconstruct mass murder in a single site and examine competing postwar narratives in judicial discourse, memory, and commemoration. We can think of such a study as a collective "biography," in that it allows generations of Buczacz residents to speak out. To be sure, this is a schizophrenic "biography," since these voices from the past often speak in very different registers about themselves and their neighbors. But it is also a representative "biography," because it stands for an entire universe of similar towns and regions in Europe's eastern borderlands, a world that was wiped out and forgotten. The interest in that world cannot reside only in the manner and causes of its destruction. It was rich and varied by its own right. We know so little of it because the voices of its inhabitants have been silenced. By letting them speak again, a careful, in-depth local study can exemplify the richness of what had been lost even as it investigates the reasons for the disaster. To the extent that we can conjure Buczacz back to life, the tragedy of its assassination is better comprehended. It is difficult to mourn a life one never knew; it is harder to accept the loss of a life intimately shared.[9]

The final eruption of external and fraternal violence in the Second World War seemed to many both shocking and inevitable. But that is reading history backward. To be sure, there had been much prior talk in nationalist as well as technocratic circles about the need to "unmix" incompatible peoples, creeds, or races.[10] But no one in 1941 could have anticipated the scale and horror of what came to pass. Still, the question must be asked: why did such unprecedented and gruesome violence seem at the same time to be a natural outcome of past events? Was this "a problem from hell," as was said about the genocide in 1990s Yugoslavia, an expression of endemic, unstoppable violence?[11] Were the various ethnic groups just waiting for the right moment to leap at each other's throats? This view is as inaccurate of Slobodan Milošević's Yugoslavia as it is of towns such as Buczacz in the 1940s. It implies that some societies are just prone to violence and there is little that more civilized nations can do about it. The fact is that while there was indeed an internal potential for violence, it was triggered by outside invaders, often representatives of those very same self-proclaimed higher civilizations, whose goals, determined independently from the peoples they occupied, could only be achieved by fire and sword.

The province that came to be called Galicia following the Austrian annexation of southeast Poland in 1772 had not experienced major outbreaks of violence since the early eighteenth century and remained relatively calm until the First World War.[12] And yet, when the Germans arrived on the scene in July 1941, they needed to do very little, at times nothing at all, to incite violence.[13] This shift from coexistence to conflict can be understood in part through a detailed local history that traces the roots of this precarious interethnic balance from the very foundations of a town such as Buczacz in the late Middle Ages to its final destruction as a multiethnic community in the Second World War. In doing so, this local history recreates the widely diverging narratives of the past told by Poles, Ukrainians, and Jews throughout the intervening centuries. These starkly different stories about the town they shared were not necessarily antagonistic; often each group simply ignored the others as it wove its own tales of history and myth, memory and legend. Yet the ever present and powerful underlying assertion of cultural, spiritual, and material difference did end up creating a sense of an essential and unbridgeable divide between the groups.

Concentrating on a single town makes it possible to use a wide variety of sources in order to recreate its evolving social and cultural fabric over time and then to zoom further in and meticulously reconstruct the violent events of its final destruction in all their complexity. One might have expected only a thin documentary record and even fewer individual accounts for this remote Galician town. In fact, official documentation by the Austrian, Polish, Soviet, and Nazi regimes is plentiful, albeit riddled with prejudice and political bias. Early "voices" of the town's residents come from local histories and tourist accounts, collections of tales and legends, diaries and memoirs, works of fiction and journalism—all reflecting their writers' individual and collective religious, social, ethnic, and ideological perspectives. As we enter the town's final agony, official documentation thins out and the voices of its people multiply a hundredfold, becoming ever more desperate, shrill, and tortured, recorded in hundreds of testimonies deposited around the world, several important published memoirs, numerous court records, and the town's Jewish and Ukrainian memorial books, providing us altogether with a cacophony of voices that can be orchestrated into a single narrative, filled with contradictions, holes, and unanswered questions, to be sure, and yet richer than anything we have had until now.[14]

Some voices reach us with force and clarity from the even more distant, opaque past. Natan Hanover's *The Abyss of Despair*, a vivid eyewitness account of the devastation wrought by Bohdan Khmelnytsky and his Cossacks in the 1648 uprising against Polish rule, tells of the Polish and Jewish citizens of Buczacz fighting side-by-side on the city's walls.[15] The German tourist Ulrich von Werdum, who visited Buczacz in 1672, wrote that despite the town's destruction by Ottoman troops, Buczacz had "been largely rebuilt, especially by the Jews, who are very numerous in this town."[16] That year the Peace of Buczacz was signed under the giant linden tree on a hill overlooking the town—where it still stands—between the Turkish sultan and the Polish king. But only four years later the French traveler François-Paulin Dalairac reported that following more fighting, "the Turks [had] accomplished a lasting destruction" of Buczacz.[17]

Yet the town was rebuilt once again. When Dalairac returned in 1684, he observed that the Ruthenian peasants had put up their shacks "next to the gate of the city and under the guns of the castle," while within the walls "live only Jews and some Poles."[18] This was to remain the demographic and occupational pattern for the next two hundred years. The eighteenth century witnessed a period of peace and prosperity. Ruled by the immensely rich and notoriously eccentric Mikołaj Potocki—a patron of religion and the arts, a womanizer, a drinker, and a brawler—Buczacz gained its impressive town hall and monastery. It also experienced the arbitrary power of a grand Polish magnate: as the poet Zygmunt Krasiński wrote, Potocki "shot women on trees and baked Jews alive."[19]

Much of what we know about the early history of Buczacz comes from an account published in 1882 by the priest and historian Sadok Barącz, a fanatical Roman Catholic and devoted chronicler of Armenian origin.[20] Many of the documents he cites were subsequently destroyed. Another ardent collector was the writer S. Y. Agnon, whose sprawling account of Buczacz overflows with tales and legends of Jewish Buczacz and its magical rabbis. Agnon's premodern Buczacz seems to have nothing in common with that of Barącz save for their identical location.[21]

The Jewish Enlightenment, or Haskalah, which promoted modern education and social integration, promised to facilitate greater Jewish–Christian interaction.[22] And, indeed, some *maskilim* from Buczacz ended up as university-trained scholars, assimilationists, or Zionists. But in the course of the nineteenth century, as nationalism began to infiltrate people's lives, it also introduced new criteria for distinguishing between one group and another. By the late 1800s the central question was: to whom does the town, the region, and the state naturally and by right belong? As Poles and Ukrainians grappled with each other over ownership of Galicia, the Jews, who could only shift alliances from one group to another, found themselves in an increasingly precarious no-man's-land.[23]

Until the First World War, the Habsburg Empire managed relations between ethnonational groups in Galicia relatively effectively; heated rhetoric rarely transformed into physical violence. Instead, nationalism pushed for greater literacy and stimulated cultural activities, political engagement, and economic progress. All this changed dramatically in the Great War and the national–ideological struggles that followed it. Little has been written on the effect of the fighting in the East on such ethnically mixed communities as Buczacz. The devastation was on a scale not seen since the seventeenth century. Tens of thousands of soldiers were killed in close proximity to Buczacz, which was occupied twice by the Russians and remained close to the front for much of the war.

The Russian occupation also brought with it murderous pogroms. The diary of Antoni Siewiński, headmaster of the boys' school in Buczacz and an anti-Semitic Polish nationalist, provides an unparalleled, albeit deeply biased, view of his town under the first Russian occupation.[24] Just as Siewiński fled in the face of the second Russian offensive of summer 1916, the Russian Jewish soldier Aba Lev arrived in Buczacz on the heels of a victorious Cossack unit. The town, he wrote, presented a "terrifying picture of destruction, vandalism, and cruelty." He went on to describe the gruesome consequences of the pogrom that had just occurred there.[25] The author, playwright, and ethnographer S. Ansky, remembered today mostly for his play *The Dybbuk*, visited Buczacz in early 1917. As he wrote in his extensive account of the Russian occupation, passing through "scores of large avenues" in Buczacz that had been "destroyed and burned down," he was stuck by the "tragic scene of the dead city."[26] Rare surviving Austrian and Russian documents and photographs of wartime Buczacz confirm these impressions.[27]

The end of the First World War did not bring peace to Galicia. As the Austro-Hungarian Empire collapsed, Ukrainians and Poles began fighting over the province.[28] In the course of the conflict, which the Poles quickly won, numerous Ukrainian atrocities against Polish civilians were widely reported.[29] Meanwhile a series of Polish pogroms against Jewish communities prompted the establishment of two international commissions of inquiry. Much of the anti-Jewish violence was linked to allegations that the Jews were taking the wrong side in the conflict, not taking any side at all, or professing Zionism. Whichever it was, the Jews clearly did not fit into the Polish or Ukrainian visions of a new nation-state.[30]

In the wake of yet another war, this time between Poland and Soviet Russia over the postwar boundaries of the two states, these national, ideological, and interethnic conflicts left a bitter legacy of resentment, suspicion, and rage.[31] Ukrainian hopes to set up an independent state had been dashed as they found themselves under Polish rule; Polish attempts to colonize the region were met with violent Ukrainian resistance, which led to even more oppressive policies; and Jewish aspirations to integrate into Poland encountered popular and official opposition. By the 1930s, the Organization of Ukrainian Nationalists (OUN), established in 1929, was becoming increasingly radicalized, not least under the influence of Nazi Germany;[32] the Polish authorities were instituting anti-Semitic measures;[33] and growing numbers of young Jews drifted toward socialism and Zionism.[34]

A mass of police reports, political pamphlets, personal letters and diaries, and postwar memoirs reflect some of these trends in Buczacz.[35] The town remained politically and culturally vibrant throughout the interwar period. It had far more restaurants and hotels, cafes and bars, than one can find there today.[36] Such figures as the historian of the Warsaw Ghetto, Emanuel Ringelblum, and the "Nazi hunter" Simon Wiesenthal began their lives there.[37] Yet the mood was growing darker. Agnon, who visited Buczacz in 1930, saw a Jewish community in decline.[38] Many were leaving. A few young working-class Jews joined a local communist party cell, but this too did not provide a space for genuine interethnic relations, and not long thereafter communist activists demonstrated their own violent potential.[39] Many younger Ukrainians were joining the OUN; some of them would later show up on lists of the auxiliary police units recruited by the Germans. Postwar investigations and trials show them as participating in the murder of their Jewish and Polish neighbors.[40]

When the Soviets took over Galicia in 1939, a brief moment of exhilaration and hope was followed by two years of political terror and economic collapse. Driven by suspicion of enemy nationalities, social classes, and integral nationalists, the Soviets deported tens of thousands of Poles, Jews, and Ukrainians. This was oppression on an entirely new scale, followed by the mass execution of mostly Ukrainian political prisoners, just as the Germans attacked in late June 1941.[41] These state-ordered murders greatly exacerbated interethnic animosity and played into the hands of the invading Nazis, who were quick to blame them on the Jews while posing as liberators from so-called Judeo-Bolshevism. The ensuing massacres of Jewish populations can be traced back directly to Soviet policies and Nazi propaganda, though their deeper origins stretch back at least to the First World War.[42]

As anti-Jewish violence became a daily routine in German-occupied Buczacz, this community of increasingly fragile coexistence was transformed into a community of genocide. Not all protagonists conformed to the roles assigned to them in conventional accounts: if many younger members of prewar Ukrainian nationalist organizations became direct participants in Nazi extermination policies, some older conservative Ukrainian political and religious leaders tried to prevent the violence.[43] While prewar Polish elites had supported the exclusion of Jews, they appear to have been more likely to shelter Jews or at least to sympathize with them than either their Ukrainian neighbors or Poles in the Polish heartland, not least because they also became targets of violence and ethnic cleansing. Conversely, Ukrainians sheltering Jews could also be seen by patriotic neighbors, local priests, and OUN members or sympathizers as betraying the national cause of creating a Pole- and Jew-free Ukraine.[44] While many peasants clearly took part in the killing, some poor villagers on isolated farms hid Jews for little or no compensation.[45] Finally, while the Germans targeted Jews as a group, the Buczacz Jewish Council and police were notorious for their corruption and despised as tools of the Gestapo.[46] Yet several Jewish police officers eventually joined the resistance.[47]

Between fall 1942 and summer 1943 the vast majority of the Jews of Buczacz and the surrounding towns and villages were murdered. Most of the killing occurred during several roundups organized by Sipo personnel from Czortków and accomplished with ample local assistance. Mass shootings occurred primarily in two sites on either side of the town—Fedor Hill, behind the magnificent Greek Catholic Basilian Monastery, and Baszty Hill, where the ancient Jewish cemetery was located. The last roundup in June 1943 also targeted the town's Jewish police, some of whose members fought back and escaped to the forest.[48] Survivors of these massacres were mostly either hidden by local villagers or employed in the few remaining labor camps and farms scattered around this region.

Then, in spring 1944, the territories surrounding Buczacz erupted into a wave of horrific and increasingly chaotic violence. The German Wehrmacht, forced to retreat from parts of Eastern Galicia in March, counterattacked the following month and drove back the Red Army. Buczacz was again under German rule. Of the approximately eight hundred Jewish survivors who had come out of hiding after the first liberation, fewer than a hundred were still alive when the Red Army returned in July 1944. In the intervening months, this remote region of Eastern Europe became the scene of mayhem and devastation, cruelty and suffering, a last frenzied upheaval after three years of total war and genocide. The Czortków Sipo outpost and its Ukrainian auxiliaries continued to hunt down and murder Jews until it was finally dismantled in early 1944.[49] As the Gestapo vacated the scene, some local German officials, along with commanders of retreating combat units, actually protected the remnants of the Jewish population from local militias and roaming bandits, disbanded Ukrainian auxiliary police, and murderous villagers.

Throughout this period, even as the Red Army and Wehrmacht were slaughtering each other, the Ukrainian Insurgent Army (UPA)—the military arm of the more radical faction of OUN led by Stepan Bandera—which had already carried out a vast ethnic cleansing operation against the Poles in the neighboring province of Volhynia, engaged in similarly bloody actions in Galicia; any surviving Jews the UPA encountered were also murdered.[50] The retreating Germans actually helped save the Poles of the eastern territories, loading them into trains heading toward the relative safety of Poland's heartland. When the Soviets finally broke through the German lines in July, they launched a massive liquidation operation geared to uproot military and political Ukrainian nationalist organizations seen as collaborators with the "German fascists" and opponents of Soviet power.[51] What the Jews perceived as liberation, many Ukrainians saw as reoccupation. The soil of Eastern Galicia was soaked in blood. But the question of who spilled the blood, and for what reason, has remained for many decades open to interpretation, obfuscation, and distortion.

Very little has been written on the fate of Eastern Galicia's few remaining Jews during these last months of German occupation and early period of Soviet rule in Poland's former eastern territories. While historians have begun to examine the ethnic cleansing of the Poles and the repression of the OUN-UPA by the Red Army and NKVD (Soviet secret police), histories of the Holocaust, including works focused on this region, have not devoted much attention to these crucial months.[52] The main reason for this seems to be that lack of official documentation and a reluctance to rely on personal testimonies have combined to deter historians from this task: most German documents were destroyed; Soviet records were inaccessible for many decades, are not always easy to come by even today, and are not particularly reliable; and documents and pamphlets by Polish and Ukrainian underground organizations, scattered in numerous archival holdings, provide only fragmented and highly partisan information.

And yet, for the few survivors of the mass murder of the Jews in this region, it was precisely these last months of the occupation that remained seared most deeply in their minds and determined to a large extent the manner in which they remembered, and the perspective from which they told their Holocaust experience as a whole. These Jewish narratives of murder and survival not only are missing from mainstream Holocaust historiography but also differ profoundly from those related by Ukrainians and Poles. From this perspective we can say that quite apart from the different manner in which the events were actually experienced by these different protagonists, the divergence in their subsequent telling and historical reconstruction has contributed to the ongoing memory wars ranging from political rhetoric to scholarly disputes.[53]

The fact of the matter is that we actually possess numerous eyewitness reports, in diaries, letters, postwar testimonies, and written accounts, as well as in judicial records and memoirs. These personal perspectives offer an extraordinarily rich source of information on the entire war, complementing official records and enabling us to sketch a detailed picture of genocide on the local level. Historians have underused these accounts, viewing them as both too subjective and too painful. This has greatly impoverished our understanding of crucial aspects of the Second World War and the Holocaust. These are reports from hell on earth, where there was little room for pity and forgiveness. Yet they also contain moments of sacrifice, compassion, and humanness, by members of the local population as well as, remarkably, some German military and administrative personnel.

In June 1943 the Germans declared Buczacz and the surrounding towns and villages *Judenrein*, or clean of Jews. All Jews not employed on the few remaining agricultural farms and labor camps could be shot on sight. As the teenager Eliasz Chalfen reported four years later, this led to a wave of killings of Jews hiding in peasants' farm, with the victims either being denounced to the Ukrainian police—who shot them on site—or killed by the very peasants who had previously agreed to shelter them for substantial fees.[54] Ester Grintal, aged eighteen at the time, recalled in 1997 that when "the Ukrainian militia passed through" the forced-labor farm where she worked, she would "hide in the toilet and count the shots, knowing by that how many people were killed." Later, "Cossacks and others who had collaborated with the Germans" appeared in the area and "began murdering" the Jews:

> They did not have enough guns, so they hanged people, or killed them with axes, etc. They came to our camp with some collaborators from the village. They locked [us up] in an empty barn ... They began beating us ... They shot a line of people with one bullet ... but the bullet didn't reach me. Again, I was put in a line, and again the bullet didn't kill me. So they began killing people with knives. I was stabbed three times.

The German army doctor who treated Grintal a few days later reportedly said: "What did the Ukrainian swine do to you?"[55] We cannot say precisely who those Ukrainians were. From Grintal's description it appears that in her specific case they belonged to units that had fought alongside the Germans. Many testimonies refer to the Banderowcy or Banderivtsy, the common Polish and Ukrainian designation for the men of OUN-UPA derived from the name of their leader, Stepan Bandera. At times this term was confused with the common German description of partisans and resistance fighters as bandits. But in 1943, the OUN, which had previously collaborated with the Germans, was turning against them, even as it saw the approaching Soviets as its real enemy. The ranks of its military arm, the UPA, were filled with men who had previously served as auxiliary policemen in German uniforms and had participated in the mass murder of the Jews. Subsequently Ukrainians who had served in the Waffen-SS Division "Galicia," crushed by the Red Army in summer 1944, also joined the UPA. And then there were also real bandits and brutalized peasants who exploited the chaos in the region to loot, rape, extort money, and murder, for whom the Jews were simply the easiest targets.[56]

Pity and empathy were rare, though not entirely extinct, sentiments during those dark times; they stood out precisely because they were no longer expected. More often, cruelty and betrayal dominated the experience of the hunted. Arie Klonicki wrote in his diary in 1943: "The hatred of the immediate surroundings ... knows no boundaries. Millions of Jews have been slaughtered and it is not yet satiated!"[57] He and his wife, who were hiding in the fields not far from Buczacz, were denounced and murdered shortly thereafter. Joachim Mincer recorded in his diary that in nearby Tłumacz, a series of "executions took place in the prison yard. The perpetrators," he stressed, "were mainly Ukrainian policemen as well as members of the [German] criminal police," and "the main perpetrator was an individual by the name of Bandrowski," who "liked to shoot Jews on the street." Bandrowski "shot the sister of [Judenrat member] Dr. Szpitzer in her yard." She, in turn, "had been denounced by young Kolewicz, a worker of the electric factory." This same "Kolewicz also shot Friedl Haber, while his friend Sytnik shot the young fourteen-year-old daughter of the Weischler family."[58] Mincer himself was killed in 1943. Yoel Katz, seventeen at the end of the war, vividly recalled many years later how the peasants surrounded his camp, shouting, "All the children out, we are going to kill you!" Some were killed with axes; others put in a row and shot with a single bullet.[59]

Conflicting memories of rescue and betrayal reflect the chaos and vagaries of fortune at the time. Edzia Spielberg-Flitman, liberated at the age of fourteen, recalled that in early July 1941 her aunt and cousins were axed to death by a group of Ukrainian villagers, including the children's female teacher, just after the Red Army pulled out and before the Germans arrived. But toward the end of the occupation, she was hidden with her mother and brother by a "poor farmer with a wife and four children." The peasant woman said to them, "It doesn't matter how long it takes, we will share our bread and potatoes with you." Yet the peasant who hid Edzia's relatives nearby betrayed them, and they were murdered by Ukrainian policemen. Later Edzia worked as a washerwoman for a German army unit but was denounced as a Jew by a Ukrainian workmate. Instead of killing them, the German commander escorted Edzia and her family to the Soviet lines, saying, "I hope you all live well." She recalled that "the Ukrainians ... were worse than the Germans," not least because in her estimation, "80 percent" of her family "were killed by the Ukrainians who were our friends."[60]

By that time, spring–summer 1944, most of the Jews of Galicia had already been murdered. But without these personal perspectives, we would have known close to nothing about this period. In 1948 Mojżesz Szpigiel, aged forty-nine, testified that in January 1944 Ukrainian militiamen had murdered most of the surviving 120 Jews on the farm where he worked, including his fourteen-year-old son: "It is important to state," he emphasized, "that this killing was not a German action, that it was performed by Ukrainian policemen and bandits." Most survivors of that massacre were butchered in yet another bandit attack. "The child orphans," reported Szpigiel, were "stacked up in a pile," while other victims were "lying with open guts." The local German administrator, a certain Vathie, had tried to protect his workers. When he left, "the Jews earnestly cried." But his replacement, a young German army officer, is said by Szpigiel to have promised them: "As long as I am here, nothing will happen to you."[61] We do not know the name of this particular officer; our only source of information about him comes from the Jews he saved. A few hundred survivors converged on the town of Tłusty, near Buczacz, where the officer was stationed, until the Red Army arrived.

Personal testimonies and interviews, many given decades later, some by elderly Christian eyewitnesses, further add to this picture. In 2003 the ethnic Polish resident of Buczacz, Julija Mykhailivna Trembach, recalled with horror the mass murder of the Jews, which she watched from her own window. But she also insisted that "our people, Ukrainians and Poles, tried to help" the Jews "however they could. They made dugouts in the ground, and Jews hid there. Secretly people would bring food to those dugouts. And God knows how much food I brought by myself." Married to a Ukrainian man, Trembach refrained from mentioning local complicity in the murder of the Jews. Buczacz, she said, was "populated mostly by Jewish people. They were cultured, wealthy, enterprising and intelligent people. All the so-called 'stone houses' in the center of the town belonged to them. Jewish people constituted the local intelligentsia."[62]

The ethnic Ukrainian Maria Mykhailivna Khvostenko was similarly horrified by the public massacres of the Jews. But while she recalled that along with the Germans, they were rounded up by "police with six-pointed stars"—that is, members of the local Jewish *Ordnungsdienst*—she left out the fact that far larger numbers of Ukrainian auxiliaries and police were invariably present at, and often participated in, such mass killings. But looking back at these horrors decades later, she did not refrain from criticizing current indifference and erasure:

> On the western slope of Fedir Hill there is a small forest where the Jewish community that was murdered in 1942–1943 by the German fascists is buried. It's time for our city—and not only the city, but also the region and the country—to pay attention to the place where the fascists murdered many Jews and to honor their memory, to put there a decent monument or a sculpture. For they were honest citizens of the city and the country, who loved our land and our city, worked for it, and suffered guiltlessly. ... We should honor and remember them so that it will never happen again.[63]

Two decades later this has still not been done in Buczacz.

For some of those not targeted, genocide proved profitable. As the Ukrainian gymnasium teacher Viktor Petrykevych noted in his diary in January 1944, most people in Buczacz were experiencing "unprecedented poverty," but "often people ... who had earned very little before the war, now profit and earn more than they would have ever dreamt possible." The source of this new wealth soon became clear: as the Red Army came closer, many "merchants, artisans, and so forth, who were living in houses that were formerly Jewish ... are moving out ... They fear Jewish revenge."[64]

To be sure, there was no Jewish revenge. The few Jews who returned to Buczacz following its recapture by the Soviets left soon thereafter. According to some accounts, they were all living in one building for fear of attacks by their neighbors. This was a violent time: reports of killings of Jews either by OUN-UPA fighters or by local bandits continued for months after the liberation. No one cared much about the survivors, let alone the dead.⁶⁵ In the area of Buczacz, as in vast tracts of Eastern Europe more generally, much of the population did not perceive the Red Army's return as liberation, and quite often considered the Soviet repression of local nationalists—who had previously collaborated with the German authorities in the hopes of furthering their own particular agendas—as precisely that much-feared Jewish revenge, which Jews may well have hoped for but were in no position to exact. The association between Jews and communists, labeled in Poland as *żydokomuna*, combined with the much more material worry that returning Jews might claim back their property from the locals who had moved in explains the continued anti-Jewish violence and the divergent memory and historiography of the postwar era in Eastern Europe.⁶⁶

And thus, the final phase in the transformation of Buczacz into a homogeneous community came with the return of the Soviets. Thanks to a wealth of hitherto inaccessible documents, it is now possible to reconstruct the liquidation and deportation policies by the Soviet authorities in 1944–9. While large numbers of Ukrainian fighters, along with their families, were sent to Gulags or exiled to Kazakhstan, most of the surviving Poles were sent to Poland in a vast Polish-Ukrainian population exchange.⁶⁷ The brutalization of the war years also left its marks. Investigations of the genocide of the Jews often culminated in summary justice. As Jewish survivor Rene Zuroff recalled in 1995 about events in newly liberated Buczacz:

> There were also hangings of collaborators in the municipality. People, both Jews and Christians, would tell who the collaborators were, and these collaborators would be rounded up and hanged in the town square. I was a little girl, and we would go for our entertainment to the hangings, and we were totally happy to go to our daily hangings of the horrible collaborators—who mutilated their victims. We saw them strung up and urinating and I'd be in heaven. My mother would come and drag me away and I begged to have my daily entertainment. There was none of all these trials with witnesses, one would say, "He did it, string him up!"⁶⁸

The inhabitants of contemporary Buczacz are former Ukrainian residents and their descendants, villagers who moved into town after the war, and ethnic Ukrainians deported from Poland. Most know very little about their town's past. The communists had subsumed the genocide of the Jews under a general narrative of Soviet martyrdom and heroism.⁶⁹ The new West Ukrainian authorities have resurrected the nationalists of the Second World War as heroic figures, neglecting to mention their role in the destruction of their Polish and Jewish neighbors. Thus the fate of the Jews has remained outside the official historical narrative.

The survivors and exiles, however, never forgot their hometown: communities of memory around the world preserved their separate narratives and passed them on to their children. A memorial association in Wrocław has published a stream of personal accounts by Polish survivors; the town's exiled former wartime mayor put together a memorial book narrating the history of the town and the region from the Ukrainian perspective; and the Jewish memorial book of Buczacz contains valuable historical scholarship and many personal testimonies but has almost nothing to say about the Christian inhabitants of the town.[70]

Jewish life has not revived in Buczacz and attempts to commemorate the victims have been largely unsuccessful. Thus the history of Buczacz and its demise must be sought elsewhere. Dozens of archives in Russia, Ukraine, Austria, Germany, France, Britain, the United States, and Israel contain vast amounts of information written in nine languages on this little borderland town, as do court records and hundreds of written, audiotaped, and videotaped testimonies, as well as interviews, which constitute an especially valuable source for reconstructing the fraught interethnic relations and the daily life of genocide in Buczacz.

In 1995 I interviewed my mother about her hometown. For the first time she spoke about her childhood, and that conversation set me off on a long historical and personal journey. We had planned to visit Buczacz together; she had not been there since leaving it at the age of eleven in 1935. But not long after the interview she fell ill and passed away three years later. When I finally reached Buczacz, I was glad that my mother had not seen the erasure of memory so blatantly displayed there. But I was sorry that she and so many other people with whom I spoke over the years about the town they loved, and who preserved cherished memories of childhood in a prewar world that seemed, from a distance, to have been an era of innocence on the eve of destruction, were no longer alive by the time I completed my study of the life and death of their hometown. In its own modest way, *Anatomy of a Genocide* was an attempt to reconstruct what had been destroyed and erased, to record the lives and memories of the lost, and to serve as a record of a forgotten past for future generations. For if we cannot undo genocide, we must at least not allow it to cover up its own tracks.

CHAPTER 4
TESTIMONIES AS HISTORICAL DOCUMENTS

Why Testimonies?

This chapter elaborates on the importance of integrating personal accounts, or testimonies, into the historical reconstruction of the Holocaust as documents with equal validity to more official sources. By testimonies I mean all forms of evidence provided by individual protagonists in historical events. These include contemporary accounts and diaries, as well as postwar interviews, written, oral, audio, and videotaped testimonies, courtroom witness accounts, and memoirs. Such testimonies were given by people belonging to all three categories we have come to associate with the Holocaust and other genocides, namely, victims, perpetrators, and bystanders. But to a great extent, one benefit of using materials of this kind is that they largely, though not entirely, undermine this very categorization. In addition, as this chapter shows, these eyewitness testimonies illuminate not only mass killing but also survival, rescue, and resistance.

The borderlands of Eastern Europe were sites of interaction between a multiplicity of ethnic and religious groups. For city- and town-dwellers, as much as for villagers, living side-by-side with people who spoke a different language and worshipped God differently was part of their own way of life and that of their ancestors. For many, their difference in ethnicity from their neighbors corresponded to different positions within the socioeconomic order, and this differentiation between those with status and wealth and those living in poverty and subjugation created resentment and envy. As new national narratives began to supplement the old religious and social differentiation between groups, they also provided a new retrospective meaning to the past and fueled a new urgency about mending the present in a manner that would conform to perceived historical rights, and correct perceived historical injustices. In the fantasy each national movement shared, the future belonged to *them*, or to no one at all. The coexistence, which had been the status quo of people's lives, with all its benefits and shortcomings, friction and cooperation, as well as occasional outbursts of violence, came to be seen as unnatural, as a problem to be solved, often by radical social surgery. Cutting out unwanted, seemingly malignant, and allegedly foreign elements would, it was said, enable the newly discovered and supposedly eternal national body to thrive.

It is, however, exceedingly difficult to understand and analyze how this transformation occurred on the ground and how it was perceived by its social protagonists. How was it that zones of coexistence were turned into communities of ethnic cleansing and genocide? To be sure, it was largely external forces, in the shape of occupying states or far-flung national movements, that determined the general course of events and provided the ideological impetus for population policies, mass displacement, and mass murder. But the way such policies and ideas were implemented on the ground had to do not only with the interaction between perpetrators and victims but also with the actions and interactions of the different local groups upon whom these policies were enacted. A close look at what happened in small communities on Europe's eastern borderlands provides us with much insight into the social dynamics of interethnic communities at times of extreme violence. Yet such a view from below of borderland communities also necessitates making use of records of the past often eschewed by historians, such as first-person accounts.

From the point of view of the historian, the single most important benefit of using testimonies is that they bring into history events that would otherwise remain completely unknown, since they are missing from more conventional documentation found in archives, which are mostly written by the perpetrators or organizers of genocide. Hence personal accounts can at times save events from oblivion. But they also provide a very different perspective on events that *are* known from conventional documentation. This other perspective has in turn two additional advantages. First, it may serve as a factual correction to official accounts; second, it provides the historian with a different vantage point and thereby helps in producing a richer and more complex—in a sense, a three-dimensional—reconstruction of the event as a whole. Finally, by virtue of being personal, or subjective, such testimonies provide insight into the lives and minds of men, women, and children who experienced the events, and thus tell us much more than any official document about the mental landscape of the period, the psychology of the protagonists, and the views and perceptions of others.

Historians have traditionally been wary of using testimonies as historical evidence. Some have eschewed their use altogether, calling them subjective and therefore unreliable.[1] Others have preferred to use only testimonies offered soon after to the event itself and have largely avoided those given decades later.[2] Others still, most conventionally, have used personal accounts only to illustrate the nature of a historical event whose reconstruction is based on seemingly more reliable documents culled from official archives.[3] This practice, to my mind, has greatly impoverished our understanding of the Holocaust, as it would that of any other historical event. There is no reason to believe that official contemporary documents written by Gestapo, SS, Wehrmacht, or German administrative officials are any more accurate or objective, or any less subjective and biased, than accounts given by those they were trying to kill. Moreover, the use of testimonies only as confirmation of events already known through other documentation condemns to oblivion events only known from testimonies. Finally, the quest to understand the mentality and motivation of the perpetrators, which has already produced a small cottage industry, would have benefited a great deal from knowing what their victims said about them and how *they* described their actions. And, of course, testimonies can tell us a great deal about the lives of those subjected to German occupation and the relations between the different ethnic groups that came under German rule.

As noted, some historians have argued that testimonies, if used at all, are more reliable the closer they are to the time of the event. Those given decades later are said to be suspect both because of the eroding effects of time on memory and because of the cumulative influence of other forms of representation and commemoration that mold the content and form of an individual's recollection. There is of course some truth to this argument. But anyone who has worked with large numbers of testimonies will know that there are two major qualifications to this assertion. First, that especially in the case of those who survived as young teenagers or even children—that is, those most likely to have still been alive six decades later—their experiences in the Holocaust could often be recounted in full only after they reached greater maturity, thanks to the healing effects of time on their traumatized souls, and only long after rebuilding their lives and establishing new families. Second, that in some, though not all cases, testimonies given decades after the event do in fact have all the freshness and vividness of a first account that one may find in some early postwar testimonies. This occurs especially in cases where the memory of the event was kept sealed inside the mind and never exposed to the light of day; without telling and retelling there is much less contamination by the "noise in the system" of external discourse and representation.

These "memory boxes" were finally unlocked and opened up due to the advancing age of the witnesses and their desire to leave a record of events, whether simply to their own children and (especially) grandchildren, or more generally to posterity, at a cultural moment more attuned to listening (designated by one scholar "the era of the witness").[4] Such testimonies are also strongly motivated by the urge to recall and inscribe in memory and history the names of the murdered that would otherwise sink into total oblivion with the passing of the witness, and at times also to record the names and actions of long-forgotten perpetrators, collaborators, and especially rescuers. Hence such testimonies contain much of the clarity and emotional impact of accounts given immediately in the wake of the events.

There has been, of course, a great deal of writing about testimonies as a form of memory, as a confrontation with trauma, a literary device, a means to gain insight into the psychology of survivors, or even as a therapeutic tool.[5] But what I am arguing for is that testimonies are also historical documents of invaluable importance that have been grossly underused by historians, especially in the case of the Holocaust, despite the fact that this is a historical event that has produced a vast amount of such materials. Clearly, personal accounts do not tell a single story and are full of contradictions, errors, misjudgments, and untruths—though no less so than any other document. They should be treated not only with the same care and suspicion as any other piece of evidence pulled out of an archive but also with the same respect, as yet another piece in the puzzle of the past. That they are concerned with traumatic events should not deter us from using them; quite to the contrary, the nature of those events must indicate to us that we would never be able to fathom them without making full use of the accounts of those who experienced them.

Integrating all these materials into a single text is clearly a difficult and complex undertaking. What one quickly realizes is that apart from such matters as chronology and geography—and not always even then—different protagonists saw and remembered the same event quite differently. Indeed, from the most elementary optical perspective, they did, since they were, so to speak, standing at different places, and because no two individuals can see the same event with precisely the same eyes. But beyond the optical perspective, such differences in view emanate from the fact that each person played a different role in the event. This, in turn, has also determined the manner in which they remembered it and in which they were willing or able to recall it in words or in writing.

There is, of course, nothing unique in this condition of historical documentation. Herodotus and Thucydides, whose different methods of treating their sources still guide us today, were already aware of this conundrum. The use of testimonies makes it more difficult to say what precisely happened at a given place and time; testimonies tell us more—perhaps more than we would like to know—about what happened, and they tell us that different people experienced, and in some cases remembered and recorded, the same events differently. We may decide to deliver a verdict on what actually happened on the basis of our documentation; or we may prefer to say that we are unable or unwilling to determine precisely what occurred and can simply report several versions or points of view.

Clearly, there are limitations to this kind of documentation. To my mind, testimonies can be most profitably used on two conditions. First, one must collect a critical mass of them, rather than relying on merely a few, if that is at all possible—although I would still argue that even a single testimony that "saves" an event from historical oblivion should and must be used. Second, such testimonies gain immensely from being focused on one locality and a relatively limited span of time and cast of characters. Within such a context, one can much more easily cross-check many testimonies that recount the same events from different perspectives, as well as integrate these individual perspectives into a historical reconstruction that uses all other available kinds of documentation. In the case of the Holocaust this would mean especially official reports by police, military, and civil administration, as well as documentation of postwar trials and, finally, scholarly secondary literature.

One last issue cannot be avoided. The use of testimonies of trauma is a very difficult exercise for the historian. It is first of all difficult psychologically because these accounts almost invariably reveal aspects of human nature that one would rather not hear or know about. They are, in that sense, traumatizing. They may also undermine our trust in the historian's craft itself, since it is ultimately based on rationalist and Enlightenment values, on the alleged ability to divine the truth of the past and to identify humanity's progress and improvement. Testimonies also make it very difficult to retain the necessary detachment from the material; in other words, they may hamper the practice of the methods and undermine the philosophical assumptions that have come to be associated with good scholarly writing since the birth of the modern historical profession.

This is possibly the more profound reason for the reluctance of many historians to use testimonies. In other words, historians want to protect their own psyche from the damage they fear might be caused it by, and to protect their profession from the undermining potential of, such testimonies. Yet these accounts are about an event that itself posed the greatest challenge to the values and methods on which the work of historians still bases itself today. These testimonies emanate from the very heart of that historical moment and site of darkness, and because they recount an historical event, they too are part of the historical record, perhaps the most crucial part of all.

Historians cannot escape the event and its implications for them as historians, as individual human beings, and as members of humankind, simply by leaving these accounts to gather dust in crumbling boxes. Historians need to face this challenge and cope with it as best they can. After all, these are accounts by individuals who were determined that what they experienced and saw and remembered should not be forgotten. Historians have largely betrayed these witnesses. By now the vast majority of them are dead. But their recorded accounts can and should still be used, not merely in order to respect those who left them behind but in order to set the historical record straight.

In what follows, I will use testimonies given by residents of the Eastern Galician town of Buczacz and by people who spent some time there during the German occupation, in order to explore some aspects of death and survival, as well as altruism and defiance, in an interethnic town at a time of genocide. In this region, the majority of the rural population was Ukrainian, while Poles and Jews constituted the majority of town and city dwellers. Buczacz belonged to Poland in the interwar period, was occupied by the Soviet Union in 1939–41, and was ruled by the Germans in 1941–4. My general argument here is that one of the central questions of historical research on the Holocaust in Eastern Europe—namely, the impact of local interethnic relations on the genocide of the Jews—must be analyzed through a close reading of testimonies by the protagonists in these events. I further suggest that this can be accomplished especially by examining a wide range of testimonies from a geographically limited locality.

I begin with an examination of testimonies on collaboration, betrayal, and denunciation, and then proceed to analyze evidence of rescue and resistance. However, as will become clear, there is both a fair amount of overlap between these categories and a degree of inner contradiction depending on the nature, the timing, and the audience of eyewitness reports.

Collaboration, Betrayal, and Denunciation

Approximately half of those murdered in the Holocaust perished in ghettos and mass executions at or near their places of residence, in open-air, often public events. Even when the shootings were conducted in slightly more isolated forests or cemeteries, the brutal roundups, which were accompanied by a great deal of gratuitous violence, took place in public view. Killing sites were frequently close enough for the shots to be heard by other residents. In most cases, locally recruited auxiliary troops and policemen actively participated.

Such spectacles, rarely portrayed in any detail in official documentation or postwar historiography, are amply documented in contemporary diaries, postwar testimonies, courtroom witness accounts, and memoirs. These eyewitness reports shed new light on interethnic coexistence and violence in Eastern Europe and reveal both the peculiarities of the Holocaust and its affinity to other instances of modern genocide. In much of Central and Western Europe, the Jews were "simply" deported to the "East," and the few who returned rarely recounted their experiences or found willing listeners for many years thereafter. Conversely, the people of Eastern Europe, Jews and Gentiles alike, were direct witnesses to and protagonists in a genocide that became an integral, routine, almost "normal" feature of daily life during the war, whether it targeted, spared, or was exploited by them.

It bears stressing what this "normality" of communal genocide literally meant. For in Eastern Europe large numbers of Jewish victims were murdered in full view of their neighbors, in public sites where Jews and Gentiles had lived side-by-side for centuries.[6] Many postwar inhabitants of former Jewish properties retained vivid recollections of the previous owners and the circumstances of their murder. This, too, is a characteristic of communal massacre, which is almost the exact inverse of industrial killing in the extermination camps. Communal massacre devastates lives and warps psyches. It belies the very notion of passive bystanders: everyone becomes a protagonist, hunter and prey, resister and facilitator, loser and profiteer. Often, in the course of events, people come to play several roles. And the resulting sorrow and shame, self-deception and denial, still infuse the way in which people remember, speak, and write about that past.

Nothing demonstrates these aspects of the Holocaust more clearly than testimonies. They expose its intimate, personally devastating effects as much as they reveal the opportunities it presented for greed and violence. Most important, testimonies repeatedly illustrate that even in the midst of the horror there was always a measure of choice, and that such choices could and did save lives and redeem souls. In these conditions, claims of indifference and passivity are meaningless, unless they include moving into your neighbors' home and sleeping in their still warm beds as soon as they have been dragged out of them and shot on the street.

Some non-Jewish residents of Buczacz, who vividly recalled the murder of their Jewish neighbors decades later, recalled their fate with much empathy: "We pitied those people," one of them said, "for they were beaten, always scared for their lives and never knowing what would happen to them next."[7] Eyewitnesses also often insisted that they had done everything they could to help the Jews despite the dangers this entailed.[8] Jewish witnesses interviewed at about the same distance of time remembered things differently, often recounting cases of local collaboration and denunciation, at times by the very people who had been hiding them. Anne Resnik's family shelter was betrayed by the barber whose shop was over it, and most of her family was murdered. Her sister was shot shortly before the first liberation by "the same people that were pretending to hide" her.[9] Similarly, Regina Gertner's sister was denounced by a Polish neighbor and killed just before the end of the occupation.[10] Yitzhak Bauer reported that the Polish dogcatchers Nahajowski and Kowalski specialized in discovering Jews and handing them over to the Germans.[11]

The sense of betrayal runs deep many decades later. John (Junik) Saunders, who had non-Jewish friends in school, remarked, "During the war you started to discover that they hate your guts … they didn't want to help us."[12] Robert Barton also had Gentile friends. He assumed a Polish identity during the war. The Germans, he noted, "could not tell who the Jew is and who is a Polack ... [but] the Polacks ... used to say ... you look like a Jew, you talk like a Jew, you walk like a Jew."[13] Jacob Heiss remembered local Ukrainians on horseback chasing and killing Jewish children.[14] Izio Wachtel recounted that in July 1941, after the Soviets retreated from his town of Czortków and "even before the Germans entered, the Ukrainians arrived at the town with ... axes and scythes and other instruments and slaughtered and killed and robbed the Jews. With the arrival of the Germans the wild killing ceased and the murder by orders began."[15]

Stories of false rescue are especially striking in this context. Shulamit Aberdam recalled in 1998 that "a Polish woman ... suggested ... [to] hide me." Her mother refused. "After the war we heard that the Polish woman had taken another girl, and after getting all the money handed her over to the Germans." Aberdam's family was ejected time and again by rescuers who robbed its members of their last belongings.[16] Fannie Kupitz, who survived as a girl by living with Ukrainians and often posing as one, commented in 1994: "They were good to me but they killed others."[17] As she told me in 2002, her German labor supervisor was fooled into thinking she was Ukrainian and wanted to send her to his wife in Germany.[18] But the locals could not be fooled so easily, and the thirteen-year-old Fannie "just decided to go on my own ... I always was afraid; I only wished I would get a bullet in my back ... I ... used to envy the people that were already dead, I used to envy when I saw a dog that is free and not afraid." When she met a Ukrainian she knew in the forest, "he said to me, 'Oh, you are still alive?'" But his wife took her in for a while. Later her rescuers returned from church citing the priest's words: "Whoever has Jews, let them go, don't keep them!" Shortly afterward she was denounced and fled into the forest.[19]

Girls, especially if they did not look Jewish, had a better chance of surviving than boys. But they were also targets of sexual abuse, rarely referred to directly in testimonies but often suggested in more subtle ways. One truck driver took Fannie into the forest.

> He says to me, "You probably had a husband." And I was so afraid, I was pulling my hair, I was breaking my fingers, I was crying, I said, "No, I don't have a husband and I am very young," I said. "Maybe you have a daughter, and somebody would do this to your daughter and what would you do?"

He then left her in the forest and drove away.[20]

Similarly, the 1945 testimony by the thirteen-year-old Rózia Brecher, who was hidden by Polish and Ukrainian women on a farm, reveals sheer terror from her main protector's brother-in-law, Hryń, a drunk and a collaborator: "Hryń came to the hayloft ... He hugged me and ... [asked if] I was once before in German hands and faced death ... and whether I was a communist. [He said] he would go to town to take part in the *Aktion*. At that moment I didn't want to live any longer." On another occasion, "Hryń climbed up to the hayloft ... He was very drunk ... and he asked who was my father and what organization [my parents] belonged to." Then again, "At midnight ... [Hryń] climbed up to the hayloft and grabbed me by the neck but I managed to scream and began to beg him to let me go. He said give me 1,000 ... [or] I will denounce you." Rózia recounts that she made "a hole in the roof [of the hayloft] and ... looked at the chickens [in the yard] and thought that soon I would be free."[21]

Much of the violence was due to greed. Fannie observed how seven of her relatives were discovered by Ukrainian police: "They knew these people ... they told them ... 'We are not going to do nothing to you, just give us whatever you have, and we will let you go.' They gave them everything, [and] when they went out, everyone separately [got] a bullet in the head."[22] Some young Jews tried to prevent this kind of killing or denouncing for profit. Alicia Appleman-Jurman recounted in 1996 how her brother's small resistance group "burned the farmer's barn or beat the farmers up ... as ... retaliation, so that ... people ... who were hiding Jews should get a message that you can't just betray them" for money. Eventually her brother too "was betrayed by a Polish boy who was ... helping out" and was hanged in the local police station. Not long thereafter, Alicia herself, who was just twelve years old, was arrested and registered by a Ukrainian police official, "my friend Olga's father ... who," before the war, "said he loved me like a daughter." On the eve of the liberation her mother was shot right in front of her after they were denounced by their Polish building supervisor.[23]

Toward the end of the German occupation, the region slipped into total chaos, and the few surviving Jews were at the mercy of greedy peasants, anti-Semitic Ukrainian militias, and local bandits of all descriptions, as well as Nazi murder squads. There is very little reliable official documentation on these last months and weeks of the war in Western Ukraine, but there are many vivid and terrifying testimonies. This is a history that can largely only be told on the basis of these accounts. It has some surprising twists and turns.

One striking account of these days was given in 1947 by the seventeen-year-old Eliasz Chalfen. This testimony implicates the Ukrainian police commander in Buczacz, Volodymyr Kaznovskyi, in taking an active part in the first mass execution there as early as August 28, 1941,[24] and goes on to describe many other roundups, in which "the Gestapo, with the help of the Ukrainian police, was trying to find hidden bunkers," and "our neighbors plundered [Jewish homes], taking everything they could," as well as collecting "valuables, gold teeth, etc.," from the thousands of victims of mass executions near the town. By the time of the chaos that preceded the German retreat, reports Chalfen, the "peasants ... were murdering Jews, taking their belongings and leaving the naked victims in the fields."[25] Yoel Katz recalled in 1995 that when the inmates of his labor camp were struck by a typhus epidemic just before the liberation, the peasants called the police to kill them, and then proceeded to massacre the Jews with axes and firearms. The Ukrainians, he concluded, "were very hard," stressing that the remnants of the inmates were eventually saved by "the Germans who came from the front [and] protected us from the Ukrainians until the Russians arrived."[26]

Who would help and who would not was often entirely unpredictable. Joe Perl, who was thirteen years old at the end of the occupation, testified in 1996 that he and his mother were hidden by a Ukrainian nationalist who was actually in charge of killing Jews and Poles.[27] Edzia Spielberg-Flitman recalled in 1995 how her mother was saved from being murdered by Ukrainian villagers by her female German friend, who was married to one of the local administrators. Indeed, like several other witnesses, she remembered that during the last months and weeks of the occupation, the few surviving Jews often ended up being protected from Ukrainian militias and bandits by German army and administrative officers. Following the liberation, when her family eventually moved to the West, Edzia recalled being "very happy to get away from the Ukrainians because they had pogroms after the war ... they were still killing us. They were so brutal."[28]

The middle-aged Mojżesz Szpigiel also testified about the surge of local mayhem and brutality in the last months of the occupation. When the forced-labor farm where he and his family worked was liquidated in 1943, they hid in the forest, where "we were attacked by peasants. The Ukrainians began to catch people, torture them, take their money." Szpigiel's father and his two nephews were killed by a Ukrainian. Returning to the farm, they found that all inmates who fell ill from the rampant epidemics had been killed by the Ukrainian police. Most of the survivors were butchered in two more attacks in early 1944 by Ukrainian militiamen and bandits using knives and pitchforks. But as Szpigiel related, when Ukrainian policemen tried once more to attack the last remaining Jews, who were now under the protection of an army unit retreating from the East, a German "major ... went [there] with his aide and hit one policeman on the head with his revolver, threw them out and ordered them to leave immediately."[29]

Izaak Szwarc, aged fifteen, reported on these same events shortly after the war. He recalled that at the labor camp, "the peasants ... wanted roundups to take place so that they could rob the Jews ... The village head forbade the peasants from giving us food. The peasants organized nightly guards around the camp so that the Jews could not escape ... The peasants supervised our work, they beat us, did not give us any water." When the camp was liquidated, "the peasants brought out hidden Jews ... In the forests Jews were attacked by bandits, and the peasants did not let us in." Under these conditions, the Jews "went to a village where the Germans were staying. We were safer there from the bandits ... We sensed that the peasants intended to remove us as witnesses to their crimes." On the eve of the liberation, as the Hungarian soldiers now stationed in the village retreated,

> the Vlasov-soldiers [former Soviet troops serving in the Wehrmacht] arrived ... They did not have any guns, only cold weapons. They murdered all the Jews they caught ... It was impossible to stay in the villages. The peasants organized roundups of Jews, killed them, discovered bunkers. Even those Jews who were hidden in bunkers at peasants' farms were killed by their hosts. The Jews began to gather in Tłusty. The [local German commander] ... promised that the Jews would not be harmed. Three-hundred Jews gathered there ... On March 23 the Soviets arrived.[30]

Rene Zuroff was only seven years old when she was liberated. In 1995, she recalled roundups in which she and her three-year-old sister would lie in the bunker and hear "the Germans ... screaming, 'Juden, Juden raus, raus!' and ... the Ukrainians and the Poles ... calling 'żyd, żyd!'" and then the "bloodbath in your house, outside the door, in the street, bodies everywhere." Her last recollections of the Holocaust are the most terrifying:

> We were hiding in the forest and our shelter was a field of tobacco ... One night we heard terrible screaming and curses in Ukrainian and running, there was a whole massacre; the Ukrainian militia came at night hunting out the Jews from the woods ... [They] were chasing the Jews with dogs and we heard this rampage and started running for our lives ... we were running blindly ... and it was the scariest thing I can remember, we saw dismembered bodies, bodies without heads, and we saw death all around us; so that was my nightmare in the tobacco fields and forest.

Rene and her family were rescued by wretchedly poor Polish peasants; the Poles by then were also being massacred by Ukrainian nationalists. They hid in a hole in a "barn ... full of rats and other vermin ... and when the animals urinated the urine would spill into the hole." But "the old polish woman was truly a saintly and wonderful human being who risked her life and that of her daughters. She gave us seven ... pirogi ... on Sunday, once a week we got food and very little in-between." Rene came to the United States in 1950, majored in foreign languages, married in 1962, and has two children, one of whom became a rabbi in Israel. She reported suffering from neuroses, hating the dark, not liking to be surrounded by people, and needing to always sit at the end of every table, "for a quick escape." She did not "have a great deal of ... trust and confidence in people."[31]

Rescue and Resistance

The testimonies cited above should demonstrate the importance of such materials for reconstructing the typical experience of Jewish victims, especially survivors, in the small towns of Eastern Galicia, and by extension in much of the rest of Eastern Europe. Such accounts also provide much insight into the psychological conditions that predominated during this period and thus help us understand both patterns of behavior at the time and the long-term effects of these events. In other words, these testimonies are crucial to any analysis of the mental makeup and resilience of those who endured the Holocaust and of the effects of trauma on memory, recollection, and witnessing.[32]

Nonetheless, the picture sketched above remains incomplete without more substantial reference to rescue, resistance, and intra-communal conflict. Relatively rare in the record as a whole, rescue features prominently in testimonies, even as they also recount numerous instances of betrayal and denunciation. If rescue was exceptional overall, it was a much more common experience for survivors on whose testimonies we must rely. Indeed, the memories of most protagonists have remained ambivalent on precisely this score: they lay blame and assert humaneness, expose betrayal, and recall altruism and sacrifice. Accounts by non-Jews often repress or marginalize Christian complicity and collaboration, while underscoring help and compassion, and in some cases blaming victims for their own fate. Jewish testimonies, quite apart from shifting uneasily between bitterness about the treachery of neighbors and gratitude for rescue by the righteous few, also alternate between repressing evidence of Jewish collaboration and corruption and expressing profound outrage and derision vis-à-vis those identified with the *Judenrat* and the Jewish police. Finally, compassion by Germans, perhaps precisely because of their local omnipotence, appears in such accounts as the strongest evidence for the possibility of choice and the potential for goodness even in the midst of genocide.

Choice constitutes the moral core of any discussion of mass murder; it also retains an underlying psychological dimension for those directly impacted by such events and for later generations.[33] Evidence of choice threatened to expose and shame those whose alibi for complicity was the alleged lack of alternative. But instances of altruism, however few, provide flashes of light in what would have otherwise remained a period of utter darkness. Such glimmers of humanness, faint and far between though they might have been, should not be removed from the historical record. They should be recounted because they occurred; they should be remembered because they give us hope; and they should be contextualized because they serve to highlight the far more prevalent phenomena of glee and greed, complicity and collaboration, violence and cruelty. And there can be no more reliable evidence for Gentile help, rescue, and sacrifice during the Holocaust than that derived from the testimonies of Jewish survivors.

Especially for children, survival depended on a combination of luck and the help of others, whether motivated by kindness or prospects of material gain. Safah Prüfer, a little girl from Buczacz interviewed soon after the liberation, recalled that her father "handed me and my little brother to a peasant we knew in our town." But following "a terrible *Aktion* ... daddy built a hiding-place in the forest ... One day the Ukrainian police arrived and shot everybody, only I alone survived. From that day on I began to fight for my existence on my own. I wandered alone for seven months, unable to find any shelter; then finally the Red Army liberated us."[34]

It is inconceivable that such a small girl could have survived the long winter without some help from the locals, however grudging. Non-Jews often claimed that such help was offered quite willingly. A Polish resident of Buczacz related in 2003 that during the war a young woman came running to her with a baby, "crying and exhausted ... At my own risk I hid them in the hayloft of the cowshed ... I fed that little girl from my own breast ... and I shared my own food with that woman." She stressed that this was not "the only case. I tried to help [the Jews] however I could, and my husband never objected."[35]

We do not know what eventually happened to that baby, though in all likelihood it did not survive. Conversely, Emil Skamene, raised as a Christian in Prague, was in fact born to the Kleiner family in Buczacz in 1941, "in a cellar of a Ukrainian peasant, who was hiding my parents." In desperation, Emil's father wrote his sister in Prague, begging her to rescue the baby. She in turn sent Rudolph Steiger, a German with "some function in the SS" who, for a fee, brought the eighteen-month-old baby "in a backpack ... over two days ... [on] the train" to Prague. Not long thereafter the peasant murdered Emil's parents in order to get his hands on their valuables. Skamene discovered his own origins only decades later; he subsequently also found out that both his adoptive parents were covert Jews. As he saw it in 1998, he owed his life to the fact that "it was very important for some people that I should survive." Even Steiger, who "originally did it for money," grew attached to the boy, becoming a regular guest at his birthday parties. His goodness paid off, since "as an SS official … [he] would have likely been killed by Czechs after the war," had it not been for "an affidavit from my parents." Steiger, concluded Skamene, "lived … his life basically in exchange for this unbelievable act of heroism."[36]

Some older children adopted a false identity, a precarious choice in a society replete with stereotypes and prejudices. The ten-year-old Genia Weksler testified in 1946 that she spent the last months of the occupation in a Polish village with her mother and sister:

> I grazed cattle … In the house they often talked about Jews. "Jews are cheaters." … The children always played … "manhunt" on Jews … we lived as Poles until the liberation. I was often told that I have Jewish eyes, Jewish black hair. I answered that if "You take a closer look it is possible that I'm completely Jewish."[37]

Bronia Kahane, who was ten when the Germans invaded in 1941, was initially hidden with her mother by a Ukrainian peasant who felt loyalty to her grandfather, even though his own son was a concentration camp guard. Later, they were saved from an execution by an Austrian SS-man thanks to her mother's excellent German and a ten-dollar bill. But in spring 1944 she lost her entire family and began working as a farmhand. She lived in a house filled with Jewish goods looted by the owner's son and was told by her employer: "You do everything like a Jew." When she returned to Buczacz after the liberation, Bronia "spoke only Ukrainian … I forgot everything." She found the few surviving Jews terrified of being attacked: "I never went back to my house … because they said … 'They're going to kill you.'"[38]

Aliza Golobov, who was fourteen when the Germans invaded, was also first saved by a German soldier, who hid her family during a roundup in 1942. Although she was denounced several times and similarly lost her entire family, Aliza was rescued by a number of Ukrainians and acquaintances of her father's in the town of Stanisławów. The lawyers Dr. Volchuk and Mr. Krochmichek, the latter's father, as well as a priest and a police inspector, provided her with false papers and protected her until the liberation, receiving no compensation and at great risk to their own and their families' lives.[39] Hilda Weitz, who was also fourteen in 1941, was sheltered by a Ukrainian family from Buczacz, despite the fact that "they were … very nationalistic" and that "two of the brothers were drafted to German army." She and her younger brother were later hidden by a blacksmith's family in a "very rough antisemitic town." The man, his wife, and their child eventually fled the village, "because they were afraid they will come to … look for Jews." Hilda and her brother were left alone: "I remember the light looked so beautiful, the sun, the nature, I said, 'Oh my God, life is so beautiful, but we will never see it anymore.' I thought this was our last day."[40] Shortly thereafter the Soviets arrived.

In some cases, love, passion, and loyalty also played a role. The sixteen-year-old Zofia Pollak jumped off a train headed to the Bełżec extermination camp near the town of Rawa Ruska, only to be arrested by the local ethnic German Polish policeman Smola. He said to her: "You are so young … and so pretty, you shouldn't be killed." He took care of Zofia for six weeks. "He was really in love with me ... But he was a married man. And his wife and two children were on vacation." When his wife returned, Smola sent Zofia back to her father and brother in Buczacz. She survived much of the remainder of the German occupation thanks to the goodwill of a Polish work supervisor on the agricultural farm in which her father, a former estate manager, was employed. Almost murdered by Ukrainian partisans, they ended up in the barn of a poor peasant who had once been helped by Zofia's father. "He said, 'Whatever I have I will share with you ...' He covered us with hay. It was very cold ... We were there in one position, we couldn't move, and this is how we were liberated on February 23, 1944, in that place."[41]

In other cases, youngsters were saved thanks to split-second decisions by strangers. Eighteen-year-old Cyla Sznajder hid in the attic of the German administrative office during the liquidation of the Nagórzanka labor camp, some 40 kilometers (25 miles) southeast of Buczacz, in 1942, and "thanks to the cleaner—a Pole, who found me by chance ... I managed to get out ... without being seen." During another liquidation action in January 1943, she hid with a friend in the backyard of a farm. The ethnic German peasant who discovered them there, "invited us into his hut ... ordered his wife to prepare warm food ... fed us ... [and] found for us some old rags." Later she and a few others were supplied with food by another peasant woman. And, toward the very end of the occupation, Cyla and several other Jewish girls hid in the attic of a cloister: "The nuns comforted us that things would not last long and brought us food."[42]

Rescuers were not all made of the same cast, and we have contradictory reports about some of them. In 1946 the twenty-one-year-old Shmuel Rosen testified that he, his two brothers, and their mother had hidden for nine months in a crypt where they "built ... a little apartment ... with the help of the undertaker" Marjan (Manko) Świerszczak, in the Christian cemetery on the slope of Fedor Hill overlooking the town of Buczacz.[43] In another testimony he provided in 1960, Shmuel described Świerszczak as "an illiterate but a very upright man," who, "in return for a fee," hid "forty Jews in the attic of the cemetery's chapel" during a roundup, refusing to betray them even when the Ukrainian police "beat him up." The Rosens paid Świerszczak "1,000 złoty every month for the supplies" in return for hiding them.[44] Shmuel's older brother Henry depicted Świerszczak in 1997 as "a gorgeous man" and "a Christian ... He would say, 'If I will turn you in, then my kids, my grandkids, and their grandchildren will have to pay for my sin.'"[45] But in March 1944, a couple of months after the Rosens moved to "a shelter under the floor" of the mortuary, "a group of German soldiers came into the house" and "the floor collapsed." The brothers managed to escape, "but our poor mother ... could not run with her sick legs. We saw ... how our mother was dragged out and shot." Świerszczak later buried her.[46]

The three boys were subsequently hidden by an old Polish acquaintance, the peasant Michał Dutkiewicz, even as some of their relatives were denounced and murdered in the same village.[47] It was thanks to them that Świerszczak's tale of heroism became known, and in 1983 he and his Ukrainian wife Maryna were declared "righteous among the nations" by Yad Vashem in Jerusalem.[48] Yet Yad Vashem's archives also contain an account written in 1947 by Moshe Wizinger, a friend of the Rosens, who had a very different recollection of the undertaker. In June 1943 Wizinger also sought refuge in the cemetery, where he encountered a "very frightened" Świerszczak, followed later by his wife, who urged Wizinger to leave or to give himself up to the Germans. Shortly thereafter he was captured by Ukrainian fighters, barely managed to escape, and returned to the cemetery. This time Maryna "shouted … that I should run away and not return, otherwise she herself would call the Germans." Remarkably, at this point Wizinger was taken in by a local Polish resistance group, whose leader, Edek, decided to punish the couple for refusing shelter to a Jew. After beating up Maryna while her husband was hiding under the bed, Edek declared, according to Wizinger, "I would have killed you like dogs for what you did to him. Only your past behavior … prevents me from doing it. Fear of the Germans cannot be an excuse for you … we will punish obedience to any German orders with death. Remember this and tell the others."

By the standards of Edek's moral code, then, as reported by Wizinger, according to which Polish honor required saving Jews, whether one liked them or not, Świerszczak did not pass the test. But Edek's group was an uncommon local phenomenon—most nationalist Polish and Ukrainian partisans were at best unfriendly to Jews—and he and the majority of his fighters were eventually killed. The only record of his heroism is in Wizinger's account, unread for decades and only recently published by me in English translation. Consequently, he received no recognition by Yad Vashem and Świerszczak's status was never challenged.

This ambiguity of heroism was even more pronounced in the case of Jewish resisters. At the end of his account, Wizinger scans the handful of Jewish fighters still left on the eve of the liberation and notes that they are "the last of a dying nation."[49] Inquiring who they were and why there were so few of them tells us a great deal about the complexities of the historical reality and the vicissitudes of memory.

An outstanding example is Yitzhak Bauer, who was eighteen when the Germans invaded and eighty when I interviewed him in Tel Aviv in 2003. Bauer recalled that "compared to other places, the Christian population" of Buczacz "was relatively all right … At least they did not harm us." Saved by a Ukrainian friend during the first roundup, Bauer ended up in a small Jewish resistance group in the nearby forest. While he acted against denouncers, Bauer maintained a nuanced view of Ukrainians, noting, for instance, that even the notorious chief of the local militia, Volodymyr Kaznovskyi, refrained from taking action upon discovering that his own father, a priest, was hiding Jews. Similarly, Bauer's Ukrainian friend Shenko, who provided the group with food, but later joined the police, explained to them that "the alternative was to enlist for labor in Germany or join the SS-Division 'Galicia.'" Not long after, Shenko's house was burned down as punishment for hiding Jews. Bauer also recalled an elderly Ukrainian family friend who invited him and his brother to his home, gave them food, and parted from them saying "I wish that you manage to survive."[50]

From a deposition he submitted to a West German court in 1968 as evidence for the trial of former Nazi perpetrators in Buczacz, however, it turns out that before becoming a partisan, Bauer had served in the Jewish police (*Ordnungsdienst*, OD). He was not the only one who made the transition from collaboration to resistance. Bauer noted that he joined the OD in November 1941. The squad, numbering some thirty men, "carried out the orders of the *Judenrat*, but during *Aktionen* ... we were put at the disposition of ... the Gestapo or the local gendarmerie." According to Bauer, on November 27, 1942, he "was assigned to participate in the cleanup of the Jewish hospital," which "was overflowing with ... about one hundred ... sick people ... The sick who could not move were shot right there and then in their beds. The others were taken out to the railroad station ... and transported to extermination in Bełżec." Bauer personally witnessed some of the shooting in the hospital, as well as during the roundup of April 1943.[51]

There is no necessary contradiction between Bauer's two accounts; it may be simply a matter of relating different segments of his experiences appropriate to the circumstances in which they were presented. But it is also possible that Bauer could not assimilate the two parts of his story into one psychological and experiential whole: to the German court he asserted his role as an OD-man, in order to establish his ability to identify German perpetrators; to me he asserted his role as partisan, thus providing his survival with the more heroic aura befitting the Israeli context. Yet many of those who lived through that period would not share our understanding of the choices made by such men as Bauer or Shenko. Gershon Gross, a tough working-class twenty-four-year-old in 1941, had only contempt for the *Judenrat* and the OD: "What was their job? ... No one wants to talk about it ... The Germans would say they need five-hundred people. The [Jewish] police went" to seize them. Gershon and his brothers refused to join the police. Of a *Judenrat* member who survived, Gershon noted dispassionately that he "had to hide, like Eichmann. If they found him, they would kill him." Jewish collaborators, to his mind, were the worst since they turned against their own. He had more sympathy for Gentiles precisely because his expectations were lower. A Ukrainian policeman, a former classmate, let him go after the OD forced him to bury victims of a mass shooting. When Torah scrolls were "hanged ... like you hang clothes" from the bridge over the Strypa River in Buczacz, "a Ukrainian priest hid one Torah in the church," retuning it to Gross after the liberation. And when one of his brothers was wounded in a partisan action, a poor Polish peasant sheltered and nursed him back to health. But Gross had no illusions. He knew that "Ukrainian police took" Hungarian and Czech Jewish refugees "to the Dniester River, tied them with wires and threw them alive into the Dniester." Closer to home, his own parents were denounced by a local Polish girl, taken out to their own yard, and shot.[52]

Moshe Wizinger was also harsher about Jewish collaborators than toward Gentile neighbors. Writing about the first days of the German occupation, he described how German soldiers led by the Ukrainian dregs broke into Jewish homes and raped young Jewish girls. But then he remarked, striking a similar tone to Gershon Gross:

> The well-known Ukrainian eye doctor [Volodymyr] Hamerskyi told a Jewish delegation headed by [the physician] Dr. Blutreich and [the attorney and former chairman of the General Zionist Party's local branch, Dr. Benjamin (Ludwik)] Engelberg that the Ukrainian intelligentsia did not support the murder of the Jews, but that they themselves were helpless, because those who were ruling now were

the leaders of the previously secret Ukrainian bands. In the end he expressed his hope that once the Germans took over, the atmosphere in town would return to normal. Meanwhile, the looting, rape, and murder increased. One night, the Great synagogue was gutted. ... The scrolls of the Torah were taken all the way to the bridge ... [and] unbound ... [with] one end ... attached to the top of the bridge while the other dangled nearly all the way to the water. This brought upon a harsh protest from the Ukrainian clergy, who categorically demanded from the leader of the Ukrainian bands, [Andriy] Dankovych, to stop profaning the Holy sites ... The abbot of the Ukrainian Basilian Monastery ... proposed to the Jews to carry the scrolls to the monastery for safekeeping.

Wizinger acknowledges that those same "Ukrainian bands" were soon thereafter "transformed into police forces," which later constituted the main local component of future mass killings. Nonetheless, it was about the Jewish leadership that Wizinger wrote most contemptuously, deriding the manner in which "the countless demands by the Germans or Ukrainians were fulfilled immediately" by the *Judenrat*. The OD, for its part, "robbed the Jews of furniture, bed linen, and clothing," so that even "in those terrible times" Jewish officials "were able to lead a very good life and to amass large sums of money," while "Jews who tried to hide their belongings were mercilessly beaten" by them. When Jews tried to escape to neighboring villages, the "peasants first robbed" them "of everything they had and then killed them," while those in Buczacz were targeted by the Jewish police: "The OD were robbing, killing, worse than the Germans."

According to Wizinger, some Jewish leaders did try to set a different moral standard. Thus when the Germans demanded 150 Jews for work in a forced labor camp, the head of the *Judenrat*, Dr. Engelberg, "announced that he would not take part in selecting the people under any circumstances." But his assistants, Dr. Bernhard "Seifer and Kramer Baruch ... proposed to exchange those who were unable to work with healthy and young workers" and "backed up their proposal with presents." As a result, "the names that were taken off the list were of those who could pay most," while Seifer and Kramer "made plenty of money ... and did not turn down jewelry either." There were some moments of heroism. Jankiel Ebenstein, "who during his few months as member of the *Judenrat* came to be hated by everyone ... was ordered to help ... looking for hidden bunkers." He initially "tried to convince the Gestapo chief that no Jews were hiding in" a certain house. But "when ... they began pulling Jews out of there," he "grabbed a hatchet, and tried to hit the Gestapo-man," only to be immediately shot down. As Wizinger commented, "that is how a man, who ... was called an agent of the Gestapo, died a hero's death. That day he was forgiven everything."[53]

The effect of German rule on intra- and interethnic relations is noted in many testimonies. Zofia Pollak "had very close ... Gentile friends" but "after the Germans occupied our city, they wouldn't even look at me because I was Jewish." As for the ghetto, "the *Judenrat* was very mean, and the Jewish police was very mean. They thought that by being very obedient to the Germans, they will save their own lives. So the very nice people became very ugly." But, Pollack concluded, "at the end everybody was killed."[54] Shmuel Rosen recalled that "the 200 richest Jewish families found their way to the labor camp," considered the last safe site in Buczacz, by paying the *Judenrat* exorbitant sums.[55] Soon thereafter the labor camp was also liquidated. Yet Rosen did think that wealth and corruption made a difference in survival rate. Of the up to one thousand (probably closer to eight hundred) Jews who came out of hiding following the first liberation of Buczacz in March 1944, "next to a handful of upright people, only dubious characters survived—denouncers, militiamen." To be sure, most of them were murdered when the Germans recaptured the town a couple of weeks later. Only a few managed to escape, and some became partisans. The Rosen brothers, for their part, joined the Red Army. By the second liberation in July 1944 fewer than one hundred Jews were still alive in Buczacz.[56]

Survivors have often been reluctant to speak about internal Jewish corruption and complicity, invoking the phrase, "one does not speak ill of the dead." Yet this was a crucial component of life during the Holocaust and of its subsequent memory. Witnesses from Buczacz also observed that the Jewish leadership opposed and hindered the creation of armed resistance. In 2002 Shmuel Rosen recalled overhearing a conversation between *Judenrat* leaders and a man called Zuhler, who had "served in the Polish army before the war ... He said to them, 'We want to create partisan groups and to go to the forest ... but we have no money for weapons.' ... So they said, 'Sir ... we will not agree to this.' And he left, and that was that."

Rosen speculated that Jewish leaders "were scared," and that while "some in the *Judenrat* ... wanted" to organize resistance, others "were together with the Germans. Excuse me for saying that, to our regret, Dr. Seifer was one." By this Rosen meant that Seifer preferred collaboration to resistance, and his willingness to name the man must have also had to do with the fact that Seifer was apparently one of only two *Judenrat* members who survived: "They say he is in Australia." Zev Anderman, another survivor, whom I interviewed together with Rosen, suggested: "Let's get off this subject, gentlemen, it is too painful." But Rosen insisted: "Look, they have to know this ... There were bad things in the *Judenrat* ... they would seize a young man for work, and they would exchange him [for another]. Who would [serve for the] exchange?" Now Anderman gave way: "One of the poor boys." And Rosen concluded: "Exactly, they would get the poor kids [in exchange for] those of the rich ..." And Anderman added: "My uncle, they got him."[57]

These are fraught and agonizing issues. Ultimately, in conditions of communal genocide, no one remained entirely apart from the events. A passing remark by Shmuel Rosen revealed that, in fact, he too had worked in the *Judenrat*, if only in the position of a "helper" ("I made tea, coffee"). Zev Anderman spoke with pride about his brother Janek's death in April 1943, when he pulled out a pistol and shot a Ukrainian policeman, only to be beaten, dragged to the town square, and burned alive. Yet other sources suggest that Janek possessed a pistol because he was or had been an OD-man. Perhaps, just like Ebenstein, his heroic end made up for his past actions in the police.[58]

Conclusion

Personal accounts of genocide, by their very nature, do not allow for the creation of a single, uniform narrative of events. Rather, they offer a multitude of perspectives, some complementary, others contradictory, which, when put together, can provide an imperfect yet multidimensional picture of past reality. At times, this may be a contentious or opaque portrait, all the more so considering the extreme circumstances of the Second World War and the Holocaust. Yet listening closely to the witnesses allows us greater depth and nuance than can be derived from the tendentious obfuscation of official accounts. Individual, personal perspectives are all the more important in reconstructing events on the ethnically mixed borderlands of Eastern Europe.

Indeed, certain internal contradictions within individual accounts carry special significance for collective memory and historiography. Generalizing statements by witnesses on the conduct of entire ethnic groups tend to conform to conventional views, which are in part reflected in the overall course of events. Yet the same witnesses often cite specific cases of individual actions that belie the generalizations and, no less importantly, were vital to the witnesses' own survival. Such instances of atypical but crucial behavior provide a corrective to widespread prejudices and undermine deterministic views of the past by introducing an element of choice.

The gap between conventional generalizations and unique individual experience makes for ambivalence. This reaction comes into particularly sharp relief in extreme situations such as genocide. Jewish accounts contain a large measure of mixed feelings about Christian neighbors, reflecting a general impression of universal betrayal and individual experiences of rescue. Precisely because denunciation and murder were so pervasive, rare instances of compassion and altruism stand out all the more. And, of course, witness accounts disproportionately represent Gentile rescue, since survival was so heavily dependent on such acts.

But testimonies also tell us that just as perpetrators occasionally showed mercy or compassion, rescuers were hardly always altruistic, as motivations for action ranged from pure goodness to cynical exploitation. While a few men with blood on their hands occasionally chose to save someone, others masqueraded as rescuers only to rob and betray those they sheltered; while many upstanding citizens became complicit in plunder and murder, some wretchedly poor peasants shared their last crumbs with the desperate remnants of destroyed communities. Some sought a postwar alibi, others paid back moral debts; generalizing about motivation is futile. Habitual killers may have acted kindly only once; others might have been transformed by that first pang of conscience. Some began with good intentions and then turned to denunciation; others acted out of greed but became attached to those they rescued. Ambivalence was hardly restricted to survivors.

Observing the dynamics of communal genocide from a local perspective reveals that not a few of those who perpetrated violence at one point became its victims at another. Ukrainian nationalists collaborated with the Germans in killing Jews and then massacred Poles of their own accord; but they had previously been targeted by the prewar Polish state, then by the Soviet authorities, and eventually also by the Germans. Poles benefited from their prewar state's discriminatory anti-Jewish and anti-Ukrainian policies; in turn, they were subjected to Soviet deportations and Ukrainian ethnic cleansing. Jewish community leaders and educated youths tried to save themselves by becoming complicit in the victimization of poorer and weaker fellow Jews, only to have their illusions of power and security dispelled as they too were murdered. Some saw this turning of tables as a kind of justice; but ultimately this merely resulted from the dynamics of unbound, unrestricted violence on a hitherto unimaginable scale.

And yet, many testimonies also contain a mélange of unspoken gratitude for the rescuers and inarticulate remorse for having failed to recognize and thank them for so long. The pervasive atmosphere of mayhem and violence, betrayal and abandonment, might have made such acts of mercy stand out all the more. Instead, they often receded into the background as survivors mourned the dead and tried to build a new life. But the testimonies tell a different story. The multitudes of the drowned have left precious little behind; yet the few who were saved have given us a detailed record of these events—of which their rescuers constituted a vital component. This is of course an unbalanced historical record. But it has the benefit of enriching our understanding of the Holocaust and its aftermath. Ultimately, beyond saving their lives, acts of rescue also saved the souls of the survivors. After all, it is astonishing that men, women, and children who lived though that era had the inner resources to rebuild their lives; and yet many of them did just that. This is testimony to their strength and resilience. But I would argue that what contributed no less to their determination to raise new families, and to their ability to instill in their children trust and humanness, was the memory of those who had selflessly saved them.

This memory remained deeply etched in the souls of the survivors. But it did not find public expression for decades, providing just enough sustenance to go on living but never completely resurfacing, perhaps because of the hardships of life after the catastrophe, or because allowing it to emerge would have brought back all the other horrors and betrayals and losses. When it did return, decades later, it came after lives had been lived, children and grandchildren had been born, and one could face the approaching inevitable end with more equanimity and sense of fulfillment. And with the memory of rescue came a recognition that those who had chosen to act then had done more than save lives and, unbeknownst to themselves perhaps, had rescued the very concept of a shared humanity—precisely that which the Nazis had set out to eradicate—by recognizing the human spark in those who were hunted down like animals.

What the witnesses I have cited here experienced hardly provides a single, one-sided lesson on human nature, or on history, or even on the events of the Holocaust. But these accounts, fraught and painful and contradictory as they are, constitute a crucial component of the past—in Buczacz and, by extension, in many other sites of communal genocide, most especially in the borderlands of Eastern Europe. Ignoring them, setting them aside, using them merely to illustrate some point or thesis unrelated to their deeper meaning not only constitutes abuse of these records of human experience, it also distorts and ultimately falsifies the historical record itself. No history should be written without listening to its protagonists, least of all the history of an event whose main goal was to silence these voices, and especially because the few who survived the disaster hoped more than anything else to transmit the memory of the events they experienced to posterity and thereby to save the multitudes of the dead from complete oblivion, statistical abstraction, and mass burial in the voluminous footnotes of scholarly publications.

PART III
JUSTICE AND DENIAL

CHAPTER 5
THE HOLOCAUST IN THE COURTROOM

The Law

In the late 1950s and 1960s a series of trials of former Nazi perpetrators took place in the Federal Republic of Germany (FRG). The best known and most influential was the Frankfurt Auschwitz Trial of 1963–5, which helped establish in the FRG a certain view of the Holocaust, the perpetrators, and the nature of guilt and accountability in the context of a state-ordered genocide. But the Auschwitz Trial was concerned with the torture and murder of inmates in a concentration and extermination camp.[1] Conversely, a series of other trials during the same period focused on the destruction of Jewish communities in Eastern Europe, many of whose members were murdered in mass shootings in or in very close proximity to their own towns, even as others were transported to extermination camps.

The perpetrators of such local killing operations were SS-men, members of various police agencies, and non-German collaborators. Unlike extermination camps' personnel, these men, as well as some women, often gained an intimate knowledge of the inhabitants of the communities to which they were posted before murdering them. They were also far less constrained by a rigid system of supervision and control, and thus had much greater opportunity for personal initiative than camp guards. They represented the "human" face of genocide: in the small and relatively insulated towns to which they were posted, contact with the people whose fate depended on the perpetrators' sympathy, rage, kindness, or cruelty was frequent, close, and occasionally ambivalent. The non-Jewish local population was another important factor in these towns: its attitude and conduct—ranging from active collaboration with the Germans to indirect profit-making from the destruction of fellow citizens, from willingness to provide shelter to the persecuted to active resistance—could be as decisive in determining the fate of the victims as was the zeal and efficiency of the Nazis. Up to half the Jewish victims of the Holocaust were murdered under such circumstances in their own towns, while others were subsequently deported to extermination camps.[2]

In prosecuting former Nazis in the 1950s and 1960s, German justice had to contend not only with the industrial killing of human beings in the extermination camps but also with the very different circumstances of eradicating local communities in German-occupied territories. For this purpose, German courts had to recreate the historical context in which these crimes were committed, often unknown to the public at the time and in many cases still quite murky today. They also had to work under the constraints of German postwar law.

Following the establishment of the FRG in 1949, the German judiciary rejected the option of applying the new legal concepts of crimes against humanity and genocide to events that occurred before such terms and laws existed. Crimes against humanity were first defined in the London Charter and the Nuremberg International Military Tribunal in 1945 and codified by the United Nations in 1946. The United Nations' Genocide Convention was adopted in 1948, and subsequently ratified by most member states.[3] But strong German legal opposition to trials based on ex-post-facto law, which denied the principle of *nulla poena sine lege* (no punishment without prior law), compelled West German courts to apply only conventional criminal law to those indicted for crimes during the Nazi period.[4]

The murder law of the German penal code, originally established in 1871 and still in force in the FRG, defines a murderer as "anyone who kills a human being: from lust for killing, to satisfy his sexual drives, from covetousness or other base motives, treacherously, cruelly, or by means endangering the community or in order to facilitate or conceal another crime."[5] The focus in this definition is therefore largely on the subjective motives of the defendant. In the case of Nazi crimes, such "base" motives could rarely be attributed to defendants who participated in a genocidal state-directed undertaking and acted within the framework of military, police, or bureaucratic hierarchies apparently sanctioned by law and in accordance with directives emanating from the highest echelons of the state.

Considering the specific circumstances of the Third Reich, soon after German courts assumed full judicial powers in the FRG in 1951, the German Supreme Court (*Bundesgerichtshof*, BGH) determined that "base motives" would include racial hatred and anti-Semitism. Thus defendants motivated by anti-Semitism to kill Jews would fall under the definition of murder, whereas those who did so merely under orders would not. This naturally led Nazi defendants to deny any anti-Semitic motivation. It is therefore not surprising that anti-Semitism appears to have rarely featured among the reported motives of Nazi perpetrators. And since it is in any case notoriously difficult to determine such subjective motives if they are not attested to by the defendant, very few murder convictions were ever reached on this basis.[6]

German defendants also tried to invoke the argument of superior orders (*Befehlsnotstand*), which the Nuremberg Tribunal had rejected. This line of defense, however, was deemed inadmissible also by West German courts.[7] Nevertheless, the need to prove subjective "base motives" for a murder conviction meant that most defendants whose cases were not entirely dismissed were eventually convicted of either manslaughter or of aiding and abetting as accomplices to murder. As of 1960 charges of manslaughter fell under the statute of limitations, whereas conviction as accomplice to murder often carried ludicrously light sentences.[8] Moreover, conduct that could be shown to have constituted treachery or cruelty, and might therefore bring a murder conviction, was attributed primarily to those rare, lower-rank sadists who were neither representative of the mass of the perpetrators nor responsible for most of the killings.

The ironic result of this legal logic was that, while a few "excess perpetrators" (*Exzeßtäter*) of the lower ranks received life sentences, many of the higher-ranking organizers of local mass killings were either acquitted or given very short prison terms.⁹ This also meant that the courts created an entirely false picture of the nature of genocide, depicting those who carried out genocidal orders as far less guilty than those who manifested sadistic traits. The implication was that the killings were the result of unauthorized actions by a few depraved individuals—quite incapable of organizing a continent-wide genocide—rather than the outcome of a well-coordinated undertaking conducted by perfectly "normal" officials following the procedures of military, police, and bureaucratic organizations. Yet without these officials' willing, and quite often, enthusiastic collaboration, the mass murder of the Jews would never have attained such a devastating magnitude.¹⁰

The Site

Historians have written a great deal on the decision-making process that led to the final solution, as well as on the concentration and extermination camps, the regional implementation of genocide and its links to policies of ethnic cleansing and economic exploitation, and the motivation of the men who carried out mass murder.¹¹ Yet research on what happened in the thousands of communities that came under German occupation, especially in Eastern Europe and the western regions of the Soviet Union, has only recently begun.¹² Considering that much of the Holocaust actually occurred in such communities, this gap in our knowledge is quite startling.

Such towns provided the social context for far more intimate and dynamic relations between perpetrators, victims, collaborators, and bystanders. Most relevant to this chapter, the study of such towns makes it possible to gain a much more intimate knowledge of the perpetrators and their relationship with the communities in which they lived, as well as with the men, women, and children they murdered. The records of these men's indictments and trials are often the most detailed and revealing sources for the reconstruction of their actions. But these records expose more than the facts of the matter. For, just as important, they demonstrate the manner in which German courtrooms constructed a view of the Holocaust that differed from the convention at the time and still remains unfamiliar today: not of detached and impersonal mass extermination in the camps but of face-to-face relations between Germans and Jews, which almost always—but often after relatively lengthy acquaintance—ended up in face-to-face killing. In undertaking this sociology and psychology of genocide, West German courts strove to locate the perpetrators on the margins of German society and culture and on the extreme end of the scale of baseness. In this manner they hoped to limit the destabilizing effect on postwar Germany that might have resulted from the courts' actual findings about the utter conventionality of many of the defendants.¹³

Location mattered a great deal also in the geographical sense. For the German occupiers and perpetrators, as well as for the German courts, the East European towns in which these massacres occurred meant very little. Conversely, for the local population, they were often sites of long histories and memories, rich culture, and deep religious roots. The German occupiers and postwar lawyers, judges, journalists—and the public—were oblivious to all that. For them the question was: how could civilized Germans behave in such a murderous fashion? Part of the answer offered was that they had strayed out of a social and cultural context that would have otherwise restrained them and preserved their civility.[14] Indeed, the courts strove to create a picture of the defendants that distanced them from the rest of German society—including the judges themselves—and postulated that such political, cultural, ethnic, or psychological distance was at the root of the crime.[15] Underlying this assumption was also the notion that the site of the crimes was essentially different, located as it was in a strange and far-off territory, where certain types of otherwise unacceptable behavior appeared legitimate.

In what follows I discuss the trials of three perpetrators who participated in the destruction of the Jewish communities of Buczacz and nearby Czortków, where the regional outpost of the German Security Police (Sipo) was located. The Germans marched into the region in early July 1941 and immediately enforced a series of anti-Jewish measures: Jews had to wear identifying armbands, their property was confiscated, and they were employed in often deadly forced labor.[16] Starting in the fall of 1941, most communities in Galicia were ghettoized; executions of the "intelligentsia" were common. Deportations, especially to the Bełżec extermination camp, began in August 1942, accompanied as of October by mass shootings on site. In the first part of 1943, Jews not employed in labor camps were ordered killed. On June 30, 1943, Police Brigadier General Friedrich Katzmann, the SS- and Police Leader (SSPF) of Galicia District, declared the area under his control *judenfrei*: only 21,156 registered Jews were still living in twenty-one labor camps. The following month most labor camps were also liquidated. Altogether, well over 90 percent of Galicia's five hundred thousand Jews were murdered. Of the sixty thousand Jews in the Czortków and Buczacz area, only twelve hundred Jews were alive when the Red Army returned for good in July 1944.[17]

This general outline of the Holocaust in Galicia was largely reflected in events in Czortków and Buczacz. A few weeks after the Germans marched into these towns, they murdered the first group of some 150 Jews in Czortków, and approximately 450 Jews in Buczacz. In both cases these victims were considered to be members of the intelligentsia who might provide leadership to the community. A year later, in late August 1942 the Jewish Ghetto in Czortków was surrounded and some three thousand people were seized and sent by train to Bełżec. Another six hundred people were deported in October; hundreds of others were shot on the spot. Mass killings in Buczacz began in October 1942; a ghetto was established in December, and the killing continued until the city was declared *judenfrei* in June 1943. Fewer than one hundred Jews were still alive in each town by the time they were permanently liberated in spring and summer 1944.[18]

The Perpetrators

Heinrich Peckmann joined the Sipo outpost in Czortków soon after it was established in September 1941. The outpost reported directly to SSPF Katzmann in Lemberg (Lwów,

Lvov, Lviv), which was attached in August that year to Governor Hans Frank's General Government (*Generalgouvernement*), the German-occupied part of Poland that had not been annexed to the Reich.[19]

Born in Parsau, Lower Saxony, in 1904, Peckmann joined the police in 1925. While serving as police sergeant-major in Cologne, Peckmann married in a church ceremony in 1932. A son was born the following year. In 1937 Peckmann was pensioned off from the regular police but managed to gain entry into the criminal police (*Kriminalpolizei*, Kripo) by joining the Nazi Party. In December 1937 Peckmann became a Gestapo official in Cologne. During his trial in 1962 Peckmann claimed to have performed some good deeds on behalf of his acquaintances while serving in Cologne.

In 1938 Peckmann completed a Kripo training course, and after a stint of keeping records of former concentration camp inmates, in 1940 he was promoted to detective sergeant and transferred to several Sipo posts in Poland. In September 1941 Peckmann arrived in Lemberg, and the following month he was sent to Czortków. Appointed deputy commander of the outpost in late 1942, Peckmann served as its commander between April and October 1943. In November 1943 he returned to Lemberg, and was eventually taken prisoner by the Soviets in Czechoslovakia in May 1945. Released shortly thereafter for health reasons, Peckmann returned to his hometown, but was interned again in 1946–7. In 1954 Peckmann rejoined the Cologne police force and served as sergeant until his arrest in 1960.

Kurt Köllner served in Czortków between December 1941 and early 1944, most of the time as the *Judensachbearbeiter* (official in charge of Jewish affairs) of the outpost.[20] Born in 1908, Köllner was raised in Bad Dürrenberg, near Leipzig, where his father worked as sales director of a cooperative. In 1922 Köllner entered a commerce school in Leipzig, and then trained as an auto mechanic. From 1926 he worked for various firms as a mechanic and a driver. Considered reliable, discreet, and sociable, Köllner soon rose to a management position, and supplemented his income by acquiring a car rental agency.

Köllner's father had been a respected member of the Social Democratic Party since 1904, and the parental home often hosted politicians of considerable status. But although the son Kurt did join a trade union, he generally preferred sports to politics. He also adhered to the Evangelical faith and married in church in 1934. In 1938 a son was born, and that same year Köllner joined the SS and the Nazi Party. In his 1962 testimony Köllner claimed that he made this step to protect his socialist father from being sent to Buchenwald. And indeed, although his father was dismissed as director of the cooperative and was evicted from his residence, no further police action was taken against him. Relations between parents and son remained good throughout the Nazi period.

In May 1939 Köllner was called up for emergency military service. Released in December, Köllner trained for three months at a border police school and was then transferred to the Sipo post in Warsaw. In August 1941 Köllner was sent to the Sipo post in Lemberg, and in December he arrived at the Sipo outpost in Czortków. Appointed *Judensachbearbeiter* in July 1942, by 1943 Köllner achieved the rank of SS-Scharführer (sergeant). When the outpost was dismantled in early 1944, Köllner returned to Lemberg, and was eventually taken prisoner by the Americans in Slovakia.

Released in June 1945, Köllner returned to his hometown and old firm. He was evidently helped by his father's influence as an old social democrat and opponent of the Nazi regime. Arrested again in August and held by the Soviets until 1950, Köllner then moved to the Saarland, where the West German authorities arrested him in 1958 and kept him in prison for most of the intervening period until his trial in 1962.

Paul Thomanek played an important role, far beyond his humble rank, in the organization and subsequent murder of Jewish forced labor in Czortków and Buczacz.[21] Born in Petershofen in 1909, Thomanek was raised in the Hultschiner Ländchen, a part of Silesia that was handed over to Czechoslovakia in 1920, annexed by Germany following the Munich accords of 1938, and returned to Czechoslovakia in 1945. Identities in this ethnically diverse region were fluid. Thomanek's father remained chief pit-foreman in Petershofen all his life; his two surviving brothers became Czech citizens after the war; his sister moved to Bavaria. At home the family spoke "Moravian," a Slavic dialect mixed with German. Thomanek began attending a German elementary school in 1916, but after 1918 his schooling was in Czech. Trained as a cabinetmaker, Thomanek was an active member of the local Catholic sports association and political party, as well as a youth leader; in 1929, aged twenty, Thomanek joined the Czech police. But after performing two years of compulsory service in the Czech army, in 1932 Thomanek joined his father's guild and began working as a mine cabinetmaker. He married a Czech woman in 1934, and their son was born the following year.

When the war broke out in 1939, Thomanek volunteered for the Auxiliary Police (*Hilfspolizei*), which recruited members of Nazi Party formations and was not part of the regular German police and security services. In his trial Thomanek claimed to have joined this force to avoid recruitment to the Wehrmacht. Thomanek served as a policeman in several German-occupied Polish towns, but in November 1939 he was sent to train with a Waffen-SS *Totenkopf* (Death's Head) unit. The following month Thomanek joined a Special Task (*Sonderdienst*) SS unit in Lublin, composed of ethnic Germans, which reported directly to the Higher SS- and Police Leader (HSSPF) Friedrich-Wilhelm Krüger, and to Governor Frank in Kraków. Frank himself called this unit a "murder squad" (*Mördertruppe*). Having meanwhile acquired Polish, Thomanek joined the Waffen-SS and was posted to Lemberg in October 1941.

Thomanek's first posting in Galicia was to the Jewish forced labor camps established to build Thoroughfare IV (*Durchgangsstraße* [DG] IV), an important transportation artery that the Germans hoped to construct between Lemberg, the capital of Galicia, and Taganrog, on the Ukrainian–Russian border.[22] Construction and repair crews were taken from many towns in the region, including Czortków and Buczacz. The work was physically exhausting, nutrition and hygiene were appalling, and disease was rampant. The death rate from illnesses and arbitrary shooting was very high. Thomanek served there for just over a year.

Still a mere private, in November 1942 Thomanek was sent to establish a labor camp for Jewish craftsmen in Czortków. Given a car for this task, Thomanek brought along "his" Jew, a Jewish police commander named Wolf. He later also hosted his wife, son, and father at his post in Czortków. By then he was already in charge of all labor camps in the Czortków region. Thomanek's position was such that in early 1943 he received a visit by none other than SSPF Katzmann, who presented him with a Finnish submachine gun and reportedly remarked that soon "things will be completely cleaned up." Indeed, on June 23, 1943, Thomanek oversaw the liquidation of the Czortków labor camp.

Thomanek was then transferred to another camp, which was also liquidated the following month. Finally leaving Galicia in July 1944, Thomanek was eventually taken prisoner by the Czechs. He was still a mere SS corporal. Returning home after his release in 1948, Thomanek was arrested again by the Czechs and deported to Germany. For several years he worked in various menial jobs in Germany and Sweden, until his arrest by the West German police in 1957.

The Crimes

These, then, are three of the men who participated in the destruction of the Jewish communities in the Czortków and Buczacz region. But what did they actually do and what were they charged with once finally subjected to West German justice?

Though obviously responsible for the murder of tens of thousands, Heinrich Peckmann, former deputy commander and then commander of the Sipo outpost in Czortków, was indicted for only two cases of alleged murder: killing the bookkeeper Jakob Seldmann during a roundup in the village of Mielnica, near Czortków, in September 1942; and killing the handicapped Levi Auerbach during a roundup in Czortków in October 1943. Although the court dismissed Peckmann's alibi of having been on leave at the time of the second killing, it also rejected as unreliable the testimonies of the two witnesses of these events.

The testimony of the first witness, the forty-nine-year-old dentist H., was dismissed on "objective grounds," namely, that he could have misheard the name of the victim, Seldmann, as that of the indicted, Peckmann, who might not have even been present at the site of the killing. The court did not question the testimony on "subjective grounds," however, which is to say that it did not assume that the witness was consciously lying. Conversely, the testimony of the fifty-one-year-old elementary school teacher R. was not only rejected on "objective grounds," but the court also implied that it had some suspicions about the witness's ability to tell the truth. The main, and somewhat extraordinary, reason for this doubt was an earlier testimony about the killing of Auerbach given by the witness to the Jewish Historical Commission shortly after the liberation of Galicia, in which the witness noted that on the same occasion Peckmann had killed several other Jews. Unable to reconcile the earlier version with the witness's later testimony that Peckmann had shot only Auerbach, the court suggested that a witness who had exaggerated in his testimony to a Jewish organization could certainly not be trusted by a German court. Peckmann was thus acquitted for lack of evidence for personally committing murder. An attempt to reopen judicial proceedings against him in 1970 also failed. By then Peckmann was sixty-six years old and seemed destined to end his life in the comfort of his own home.[23]

The case of Kurt Köllner was far more complex. For here was a man who not only claimed, as we have seen, to have joined the SS merely to protect his socialist father, but who also told the court that he had maintained amicable relations with some Jewish families throughout the 1930s and had even "helped" one of his Jewish acquaintances to emigrate by buying up his possessions—no doubt for a suitably meager sum considering the galloping "Aryanization" of Jewish property at the time. Köllner also claimed that he had openly criticized the *Kristallnacht* pogrom of November 9, 1938, and that he saved some other non-Jewish friends who had gotten into trouble with the authorities. Yet his nickname, "*Mäuschen*" (mousy), suggests another aspect of Köllner's personality.[24]

Even while serving in the SS, Köllner supposedly kept intervening on behalf of Jews. As he asserted, he had received special praise from his superior at the Sipo post in Warsaw, detective superintendent Engels, for curbing Polish and Ukrainian extortions from Jews. Indeed, it would seem that in Engels he found yet another friend of the persecuted. Once he arrived in Lemberg and was employed in the construction of the DG IV, Köllner reportedly opined to SSPF Katzmann that without sufficient food, accommodation, and clothing, Jewish forced labor would not be productive. He also noted that, thanks to their preponderance among Galicia's craftsmen, the Jews were indispensable to the military. Unfortunately, Katzmann paid no heed to these arguments since he saw the road-building project as nothing but *Vernichtung durch Arbeit*—extermination through labor of the local Jewish population.[25]

According to Köllner, it was because of his "defense" of the Jews that he was transferred from the comforts of Lemberg to the muddy streets of Czortków. Arriving there just before Christmas 1941, Köllner compensated himself for this punishment by bringing along his wife, who later took over the outpost's registrar office. Appointed *Judensachbearbeiter* in summer 1942, Köllner again "befriended" the local Jewish community, exercising his newly acquired power through contacts with the Czortków Jewish council and Jewish police. On the eve of the first roundup in Czortków in August 1942, Köllner promised the Jewish council that he could spare people from deportation by stamping their work cards. This facilitated Jewish collaboration and brought in a handsome profit from bribes for these life-saving stamps. Meanwhile, Köllner deceived the Jewish council about the timing of the roundup. Consequently, the community was caught unprepared: some three thousand Jews were deported to Bełżec, and another three hundred were shot on the street.[26]

Köllner's subsequent record reveals few traces of amicable relations with Jews. In early October 1942 he participated in another roundup in Czortków, involving the deportation of a further six hundred Jews to Bełżec. During that time Köllner also organized deportations of many other Jewish communities in the area.[27] Yet such general responsibility for genocide was not sufficient to bring about conviction in German courts. As we have seen, it was necessary to prove that the defendant was directly guilty of specific murders; that he had acted with "base motives," such as sexual lust or sadism; and that his actions were on his own initiative or in awareness of being in fulfillment of clearly unlawful orders.

In the end, Köllner was charged with eleven separate cases of murder. In August 1942 he shot the fifteen-year-old Haim Morgenstern with his pistol from a distance of about 8 meters; the youth had tried to escape from the Czortków police station courtyard, where scores of incarcerated Jews were about to be executed. Around the time of the second Czortków roundup of October 1942, Köllner shot the handicapped woman, Rifka Schwebel, point blank in the back of the head for failing to keep up with the other deportees. On October 4 he shot the elderly Schlomo Herschkowicz in the head from a distance of 3–5 meters under similar circumstances. In June 1943, during the liquidation of the Czortków Ghetto, Köllner shot the plumber Schorr, his wife, and the child she was holding. A few days later, Köllner detected the youths Emil Kitaj and Hania Adler trying to enter the labor camp in Czortków—the only remaining safe place for Jews in the town. Accompanied by a five-year-old child who was almost certainly his own son (born in 1938), Köllner shot the youths point blank as they fell to their knees and begged for their lives.

Köllner was also active in Buczacz. On October 8, 1942, he shot and killed Jakob Halpern, who suffered from a severe intestinal illness, for failing to pull himself up into the deportation train during the first roundup in Buczacz. In November 1942 Köllner shot the elderly Julia Hirschkorn, who had been dragged out of her apartment and proved unable to walk. In March 1943 Köllner shot the Jews Mandel and Fuchs, after they were evicted from the Buczacz hospital. The following June, during the "extermination action" in Buczacz, Köllner hauled the elderly Rosen couple from their apartment, made them run ahead of him, and then shot them in the head with a submachine gun.

Additionally, Köllner was charged with killings in other sites in the region. In early August 1943, during the liquidation of the labor camp in nearby Nagórzanka, Köllner discovered three youths hiding in a barn. He chased and shot the fleeing Mojsze Waisman, and then shot Bina and Gisela Horowitz point blank in the head as they knelt in front of him tearfully begging for their lives. Finally, Köllner was charged with a mass execution that took place in October 1942 in the town of Borszczów. Arriving there by car in the morning, Köllner arranged the roundup with the Jewish council and waited at a local restaurant while Ukrainian militia assembled the victims. He then followed the twenty-eight Jewish men and women and the militia some 600–800 meters out of town and monitored the execution.[28]

Paul Thomanek was acquitted at his first trial by the Jury Court of Hagen in 1957, but soon thereafter he was indicted again for "having killed Jews in numerous cases on his own initiative, in part together with others, out of bloodthirstiness or otherwise with base motives and partly also in a gruesome manner, in the period from November 1941 to July 1943." Relenting from his complete denial of any complicity at his first trial, during his second trial in 1960 Thomanek admitted that he had been present at shootings and mass executions but denied taking part in them. He also admitted to having been in charge of several camps in the Czortków area and to participating in the liquidation of the Czortków labor camp, but claimed that he shot Jews only in self-defense, or in compliance with his superiors' orders. Thomanek submitted to the court that "today he knows that it is a terrible crime to eradicate an entire race. But at the time he could not refuse orders, since it was said, 'Whoever doesn't cooperate with us is against us.'"[29]

Thomanek was charged with a long series of crimes. As SS-man in the Kamionki forced-labor camp near Tarnopol, set up as part of the construction of the DG IV, in November 1941 he shot the sick Jewish inmates Kleiner and Eisen, and killed Dr. Bela Blum, who was wounded in a melee during the food distribution. In December he shot a woman named Sala who brought food for her incarcerated husband. In March 1942 Thomanek ordered two Ukrainian guards to flog Aron Schwarz seventy-five times, while he pressed his foot on the inmate's head. He then shot Nahum Klein, who tried to eat the snow by the fence, having received no food or water for several days. Shortly thereafter he shot six sick inmates during a roll call. Several weeks later he shot the inmate Byk who was too sick to attend roll call.

For these and other cases in nearby Tarnopol, the court relied on several witnesses. They included Dr. R., who was working at the time of the trial as head doctor in Israel and had served as a physician in the Kamionki camp. The doctor described Thomanek as the second most powerful man in the camp, noting that the inmates called him "Der Erschiesser" (the shooter). Born in 1908 in Tarnopol, Dr. R. had studied in his hometown as well as in Vienna, Prague, and Italy, and was raised speaking German. These credentials convinced the court of the veracity of his testimony. The court found the testimony of the witness G. reliable for similar reasons: born near Kamionki in 1913, he had obtained a law degree in interwar Poland. According to G., the defendant was known at the time as "the red dog Thomanek" because of his red hair and brutality. The witness O., born in 1891, had studied law in Lemberg and Vienna, had served as an officer in the Austrian-Hungarian army, and was the owner of a lumberyard and brick factory in Tarnopol in the interwar period. He described the arbitrary shooting by Thomanek of his twenty-one-year-old nephew, Osias Seräth, who was kneeling with a group of other youths in the town square of Tarnopol during a roundup. The court accepted his testimony without reservation.[30]

Once he was appointed commandant of the labor camp in Czortków in November 1942, Thomanek reported directly to SSPF Katzmann in Lemberg, and was thus not under the control of the Czortków Sipo outpost. This gave him absolute power over some three hundred male and female Jewish workers along with several children. Shortly after his arrival Thomanek shot the grocer Bonia Hertmann and the cap-maker Wachtel for no apparent reason. Yet witnesses concurred that initially Thomanek was primarily concerned with his own well-being rather than with brutalizing the inmates. For instance, as Dr. Izrael Schorr testified at the trial, Thomanek threatened to confiscate his X-ray machine unless he provided him with regular supplies of pork and milk, which the doctor received from local peasants in return for his medical services. Born in 1898, Dr. Schorr had practiced as an X-ray specialist before the war; after the liberation he assisted the Soviet Extraordinary Commission for the investigation of Nazi crimes, which exhumed the mass graves in the vicinity of Czortków. By the time of the trial, he was practicing again in Israel. The court found him entirely reliable.[31]

In spring 1943 Thomanek, possibly following Katzmann's visit earlier that year, became noticeably more brutal. In May Thomanek publicly shot Sofia Wolf, Baruch Kratter, and Glaser Diamant. As she was led to the execution, Sofia Wolf, whose "offense" consisted of speaking through the camp's fence with the Polish woman caring for her child, turned around and called: "Herr Camp Commandant, spare my life, I have a small child." Thomanek shot her in the face and she fell dead to the ground. He then shot the other two men in the back. Some witnesses suggested that Thomanek merely wanted to try out the new Finnish submachine gun he had been given by Katzmann.[32]

On June 23, 1943, Thomanek liquidated the labor camp with the help of German gendarmes and Ukrainian auxiliaries. At the roll call of the entire camp population, Thomanek separated the men from the women and ordered everyone to lie on their stomachs and not to raise their heads. He then sorted out some forty to fifty Jews to dismantle the camp's workshops. At this point the inmate Mania ("Papusch") called out to Thomanek: "Herr Camp Commandant, take me too, I am your barber after all." Thomanek killed him on the spot with his submachine gun, also fatally wounding the inmate Bergmann, who was then shot to death by the gendarme Schultz. The rest of the Jews were transported in groups by truck to a former airfield and were all shot. When the brothers Gotesfeld refused to climb on the truck, Thomanek shot them dead. He also severely beat and then shot Max Lineal, whom he found hiding in the barracks. When the women's turn came, a seventeen-year-old blond girl named Jäger begged Thomanek to spare her life. She too was shot on the spot.[33]

Thomanek's version—that he had tried to save the people he knew by selecting them but had been compelled to defend himself when a Jew wielding a pipe-wrench attacked him—was rejected by the court. The court also dismissed Thomanek's assertion that he merely collected the victims' valuables at the airfield rather than participating in the shooting.[34] Indeed, as it turned out, Thomanek was involved in killings throughout the region.

In February 1943 Thomanek participated in a mass execution on Fedor Hill, near Buczacz, in which some five hundred Jews were shot in groups of ten into a predug trench after being forced to undress. In April 1943, during another killing operation in Buczacz, Thomanek and the chairman of the Jewish council, Baruch Kramer, encountered four young Jews who were caught trying to escape, being led down the main street of Buczacz. One of them, Akiba Weissmann, called out to Kramer: "Baruch, save me, I want to live." Kramer responded: "I can't help you." But as Weissmann persisted, Thomanek pulled out his pistol and shot him point blank.[35] A few days later, accompanied by a young Ukrainian woman, Thomanek and another SS-man raided a restaurant near Buczacz. The woman, who worked there as a waitress, had apparently denounced the new Ukrainian owner of the restaurant for hiding Jews. And indeed, the two SS-men found ten Jews in hiding, including the former owner, Leonie Folkenfolk, his wife, and their nine-year-old son; Dr. Fonki Neinan, his wife, their five-year-old child, his mother-in-law, and his brother-in-law; and a man named Tischler together with his pregnant wife. Thomanek stripped the Jews of their valuables and shot them all with his submachine gun. The last to be shot was the pregnant woman, who threw herself at his feet and begged for her life.[36]

At his trial, Thomanek denied all charges. While recalling what he termed the "assembly-line" killing on Fedor Hill, Thomanek claimed to have merely helped collect the victims' valuables, and even remembered saying to a fellow SS-man on the drive back: "Look at these beautiful flowers and yet so many people have to die." But Jewish survivors could detect no such compassion. The witness Rabinowicz noted that Thomanek was well known in Buczacz. A large man with red hair, Thomanek spent many days in the town, where he had his own room and made numerous demands, not least to be provided with "girls." Whenever Thomanek appeared he would spread fear, for people knew that "something was going on." The witness Kleiner also recalled with terror the man whom they called "Automaniuk."[37]

The court accepted the testimonies of the Jewish survivors. Here too a personal profile of the witnesses served to establish their reliability. Rabinowicz, who was one of the young Jews present when Thomanek shot Weissmann on the street in Buczacz, was born in 1916 and was working at the time of the trial as an engineer in the food industry in Israel. Son of a well-known merchant and city councilor in Buczacz, Rabinowicz had served in the Polish army in the Second World War, escaped from German captivity back to Buczacz, and worked with his father under the Soviet occupation as manager of a grain storage depot. Because they had helped Kramer under the Soviets, the latter helped them out when he was made head of the Jewish council by the Nazis. The court was impressed with Rabinowicz, who "speaks very good German" and "gave his testimony in a calm, informative manner." As the court noted, "There was no indication whatsoever that he exaggerated, let alone provided any false information under to the pressure of his emotions."[38]

The court also had a positive view of Kleiner, who was sixty-two years old at the time of the trial and worked as a spice merchant in New York. Before the war, Kleiner too had belonged to the wealthy grain merchants of Buczacz. The court noted that Kleiner, "due to his temperament, gave his testimony in a more animated, even agitated manner, compared to Rabinowicz." It insisted, however, that the witness, "whose profound and genuine Jewish faith was visible, left the impression of an uncompromising love of truth." Thus social class, professional training, business success, European and German culture, and religious faith were all important elements in accepting the testimony of Jewish witnesses.[39] But it was just as valuable to be able to report in a detached, "objective" manner about the horrors that one experienced or witnessed. Any demonstration of excessive emotion was seen as suspect by the court.

This judicial preference for lack of emotions can be glimpsed from the following case. In early 1943, Thomanek discovered the teenagers Binka and Nuzia Steigmann visiting relatives at the Nagórzanka labor camp under his command, next to the town of Jagielnica. The two young women threw themselves at his feet and begged for their lives. Thomanek shot them one after the other in the head. The event was witnessed by Schlomo Wołkowicz, who testified about it to the court. Born in Jagielnica, near Czortków, in 1922, Wołkowicz was trained as a technical engineer and was working in this capacity in Israel during the trial. What made his testimony credible to the court was not only his professional and social status but also the fact that he depicted in what the judges called a "heart-wrenching manner" how he survived a mass execution in the town of Złoczów, crawled from under the pile of bodies, and made his way back to Jagielnica in time to see the murder of the two teenaged girls. That he could report all this in a calm and composed manner was evidence of his truthfulness.[40]

And yet, even the setting of the court could not entirely obscure the terror that Thomanek instilled in his victims. During an inspection of the Jezierzany camp in June 1943, Thomanek hauled the elderly Rosen couple out of the barracks, led them to a small hill, and shot them with his submachine gun. As the fifty-nine-year-old witness Dr. W., who had worked as a lawyer in interwar Poland and practiced in Israel at the time of the trial, succinctly put it, "the defendant with his red hair was at the time an apparition that one would never forget." The witness C., who was born in 1930, recalled the terrifying cry "Thomanek is coming!" when his tall, fat, red-haired figure was detected in the camp.[41]

The Judgments

How did German courts evaluate the guilt of the indicted? What understanding of the historical and political context of these events did the judges demonstrate and what role did this context play in sentencing the defendants? In other words, what relationship did the courts establish between personal guilt and state-directed genocide?

In considering the charges against Kurt Köllner in 1962, the State Court of Saarbrücken took several factors into account: first, that since the events occurred twenty years earlier, memory could have faded; second, that the witnesses' perception might have been distorted by the extraordinary nature of these occurrences; third, that the witnesses could have been motivated by feelings of hate or revenge; and fourth, that the witnesses might have conspired with each other to condemn the defendant. The court concluded its review of witness testimony with the following statement:

> During the entire proceedings the court paid special attention to all such issues that were of the greatest significance to the credibility of the witnesses and, in view of these special circumstances, the court employed the strictest standards in weighing the credibility of the witnesses. The witness testimonies were therefore carefully scrutinized and assessed. The judgment was based only on witness testimonies in which errors caused by flawed observation or flawed memory as well as untrue statements could be ruled out with certainty.[42]

Köllner denied all charges. Not only did he stubbornly maintain that he had always had good relations with the Jews of Czortków, but he also went so far as to claim that some Jews had willingly revealed to him the locations of their hiding places. Just as he asserted that his transfer from Lemberg was punishment for his criticism of anti-Jewish actions there, Köllner also claimed that his kindness to the Jews of Czortków got him into trouble. In May 1943 he was called to an SS and police interrogation in Lemberg, and meanwhile his house in Czortków was searched. Jewish witnesses, however, noted that Köllner's alleged kindness derived from sheer greed: he did release some Jews from imprisonment, but only for exorbitant bribes. Indeed, it was these bribes that triggered the SS inquiry into his conduct. The court thus rejected this line of Köllner's defense.

Köllner's attempt to plead mistaken identity and to incriminate a fellow SS-man also failed. He then claimed to have been on sick leave when many of the crimes in the indictment were committed. His wife provided an alibi for this assertion, but the veracity of her testimony was completely discredited by her extraordinary assertion that during her lengthy stay in Czortków she never knew about the mass killings of the Jews there.[43]

The court found Köllner guilty of most of the crimes as charged. Its findings concerning the Borszczów execution of twenty-eight Jews are especially instructive, considering that in this case Köllner had not personally shot anyone, and that neither Köllner nor Peckmann were charged with the organization and supervision of the mass killing of tens of thousands. According to the court, Köllner had conceded during an earlier interrogation that he had in fact been in charge of the execution squad. Moreover, the court rejected Köllner's assertion of moral qualms. The closing statement noted that the court

> does not believe the defendant that he had inner reservations against taking part in the execution action. What contradicts this claim is first, that by that time he had already shot many Jews, even on his own initiative; second, his entire attitude toward the Jews proves that he had no humane considerations in his treatment of the Jews.[44]

In explaining Köllner's motivation, the court referred to a comment made by his father after the war, namely, that "now his son must put out of his head his previous attitude and previous conduct." This, the court noted, indicated "especially clearly the defendant Köllner's moral transformation and the hold of National Socialist ideology over him." Finally, Köllner's argument that he could not evade orders was also rejected. The court pointed out that Köllner "generally did not shy away from avoiding his superiors' orders when it suited him [as] can be seen from the fact that according to his own testimony, in early October 1942 he went on a private trip with Detective Superintendent Engels instead of participating in an Aktion that had just begun."[45]

The court's concluding observations about Köllner's guilt and its implications for the rest of German society, however, were simultaneously damning and ambivalent. Crucially, even as the judges insisted on Köllner's responsibility for his actions, they described him as a victim of circumstances. The guilty party was ultimately Hitler's regime. Yet the middle-class values instilled in Köllner at home and in school should have immunized him against the evil of Nazism. The Third Reich, in this account, appeared to have nothing in common with German decency, education, upbringing, or traditions. Hence Köllner's personal guilt lay in failing to apply these values to the new political situation and his willingness to be seduced by the promises and opportunities of Nazism:

> [Köllner] received a completely normal education in his parental home and at school and was raised in a democratic state. ... [H]e recognized quite early the danger of National Socialism ... [and] remained inwardly unmoved by [its] ideas and goals ... even after he joined the SS. ... All this indicates that the defendant ... would have probably continued to lead an ordinary bourgeois existence, had he not increasingly succumbed to the temptations of National Socialist ideology

following the transformation of the political conditions. In this sense he became—like many others—a victim in the wider sense of the circumstances of the time.[46]

Speaking directly to the vexed issue of personal guilt within what was, after all, a criminal state, the court presented Köllner as a man who knew that he was committing a crime and yet did so for personal gain:

> [Köllner's] guilt consists ... in the fact that he sacrificed his previous moral and human restraints and that in the effort to promote his own advancement and profit as much as possible, he became a compliant and pliable instrument of the regime of the time, especially in the planned eradication of the Jews, even though, according to his own description, he knew precisely "that this is murder."[47]

Moreover, the court argued that Köllner's conduct served the goals of the Nazi regime and implied thereby that it was precisely opportunists of his ilk who were the instruments of Nazi power and genocide. But again, a certain degree of ambivalence crept into the judges' attempt to distinguish between opportunism and conviction; for while Köllner was said to have acted "only" for personal gain, the court attributed to him racist and thus potentially ideological sentiments as well:

> Through his deeds he consciously sustained and strengthened the National Socialist dictatorship's rule over the Jews. He thereby made himself into the arbitrary master over life and death of his Jewish victims in his capacity as *Judensachbearbeiter* and by this means disseminated fear and terror. This is not to deny that in individual cases of momentary caprice he showed kindness to his favorites and to such persons from whom he could expect material profit. The court is convinced that this too happened only out of calculation and for his personal profit. The defendant acted out of this general attitude and out of a feeling of supposed racial superiority.[48]

Kurt Köllner was consequently found guilty of nine counts of murder and was sentenced to life imprisonment. In reaching this verdict, the court noted that "these acts were perpetrated in a period in which the actions of the regime of the time extensively effaced the concepts of justice and injustice and in which the respect for human life had largely vanished." Nonetheless, the court insisted that "the defendant committed offenses against defenseless people and that he pitilessly and without any scruples destroyed or wanted to destroy the lives of elderly and in part ill persons as well as the lives of young people."[49] Thus the ambivalence of punishing a murderer who acted "normally" in abnormal times, or of bringing to justice an otherwise perfectly "normal" person who had been transformed into a murderer by the circumstances of his time, remained at the heart of the judgment. We might say that it is still there, not only regarding the Holocaust but also many of the subsequent genocides the world has experienced.

Paul Thomanek's defense rested on his assertion of having acted on orders of his superiors or in conformity with SS instructions concerning the treatment of Jews. The

Jury State Court of Hagen conceded that SSPF Katzmann had indeed ordered the killing of Jews unable to work. But the court argued that since this was a general instruction, it left a great deal of "free-play" for the actors in the field. As proof, the court cited Thomanek's own statement that, "no one in Lemberg cared about me [in Czortków]." Moreover, the court asserted that since Katzmann's "order" was aimed at implementing a criminal undertaking it could not be seen as binding: "It is the basis of any moral order that the life of an individual who is not guilty of anything is inviolable."[50]

According to the court's logic, Thomanek's guilt therefore had to derive from his ability to distinguish between criminal and lawful orders, or, more generally, between Good and Evil. As in Köllner's case, the court assumed that Thomanek had acquired this ability at home and in school:

> The defendant was raised in well-ordered family circumstances. ... He was educated according to the general moral teachings ... [and] he had a confessional commitment. ... Through this personal development the inviolability of human life was always presented to him, so that this fundamental concept of morality was drilled into his consciousness. The defendant was also educated in the then democratic Czechoslovakia ... in which there was no racial hatred ... until he joined the Waffen-SS, he had no contact with Jews.[51]

Because of this background of moral education, argued the court, "the defendant should have recognized ... that the Katzmann order was a monstrous injustice." The court then examined Thomanek's explanation as to why he nevertheless complied with these instructions. Thomanek had argued, wrote the judges, that initially Katzmann's order "made a terrifying impression on him." And yet, "as Katzmann went on to say that the Jew was the worst enemy, [Thomanek] thought to himself, if so many millions of people cheer for Hitler, then what the general says must also be right. Apart from that he [Thomanek] was also afraid of refusing orders."[52]

The judges had no time for such arguments. As they forcefully put it: "This assertion by the defendant that he initially had doubts, but then became convinced that the order was just, is pure evasion." According to the court, "the basic ethical rules, which were taught to the defendant for many years, could not and were not undermined and extinguished by the brief statement of an SS general." What, then, was the true reason for Thomanek's compliance? The judges' view was unequivocal: "The conviction that the actions of the SS against the Jews were just could only exist—if at all—in people into whom National Socialist ideology had been drilled for many years." And yet, they continued, "This was not the case of the defendant. He was a grown, mature man ... who ... had been educated in a Christian and democratic spirit."[53]

Here, then, was the moral and legal conundrum. A man educated outside Nazi Germany according to fundamental humanitarian principles chose to obey blatantly criminal orders. The court was thus conflicted between, on the one hand, its finding that a man who should have internalized an ethical worldview became a heartless murderer and, on the other hand, its need to demonstrate Thomanek's ability to distinguish Good from Evil in order to find him guilty of betraying his conscience. It thus insisted that "the defendant recognized the unjust nature of the Katzmann order," as evidenced by the fact that on the eve of one labor camp's liquidation, Thomanek "consciously drank himself senseless, so as not to be present at the liquidation, as this already 'disgusted' him." The court concluded that this "is not the way a man behaves when he is convinced that he is doing the right thing."[54]

This is of course a problematic assertion. It assumes that those who were convinced and committed Nazis could not tell Good from Evil. According to this logic, however, such absence of any ethical perspective would make ideologically committed murderers less guilty of the crimes they perpetrated than those who, presumably like Thomanek, had previously internalized a moral worldview. In fact, we know that SS-men and policemen who killed hundreds of thousands of Jews often got drunk before, during, and after their actions.[55] Did this mean that they were all unconvinced of the justice of their actions? If they were not convinced, who was? Could the entire genocide of the Jews have been carried out by men who were filled with doubts? What would be the meaning of such a statement? Can one envision a genocide that would be even worse because it was carried out by truly committed, sober men, who never needed a drop of alcohol to soothe their conscience since they had no doubts? Is it necessary to be convinced in order to commit genocide? And what, then, is the relationship between ideological conviction in a genocidal ideology and confronting the reality of mass murder?[56]

There are no simple answers to these questions, and the court was certainly not called upon to address them. Nevertheless, the judges' assumption that overconsumption of alcohol indicated moral revulsion and served to either blunt one's moral sensibilities or evade massacre altogether is quite revealing. In making the dissolute into people of conscience and absolving the ideologues by denying their moral choice, the court's argumentation sheds light on the much wider issue of German confrontations with complicity in genocide and the uncomfortable role of conviction in "coming to terms" with the national and personal Nazi past.

Less problematically from a moral point of view, but of major legal significance, the court also rejected Thomanek's assertion of superior orders (*Befehlsnotstand*). This was the most common argument raised by former Nazi perpetrators after the war, even though the Nuremberg Tribunal had already dismissed it in 1945.[57] In Thomanek's case, the judges noted that "the situation of the defendant at the time was not such, that he could only save himself from a threat to his own life and body by acting as he did." In fact, the court argued, it had not been shown that all SS-men followed Katzmann's order to the letter, or that in the Kamionki camp "an SS man who did not take part in executions of Jews faced danger to his own life and limb." The court conceded that had Thomanek refused to shoot Jews, "he would have had to reckon with being dismissed from his post and possibly being sent to the front." Obviously Thomanek did not cherish this prospect. But the threat of being forced to do what millions of other Germans were already doing certainly did not justify compliance with criminal orders.[58]

The Hagen court found Thomanek guilty of twenty-six counts of murder and sentenced him to life imprisonment. But in explaining its reasoning for this decision, the court described Thomanek's guilt using precisely the same logic that the Saarbrücken court had employed in the case of Köllner. For here too, Thomanek was said to have been a victim of his time and circumstances. This argument referred not only to Thomanek but, by extension, to an entire generation of Germans, including the court itself. "The question of the defendant's motivation for his deeds," wrote the judges,

> can only be answered by reference to his career, his personality, and his attitude to National Socialism. The defendant was ... raised in a Christian spirit and grew up in a democratic state. The fundaments of a general ethical teaching were planted in him. ... The court is ... convinced that in all likelihood the defendant would have continued to lead a decent life, had he not come into contact with the horrible ideas and plans of the SS leadership through the transformation of the political circumstances and especially through the war. Clearly he does not carry any responsibility for these ideas and plans as well as for the transformation of the political circumstances and the war. To this extent he became—like many others with him—in a wider sense also a victim of that time.[59]

Following this general justification of complicity in Nazi crimes, the court elaborated Thomanek's particular circumstances: whereas in Köllner's case it was his socialist home that provided the foil against which his actions were measured, for Thomanek it was his ambiguous ethnic identity that featured most prominently. Indeed, this mixed identity helped distinguish between Thomanek and most "ordinary" Germans, even as these "ordinary" Germans' complicity had already been explained away by the court's interpretation of circumstantial victimhood. Thomanek, argued the judges, was primarily motivated by an urge to become an even better German than his purely "Aryan," true Reich-German comrades. Not merely a victim of the political circumstance of Nazi rule,

> his fate was formed also by the circumstance of being a resident of the borderlands [dass er ein Grenzbewohner war], a man whose national identity [Volkstumszugehörigkeit] could have been seen as somewhat questionable. The defendant declared ... that the Czechs did not see him as a fully rightful citizen, because he was German, and that the Germans had also initially not seen him as a fully rightful German, because he had previously lived in Czechoslovakia. These circumstances stimulated many of these border- or ethnic-Germans, once they were back under German rule, to endeavor to demonstrate and prove from that point on that they were especially reliable and especially "good Germans." The defendant also made such an endeavor.[60]

Yet if Thomanek's circumstances explained his motivation so well, where, after all, lay his guilt? Here too the court employed a remarkably similar rhetoric to that used to condemn Köllner. But while Köllner's opportunism was one of power and material enrichment, Thomanek's was focused on establishing his identity, which would then also ensure him of a more secure status and greater material comfort. "The guilt of the defendant," argued the judges,

> consists in that, as a result of his weakness of character, he subordinated all the basic teachings he had earlier acquired to the effort to prove himself to be a "reliable" German, and that he went so far in this effort ... as to offer himself ruthlessly and unconditionally to his contemporary superiors ... not because he was convinced of the moral justification of this conduct, but because he saw it as serving his own personal interest. He clearly understood the dreadful injustice that would be carried out against the Jews. ... But he also saw that the National Socialists, especially the SS with their program and their actions, were in power and in a certain sense were "masters of the world." He saw ... that he could share that power and that when he behaved in the manner required and expected of him by his superiors, things went well for him personally. ... He led a good life both in Kamionki and later in Czortków. He had his own house in both places and even had his own room in Buczacz. In Czortków he owned a car and had a batman, who for his part also had an assistant [one of the Jewish witnesses]. For a certain time he was in a position to accommodate his wife and child and even his father. These are privileges that would have normally not been reserved for a simple SS man. ... The defendant was offered them because he excelled in the "treatment" of the Jews ... For this reason he was also then given command of the camp in Czortków and ... [of] other camps in the area ... all while still a mere private. This gave him a position of enormous power beyond any proportion to his rank. ... [He] did not want to be called up by the Wehrmacht and be sent to a frontline unit. Motivated by these selfish reasons the defendant thus became a compliant accessory of the National Socialist dictatorship.[61]

Thomanek was therefore guilty precisely because he could tell Good from Evil and chose to serve the latter in order to further his own selfish interests. In this Faustian bargain, he acted neither under compulsion nor was he incapable of evading the circumstances in which he found himself. He joined the police in order to avoid the front; he brutalized others in order to gain his superiors' favor; he killed on his own initiative in order to enhance and maintain his power. He also formed his own understanding of what becoming a "good German" meant: he believed that his German identity could only be ensured by carrying out the genocidal plans of the regime. And yet, in the eyes of the court, he also remained a victim of his circumstances.

Elusive Justice and Historical Truth

The court's characterization of this SS perpetrator contained other contradictions. The court condemned Thomanek for having chosen to kill Jews rather than risking his life at the front. This would imply that, had he gained a better understanding of what it meant to be a "good German," he would have refused the orders of the SS and participated instead in the Wehrmacht's attempt to subjugate Europe and Russia to German rule. Thus the court posited that compared to Himmler's troops, Hitler's soldiers were decent and upright patriots.[62]

Furthermore, if Thomanek had been motivated by his ambivalent status as an ethnic German, could one extrapolate from his case and say that ambiguous Germans were more likely to be Himmler's willing executioners than "real" Germans? Or that Nazi indoctrination did not matter, since those who had not been subjected to it were just as bad, or even worse? And consequently, was one to conclude that such decent men as perhaps the judges themselves, who had presumably lived under Hitler's rule during the war, either practicing the law or serving in the Wehrmacht, were not as likely to act like Thomanek, the *Mischling* Czech-Moravian-German who evaded service at the front and had to prove his Germanness by killing Jews?

The three men examined here were at the sharp end of the Holocaust. Peckmann was a middle-class professional policeman; Köllner was a small businessman from a well-connected socialist family; Thomanek was raised in a working-class family in Czechoslovakia. The professional policeman Peckmann, who in another historical context would have been the most representative of "ordinary Germans," but during the war was one of the commanders of the Sipo outpost in Czortków and thus responsible for the murder of many of the region's sixty thousand Jewish victims, was acquitted. Köllner and Thomanek, one stemming from the compromised left-wing milieu, the other a son of Germany's ambivalent borderlands, could hardly be seen as the embodiment of the German geographical and social "heartland," where ethnicity was predominantly German and the elites largely continued to hold patriotic and conservative views, and were still perceived as the source of authority and morality in the Federal Republic of the early 1960s.

At first sight, Thomanek appears to fit the stereotype of the typical low-ranking Nazi perpetrator: crass, brutal, and sadistic. But as the Hagen court discovered, he was only partly German, was raised as a good Christian in a decent family, and acted out of overzealousness to be accepted into the fold of the German nation. Köllner too seemed initially like a typical Nazi; less brutal and slicker, but otherwise quite true to type. But as the Saarbrücken court revealed, he came from a family with deep socialist roots. Neither of these men would have become a mass murderer had the Nazis not come to power. But then of course the Nazis came to power, maintained it, and used it to perpetrate genocide, precisely because such men as Köllner, Thomanek, and, not least, Peckmann were so willing to help them. Or rather, "the Nazis" were such men as Köllner, Thomanek, and Peckmann.

The judges struggled with this conclusion, because ultimately it implicated large numbers of Germans, including, possibly, themselves. They had to show that decent men could become killers if in evil times they abandon their humanity for opportunistic reasons. But of course, there were very few people in Nazi Germany who did not exercise a measure of opportunism, and the vast majority sacrificed a greater or lesser portion of their humanity. This was a question of degree, and of circumstances. And even after the fact, most men walked free, men like Peckmann, who continued to enforce law and order in the Federal Republic, and innumerable other lawyers, judges, physicians, professors, biologists, anthropologists—and so on. These men became the mainstay of postwar society for another generation and were treated with at least as much respect as those Jewish witnesses who had earned medical and law degrees at prewar European institutions.

On the one hand, the perpetrators remain elusive figures: the convicted were not typical, and the typical were not convicted. On the other hand, when we observe such an apparently unfathomable event as the Holocaust at the local level, we realize its human dimensions, even at their most inhuman. The peculiarities of the German criminal code allowed many of those who had organized genocide to avoid punishment and created a stereotype of a Nazi perpetrator who seemed very different from "ordinary" Germans. But these trials also provided valuable insights into the workings of genocide and the relationship between the killers and the killed. Ultimately, much of what we would like to think about the Holocaust turns out to be different when observed close up: the perpetrators often knew the victims; they were motivated by the most conventional urges and desires even if they committed the most abominable crimes; the killing was both systematic and gratuitous, often without any specific motive apart from a sense of power and impunity; the killers knew that they were committing murder even as they were killing, and chose to act as they did because they hoped to gain from their actions—as indeed they often did—just as they hoped never to pay a price for their crimes, which indeed rarely happened. Even when the reckoning finally came, it arrived belatedly, often in much diluted form, and invariably carefully wrapped in layers of rationalizations that protected society from being drawn into the scene of the crime.

CHAPTER 6
MEMORY LAWS AS A TOOL OF FORGETTING

Ukraine and Israel—Legitimizing Genocide

The enactment of laws criminalizing or penalizing certain versions of the past and, more generally, the struggle over competing historical narratives and the status of victims and perpetrators, national heroes and internal or foreign villains, have become an increasingly prominent feature of the last few decades, both in Europe and in other parts of the world. The predilection to criminalize unwanted or objectionable representations of past events is often related to differing interpretations of the events of the Second World War and its immediate origins and aftermath, although in some cases, most prominently perhaps the genocide of the Armenians, memory laws stretch back to the First World War.[1] Such interpretations, in turn, are usually related to the roles played not only in the war but also in the pre- and postwar periods, by different national, ethnic, religious, and ideological groups, as well as to the political arrangements reached by or imposed on the states that emerged from the conflict. Subsequent changes in official and popular versions of the past and the relevant legislation of historical perspectives have similarly reflected the transformation in the political order—not least since the fall of communism—as well as the emergence of new postwar generations and an ongoing tension between a desire to expose the obfuscations and denials of past wrongs and a no less potent urge to reassert national honor and dignity, even at the price of suppressing or outlawing historical facts that threaten to undermine the favored perception of the nation's history.

Much has been written on this issue in recent years and there is little point in recapitulating it here.[2] What interests me in this chapter, rather, is the interdependence of recognition and criminalization of several distinct national discourses. Thus, for instance, in 2006, Ukrainian President Viktor Yushchenko proposed a law that both recognized the Holodomor—the Stalinist state-directed famine in Ukraine—as genocide and introduced penalties to its denial. To its credit—but also largely because of the fraught internal politics of memory in Ukraine at that time between the pro-Russian (formerly Soviet) east and the pro-nationalist anti-Russian west—the parliament refused to adopt concrete penalties for denial even as it signed into law the following unequivocal statement:

> The 1932–1933 Holodomor in Ukraine is an act of genocide of the Ukrainian people.
> Public Denial of the 1932–1933 Holodomor in Ukraine shall be recognized as desecration of the memory of millions of victims of the Holodomor as well as disparagement of the Ukrainian people and shall be unlawful.[3]

The following year, Yushchenko traveled to Israel, where he visited the Holocaust memorial at Yad Vashem as well as the Western Wall, reportedly stating there that his trip was intended "to express identification with the Jewish people and its heritage and to pray in the holiest site of the Jewish people." In his speech to the Knesset (the Israeli parliament), the Ukrainian president also condemned anti-Semitism, but did not make any apology for the role of Ukrainians in the Holocaust. Conversely, standing alongside Knesset Speaker Daliah Itzik, Yushchenko condemned the massacre of Ukrainians by Stalin's regime. For her part, even as she stressed that "many Ukrainians are among the righteous of the nations who risked their lives to save Jews," Itzik also added, "we cannot accept the commemoration of the actions of Ukrainian individuals who, in the course of the national struggle for Ukrainian independence, took part in mass murder of Jews."[4] Ultimately, just as Ukraine did not formally assume any responsibility for collaboration in the Holocaust, Israel did not formally recognize the Holodomor as genocide, apparently one of Yushchenko's main goals in his visit.

In part, Israel's reluctance to use the "G" word in this context can be attributed to its relations with Russia. Almost a decade later, in 2016, Russia's deputy ambassador in Tel Aviv, Leonid Frolov, warned Israel against passing a proposed law that would formally recognize the Holodomor as genocide: "This is not a good time to discuss such a proposal," he said. "It will be bad. It will be (the) wrong step."[5] But beyond the constraints of policy there clearly was and remains a more profound reason for refusing to take this step. For Israel, recognizing the Holodomor as genocide would put it perilously close to the Holocaust; hence, Ukrainians and Jews might be seen as equal victims. Yet for Israel, not only does the claim of being the answer to the Holocaust serve as its cardinal raison d'être, the insistence on the Shoah as a unique historical event elevates Israel above all other national entities and puts it on a higher moral plane than those who might either reject its existence or even criticize any of its policies. It is precisely for this reason that for Ukraine recognition of the Holodomor as genocide by Israel is of greater importance than by any other state, providing a uniquely powerful stamp of approval by the self-proclaimed successor state of the Holocaust. Additionally, especially because of Ukraine's checkered history vis-à-vis its Jewish inhabitants, acquiring the status of a fellow genocide victim from the Jewish state would go a long way to redressing a perceived moral imbalance, liberating Ukraine from the ghosts of the past more effectively than could be expected from a more conventional international declaration.[6] In other words, precisely because of Israel's success in making itself into the universally recognized representative of Jewish victimhood, an official statement by its leaders on the Holodomor as genocide would have ranked as a major accomplishment by a Ukrainian president who was trying to rewrite his nation's history. Which is, ultimately, exactly why the request was denied.

Collective Israeli and Jewish memory had a great deal to do with this as well. For many Jewish survivors stemming from Ukraine, especially from those parts of Eastern Poland that subsequently became postwar West Ukraine, the Ukrainians were "worse than the Germans." Memories of Ukrainian slaughter of their Jewish neighbors, perpetrated by Ukrainian auxiliary police units under German command, Ukrainian nationalist militias, and other paramilitaries, as well as bandits, acquaintances, and villagers, fill the testimonies of Jewish survivors.[7] The sense of bitterness over betrayal by neighbors, colleagues, and friends is palpable even decades after the event. What complicates matters even further is Ukraine's post-communist veneration of its freedom fighters and liberators, whose cult, especially popular in West Ukraine, concerns mostly the fight against the reimposition of Soviet rule in the wake of the German occupation in the Second World War, recently provided with additional fuel by the Russian annexation of Crimea, incursion into Eastern Ukraine, and finally its wholescale invasion of Ukraine on February 24, 2022.[8] The problem with the resurrection of these national heroes' memory since Ukrainian independence in 1991 is, however, that it also entails the denial or suppression of their darker side, namely, their collaboration with the Germans in the mass murder of the Jews and, no less important in the regional politics of memory, their entirely independent campaign of ethnic cleansing of the Polish population in Volhynia and Galicia.[9] From this perspective, then, while Israel might have been in the best position to legitimize the categorization of Soviet crimes in Ukraine as genocide, it simultaneously threatened to hamper the glorification of Ukrainian nationalists precisely because of its self-perception as the main bulwark against Holocaust denial.

Indeed, for the state of Israel, the Holocaust exists not only as a past event whose memory must never be denied or erased but also as the most powerful tool in its arsenal in the constant struggle to legitimize its existence and policies. Before visiting dignitaries sit down to negotiate with Israeli officials, before they perhaps gingerly raise sensitive questions about settlements, occupation, and the treatment of Palestinians, they must first attend Yad Vashem, the state's official shrine to the Holocaust in Jerusalem. There they are forcefully and unambiguously reminded that the entire Jewish people, for which Israel claims responsibility no matter where its sons and daughters may reside, will and must never again become the target of genocide. They are also told in no uncertain terms that all nations of the world must be committed to the defense and might of Israel because of the guilt they bear for the abandonment of the Jews in the Second World War.[10] And, almost in the same breath, so to speak, the memory of the Nakba, the expulsion of the vast majority of the Palestinians from what became the state of Israel in 1948, is expunged. For one cannot speak about the fate of the Jews and the fate of the Arabs at the same time, and any mention of the Nakba evokes the automatic and officially sanctioned response of "How can you compare?" and is immediately perceived as casting doubt on the very right of Israel to exist, and thereby as in fact promoting another Holocaust.[11]

Poland and Ukraine—Heroes and Villains

The relationship between Ukraine's desire for an Israeli stamp of approval over the Holodomor's status as genocide and Israel's insistence on the Holocaust as a unique crime in the annals of human history is further complicated by Poland's similar claims of being the "Christ of nations." For Poland, the Jewish/Israeli claim of unique victimhood not only stands in competition to its self-perception but also undermines Poland's victim status by suggesting Polish complicity in the Holocaust. The Polish sense of victimization is further exacerbated both by the fate of the nation in the latter parts of the Second World War, when Polish residents of Eastern Poland were subjected to massive ethnic cleansing by Ukrainian nationalists, and by the imposition of a decades-long communist regime often associated with so-called Judeo-Bolshevism, or *żydokomuna*, denoted as Jewish sympathy for the Soviets and complicity in their rule.[12]

Poland's memory laws have therefore attempted to confront the conundrum of pre-1989 communist obfuscation, competition of victimhood with the Jews and rejection of any hints of complicity in the Holocaust, and provide a response to Ukraine's nationalist glorification of its Second World War liberation fighters by claims of Ukrainian genocidal actions in the Polish borderlands, precisely those majority Ukrainian lands seen by Ukrainians as sites of Polish colonization and suppression of national aspirations.

In 1998, Poland legislated the first memory law in Eastern Europe, stipulating that "He who publicly and contrary to facts contradicts the crimes mentioned in Article 1, clause 1, shall be subject to a fine or a penalty of deprivation of liberty of up to three years." These were specified as "crimes perpetrated against persons of Polish nationality and Polish citizens of other ethnicity, nationalities in the period between September 1, 1939 and December 31, 1989," including "Nazi crimes," "communist crimes," and "other crimes against the peace, crimes against humanity, or war crimes."[13] As noted by Nikolay Koposov, this law put Nazi and Soviet crimes in the same basket of crimes against humanity, while eschewing any direct reference to the genocide of the Jews, referenced only by the phrase "Polish citizens of other ethnicity, nationalities," thereby adopting the Soviet formula of subsuming the Holocaust under the general category of "crimes against the Polish nation," a vague definition at best.[14]

Moreover, definitions of what constitutes such crimes, who committed them, and what are the parameters of denial, have been shifting between the fall of communism and the present day. In 2018, the Polish parliament passed an amendment to the Act of 1998, which was signed into law by Polish President Andrzej Duda later that year. As the new version states,

> Whoever claims, publicly and contrary to the facts, that the Polish Nation or the Republic of Poland is responsible or co-responsible for Nazi crimes committed by the Third Reich … or for other felonies that constitute crimes against peace, crimes against humanity or war crimes, or whoever otherwise grossly diminishes the responsibility of the true perpetrators of said crimes—shall be liable to a fine or imprisonment for up to 3 years.

Here, then, is not only denial of Nazi and Soviet crimes against the Polish nation criminalized but also the assertion that Poles might have been in anyway complicit in Nazi crimes (or other crimes, presumably by communists, although those are not explicitly stated for the obvious reason that the legislators were perfectly aware of the fact that the communist regime in their country was run by Poles).

Additionally, and significantly, the law expands both the timeline of crimes committed against the Polish nation and the list of perpetrators. As the revised Article 1 reads, these crimes include the following:

> Nazi crimes, communist crimes, crimes committed by Ukrainian nationalists and members of Ukrainian units collaborating with the Third Reich, and other felonies that constitute crimes against peace, crimes against humanity or war crimes, committed against persons of Polish nationality or Polish citizens of other nationalities between November 8, 1917 and July 31, 1990.[15]

As the legislator notes, the law was amended specifically with a view to "protecting the reputation of the Republic of Poland and the Polish Nation," namely, in order to act against any accusations of Polish complicity in the genocide of the Jews, an issue that became especially heated following the publication in 2000 of the Polish-language original of Jan Tomasz Gross's book *Neighbors* on the massacre of the Jewish inhabitants of the village of Jedwabne by their own Polish neighbors. More recently, Polish officials have become increasingly obsessed with vehemently (and justifiably) rejecting any use of the term "Polish death camps," as was done most prominently by President Barack Obama in 2012 (for which the administration promptly apologized).[16]

But the amended law had another intent, generally ignored by Western commentators. This time, the law specifically stated that

> crimes committed by Ukrainian nationalists and members of Ukrainian units collaborating with the Third Reich constitute acts committed by Ukrainian nationalists between 1925 and 1950 which involved the use of violence, terror or other human rights violations against individuals or population groups. Participating in the extermination of the Jewish population and genocide of citizens of the Second Polish Republic in Volhynia and Eastern Małopolska [Lesser Poland] also constitutes a crime committed by Ukrainian nationalists and members of Ukrainian units collaborating with the Third Reich.[17]

Hence, the law not only included Ukrainian nationalists, along with the Nazis and the Soviets, as committing crimes against humanity and genocide against the Polish nation but also viewed accusations of collaboration by Ukrainians in Nazi crimes as legitimate even as it simultaneously criminalized similar allegations against Poles.

This controversial amendment therefore refers to two important episodes in the period since the fall of the communist regime. One, which has drawn much greater public attention, is the case of the Holocaust. While several scholars, including not a few Poles living in Poland and elsewhere, have documented Polish complicity in the murder of the Jews, sparking what had been seen as controversial but fruitful Polish confrontations with the past, this law seems to criminalize any further investigations into the murkier aspects of the German occupation, its immediate aftermath—which included several major massacres of Jews by Poles—and Poland's prewar increasingly anti-Semitic 1930s.[18] The second aspect of this law, which, as noted, drew much less international attention but enraged many Ukrainians, greatly exacerbated Poland's fraught relationship with Ukraine, which up to that point seemed to have been resolved thanks to mutual efforts by the two states following the fall of communism. Thus on May 21, 1997, the presidents of Ukraine and Poland issued a joint statement "On Concorde and Reconciliation"; on July 11, 2003, another statement was issued "On Reconciliation on the Sixtieth Anniversary of the Volhynia Tragedy" (i.e., the ethnic cleansing of the Poles by nationalist Ukrainian paramilitaries in 1943–4); and on April 27, 2007, yet another mutual statement was issued on the occasion of the sixtieth anniversary of the "Vistula Operation" (i.e., the deportation of ethnic Ukrainians by the postwar communist Polish regime). These proclamations by the heads of the two states were accompanied by several statements of reconciliation between Ukrainian Greek Catholic and Polish Roman Catholic bishops in 2005 and 2013.[19]

But these concerted efforts were thwarted first by Ukraine's adoption in April 2015 of the so-called de-communization package, a set of four laws, which included the "Law on the Legal Status and Honoring the Memory of Fighters for Ukrainian's Independence in the Twentieth Century," namely, precisely those individuals associated with what the Poles perceived as acts of terrorism against their rule in the interwar period and especially the ethnic cleansing operation in Volhynia and Galicia in 1943–4 (as well as complicity in the genocide of the Jews in these regions). The Ukrainian law, for its part, proclaims that Ukraine "considers as legal all forms and methods of struggle for its independence in the twentieth century," and states that it would hold responsible those who "publicly display a disrespectful attitude" toward its heroic liberation fighters, including members of the fascist OUN and its military arm, the UPA, and those who "publicly deny the legitimacy of the struggle for the independence of Ukraine." Specifically, the law states that "Ukrainian nationals, foreigners and stateless persons who publicly express disrespect for those stipulated in Article 1 of this law," namely the "fighters for Ukrainian independence in the twentieth century," would "bear liability in accordance with current Ukrainian legislation. Public denial of the legitimacy of the struggle for Ukraine's independence in the twentieth century is deemed desecration of the memory of fighters for Ukraine's independence in the twentieth century, denigration of the dignity of the Ukrainian people, and is unlawful."[20]

No wonder, then, that in July 2016 the Polish parliament adopted a resolution "On the Perpetuation of the Memory of Victims of Genocide Committed by the Ukrainian Nationalists Against the Citizens of the Second Republic in 1943–1945," which specifically described the massacres in Volhynia as a "genocide" and declared July 11 as a "National Day of Remembrance for the Victims of the Volhynian Genocide."[21] This was followed, as we have seen, by the criminalization of any denial of Ukrainian nationalist crimes signed into law in January 2018. The extraordinary attempts made by both nations, whose history of mutual animosity dates back to the seventeenth century, to bring about mutual reconciliation in the wake of the disintegration of Soviet rule, was thus undercut by the nationalist memory warriors on both sides. To be sure, even before the Russian invasion of Ukraine in February 2022, there was no imminent prospect for armed conflict or irredentist claims between Poland and Ukraine, and the extraordinary willingness of the Polish population to help millions of Ukrainian refugees entering their country will likely play a role in reversing the trend outlined here. Nonetheless, the uncertainty about Ukraine's future independence, and the increasingly nationalist and antidemocratic trends in Poland, which include the undermining of the judiciary's independence, do not bode well for the future.[22]

This is also a particularly dispiriting moment since, until quite recently, Poland had made major strides toward facing up to its past, serving as a model for other post-communist East European countries. Indeed, Poland has gone out of its way in recognizing its rich history of Polish-Jewish coexistence, beautifully exhibited in the new POLIN Museum as well as in the reconstruction of Jewish sites throughout the country.[23] And yet, Polish officials have increasingly insisted that while millions of Jews were murdered on its soil, anyone claiming that Poles were in any way involved is engaging in fake history. The "bloodlands," it is argued, were the product of external invaders from East and West, and Poles as much as Jews were their common victims. This is, in fact, also the underlying argument of the POLIN Museum itself, despite, but also consistent with its emphasis on harmonious Polish-Jewish relations.[24] Yet now the museum itself has been coming under attack, while scholarly works exposing Polish collaboration in the Holocaust and local murder of Polish Jews by their Christian neighbors have elicited outrage among nationalist politicians and other defenders of the national pride. If denying the event is illegal, excavating the manner in which it actually happened on Polish soil can be not merely embarrassing but also downright unpatriotic and therefore ultimately illegal, since it sullies the name and reputation of the Polish nation.[25]

The Duty to Remember and the Urge to Forget

There is, therefore, a bond of blood, of victimization and perpetrations of violence between Poles, Ukrainians, and Jews, just as much as a history of centuries-long coexistence and mutual cultural exchange. There is a bond of memory and vengeance, of commemoration and erasure. But while the Poles and Ukrainians remain on either side of their mutual border—their minorities within the other nation having been murdered, expelled, or "exchanged"—the case of the Jewish state is different. For even as Israel is committed to the memory of the Holocaust, it is also founded on a tale of heroism and erasure that both links it to Poland and Ukraine and, at the same time, contains its own regional narrative of glorification and forgetting.

Are these simply three cases that bear similarity to each other or are they intrinsically linked? After all, we can cite many other such examples, not least in the United States, where the glorification of fallen heroes proceeds independently from their actions as instruments of policies that not infrequently produce large numbers of civilian deaths in other nations, as in the cases of Vietnam and Iraq. Merely mentioning civilian victims in the same breath threatens to diminish both the individual glory of the fallen and the good name of the nation that sent them on such missions. Hence, for instance, the Vietnam memorial in Washington, D.C., makes no reference to the hundreds of thousands of civilian Vietnamese killed in the war.[26] Nevertheless, I would maintain that in the case of the Ukrainian-Polish-Israeli triangle, the mechanism whereby remembrance facilitates denial, criminalization of denial enables erasure, and erasure creates space for the mobilization of self-righteous victimhood is particularly visible precisely because of the complex links between the three nations' narratives of victimization and self-assertion.[27]

Crucially, then, the "duty to remember" and the urge to forget are inextricably linked within each of these national discourses, just as they are also dependent on competing national narratives. This relationship, as noted, actually goes all the way back to the "never again" slogans of the immediate postwar era; but the discourse of anti-fascism has been replaced since the 1990s by a post-communist ethno-nationalist rhetoric that often masquerades as or creates strange alliances with anti-neoliberal and anti-globalization discourses. In the specific cases of Poland, Ukraine, and Israel, I would reiterate that laws enforcing remembrance and censuring denial, just as much as those enforcing denial by way of restricting the content of legitimate remembrance, are linked to each other not only conceptually but also historically. If popular presentations of Soviet crimes in Poland and Ukraine are often associated with Jews, popular Israeli views of the Nazi crimes in Eastern Europe are just as often associated with Poles and Ukrainians. Indeed, in all three nations distorted popular perceptions are used to their own benefit by politicians and demagogues. In other words, such laws are never merely against denial but also invariably seek to utilize it. By the same token, the insistence of such laws on exposing the truth about the past is also always invariably about forgetting and erasing its more inconvenient components. Remembrance and erasure in Israel is a case in point.

Israel's Foundational Denials

Having spent two decades studying Jewish-Polish-Ukrainian coexistence and violence from the perspective of one small town, and as a member of the generation born in Israel in the immediate aftermath of the Second World War, the Holocaust, and the establishment of the state, my interest here is not only in official commemoration and eradication but also in collective, communal, and personal engagement, trauma, and memory; not only in criminalization of denial but also in the perhaps more powerful effects of public and social censure of what must not be denied (or must be remembered) and what must be denied (or may not be remembered).

Jewish children—matters were very different in the case of Arab Palestinians of that age group—of European (largely Ashkenazi) background growing up in Israel of the 1950s and 1960s had to contend with two major denials. First there was the denial of the Diaspora, or *shelilat hagalut*. For those born in the wake of the 1948 War, this fundamental tenet of Zionism was associated not with criminality but with something both very far and unknown and at the same time familial and familiar: grandparents, the sounds of spoken Yiddish and Polish around us, remnants of religious practice in generally secular spaces, as well as old age, foreign and embarrassing mannerisms, along with evocations of names of people and places we could not pronounce or locate. These were, in other words, vicarious memories we neither had nor wanted to have: alien, unpleasant, vaguely threatening, yet simultaneously intimate; something from which we had been liberated and refused to be dragged back into, whatever it was (which we didn't really know), but also at times alluring in a menacing sort of way as forbidden fruits and neglected graveyards tend to be, especially for the young. We, after all, were the first generation of Israelis, the very embodiment of the "new Jew," so new, indeed, that we were said to have been "born from the sea" and to have none of the burden of those long, dark millennia of exile.[28]

The second great denial was that we had inherited another people's place. We grew up next to remnants of villages, often unnamed, misnamed, or renamed, and eventually bulldozed away: we grew used to the new names for sites whose origins we did not know or want to know, even as the older generation still used the previous names without ever recalling, or telling us, that they had once stood for sites of habitation filled with now vanished men, women, and children; we played next to sabra fences, whose locations and purpose were never explained; we skirted the fading boundaries of cemeteries, unfamiliar and overgrown. For us the Nakba, as a word and an event, did not exist; or if it did, it was merely as a distant rumor, inarticulate, hidden, unpronounceable and shameful, if not downright offensive.

These two denials were at the core of the first generation's identity, and thus the founding truth, the national blind spot, the tunnel vision through which everything was seen and understood by the Jewish state's founding native generation. These same two denials were simultaneously rooted in two fundamental, constitutive events, fated to be commemorated, celebrated, and codified. The first was the Warsaw Ghetto Uprising and all that it symbolized as the defiant act of a nation both dying and being reborn phoenix-like in the fire and sword of the Holocaust. The second was the first's natural product, the War of Independence, in which the few heroically vanquished the many, against all odds, a replay of the Warsaw Uprising but with the opposite result. Anything that might threaten, belittle, or undermine this memory had to be denied—not by law but by society at large. The Uprising was the core event of the Holocaust: the masses who went "like sheep to the slaughter" were on its margins; the victory by the few and the transformation of the Jewish minority of the Yishuv (pre-state community) into a majority in the new state of Israel was a redemptive miracle: the violence of expulsion and eradication of Arabs was mere collateral damage that could not be allowed to mar the magnificence of national rebirth.[29] Grandparents might have had sentimental memories of the Diaspora, and young men and women might have been haunted by the atrocities committed in 1948. But with few exceptions that proved the rule, in the public sphere these remained unspoken, repressed, and denied.[30]

Memory, denial, and law have a complex relationship. Legislating remembering can lead to forgetting; prohibiting denial can be the best way to let it back in. In 1956 Israeli border guards murdered over forty residents of the Arab village of Kafr Qasim. In the trial that followed Judge Benjamin Halevy determined that the troops had obeyed an unlawful order that they had a duty to refuse: "The hallmark of a 'manifestly unlawful' order," he stated in 1958,

> must fly like a black flag over the given order, as a warning sign that says, "Forbidden!" What matters here is not a formal illegality, obscure or quasi-obscure, not illegality that can be discerned only by legal scholars, but rather: a visible and distinct violation of the law, a certain and inescapable illegality that appears on the face of the order itself, a clear criminal nature of the order or of the actions that the order demands to carry out, an illegality that pierces the eye and revolts the heart, if the eye is not blind and the heart is not impenetrable or corrupt—that is the measure of illegality needed in order to override the soldier's duty to obey and to impose on him criminal liability for his actions.[31]

The event was recalled publicly less as an atrocity and much more as a triumph of Israeli justice and a demonstration of the purity of the arms (*tohar haneshek*) of the Israeli Defense Forces (IDF). While it has become part of Israeli lore and repeated claims that the IDF is "the most moral army in the world," it has never formed a constituent element of military practice.[32] Indeed, even at the time, most of the Israeli public came out against Halevy's ruling, and subsequent judicial actions radically reduced the sentences; by 1959 all involved had been pardoned.[33] Halevy's ruling was not invoked, for instance, after the Gaza operation in July–August 2014, euphemistically named "Protective Edge" (Mivtsa Tsuk Eitan), in which approximately 2,200 Palestinians were killed, including close to four hundred children under the age of fifteen, and up to five hundred thousand local residents were displaced from their homes as large parts of the built-up area were flattened by aerial bombs and artillery.[34] In Israel of the twenty-first century the mere evocation of the term "war crimes" or "crimes against humanity" in this context is anathema, considered by many as treasonous and anti-Zionist, if not anti-Semitic.[35]

Born in Germany in 1910, where he received a doctorate in law in 1933, Halevy was also the judge in the so-called Kasztner trial of 1955, in which he declared that Rudolf Israel Kasztner, who negotiated with Adolf Eichmann in Budapest during the Holocaust, had "sold his soul to the devil" since he collaborated with the Nazis, a ruling that led to Kasztner's assassination. And although the Israeli Supreme Court subsequently ruled that "Kasztner would be judged by history and not by the court," the question of Jewish collaboration in the Holocaust persisted as a troubling and disruptive component in the struggle between memory and forgetting, commemoration and denial: a constant reminder—relentlessly denied—of the cost entailed in the attempt to derive moral superiority and ethical license from victimhood.[36] Indeed, Halevy also served as one of the three judges in the Eichmann trial of 1961-2 in Jerusalem. It was this trial that exposed the Israeli public, and especially members of my generation, for the first time to the Holocaust not as a shameful event in which the Jews went like sheep to the slaughter and were redeemed only by the allegedly Zionist rebels in Warsaw, but as an unfathomable genocide that still haunted its survivors, men and women who turned out to be our neighbors and family members.[37]

But it was also during this trial that Halevy interrogated Eichmann on the question of Jewish collaboration in the organization of the "final solution," speaking to the defendant, as he put it, "in his own language," namely German. Was it true that "the Jewish functionaries were given the task of registering the members of their communities for the purpose of emigration, settling property matters, and exercising fairly stringent controls here, which greatly facilitated emigration?" he asked the defendant. "Jawohl, das stimmt" (yes, that is correct), responded Eichmann. "And then," continued Halevy, "that could be switched rapidly and smoothly to deportation?" Again, Eichmann responded with "Jawohl." Halevy persisted: "Then there was the idea of the Jewish councils ... As instruments of German policy regarding the Jews, these Jewish councils—shall we say—considerably facilitated the implementation of measures against the Jews?" Eichmann agreed: "Jawohl." This, stated Halevy, "saved a great deal of manpower and staff." "Jawohl," Eichmann responded. Hence, concluded Halevy, the Jewish councils "made it possible, by misleading the victims, to facilitate the work, and also to harness the Jews to work for their own extermination." Eichmann appeared almost relieved; finally, the court had understood: "Jawohl, das stimmt," he confirmed.[38]

Whatever might have been Halevy's purpose in pursuing this line of questioning, he clearly exposed the danger of trying to use absolute evil as justification for the actions of its victims and survivors. And yet the emergence of the Holocaust from denial to memory, supported by the growing prominence of Yad Vashem, created by law as a national institution to commemorate the Holocaust in 1953, facilitated denial just as much as it institutionalized remembrance.[39] The vast shadow the Holocaust increasingly cast over the entire land made the war of 1948 appear all the more miraculous, the existence of the Jewish state all the more precarious, and the fate of the Palestinians and their rapidly vanishing villages, bulldozed systematically by the authorities as a prelude to allegedly conquering the wilderness and greening the wasteland, appear ever more marginal.

The Past That Will Not Pass

Memory and forgetting, marginality and centrality, consciousness and unconsciousness: I recall jumping a gate in the small German town of Kornelimünster in 1981. I had heard there was a Jewish cemetery there, but the gate was locked. The overgrown space was filled with tombstones, mostly inscribed in German. Those Jews who were still living in the town under Nazi rule, my landlady recalled, were carted off in 1942, including her best friend, Ruth. She remembered Ruth fondly, and how the Jews in the town were assembled in its beautiful medieval square one day and taken away, never to return. She also had fine memories of the Third Reich, as she told me over Kaffee und Kuchen: she was a member of the *Bund Deutscher Mädel* (BDM, the Nazi League of German Girls), where they learned how to make Eintopf, a stew into which you could throw anything you had in the kitchen and that brought everyone together. These were times of scarcity, but also of fraternity, pride, and decency, she said.

No one spoke openly about those matters at the time in such small German towns, but things have since changed a great deal. Two decades later I visited for the first time Jewish cemeteries in West Ukraine, formerly Eastern Galicia, including the cemetery in my mother's hometown of Buczacz. There were no gates and fences; goats were grazing among the derelict tombstones, where local residents deposited their garbage. It took me all those years to recall the Muslim cemeteries of my childhood, as I tried to see the remains of my ancestors through the eyes of Ukrainian children playing in the ruins.[40] Questions about that past were not welcomed. Memory has a price, usually gauged more in terms of property than shame. Silence was definitely safer, as one walked through graveyards, forests, and creeks, where thousands of bodies lay buried in shallow graves within earshot of the town center. Here there was no need to legislate either for or against denial: everyone was in agreement not to talk, not to remember, not to commemorate.

Yet by then commemoration was all the rage. With the communists gone, one could finally remember. Those who had been maligned and discarded returned, proudly stepping back into history. And just as at the time when they were living, what was recalled about their deeds and what was forgotten had to be balanced between historical reconstruction and political need. As the surviving old men and women of the OUN and the UPA gathered to remember their heroism and suffering, many of them having spent years in gulags and prisons, they also recalled how they had fought for freedom from Poland and the Jews, Germany and the Soviets. They had nothing to be ashamed of and had paid a heavy price. Others, too, were victimized, but they had worked with the enemy and were justly punished. And in any case, it wasn't us who killed the Jews.[41]

Criminalizing Holocaust denial in Ukraine and Poland comes wrapped together with criminalizing denial of communist crimes and defaming the nation. Yet the manner in which we remember one defines how we remember the other, and the vision we wish to have of the nation and its honor is the prism though which we filter these public recollections. Who were the communists who committed crimes against Poles and Ukrainians? And who were those who committed crimes against the Jews? In public memory, the communists are associated with the Jews, while the murderers of the Jews are associated with the Germans. The Jews, in other words, were, and must be remembered as having been murdered by others, those who marched into the "bloodlands" from elsewhere;[42] our own people, real Poles and Ukrainians, were murdered not just by external outsiders but also by our own internal enemies. It is, ultimately, the memory of Judeo-Bolshevism, that infamous żydokomuna, that helps organize all these other memories, denials, and erasures.

But for the Jews who came to Palestine, much as they wished to negate the Diaspora, it was precisely the Diaspora experience that determined the manner in which they remembered and denied their own actions. The vocabulary was already in place, the need was even more urgent, and the opportunity could not be missed. What was denied to us had to be denied to others; what was forgotten and erased had to be remembered and reconstituted, albeit elsewhere; the victims of injustice could not be guilty of committing crimes, and the victims of forgetting, those who vowed never to forget and always to remember, could not be blamed for erasure.

This was and remains the mechanism of repression of the events of 1948. The state of Israel was built around the notion of "never again" and "we shall never forget." And the process of its very making, the war in which the vast majority of the Arab Palestinian population of Palestine was expelled from the territory of what became the state of Israel, was legitimized by these very slogans: only by creating an independent majority Jewish state would another Holocaust be prevented, and any objections to the manner in which this goal was achieved would be pushed aside by the overwhelming memory—never to be forgotten—of the genocide of the Jews. But at the same time, the constitutive events of 1948 were based on the precise opposite—the mirror reflection, if you like—of these slogans: the process of expulsion, the Palestinian Nakba, was not merely an event that would never happen again, but became an ever-recurring, never-ending event, whereby an entire people remains either exiled or under various forms of oppression. The "never again" in this case became "again and again," an interminable effort to "complete the job" in the face of a stubborn insistence to hold out, either as "*sumud*," that is, holding fast to the land, or as in never giving up the aspiration to return to it. And thus the slogan of "we shall never forget" was turned on its head as regards the Nakba, an event which for the Jewish state is one that must always be repeatedly forgotten, just as it must be eternally remembered by those subjected to it. In this sense, the evident and bitter irony is that just as the insistence on remembering the Holocaust has encountered repeated attempts to forget, "contextualize," marginalize, or blatantly deny it in different countries in which it occurred throughout the past eight decades, so too the mounting scholarship on the actual events of the expulsion of the Palestinians has only increased the efforts by the state of Israel and many members of its political, media, scholarly, and intellectual community to forget, "contextualize," marginalize, or blatantly deny it.

Outlawing the Past

From this perspective, then, the infamous recent "Nakba law" should come as no surprise. In a sense, it merely attempts to legislate a long-term convention in Jewish-Israeli public discourse, namely, that the state celebrates its war of independence in 1948 and that any talk about those who paid the price for this accomplishment is at best irrelevant and at worse downright seditious.

The so-called "Nakba Law" specifically originated in a bill proposed in 2009 to criminalize the commemoration of the Day of Independence or the establishment of the state of Israel as a day of mourning. This bill was supported by the government but encountered a great deal of public opposition as well as criticism abroad. As a result, the criminalizing element of the bill was removed, and a new version of it was smuggled into the state budget legislation as amendment number 40 in March 2011. The law passed that year states that the minister of finance would be allowed to deprive an institution funded or supported by the state of some of its funding (up to three times the amount of the disallowed expenses used by that institution) if that institution engaged in any of the following:

1. Denying the existence of the State of Israel as a Jewish and democratic state.
2. Incitement to racism, violence or terrorism.
3. Support for an armed struggle or act of terror by an enemy state or a terrorist organization, against the State of Israel.
4. Commemorating Independence Day or the day of the establishment of the state as a day of mourning.
5. An act of vandalism or physical desecration that dishonors the state's flag or symbol.[43]

In May 2011 the Association for Civil Rights in Israel and Adalah, the Legal Center for Arab Minority Rights in Israel, launched a public petition against the law. The petition noted that as a result of the so-called Nakba Law,

> academic bodies, educational and cultural institutions, local municipalities, and other funded bodies find themselves at the moment conflicted over the question whether an event that would include reference to the very occurrence of the Nakba could expose their budget to monetary diminution ... Such a conflict may bring about self-censorship, thereby causing severe damage to the freedom of expression and restricting democratic discourse ... In our opinion, the law causes severe and scandalous damage to the right of equality, the freedom of political and cultural expression, the right for personal and group dignity and other constitutional rights ... Clearly this law cannot be seen separately from the rising tide of anti-democratic legislation in the Knesset, which in many cases is aimed to harm the rights of the Arab citizens of Israel.[44]

That same month these two organizations appealed to the Israeli Supreme Court, on their own behalf as well as on behalf of several other institutions, including the parents and students of a bilingual Jewish-Arab school in the Galilee. The appeal argued that "the law causes unprecedented harm to historical memory by using the power of the majority in order to try and erase and repress minority narratives about events, facts, emotions and ideologies," and "seeks to suppress essential ideological disputes that concern the fundamental questions of Israeli society." The main effect of the law, it was noted, would be "on Arab citizens—who as a national minority should in fact be provided with greater constitutional protection of their right for full civil equality." Finally, and importantly, the appeal noted that "the immediate effect of the law" would be "a chilling effect on a large public in Israeli society," not least because "the law employs opaque and vague terms, increasing the uncertainty as to how they will be interpreted by the Minister of Finance and the legal authorities."[45]

On January 5, 2012, the Supreme Court turned down the appeal. In endorsing the ruling by Justice Miriam Naor, the president of the court, Justice Dorit Beinisch, noted that the appeal "raises complex issues of public significance," which "may under certain circumstances touch on the roots of the problems that divide Israeli society." But, she concluded, the appeal "is not mature for a legal debate. On the declarative level the law does indeed raise difficult and complex questions, but the constitutionality of the law depends first of all to a large degree on the interpretive content given to its instructions, and this will be clarified only upon its implementation."[46] What the court did not address, therefore, was the "chilling effect" of the law on publicly airing a historical narrative that undermined the conventional perception of Israel's constitutive event of 1948. Indeed, the court showed no interest in this debate and thereby implicitly accepted the state's right to impose its own—and generally the Jewish majority's—view of the past. While alternative views were eventually not criminalized, within the context of an ongoing conflict over the land and the state's overwhelming power over its Arab citizens, this could be seen as nothing less than an agreement to stifle the collective memory of a fifth of the state's population.[47]

A nation built on a cult of resurrection and memory could not possibly allow the summoning of the memory of its own birth in sin.[48] One can go back to the desolate remnants of Jewish civilization in Europe and gain an understanding of the cruelty of history: but this understanding can breed either empathy and compassion or determination and ruthlessness. To remember, and to forget: perhaps no other nation has internalized that lesson more powerfully.[49] But it is a brittle tool; the mightier the edifice, the more likely it is to crack and disintegrate if built on doubtful foundations. Laws trying to suppress the event, memory, and commemoration of the Nakba are the dark side of legislating Holocaust remembrance. Their roots reach back to all those other attempts to remember and forget for which the Jewish state was supposed to have been the answer: as long as denial of the Diaspora and denial of the Nakba remain at the core of Israeli identity, no law will be able to liberate the state and its people from their own false memories, free them from premonitions of catastrophe, and allow them to contemplate the possibility of coexistence with the Palestinian inhabitants of the land.

From this perspective, too, the Polish-Ukrainian-Israeli triangle can both be broken down into its constitutive parts and be reprioritized. Poland and Ukraine's relationship to the Holocaust and ethnic cleansing in the Second World War is about confronting the past. It matters, of course, for nations to be able to look back to the darker episodes of their history clear-eyed and critically: not only in order to understand their own making but also so as to build a better, more open, and more just society in the present, free of lies and obfuscations. But ultimately, the borders between Poland and Ukraine are unlikely to be disputed, disagreements about the past are unlikely to cause major conflict, and the minorities that were at the core of those past horrors have been either murdered or expelled.[50] As part of this process, the Jewish component of that era is now largely represented by the state of Israel as the third side of that previously uneven triangle. But in the battles of memory, Israel is in a very different spot vis-à-vis the Palestinians. Here the conflict is far from over, the borders have not been determined, and the populations are mixed as never before. Here memory rises from the recesses of the past fully armed, populating the battlefields of the present as a concrete, lethal presence. One can try to ignore it, avert one's eyes, deny its existence or veracity. Yet it will be disarmed not by erasure but only through recognition and acceptance.

PART IV
FIRST-PERSON HISTORIES

CHAPTER 7
H. G. ADLER'S (UN)BILDUNGSROMAN

H. G. Adler was born in 1910 to an assimilated, German-speaking Jewish family in Prague, shortly before the First World War shattered that universe of multiethnic, multilinguistic existence. In 1948, in the immediate aftermath of yet another cataclysm that irretrievably wiped out all that had remained of his world along with its memory, Adler completed his extraordinary novel-memoir, *Panorama*. Not published until two decades later, *Panorama* peers back through the thick glass of time and forgetfulness into the making and unmaking of its author.[1] Can one reassemble the fragments of a past life into a meaningful existence after the very notion of shared humanity was dismantled in the camps? What are the ingredients that make up the reconstituted self, the exceptional survivor, that allow self-recognition as the person who had once been, coexistence with the memories of horror just experienced, and reintegration into a world oblivious of the abyss that had just been detected under the thin crust of civilization?

Panorama tells the story of one person in the form of a *Bildungsroman*, or perhaps more accurately, a faux or *Unbildungsroman*, depicting the protagonist's making, unmaking, and possible remaking. It is an *Unbildungsroman* in that it does not relate the education and coming to an understanding of the world of a child and young man, but rather it chronicles his un-education and not-coming to an understanding of the world. Instead of relating the opening of a child's soul, it traces the process of shutting it off and out. That the notorious Nazi perpetrator and the last commandant of the Bergen Belsen concentration camp, Josef Kramer, shares the name of *Panorama*'s main character may be either coincidence or intentional, but the near-dehumanization of Adler's Josef suggests the potential of this being a novel about the making of a beast just as much as about the unmaking of the human.[2] For while the modern *Bildungsroman* increasingly ends up in an unsuccessful integration of the hero into his or her social milieu, be it because of the protagonist's qualities or the nature of society, in *Panorama* the world into which Josef is plunged is such that both integration and lack thereof may strip him of his humanity.[3]

The world we see through Josef's eyes is one from which he remains absent even as he finds himself in its midst. He looks at History (with a capital *H*) as a detached observer, but what he sees is his own self being subjected to History's fury and barely surviving being mauled to death by it. Hence Josef remains divorced from what are simultaneously the very forces that make him into what he is, even as they deprive him of all that he had been before. In that sense, Josef is akin to Albert Camus's first man, a human soul that strives to remain independent from the events that are its entire universe and outside of which it cannot exist.[4] To be sure, every *Bildungsroman* has the quality of a panorama, of the author peering at the tableau of his life through a separating glass, reconstructing in his mind's eye the scenes and events, sounds and smells of a distant past, and trying to understand the road traversed from one side of the glass to the other. But in *Panorama* the distance between the bucolic scene of childhood and the adult man's experiences is so vast, and the glass separating them is so thick, that self-recognition demands an immense effort, a huge leap of the imagination, a shedding of the previous self that leaves the observer bereft of his past and shivering without cover in a new and alien world.

In one of the labor camps Josef meets Dr. Siegler, who believes that "the world is going to pieces, such that the only thing that can be sensibly described is what we each experience alone." In Siegler's view,

> We indeed learn from fate, if only in the sense that we learn that life continues on despite its dissolution, and that in truth man cannot cut himself off from it, but instead must immerse himself, meaning that he may indeed be a victim, but he is also a witness, and through that each can—whether through his own disposition or caprice—find a certain freedom, namely the freedom of knowledge or the ability to know. The difference between men may well lie only in the degree to which someone takes hold of this freedom, versus those who deny it, despite whatever reason there may be for seizing hold of it. (*Panorama*, 343–4)

But Josef wonders

> whether it's because there is not an obvious cause to rise to, no clear act or even a way to prepare for it, whereby one's inner tendency remains independent of any possible or actual dissolution, meaning an act that one could accomplish and can accomplish in order to devote oneself to it and thus arrive at an overall sense of purpose that potentially leads one through any catastrophe.

What Josef insists on is "the need to maintain an unwavering intent that is not entirely tied to the general course of daily events but instead keeps its eye on an ideal that helps one become independent, no matter what goes on in the world, as well as remaining independent of the web of relations we find ourselves ensnared in" (*Panorama*, 344).

If Josef still believes in purpose and intent, Siegler trusts only the solace of memory, which

> gives rise to images ... with foregrounds and backgrounds and, even more so, moving images that continually change, as in a panorama ... a precursor to the cinema, it being obvious that one can't jump into such images but instead you stand before them ... this world of images lending the viewer something to hold fast to.

For Siegler, then, "Whoever does not hold such a world within himself, whoever can't save it, he is today lost before he is even killed, for all will be killed." And yet, Siegler "hopes for the strength to be able to maintain such solace right up until that last horrible moment." (*Panorama*, 344–5)

What Adler offers us are two kinds of distancing mechanisms: Siegler's method comforts or distracts the person experiencing an event by simultaneously recalling another universe, another existence, and holding on to it as solace for as long as possible, until the eventual and inevitable end strikes one down. Adler's own method creates a distance between the event and its observer, whether while it is actually happening or in memory, after it had already occurred and is now being seen again, as in a posttraumatic repetition of the moment of trauma. This second type of distance between the observer and what is being observed, which is, after all, what is being done, or had been done, to the observer—this insistence on being outside of the event—enables one to view it as a panorama and thus to maintain one's independence from it, in this sense ensuring one's survival on the other side of that glass. This distance is not the same as the detachment from the event required by historical scholarship, which is based on not having been there in the first place, and consequently on the ability to feel empathy without losing a sense of objectivity.

Rather, Adler's panoramic detachment is akin to what we find in Roman Polanski's childhood memories, briefly related in a memoir published four decades after the war, and giving the distinct impression of having been experienced by someone else, as if the author was unable to imagine himself into his own past.[5] As a filmmaker, Polanski chose not to make a cinematic representation of his childhood but instead to produce Władysław Szpilman's memoir in his 2002 film, *The Pianist*, six decades after his own survival. That film, in turn, preserves the detached tone of the memoir, originally published in the immediate aftermath of the war but soon suppressed by the Polish communist authorities and reissued to general acclaim only in the late 1990s, first in translation and then also in Polish.[6] Twice removed from his childhood trauma, having filtered it through Szpilman's story, Polanski seems to adopt Josef's mantra—"the need to maintain an unwavering intent"—as pianist, as artist, as filmmaker—"an act that one could accomplish and can accomplish in order to devote oneself to it and thus arrive at an overall sense of purpose that potentially leads one through any catastrophe" (*Panorama*, 343–4). One survives so as to practice one's craft, and one practices this craft so as to survive.

I have long been preoccupied with the relationship between History with an uppercase *H* as a chronicle of past events and history with a lowercase *h* as individual experience. This preoccupation stemmed from a growing dissatisfaction with the historical profession's predilection to separate professional history, on the one hand, from personal accounts, as well as autobiographical and historical fiction, on the other hand. As a young historian, in the second half of the 1980s and the early 1990s, I had attempted to maintain that division, publishing two English-language works of scholarship and two Hebrew-language novels containing strong autobiographical elements.[7] But unlike Adler, who persisted in writing across genres, I eventually found that doing so made it difficult to write either at the level or with the focus to which I aspired, and I opted for (admittedly increasingly personal) historical scholarship.

But having grown up in a human landscape where the history I ended up writing was part of most people's lived or transmitted biography, I was also keenly aware of the fact that in that context, writing scholarship about the Holocaust with the necessary called-for distance and objectivity was largely a contradiction in terms.[8] It was precisely that contradiction that intrigued me, as expressed in the tension between historical reconstruction and the individual's experience and perception of reality, themselves the products of internalized ideas and images, and confrontation with the external world, where one is perpetually acting and the object of others' actions. In other words, I remained always interested in the stories that people told about their lives in the world, their inner voice relating to them what was occurring to them and what was being done to them, what they were seeing, what they were feeling, and what they did and would remember and relate thereafter.[9]

Shortly before reading *Panorama* for the first time, I decided to explore this relationship between History and individual experience in a classroom setting. In the spring semester of 2012, I taught a graduate seminar titled "First Person History in Times of Crisis: Witnessing, Memory, Fiction." Postulating that historians could learn a great deal from juxtaposing historical reconstructions of the past with accounts of how that past was experienced by its protagonists, the seminar focused on the complementary and contradictory aspects of this often-fraught relationship especially under conditions of war and genocide. Materials for the seminar included diaries, postwar testimonies, trial records, memoirs, historical fiction, and films.[10] As a first attempt to grapple with the incongruities and conundrums of mixing history, personal accounts, and fiction with a group of budding scholars, this was a fascinating and intellectually productive, albeit at times frustrating undertaking. I have since taught this seminar a few more times, and have made considerable changes to the readings, as well as engaging the students in offering relevant first-person readings from their own fields of research. But partly because of the additional readings proposed by the students, and partly because we dedicated much of our time to documentation, testimony, and postwar representation, I found myself repeatedly compelled to exclude several profound ruminations on the very nature of first-person history in times of crisis, each of which would have required close reading and sustained discussion beyond the framework of that particular class. Indeed, as I write this, in the coming years I still hope to teach a rather different incarnation of the seminar, this time dedicated primarily to twentieth-century first-person writing on loss, trauma, and memory. In such a class, one of the cardinal texts, perhaps the very leitmotif of the course as a whole, would be Adler's *Panorama*. Along with it, and in the same spirit, I would include Albert Camus's *The First Man* (*Le premier homme*), Charlotte Delbo's *None of Us Will Return*, Primo Levi's *The Reawakening*, Saul Friedländer's *When Memory Comes*, Georges Perec's *W, or the Memory of Childhood*, and W. G. Sebald's *Austerlitz*.[11]

The reasons for associating these titles—and quite a few others could be added—with *Panorama* are too complex and intricate to be fully elaborated here, but alluding to a few of them may shed some light on why Adler's still relatively unknown novel is both unique and part of a particular genre of writing on loss, trauma, and memory.[12] These authors belong to three historical generations. Camus and Delbo were born in 1913, and Levi in 1919: they were all young adults at the outbreak of the Second World War. Friedländer, born in 1932, and Perec born in 1936, were children during the Holocaust. Finally, Sebald was born in 1944, and therefore had no direct memories of the events of Nazism and the war.

Camus' *Le premier homme* was published over three decades after its unfinished manuscript was found following the author's death in a car crash in 1960. The reasons for its delayed publication apparently had to do with the fact that this was a childhood reminiscence about Algeria by a *pied-noir* (Algerian of European ancestry), who had subsequently adopted controversial views about the Algerian War, a conflict still raging when he was killed. But *The First Man* also attempts to recapture the lost memories of a child whose father had died in the First World War shortly after his birth and whose mother was partially deaf and illiterate. Between that time and the writing of the manuscript, Europe had been convulsed by two murderous wars and France had become engaged in a horrific colonial struggle. Between the writing of the manuscript and its final publication, the memories and traumas that Camus had evoked were re-suppressed and re-forgotten. This extraordinary rumination on the loss of things past, this attempt to regain access to a childhood barred to the author by personal tragedy, reaching back beyond the collective catastrophe of war, massacre, and genocide, is thus linked in several ways to Adler's *Panorama*.

Just like Camus, Delbo was born only three years after Adler. Similarly to their works, her writing is concerned with the inability to bridge between the lived present and the remembered past because of the chasm of catastrophe from which no one could ever return, not even those few who actually "came back." She, too, did not publish her work on the camps and the survivors' inability to survive that experience for two decades after writing it.[13] And while such a delay in publication—possibly making for a protective gap of time between the event and the public's exposure to its representation—did not occur in the case of Primo Levi's *If This Is a Man* (now known in English as *Survival in Auschwitz*), its exposure to public view appears to have indeed been premature. Levi's account of his incarceration in Auschwitz was published in 1947, but few readers were interested, and not even all the copies of that limited edition were sold. It was only after the successful publication of *The Truce* (known in English as *The Reawakening*), which recounted his way back from hell to his hometown of Turin, that Levi's reputation allowed for a second look at that early memoir, now considered a classic of this genre.[14] As Levi noted in his introduction to the Hebrew translation of *The Truce*, he could understand why people preferred the story of a reemergence from the camps to that of his descent into that murderous universe.[15] The English titles of his books certainly indicate the publishers' view that Auschwitz should be told as a story of survival, and the way back should be related as a true return rather than a mere pause between repeated bouts of inhumanity.

Perec was only nine when the war ended; by then he had lost his father in the war and his mother in Auschwitz. His profession as an archivist and his faint memories of a childhood whose traumas could not be accurately reconstructed finally led him, three decades after these events, to compose a harrowing memoir-fantasy that both attempts to put together what can still be remembered and recorded and takes flight into an imagined world of horror and cruelty. This nightmare universe reflects the inability of the grown author to recapture the details of the past and his insistence on recreating them, if only by way of a grotesque fantasy, in order to come to terms with what he knows had happened but which he will never quite remember experiencing. This strange world is Perec's panorama, observed through the prism of time past and lost and the eye of a horrified, uncomprehending child. It is a belated, merciless, yet also loving glimpse, but one that constantly averts the eye from memory to nightmare and to memory again. These are the memories of childhood that no man or woman should ever have, yet so many people to this day are still subjected to, if they are lucky enough to survive their childhood.

Friedländer, four years older than Perec and thirteen years old at the end of the war, trained as a political scientist and a historian; he waited for more than three decades before writing his own memoir of childhood. When memory returned, it was both vivid and detached. Friedländer knew the History of that time in detail, having dedicated the intervening years to studying and writing about it. But he had to probe into his own memories in a manner entirely different from that of the scholar to reach back to that lost childhood, that moment at which, as a boy, he lost his parents forever and with them any reliable reference point to the years that preceded their murder. This is a memoir located half-way between the emergence of the child from the French monastery that kept him safe from the Nazis and the completion of his magnum opus, *Nazi Germany and the Jews*;[16] it is an introspection that may have been necessary before launching back into that upper-case History of the event itself. But it is also guarded, cautious, controlled, never allowing fantasy or nostalgia, let alone sentimentality, to impinge on the careful reconstruction of memory and the acknowledgment, often quietly painful, of all that cannot be remembered.

More recently, Friedländer has published a study of Franz Kafka, linking him geographically and metaphorically to both Sebald and Adler.[17] With Kafka, Friedländer returns to the Prague of his birth, the city where Adler was born just over two decades earlier, and the presumed birthplace of the fictional Austerlitz, the protagonist of Sebald's eponymous novel, who is perhaps only slightly younger than Friedländer. Prague is reality and fantasy; it was a meeting place of cultures, a cradle of literature, an island within an island of German-speaking Jews in the heart of a dying multiethnic empire and the emergence of unrelenting nationalism. It stands now as a symbol of what had once been and is no longer, what could have been but was eradicated, for all the memories of things that are not only past but also perhaps never actually happened. That is Sebald's world, the universe of a voluntary German exile born in the closing months of the war in a distant Bavarian village and overwhelmed with memories of events he never experienced. Somewhat akin to such French Jewish writers as Patrick Modiano (born in 1945), Henri Raczymow (born in 1948), and Alain Finkielkraut (born in 1949), much of whose work concerns the great catastrophe they had barely missed,[18] Sebald is obsessed with putting together the fictional identities of those who had been disaggregated and dispersed by Nazism. Austerlitz, raised without memories in Wales, and his creator, Sebald, who cannot remember what he has not lived through, together set out on a mission to recreate the protagonist's past, finally bringing him back to his childhood in Prague, though little can be found and even less remembered. It is a reference point, but it is not a recovered life.

These works help us grasp the human catastrophe of the world wars and the Holocaust in ways that are inaccessible to conventional historical scholarship. The link between fiction and scholarship, memoir and documentation, and analysis and reflection is essential in any attempt both to understand that cataclysm and to read the world that emerged from it and in which we still all live, whether oblivious or not to its origins. These works are also about the relationship between destruction and creation, the relentless urge of nihilism, and the fragile yet stubborn spirit of the artist.[19] In this sense, Szpilman's memoirs reflect Polanski's notion of the need to survive a catastrophe not only physically but also as a soul capable of producing and reproducing art. Yet this art eventually folds upon itself to recreate that very same event with that same detachment, now twice over, separating both the protagonist and the filmmaker from the event that is at the heart of the work, the trauma that the two men had in fact undergone themselves. It is the same detachment that we find in Friedländer's memoir, as his eye observes from afar the child who is to become the man who is writing the memoir without ever entirely stepping into the event, or into the soul of the child who had experienced it. And it is this detachment that then leads the scholar Friedländer to write and rewrite the event, finally re-creating it as *Gesamtgeschichte*, echoing Richard Wagner's notion of *Gesamtkunstwerk* (total work of art), but written as a total history of the Holocaust, twice removed from that child who had been led away from his parents, never to see them again.

Never, as Adler writes in *Panorama*, is Josef able to

> head home ... home to where? This question is hard to answer, but it is also idle, since for Josef no return home is possible, that would also mean a step backward to the presumption of a home that doesn't exist for him, there being no way to feel at home, but instead of something else, a kind of order that allows oneself to find oneself, even if it doesn't involve finding one's way back but instead involves indeed finding something, a location, and that is a state that presumes habit and habitation, and so it happens, and this stands for what other people call returning home, and is what Josef accepts. (*Panorama*, 431–2)

For Adler, as for all the others, practicing one's craft must be the alternative; for none of them can return home, not Friedländer and not Camus, but also not Levi or Delbo, who seem to return but will never again be at home, and whose homelessness becomes the core of their writing, and not even Perec, who never left but whose home was torn out of his childhood to return only as nightmare. For, as Adler writes,

> The sober, dissembling gaze into what's behind the images is not allowed, as that would break the last law that keeps him attached to his surroundings. He considers

a peek behind the images to be an incursion known as death, or no, it's not the onrush of death, it's suicide, and Josef has not survived until this day to do that. (*Panorama*, 432)

This removal of the self from within the event and from without it, the perspective of the distanced witness and of the detached historian—Adler being the author of a vast scholarly study of the camp—is at the heart of the conundrum of separation between fiction and scholarship, lived experience and historical reconstruction.[20] In some ways, Adler is closest in his biographical fiction writing to Sebald (as is Sebald to Adler)—both casting their glance at the dissolution of individual identity even as they gaze at it from within, putting up a thick glass between themselves and the person on the other side who is also their own recognizable yet simultaneously entirely different self. But Adler writes from within his own experience, even as Sebald, having just been born toward the end of the war, writes from without. Having no personal recollection of the events and belonging to a literary and intellectual heritage—against which he rebels—that constructed an inverse view of those time—a German, bystander-victim perspective—Sebald, from his self-imposed English exile, perfects an extraordinary capacity for empathy with his all-too-real fictional character Austerlitz.[21] This accomplishment is matched asymmetrically by Adler's own extraordinary ability to accomplish what I can only call empathetic detachment from the specific fate of the Jews—indeed from the life of Josef as a Jew in prewar Prague and for much of his wartime experiences as well, the word *Jew* appearing for the first time on page 200, then again on page 295, and only in the latter parts of the 450-page English translation of the novel, making slightly more frequent but still only occasional appearances. This absence—of the man, the Jew, the person—makes *Panorama* into an odd yet powerfully effective example of first-person history.

Some years ago, one of my students who had just read Primo Levi's *Survival in Auschwitz* wrote in a paper that now she had finally understood what "it was like." That is the strength and the weakness of Levi's account, which he understood and lamented years later in *The Drowned and the Saved*. Levi had written an account that was meant to document as clearly and dispassionately as possible the reality of a world referred to elsewhere politely as *anus mundi* (asshole of the world). It was an astonishing achievement, so soon after the events he had witnessed and experienced, to recreate that "other planet" with such attention to both material and emotional detail without even once slipping into pathos, self-pity, or rage.[22] Perhaps this was why readers could still not accept his writing, even though most of them had not lived through that experience, or precisely because they had not and therefore preferred to think of it as unimaginable rather than mundane, as a Bosch-like fantasy of monsters rather than a site where normal human beings systematically dehumanized and murdered other normal human beings, which was what Levi was trying to say. But some decades later, when the threat that one might have ended up in such sites as victim or perpetrator had receded, readers took something else from *If This Is a Man*; they now thought they understood what it was like, and thanks to the deceptive transparency of Levi's prose could also devise for themselves ways in which they would have faced up to that situation. Levi recalls speaking to a fifth-grade classroom about his book: "An alert-looking little boy, apparently at the head of the class, asked me the obligatory question: 'But how come you didn't escape?'" Levi explains, drawing the plan of the camp on the blackboard, "the watch towers, the gates, the barbed wire." In response, writes Levi, the boy "presented to me the plan he had worked out," and having explained it all, "he added seriously: 'If it should happen to you again, do as I told you. You'll see that you'll be able to do it.'"[23]

As Levi saw it in the mid-1980s, shortly before his death, possibly by suicide, "This episode illustrates quite well the gap that exists and grows wider every year between things as they were 'down there' and things as they are represented by the current imagination fed by approximative books, films, and myths. It slides fatally toward simplification and stereotype, a trend against which I would like here to erect a dike." But he goes on to say,

> This phenomenon is not confined to the perception of the near past and historical tragedies; it is much more general, it is part of our difficulty or inability to perceive the experience of others, which is all the more pronounced the more distant these experiences are from ours in time, space, or quality. We are prone to assimilate them to 'related' ones, as if the hunger in Auschwitz were the same as that of someone who had skipped a meal, or as if escape from Treblinka were similar to an escape from an ordinary jail. It is the task of the historian to bridge this gap, which widens as we get farther away from the events under examination.[24]

This is the conundrum of representation: when clear, plastic, and transparent, it gives us the illusion that we understand the event and would be able to prepare for and confront it; when distant, bizarre, and alien, it makes us believe that it has no relevance to our own lives. Here, too, is the role of empathy; not the kind of empathy that makes us comfortable and intimate with the protagonist or the event, but one that allows us to both imagine ourselves into that situation and to realize that we can neither make a difference to a world that is out of our reach nor could have overcome the obstacles faced by the protagonist had we actually been transported to the other side of the glass, for then we would no longer have been ourselves but that other figure we are watching from afar. The historian's empathy, that necessary ability to feel oneself into those distant events of the past, must always be balanced against the knowledge that what happened cannot be altered, and that had we been present at the time, we cannot know how or whether we would have made a difference, since we would have been of that time and not of our own. And yet things did not happen because they were predetermined, and the historian's task is to reconstruct why they occurred as they did.

But in the case of such cataclysms as the Holocaust, literary and scholarly tools often fail to provide more than the most superficial and insufficient explanations. Like Levi, we are torn between the desire to tell it as it was, and the knowledge that we cannot do so without that very simplification of which Levi speaks. We then turn to Adler, who, at the end of *Panorama*, leaves no one with the illusion that they have finally understood, or learned their lesson. But he also refuses to plunge into endless personal or universal despair. "How is it," Josef asks in the aftermath of the war, "that one comes to survive his own destruction?" (*Panorama*, 410). He would like some kind of "commemorations to effect a deep transformation, for posterity cannot simply weave a wreath for such suffering, because even if it is not one's own one can surely empathize with past suffering, yet it no longer burns in your heart like a glowing thorn from having survived those times of extermination" (*Panorama*, 400). But he

> realizes how unreal it all is when one gets involved with past suffering, most pieties being disingenuous, since they mix the pure feeling of the honored ones with a certain strangeness that they can never penetrate, and which they never fulfill and know that they don't, veneration an odd game in which nothing is so sacred that it is spared. (*Panorama*, 401)

And so Josef remains suspended between "a readiness for acceptance that is often condemned in human history" as "passivity or fatalism"—a criticism he rejects, for "what can one really do?"—and a realization that "the great hopes that existed at the end of the war and which were tied up with the downfall have already and easily been trampled under," and that although "only a little more than three years have slipped by," already "the misery that has hardly passed" has now been "reduced to a myth, for new pressing concerns always turn the too-weak heart full of its greedy demands away from the horror of yesterday's atrocities." And yet, he

> is not satisfied with remaining just an observer, he wants to be an active observer … it no longer being good enough to simply look on, but instead you have to examine closely, the panorama now turned around, the right to impartial observance is now forfeited, the spotlight is on and there is nothing for you but to wait and see whether it suits others to come and observe as well, but nonetheless impartiality has been destroyed … the role of the guest now over. (*Panorama*, 409–12)

And yet, matters are not so simple. For ultimately, "each person is beyond the border of those closest to him," although "there should be something that binds one person to another … something that is not simply asserted by one's ego but which instills something into that ego in order that it also exist in the other without killing itself." But Adler believes that this kind of empathy is, in the end, "inconceivable, even in feeling, it being the equivalent of the panorama that no amount of will can allow one to escape," the panorama being "perhaps just another name for the root of all evil" or "the defeat of one's humanity." Josef thinks, "If indeed a man survives and can look at himself the way that others do," then his "idea of the panorama prevails, namely that one can see others but never reach them" (*Panorama*, 417–19).

Before the catastrophe, Josef had wanted "to pursue a dreamed-of better world," but soon enough "oppression returned to the country, the handling of individual people often manifesting itself as crass and senseless, it not mattering what he did, fate had already begun to play with him, taking charge of him, he having been taken charge of." But "now all that is over … and so Josef sleeps." He is, of course, Josef the dreamer, and no one will any longer approach him "to order, 'Josef, get up, get a shovel and dig your own grave!' " But he has been betrayed: "The brothers had not strangled him, so that they could say that an evil animal had eaten him, but instead they had sold him into slavery." As Josef sleeps, he dreams of a better world, where "even a minimum of grace would be able to completely dissolve the contradiction between the two worldly principles of matter and essence" (*Panorama*, 421–3). But as Adler notes, "It's good that Josef sleeps," because he "should wait and know that his clever words are only the helpless attempts of one who has been abandoned and wishes to overcome his loneliness, as he doesn't always want to remain an onlooker, though he should indeed realize that he will always be only a viewer. He sits before the glass panes of the panorama" (*Panorama*, 425).

But things are changing, despite Adler's skepticism and Josef's helplessness. From a certain point, Josef is "able to preserve what he once experienced. Now he can look on and realize that the tables have been turned, he is the embodiment of all that has happened to him." For Josef, the act of observing his torture is being transformed into memory. His urge is now "to conquer the past for good, to bury it." He wants no "monuments set up to it, no memorials … no painted plaque, but instead allow the site of suffering to sink into soothing, blessed forgetfulness, leaving only what is felt in the heart, but no thoughts of any places through which one can just naively stroll" (*Panorama*, 427–8). Eventually Josef "wakes up and looks around him with eyes wide open." Has his sleep soothed and enlightened him, or is he waking from the nightmare of recent events, the atrocity of his brothers' betrayal? Josef "waits patiently, awakening takes time, a temporal activity, since it is steeped in memories." Indeed, notes Adler, "Every awakening is a trip to a past that must be reviewed if it is to be completed" (*Panorama*, 435).

And so, for Josef, his "memory remains the only memorial, but this memory will leave with him," as he departs from his place of rest in the English countryside to begin a new life (*Panorama*, 438). He feels that "he is now in his own way without a past, it not forgotten but rather lost, he having to strain himself to see it through a veil." He had once considered his past a "possession," but now it is "alien and unrecognizable." Josef also "doesn't know whether what history has to say has anything to do with him … because the past is so transparent in its intrusion that it no longer relates to any so-called 'I' or 'you.' " He feels just as unsure "whether he is someone who has acted or is a witness or a victim, or whether he is all of these together in having been part of history or if he simply overheard a bunch of tales." What he finally realizes is that "everything that happens is the price paid for living in the present, if only the individual accepts it," which he does, since "otherwise he wouldn't be able to go on" (*Panorama*, 440).

Adler thus asserts that the only true memory of the event is that which is contained in the mind of those who had experienced it. From that perspective, memorials are at best meaningless, at worst false sites of commemoration constructed to comfort those who had been spared the atrocity of the past. But the personal memory will fade with its carriers; indeed, his own memory already casts a veil over the events he had experienced. He no longer sees them in the frozen clarity of a panorama, but as "alien and unrecognizable." Conversely, History is vivid and transparent, raising few questions of detail but simultaneously having close to nothing to tell him about himself; it is no more telling or objective in that regard than "a bunch of tales." Adler has learned that he must accept the past as the price of living through it and that only such acceptance will allow him "to go on." And we, the readers, are tempted to believe that with this, he has made his peace with History as well as with his personal trauma. But, as it turned out, history had no clarity or transparency, memory refused to go away, and acceptance of the past, by those who recognize it, let alone those who deny it, is excruciatingly painful and has always remained controversial. That Adler spent much of the second half of the twentieth century writing and rewriting the History of the Nazi genocide and lifting the veil over his own personal memories of those terrible years is testimony to the continuing presence of that past.[25]

CHAPTER 8
LEAVING THE SHTETL TO CHANGE THE WORLD

H. G. Adler, as we recall, was born in Prague just four years before the war that destroyed the multiethnic universe of Eastern Europe's borderlands. His generation experienced the disasters that followed that transformation. The great paradox for the previous generations of Europeans, those born in the period between 1848—known as the "spring of nations"—and the end of the nineteenth century, was that many of them experienced it both as a time of unprecedented new opportunities for self-realization and collective liberation and, simultaneously, as one in which individual and collective identities came to be progressively constrained within national boundaries. History, as it subsequently unfolded during those years of great hopes and looming despair, was not predetermined, and the citizens of many towns such as Buczacz in the remote Austrian province of Galicia had more choices than ever before or after. A new world was emerging, and the restraints of the old were falling away: tradition had weakened, religious faith was waning, and authority was loosening its grip on family and society. Travel became easier, and people could go farther, change identities more easily, aspire to previously unthinkable goals, and embrace radical, exciting new worldviews.

But, at the same time, as groups and individuals began identifying themselves nationally and ideologically, they also increasingly perceived others through different eyes, distinguishing them not only by religion and ethnicity but also by whether their history gave them the right to continue living where they were. By the same token, those who adopted nationalist discourse restricted their own horizons by determining who they were, where they belonged, and what they could and should hope and struggle for. In this brave new world, vast collectives were being transformed into communities of fate, whose history and future were determined by national affiliation; it was a fate from which others were excluded by definition, and yet one from whose repercussions there was no escape.

In the wake of the 1848 revolution, the Habsburg Empire abolished serfdom in Galicia. Over the next few decades, a new nation emerged from the Ruthenian (later known as Ukrainian) peasants in the larger, more populous eastern part of the province. It was a long process: most of the former serfs remained wretchedly poor, illiterate, and the target of ruthless exploitation by the landowners. Instilling "national consciousness" into the rural masses and crafting them into a nation that would eventually claim Eastern Galicia for itself was the singular accomplishment of an increasingly radical national movement.[1]

The Jews of Galicia were also transformed into a modern nation in the second part of the nineteenth century. Jewish activists initially focused on civil, rather than national emancipation. Emperor Franz Josef's "constitution" of 1867 had guaranteed equal rights to all citizens and thereby emancipated the Jews.[2] This fundamentally changed relations between Jews and non-Jews. Efforts by the Ukrainian national movement to educate peasants coincided with the return of Jews to the countryside after restrictions on occupation and residence were lifted. As rural Ukrainians were being nationalized, the growing presence and economic role of Jews in the villages created a popular sense of material exploitation and cultural decimation. Jews were presented as fleecing the ignorant peasants, tricking them into alcohol and tobacco addiction, and lending them money at cutthroat rates. Some accused the Jews of retarding the development of a healthy Ukrainian nation, and anti-Jewish comments in the new Ukrainian press soon surpassed attacks on Polish landlords.[3]

Ironically, then, the realization of the Enlightenment's lofty aspiration of liberating the individual from collective feudal constraints culminated in the unleashing of forces that undermined the very core of humanism. As nationalism became the carrier of ideologies that often generated mass violence, one of its central obsessions entailed unmasking assimilated Jews, perceived as a major obstacle to the creation of ethnically homogeneous nation-states.

The Ukrainian author Ivan Franko was among the most influential advocates of national independence in the latter years of the nineteenth century in Galicia. Born in 1856 in a small village near the town of Drohobycz, Franko was deeply engaged with the links between social and national oppression and, in his works of fiction, relentlessly defended the rights of the peasants for dignity, identity, and material well-being. Simultaneously, he produced a series of stark literary representations of Jews as parasites sucking the blood of the Ukrainian nation in the service of Polish landowner exploitation and oppression. Still widely read in Ukraine, Franko's fiction has been influential in creating an image of "the Jew" as young Ukraine's explicit "other" within the setting of a social-realist depiction of Galician rural and small-town life at the turn of the nineteenth century.[4]

It was for that reason that Franko responded enthusiastically to the publication in 1896 of Theodor Herzl's *Der Judenstaat* (*The Jewish State*): his preferred solution to the "Jewish question" was the Jews' departure from Ruthenian lands, and he believed that Jews choosing to remain in a future Ukrainian state should be categorized as "aliens" with restricted political and civic rights.[5] Franko's Jewish contemporary, the social-realist author Karl Emil Franzos, had a rather different view of this matter. Born in 1848, Franzos spent his childhood in the town of Czortków, some twenty miles east of Buczacz; it was there, as we saw in previous chapters, that a century later the German Security Police establish an outpost charged with murdering the Jews of the region. As the son of a physician, he had an atypical upbringing and sense of identity. Decades later, he still recalled his father's admonition: "Your nationality is not Polish, nor Ruthenian, nor Jewish—you are German," but, "as for your faith, you are a Jew." In providing him with that hybrid identity—hardly sustainable in a mid-nineteenth-century shtetl—his father's goal was "that I should not see Galicia but rather the West as my homeland," concluded Franzos.[6]

As a child in a largely Hasidic town, Franzos attended school in the Dominican monastery, had little contact with other Jews, and never went to synagogue. At age ten, following his father's death, Franzos was sent to secondary school in the city of Czernowitz, a site of increasing Jewish assimilation into German culture. And while "it was entirely out of the question that I would ever even think of changing my faith," he stressed, "I thought just as little that Judaism would play a decisive role in my life."[7]

Shortly thereafter, Franzos was denied a government scholarship to study Classics at Vienna University. His Jewish identity, he now wrote, had demanded "a terrible sacrifice from me: that I give up the profession I chose." While he went on to study law, he decided to learn more about Jews and, as a consequence, ended up as an author whose novels were largely dedicated to explaining the fate of Galician Jewry to German readers. To be sure, stressed Franzos, he "did not become pious," yet his "feeling of belonging to the impoverished caftan-wearing Jews" of the province "became incomparably greater than before." It was this sense of belonging, yet also of peering from afar, that became the core of his entire oeuvre.[8]

Franzos had no qualms about railing against the tyrannical hold of Jewish religious leaders in Galician towns over the lives of young men and women, their dismissal of love as a poor substitute for a well-arranged marriage, and their vehement opposition to any intimate relations with Gentiles.[9] But, unlike Franko, he did not call for Jewish national consciousness and reassertion; instead, he sought a trans-European culture of openness and mutual understanding, and the fulfillment of individual aspirations divorced from ethnic identification. The tragic content of his writing is derived from the impossibility of realizing these goals in Galicia.[10]

Franzos's greatest literary achievement is his novel *The Clown of Barnow* (*Der Pojaz*), an inverted *Bildungsroman* about a Jewish youth's failed quest for self-emancipation.[11] The main protagonist is Sender, the son of a famous wandering jokester, who inherits his father's extraordinary acting talent. But while the father represents the quintessential "wandering Jew," the son pines to play Shylock, the archetypical Jew of the Christian imagination. Paradoxically, in order to be allowed to act the Jew on the European theatrical stage, Sender must first become European by shedding his Jewish attributes, a transformation he fails to accomplish.

For Franzos, Shylock was the ultimate embodiment of irreconcilable yet complementary perceptions of the world.[12] When Sender proposes to play Shylock in a wandering theater troupe, the director exclaims enthusiastically that *The Merchant of Venice* "is a play for Galicia. It is interesting for Jews and Christians and both can be pleased or angry about it to their hearts' content. Shylock is always a sellout." If Christian audiences see a money-grubbing, parasitical, self-hating, and vengeful Jew, the Jews see in Shylock a personification of their predicament, eternally dependent on the tender mercies of the Gentiles no matter how much wealth he acquires. As the dying Sender watches his idol, the great actor Dawison, perform Shylock's soliloquy in Lemberg, "If you prick us, do we not bleed? If you tickle us, do we not laugh?" he observes: "This was no longer an actor, but rather a poor, unfortunate man who had long kept his and his brethren's misery bottled up within himself, who had long suffered without complaint, and who had suddenly found words for his terrible pain."[13]

This appears to have been Franzos's own state of mind when he wrote the novel. Completed in 1893, *The Clown of Barnow* was only published in 1905, after its author's death.[14] By all accounts, Franzos delayed publication in response to the rise of anti-Semitism in Central Europe. As a prominent proponent of Jewish integration into the mainstream of European culture, Franzos was shaken by the growing tide against emancipated Jews in the culture and nation he had adopted. Ironically, when the novel was published, despite its commercial success, German critics greeted it as "too Jewish," and Zionist detractors saw it as "too German."[15]

Both Franko and Franzos felt that, by accurately yet both critically and empathetically describing the ills of the present, they would motivate society to progressive action. For Franko, the purpose of the historical novel was "to lay bare the human heart, its fervent aspirations and consuming passions, its struggles, triumphs and defeats … portrayed against the backdrop of a historical event."[16] Franzos, who called himself "the historian of the Podolian Ghetto" and referred to the Galician world he had come from as "half-Asia," insisted that despite his "great desire to give these stories an artistic form," he would never do this "at the cost of truth … I am confident," he wrote, "that I have described this strange and outlandish mode of existence precisely as it appears to me."[17] But these two writers saw the same world through utterly different eyes: their very insistence on factual accuracy betrayed the gaping fissures between the perceptions of reality by their respective ethnic groups, which eventually widened to unbridgeable chasms, irretrievably shattering that entire universe.

Unlike Franzos, most Jews of his generation had to chart their own course into the world directly from a traditional Jewish upbringing. Some, such as David (Zvi) Heinrich Müller, who was born in Buczacz in 1846 and was the author S. Y. Agnon's maternal cousin, made subsequent use of the skills they had acquired as children and youths. They also always retained a whiff of foreignness about them, and much as they were admired by the communities they left behind, they were suspected both by the Orthodox and by the emerging Zionists of having abandoned the fold: too Jewish for the Germans, too German for the Jews.

For a man of his generation, Müller was a rare exception. By the time of his death in 1912 he had become a renowned scholar, a university professor, and the holder of a heredity noble title, all without abandoning his Jewish faith, as was conventionally required for such official recognition. A child prodigy, Müller was banished from his father-in-law's home because of his interest in the *Haskalah*, and set out on an educational journey throughout Europe, ending up at the age of thirty-one as an assistant professor of Semitic philology at Vienna University, where he remained for the rest of his life.[18]

To be sure, not everyone admired Müller. The Palestine-based Zionist newspaper *Hatsevi*, for instance, accused him of having betrayed the cause of Hebrew and "worshipping only German literature."[19] Conversely, the Berlin-based liberal Jewish monthly *Ost und West* described Müller as "a sharp-witted grammarian, text critic, decipherer of ancient inscriptions and texts, editor and cultural historian."[20] Müller's most important contribution was his assertion that the Hebrew Bible had a major impact on later sacred and secular European writing, which flew in the face of the contemporary wisdom, according to which the Bible was largely a derivative of earlier Assyrian and Babylonian texts. In 1903 he published an annotated German and Hebrew translation of Hammurabi's Code, discovered two years earlier in Persia, where he showed the vast differences between Mesopotamian and biblical concepts of law and morality.[21]

Learned in Jewish and secular scholarship, equally comfortable in the company of rabbis and professors, committed to traditional erudition and to the *Haskalah*, and publishing in both German and Hebrew, Müller had all the makings of the ideal modern Jew. Contrary to the reproaches of his Orthodox and Zionist detractors, he spearheaded the establishment of the Jewish Theological Institute in Vienna, where he began teaching in 1893. As *Ost und West* noted, Müller also encountered much "resentment and envy" from "Protestant German colleagues eager to deny a Jew the right to have a word on Biblical questions," especially at a time when "antisemitism raged at its fiercest in Austria." While the journal insisted that Müller had prevailed over his opponents, *Hatsevi* claimed that Christian scholars had eventually adopted Müller's views only at the price of denying his original contribution and even accusing him of plagiarism. Indeed, the old professor was said to have been so "consumed by rage" that "his health was destroyed." As "this Jew descends to the Netherworld in discontent," concluded *Hatsevi* in its 1913 obituary, "his entire intellectual work will be ignored by the sages of Semitic languages."[22]

Müller's hometown also viewed him with a mix of admiration and resentment. In 1893 Müller was sent word by his mother "that an evil rumor has come to the city of Buczacz and that informers have denounced and slandered me and that she would rather die because of this affair." Deeply distressed, Müller responded that he was "the strong pillar upon which the house of Judah rests," and that "the whole congregation of Vienna honors me and the Name of God is sanctified through me." But there is little doubt that, for some of those who stayed behind, his very accomplishment on the European stage cast doubt on his commitment to Jewish faith and tradition.[23]

For others, not least Agnon, Müller was "a great and famous sage of whom all Galicia was proud." In 1908 the twenty-one-year-old Agnon was instructed by his mother to visit their relative in Vienna on his way to Palestine. Perhaps the mother hoped that the venerable scholar would dissuade her son from this adventure. Indeed, as Agnon recalled in his autobiographical novel *Hemdat*, Müller impressed on him that "settling the Land of Israel is a great deed, but its climate is harsh, and its inhabitants suffer, and you will not be able to withstand the suffering of the land. Better that you settle down in Vienna and prepare yourself for the university and I will support you." Agnon did not heed this advice. But four years later he abandoned Jaffa and moved to Germany, where he stayed for well over a decade.[24]

Although Agnon's later writings betray the influence of Sigmund Freud, who was also teaching at Vienna University, he is unlikely to have heard of him at the time, or to have known that he, too, was linked to his hometown.[25] In fact, Freud's paternal grandfather and great-grandfather were born in Buczacz and there is evidence to suggest that both were rabbis, while his father was born in the nearby town of Tyśmienica (Tysmenitz, Tysmenytsya), moving later to Freiberg (Příbor) in Moravia, where Sigmund was born to his second wife Amalia. The family settled in Vienna four years later, where Freud was raised, having had no direct contact with Buczacz.[26]

But a century later, in 1958, Freud's sixty-nine-year-old son Martin recalled his grandmother Amalia, who "came from East Galicia" and was of "Jewish stock." These "Galician Jews," he commented, "were a peculiar race, not only different from any other races inhabiting Europe, but absolutely different from Jews who had lived in the West for some generations." On the one hand, they "had little grace and no manners; and their women were certainly not what we would call 'ladies.' They were highly emotional and easily carried away by their feelings." On the other hand, "they, alone of all minorities, stood up against the Nazis" and "fought the German army on the ruins of Warsaw." Martin firmly believed that "whenever you hear of Jews showing violence or belligerence, instead of that meekness and what seems poor-spirited acceptance of a hard fate sometimes associated with Jewish people, you may safely suspect the presence of men and women of Amalia's race."[27]

Martin Freud had served as an officer in the Austro-Hungarian army in the First World War and in the British Army in the Second World War. As tall and broad-shouldered as his paternal grandfather, he appreciated physical resistance to one's enemies, and took pride in what he believed to be the laudable qualities of his heritage, about which he otherwise knew close to nothing. One can imagine that Martin acquired some of his views of Jews from his father. The rabbi and ethnographer Max Grunwald, who encountered Sigmund Freud a few times, has left us some telling observations on the topic.[28] At their first meeting, following a lecture he delivered in Vienna in 1898, Freud remarked that he was "pleasantly surprised" to see Grunwald in "an elegant tailcoat," since "he had imagined a Jewish rabbi in the image of John the Baptist, wearing a shaggy coat, with unkempt hair and tormented features." Several years later Grunwald attended a lecture by Freud on Hammurabi's Code, where Freud rejected his colleague Müller's views and insisted that the Hebrew Bible and thus Judaism as a whole were derived from ancient Mesopotamian mythology. Raising the issue again at their third and last encounter, Freud asserted "resolutely that the Jews had given nothing to culture" in recent times as well.[29]

One cannot but be struck by the irony of Freud's statement considering his own incalculable impact on modern culture. Freud's discernible influence on Agnon is only one, albeit significant instance, both in terms of Hebrew literature in general and, more to the point of this chapter, by way of linking these two singularly creative offspring of late nineteenth-century East European Jewry to each other. Freud, as we know, also shared with Müller a fascination with ancient Jewish mythology. These two Jewish men had made the most of the opportunities that had opened up to members of their generation, however differently they related to their own heritage, yet their personal fates were the function of changing times and circumstances: Müller, ten years older, died just before the First World War as a respected Austrian scholar. Freud fled Vienna as a hunted Jew shortly after the *Anschluss* with Germany in 1938 and lived just long enough to witness the outbreak of the Second World War. His four sisters were murdered in the camps. One of his last books was *Moses and Monotheism*.[30]

Most of those who left their Galician hometowns never came back, but some did. They brought with them a trace of the new world and the possibilities of a different life, as well as books, newspaper subscriptions, ideas, and opinions. But they also found themselves irretrievably back in the drudgery of provincial life. Their children, growing up among those books and magazines, ideas and disillusionments, at times decided to act where the fathers had not: to transform not just their hometowns but the entire world. They were often adventurous, reckless, and tragic figures: their high hopes were irreparably dashed, their firm beliefs betrayed, the world of their youth wiped out, and the one that replaced it turned out to be infinitely crueler and more cynical. Many died young; some of the survivors adapted to the new reality and served its masters, while others ended their days sheltered in the margins of irrelevance. They tended to be bitter and, toward the end, were occasionally given to rather unrevolutionary nostalgia. The youngest among them belonged to my grandparents' generation.

This generational trajectory is well illustrated by the case of the Nacht family. The father, Fabius, was born in Buczacz in 1848 and raised in an affluent, German-speaking home already touched by the Haskalah. After matriculating from the Polish-language state gymnasium in Stanisławów, Fabius went on to study medicine at the University of Vienna. (He had originally aspired to acquire a degree in mathematics but abandoned that quest when he found out that Jews were not allowed to teach it in schools.) In 1879 he came back to Buczacz and opened a private medical practice. Fabius was soon recognized as one of the most respected members of the Jewish community on account of his university degree, his position as a doctor, and his "higher" German culture.[31]

But as his son Max recalled almost a century later, in response to the limitations imposed on him by "the reactionary, church-ridden Vienna regime," Fabius Nacht had also become a socialist in the early 1870s. Indeed, it was from his father, wrote Max, that "I got my first radical indoctrination."[32] Yet unlike Franzos, his exact contemporary, who was forced to study law but never practiced it, Fabius dedicated himself to his role as the most prominent medical authority in Buczacz. In 1891 a modern hospital was established in Buczacz under the direction of Fabius Nacht, a position he held for thirty-four years, until his retirement at the age of seventy-seven in 1925. He was fortunate to pass away just before the war. In 1942 the German occupiers, together with Ukrainian and Jewish policemen, deported the approximately one hundred patients to the Bełżec extermination camp, while shooting those too sick to move in their beds. Nowadays all that is left of the hospital is an empty lot.[33]

An obituary published in the Polish Socialist Party's weekly in 1938 acclaimed Dr. Nacht as "a socialist out of conviction, a freethinker without hateful intolerance ... a rationalist filled with deep feelings, [and] an internationalist who sympathized with all liberation movements." Even toward the end of his life, the doctor's "desk was overflowing with piles of socialist newspapers and magazines of all shades and languages."[34] It was in this home that Fabius Nacht's sons were raised as members of the first activist socialist generation in Buczacz.

In his vast posthumous "biography" of Buczacz, *A City in Its Fullness* (*Ir u-Melo'ah*), Agnon depicts those early days of social mobilization: "An explosive new word is making the rounds in Buczacz and it is socialism." Suddenly, those who used "to work for you as servants" assert that "every person is his own master and does not belong to anyone else"; they "used to work from daybreak till midnight," but now they "stop working after eight hours." As Agnon observed, in this struggle for social justice, not a few Jewish "sons of the wealthy who appeared to want for nothing ... joined the socialists, and no father could be certain that his son would not carry out some action that would land him in prison or that he would not marry the daughter of a worker." All those who thought that "Zionism is the worst of all upheavals in the world" now "discovered that there are even greater upheavals," since Buczacz had become "a city of socialists."[35]

One center of political ferment was Fabius Nacht's home, described in his obituary as "the meeting point for socialist youths of all nationalities."[36] The local leader was Anselm Mosler, whom Max Nacht recalled as "the only citizen of our town ever to accomplish" the "intellectual feat" of earning two doctorates from Vienna University, in law and philosophy. Having spent eighteen months in a Russian prison for smuggling illegal literature, Mosler returned to Buczacz and organized a socialist association which, despite its Ukrainian name, was, according to Max, "exclusively Jewish, for the Gentile workers, Roman Catholic Poles and Uniate Catholic Ukrainians were under the influence of their respective clergymen and would not join such a society." In any case, as he pointed out, the majority of the population in Buczacz "consisted of Yiddish-speaking Jews," while the remaining Polish and Ukrainian inhabitants "hated and despised each other even more than they did the Jews."[37]

Born in Buczacz in 1881, Max Nacht became a Marxist by the ripe age of fourteen and was an early member of Mosler's group. He and his older brother Siegfried attended public school, where they learned Polish and Ukrainian. Siegfried soon joined the social democratic movement and was expelled from two secondary schools in a row for conspiratorial activities before finally matriculating in the larger city of Stanisławów in 1895.[38]

By then, Max, too, had become radicalized; turning to anarchism, he broke with his former idol Mosler, whom he accused of wanting to go "beyond cultivating his own garden, with its few scores of Jewish tailors, carpenters, locksmiths, salesmen, butchers, and shoemakers," so as "to play a more important role," especially "in the Polish section of the Austrian Socialist party." Yet Mosler's "first bid for leadership," recalled Max, "met with such bitter abuse that he resigned from that party and joined the newly organized Jewish Social-Democratic Party," formed after it had been denied recognition both by the Austrian socialists and by the Polish section. To Max, writing about these events six decades later, this demonstrated the effects of Polish and Austrian socialists' anti-Semitism, leading to Mosler's "utterly ridiculous ... sudden conversion to Yiddish separatism," considering that he was a former "assimilationist who was unable to speak Yiddish."[39]

In fact, Mosler had not entirely given up on trying to revolutionize the local population. In 1905 he began publishing a bilingual Polish-Ukrainian monthly newsletter directed at the "farm laborers of the Buczacz district and other districts of Podolia" with the goal of enlightening the largely illiterate peasants about their rights and helping them resist abuse and exploitation.[40] Yet as many of the peasants' letters to this short-lived newsletter show, their sense of injustice and resentment often translated into rage against the Jews. Disillusioned and impoverished, Mosler finally put an end to his career as an agitator and receded from the scene. Living in Vienna during the First World War, he finally succumbed to the tuberculosis he had contracted in the Russian prison as a young revolutionary.

But Mosler did make one last ghostly appearance in Agnon's great novel, *A Guest for the Night* (Ore'ah natah lalun), over two decades after his death, under the evocative fictional name Knabenhut (which can mean both a boy's cap and a guardian). Based on Agnon's last visit to his hometown in 1930, the novel depicts his protagonist's encounter with Aharon Schützling, a character bearing a striking resemblance to Max Nacht. Both the narrator and Schützling had left Buczacz many years earlier and are keenly aware of how profoundly both the city and their own outlooks had changed since their departure. "Although we differed in our opinions," observers the narrator, "for I was a Zionist and he an anarchist, we were glad to talk to each other."[41]

As they contemplate their respective disillusionments, they remember Knabenhut, who is "dead and gone." Schützling is beset with nostalgia: "Days like those will never return. Strikes during the day and wild parties at night." But then he recalls a chance meeting with Knabenhut in wartime Vienna. The latter, he says, had "fumed at me for becoming an anarchist, and some said that he had denounced me to the authorities, and I had to flee to America." This time the disheveled Knabenhut lectured him "about the war and the destruction that is in store for us and the entire world." He was gravely ill, and his last words were just a whisper: "The generation that is about to come will be worse than all the generations that preceded us," he prophesized. "The world is becoming ever uglier, uglier than either I or you had ever sought to make it."[42]

This prophecy expressed Agnon's own foreboding at the time of the novel's publication in 1939. His narrator recalled how Knabenhut had empowered the "wretched boys" of Buczacz, "who were treated like cattle, tyrannized day and night by their masters." But the anarchists blamed him for refusing to accept that "the world can only be repaired through eradication," whereas he viewed them, in Agnon's words, as "rabid zealots, ready to sacrifice themselves and the whole world as well."[43] To be sure, while the fictional anarchist Schützling somehow wound his way to wartime Vienna, the real Max and Siegfried Nacht were already in the United States by the time the war broke out, having also given up on their efforts to change the world after years of revolutionary activities across Europe.

In the years between his departure from Buczacz and immigration to the United States, Siegfried was transformed into an itinerant revolutionary. Having acquired a degree in electrical engineering in Vienna, he could not find an appropriate position because of his Jewish background and socialist politics. At the same time, as a member of Austrian Social Democracy, he came out against Zionism and, in 1897, officially left the Vienna Jewish community. But shortly thereafter he also grew disenchanted with what he perceived as the nationalism, anti-Semitism, and parliamentarism of the Social Democrats, embraced anarchism, and moved to Berlin, whence he traveled, mostly on foot, from one revolutionary cell to another. In April 1903 he crossed into Gibraltar and was promptly arrested on suspicion of plotting to assassinate King Edward VII during his planned visit to the British territory. The pistol he regularly carried did not help matters.

Siegfried's arrest made waves throughout Europe. Polish émigrés in Paris and Ruthenian socialists in Vienna protested. In London a committee was formed under the leadership of Russian anarchist Peter Kropotkin and the philosopher Herbert Spencer (who died just a few months later). Siegfried's younger brother Max described the response to the arrest in Buczacz, noting sarcastically that overnight Siegfried was transformed from "the disgrace of the town" into "a national hero, the fame and pride of the place." Moreover, Siegfried was called "an engineer" and "an author" in Polish newspapers and was said to have come under the protection of "a former minister, a real countess," and "an actual prince." With such credentials, commented Max, the town of Buczacz came to view Siegfried as nothing less than an "eighth wonder of the world." In Agnon's *A Guest for the Night*, Siegfried appears as Sigmund Winter, "the son of a doctor and one of Knabenhut's disciples," who "was distinguished among his friends by his black hair and beautiful eyes that he would make at young women." The narrator recalls Winter's victorious visit to his hometown following his release for lack of evidence a few weeks after his arrest in Gibraltar. He was "holding his head high like a prince, a black cape over his shoulders with its hem flowing down below his knees, a black hat on his head slightly tilted to one side, his moustache rolled upward and his beard descending in the shape of a half Star of David." Indeed, the young revolutionary "was walking as if" the whole city "belonged to him," surrounded as he was by "beautiful maidens from the best families" with "all the officials making way for him." It all sounded a little like Mordecai the Jew's triumphant march through the city of Shushan following his victory over Haman the Agagite.[44]

This was Siegfried's finest hour. In 1912 he immigrated to the United States and was joined there by his brother the following year. Max had begun studying law at Vienna in 1900, but he soon teamed up with fellow student Mykhailo Lozynsky, a Ukrainian poet, journalist, and political agitator, to produce a single issue of a projected anarchist periodical, leading to Lozynsky's arrest and indictment for high treason by the Austrian authorities. Max, who manage to escape to Switzerland in the nick of time, ruminated years later that, had it not been for this event, "I most likely would have remained in Austria to die for my Emperor during World War I, or, in case of survival, to be gassed by Eichmann during World War II." By then, he rationalized his adoption of anarchism as "compensation for the personal sense of inadequacy and insecurity of the impractical son of a radical Jewish physician." Conversely, he saw his Ukrainian comrade's anarchism as the "expression of a nationalist intellectual's protest against the Austro-Polish landed nobility," who "were oppressing four million Ukrainian peasants" in Galicia. Yet in the wake of the First World War, Max noted, Lozynsky "capitulated to Moscow, taking a job with one of the Ukrainian scientific institutions in Kiev." Nevertheless, during the Great

Purge of the late 1930s he "was shot along with all the other well-known Ukrainian intellectuals who had ever shown any Ukrainian nationalist inclination."[45]

In the United States the brothers changed their names to Stephen Naft and Max Nomad and lived most of the rest of their lives in New York City.[46] Max achieved certain notoriety in the American Left. The eminent critic Edmund Wilson wrote an introduction to Nomad's 1961 book, *Aspects of Revolt*, where he described him as a "connoisseur of radicals," not least because he was, in his own words, "a Socialist in my high-school days, an Anarchist as a college student, a Syndicalist *sui generis* during the years of my romantic and not-so-romantic vagabondage, and finally a Soviet sympathizer some forty years ago when Lenin and Trotsky were still glorious legends, between 1917 and 1920."[47]

To lifelong professional revolutionaries, Mosler and the Nacht brothers would have appeared as mere dilettantes who ended up betraying their ideals. Adolf Langer, born in Buczacz in 1892, just eleven years Max Nacht's junior and five years younger than Agnon, had the temperament and perseverance of the numerous apparatchiks who have populated so much of the twentieth century. After his death, his communist colleagues noted vaguely that he was raised "in an atmosphere of patriotism and democratic ideals." In fact he was the son of Joachim Langer, director of the Baron Hirsch School, where classes were held in Polish, but German, Ruthenian, and some Hebrew were also taught; Joachim's wife, described by one of her former students as "a beautiful blond," taught there as well, while he offered additional extracurricular classes on Jewish religion at the Buczacz state gymnasium, which his son Adolf also attended.[48] In the small universe of Jewish Buczacz most people knew each other: Markus (Mordechai) Kanfer, a teacher at the Baron Hirsch School and an essayist for Hebrew-language magazines, also taught Agnon German and some Polish; Markus's son Mojżesz (Moshe) attended gymnasium with Siegfried Nacht and later became an important intellectual figure in interwar Kraków. He and his wife were murdered in the Holocaust but their daughter, Irène (Irma) Kanfer, became a well-known postwar French poet. Markus Kanfer's daughter Sabina (Sara) became romantically involved with, and apparently married Max Nacht; their son was born in Paris after he left for the United States. I met Alain Kanfer, a retired physician and Sabina's grandson, in 2001 in Paris: raised as a Roman Catholic, he was trying to recover his roots in Jewish Buczacz, only to discover that his grandfather, whose name was never uttered in the family, was Max.[49]

By the time Adolf enrolled as a philosophy student in Vienna University in 1914, he had become a member of the Austrian Social Democratic Party, but two years later he shifted his loyalties to its "revolutionary left wing grouped around Lenin."[50] A founding member of the Austrian Communist Party in 1918, Langer led the establishment of the Communist Party of Eastern Galicia the following year. In 1921, he chaired its national conference in Lwów, where the mostly Ukrainian Galician communists clashed with the Polish representatives over the demand to retain their autonomy in newly independent Poland. Ironically, the twenty-nine-year-old Jewish communist Adolf Langer, now known by the more Ukrainian- and Polish-sounding name Ostap Dłuski, was charged with resolving this largely ethno-national crisis within the new Polish communist party.[51]

Not unlike Mosler, and despite being a loyal communist, Dłuski had much sympathy for the Ukrainians, spoke frankly about Poland's "brutal suppression of the Ukrainian nation" in 1919, and stressed that even the Polish communists "came to us not with a vehement, all-inclusive protest against the horrors that were committed, but rather with the slogan 'Polish Soviet Republic,' which to us was incomprehensible, alien, and aroused suspicion." In fact, while three-quarters of the Galician communists were Ukrainian, and Jews were prominent among the leadership, the majority Ukrainian population of Eastern Galicia, mostly made up of peasants, was strongly anti-Polish. As Dłuski noted at the time, the "simple Ukrainian" responded to Polish Communist assertions that "this was one state," by saying, "You are nationalists, you are exactly like the other bourgeois parties."

The 1921 conference came to an abrupt end when the Polish authorities arrested all the delegates. At the trial, Dłuski unflinchingly professed his belief that "only communism could eliminate the oppression, poverty, and misery of humanity," and that the Soviet Union marked "a new beginning in the progress of humankind."[52] Throughout his life, at least publicly, Dłuski never wavered from this position, and following his release from prison in 1923 he made a career in the Polish Communist Party, becoming a member of the Central Committee and later head of its National Secretariat. In 1936 he moved to France in order to liaise with the French Communist Party.[53] When the Polish government dissolved the Communist Party in 1938, Dłuski remained in France, resuming underground activities following the German invasion of the Soviet Union in 1941. With the French police hot on his heels, in 1942, he went into hiding in a shack owned by Dr. Edgar Longuet, Karl Marx's grandson and mayor of Alfortville near Paris, where he spent several months composing a lengthy German-language indictment of Nazism. In his only known written reference to the ongoing Nazi genocide, using the pen name Oswald Ostenrode, Dłuski condemned Hitler's "bloodhounds," who "drag millions of unarmed Jews in all occupied lands out of their houses, bring them to Poland, and heinously slaughter them there in slaughterhouses built especially for this purpose, among them hundreds of thousands of Jewish children."[54]

By 1943 Dłuski was back in action, organizing a Ukrainian underground in France, editing the Ukrainian-language magazine "Fatherland," and justifying Stalin's takeover and reordering of Eastern Europe in a series of French-language articles. The Soviet Union, he asserted without a trace of irony, "had made the principle of liberty and independence of peoples into the basis of its *raison d'état* and of its foreign policy," because "a nation that oppresses another people cannot be free."[55] In a victory speech he delivered in liberated Paris in 1945, Dłuski blamed the recent crushing of the Polish uprising and the destruction of Warsaw by the Wehrmacht as the Red Army stood by on "the egotistical politics" of those who "wanted to drive a wedge into the Allies' front," to which "the heroic people of Warsaw fell victim."[56] He made no reference to the Warsaw Ghetto uprising of 1943 or to the extermination camps overrun by Soviets.

Dłuski's firm Stalinism seems to have been shaken only once. On July 4, 1946, the bloodiest postwar pogrom in Europe took place in the Polish town of Kielce; over forty Jewish survivors of the Holocaust were butchered. Altogether between five hundred and one thousand five hundred Jews were murdered in Poland in the immediate aftermath of the war.[57] Back in Warsaw as a member of the Central Committee, on July 29, Długoski proposed to his colleagues "that an institution be established which would facilitate departure of the Jews from Poland, so that they could join their families." He went so far as to take note of the Jewish community's disappointment with the lack of democracy in Poland and the fact that Władysław Gomułka—at the time deputy prime minister and de facto ruler of Poland—had not made a single reference to the situation of the Jews in a five-hour speech to the communist party.[58] In 1968 Gomułka, by then leader of the renamed Polish United Workers' Party, expelled the remaining Jews from the country.[59]

Długoski's brief preoccupation with anti-Semitism in Poland may have been mostly motivated by the communists' attempt to accuse their enemies at home and abroad of inciting anti-Jewish sentiments, but it is at least possible that he was also personally shaken by the violence that followed the destruction of the world into which he was born.[60] Subsequently Długoski became engaged mainly in propagandistic humanitarian activities.[61] When given the opportunity to speak publicly about Nazi crimes, such as on the occasion of Wolfgang von Goethe's two-hundredth anniversary in 1949, Długoski refrained from any mention of Holocaust.[62] Conversely, after Stalin's death in 1953, which put an end to the anti-Jewish campaign he had just unleashed, Długoski depicted his memory as "eternally alive, warm and sincere," and described the Bolshevik Party as representing "the highest achievements of advanced human thought."[63] No wonder that following his death in 1964 at the age of seventy-two he was described as "a model communist."[64] He certainly had impeccable timing; four years later he would have likely been "unmasked" as the crypto-Jew Adolf Langer and expelled from Poland as a fifth column Zionist.

Still, for all the ideological baggage Długoski piled up between himself and Buczacz, he always remained within the Polish sphere on whose periphery he was raised. Others, who had wandered much farther, remained attached to the world they had striven to leave behind. Max Nacht acknowledged toward the end of his life that his worldview had initially been forged in Buczacz. Müller, whose move across the Carpathians to a Vienna professorship was a giant step for members of his generation, drew greatly on his early years in Buczacz and was pained by rumors about his lack of loyalty to its community. Agnon spent a lifetime writing about Galicia; had he lived longer, he might have continued compiling ever more stories about Buczacz, because in the aftermath of destruction, "building a city," as he depicted the writing of *A City in Its Fullness*, could not but be a never-ending labor of love:

> For if my city has been wiped out of the world, its name exists in the poem that the poet has written as a sign of my city. And if I do not remember the words of the poem because of its greatness, the poem resonates in the heavens above among the poems of the holy poets beloved of God.[65]

In different ways, they were all trailblazers: coming from the margin they struggled to make themselves known to the world and in the process became part of its remaking.

PART V
WHEN MEMORY COMES

CHAPTER 9
RETURN AND DISPLACEMENT IN ISRAEL-PALESTINE

In Zionist historiography, the year 1948 appears as the culmination of the long Jewish quest for rights and justice, which reached its climax in the immediate aftermath of the Second World War and the Holocaust. Following the completion of my two-decade research project on the transformation of an Eastern European community of ethnic and religious coexistence into a community of genocide, I have come to consider the cardinal year of 1948 from a rather different perspective.[1] Indeed, I would like to suggest here that the links between the fate of the Jews in Europe, especially in its numerous multiethnic towns in the eastern parts of the continent, and the fate imposed by the triumphant political and military leadership of the emerging Israeli state on the land's Palestinian inhabitants, transforming a community of increasingly fraught coexistence into a community of ethnic cleansing and Jewish national hegemony, are both extraordinarily complex and filled with profound ironies.[2]

Two Catastrophes

Israeli politicians, scholars, poets, and writers have repeatedly invoked the relationship between the Holocaust and the establishment of the state of Israel, often for vastly different purposes.[3] Yet some of the more intricate aspects of these links have never been sufficiently explored, not least because they have to do with two incontrovertible and yet irreconcilable ideological axioms: first, that the mass murder of the European Jews demonstrated the urgent need for a Jewish nation-state; and second, that Jewish national hegemony was established by transforming the Arab majority in those parts of Mandatory Palestine that became the state of Israel into a minority through mass expulsion. In both cases, the clock of history was reset to begin counting only after the catastrophe: the Nazi genocide of the Jews was presented as an inevitable consequence of the Diaspora, which therefore had to be relinquished and forgotten, and the near-total destruction of Palestinian civilization had to be followed up with the erasure of its remaining material traces and the wiping out of its memory, thereby allowing the newly created status of an "Arab minority" to appear as if it had always been such.[4]

The logic of this vast transformation was, so to speak, imprinted on the identity of the state at the very moment of its birth. As the Declaration of the Establishment of the State of Israel of May 14, 1948, popularly known in Israel as the Declaration of Independence

(*Megilat ha'atzma'ut*), put it, this would be "a Jewish state in Eretz Israel, which is the state of Israel."⁵ This state, it was declared, would "be open to Jewish immigration and the gathering of the diasporas." It would also "strive to develop the land for all its residents, [would] be based on the principles of liberty, justice, and peace as was envisioned by the prophets of Israel," and would "maintain complete social and political equality for all its citizens without any religious, racial, or gender distinction." Indeed, the new state would "ensure freedom of religion, conscience, language, education and culture," and would "protect all the holy sites of all religions." The Palestinians, however, were mentioned only in a different, separate paragraph, which depicted the local population as hostile to this endeavor and yet magnanimously promised to tolerate its existence nonetheless:

> We call—even in the midst of the bloody attacks conducted against us for months—upon the sons of the Arab people who are residents of the state of Israel to keep the peace and to take part in the building of the state on the basis of full citizenship and on the basis of appropriate representation in all its temporary and permanent institutions.

In other words, even as the state was being formed and hundreds of thousands of Palestinians were being expelled, the state promised those who might be able to remain in the country, a minority within a Jewish nation-state, equal individual (but definitely not national) rights.

Thus the Holocaust and the Nakba were both parallel and irreconcilable events. In the wake of the Holocaust, nothing could sound more just than the demand of the Zionists to have a state of their own. As the Declaration stated unambiguously,

> The Holocaust that has recently occurred to the Jewish people, in which millions of Jews were slaughtered in Europe, proved definitively once more the need for a solution for the Jewish people, deprived of homeland and independence, by renewing a Jewish state in Eretz Israel, which will open the gates of the homeland to every Jew and endow the Jewish people with the status of a nation of equal rights within the family of nations.

And yet, in the wake of the Nakba, nothing could sound more just than the demand of the Palestinians to be allowed back into their own land, from which they were brutally expelled. As the Palestinian Declaration of Independence of November 15, 1988, stated,

> The occupation of Palestinian territory and parts of other Arab territory by Israeli forces, the uprooting of the majority of Palestinians and their displacement from their homes by means of organized intimidation, and the subjection of the remainder to occupation, oppression and the destruction of the distinctive features of their national life, are a flagrant violation of the principle of legitimacy and of the Charter of the United Nations and its resolutions recognizing the national rights of the Palestinian people, including the right to return and the

right to self-determination, independence and sovereignty over the territory of its homeland.[6]

The strength of these two arguments is demonstrated by their astonishing resilience, which is, in turn, sustained by their interdependence. Even as the Holocaust has come to play an increasingly central role in Israeli political rhetoric and has, moreover, become a major element of political discourse at least throughout Europe and the United States, so too the Palestinian discourse of victimhood, resistance, and the right of return has persisted through numerous mutations and adaptations as a central focus of political and cultural discourse throughout the West and the Arab and Muslim world.[7] Considering that, even after its 1967 expansion, Israel still takes up a minuscule space on the globe, while Palestinian refugees, notwithstanding the quadrupling of their population since 1948, are numerically overshadowed by more recent refugee and migration crises, the intense international focus on this conflict may seem disproportionate. That this interest has not diminished is due not only to the objective dangers that the conflict poses to the region and beyond but also, I would argue, to its inherent nature as a confrontation between two assertions of extreme victimhood and righteousness that appear to keep producing endless wrongs and injustices.

Yet another reason for the difficulty of sorting out the links between Jewish fate in Europe and the unfolding of events in Palestine is that they have often, indeed almost exclusively, been examined and analyzed by very different scholarly communities and have appealed to rather disparate constituencies. This too is somewhat ironic, considering the frequency with which one set of events has been rhetorically and politically pitted against the other, not to mention the fact that a considerable number of the protagonists of one event literally traveled to and participated in the other. Arguments such as "how could the Jews have done to the Palestinians what the Germans did to them" or "Israel will never let the Arabs carry out another Holocaust" clearly reflect the instrumentalization of the Holocaust, whereby either the Zionists or the Palestinians and other Arabs and Muslims are presented as the new Nazis. But beyond such vacuous demagoguery, thinking in more depth and with greater nuance about the effects of the realities and perceptions of Jewish life in Eastern Europe on the violent creation of the Jewish state in Palestine, and considering how both have been subsequently presented in scholarship, political rhetoric, and popular discourse, can help us disentangle some of the murkier subplots that make up the largely exclusionary national narratives of 1948 and its long posthistory.[8]

Jews and Others in Eastern Europe

At the core of the modern Jewish experience in Eastern Europe was the question of nation and territory. East European nationalisms were all about land. The beginning of nationalism in the second half of the nineteenth century pitted peoples against monarchs and unleashed national movements throughout the territories of the great multiethnic empires that straddled the lands of Eastern and Southeastern Europe. In the Balkans, these forces eventually pushed the Ottoman Empire out of Europe in a series of increasingly bloody wars and massacres. In the Habsburg Empire's Galicia, abolishing serfdom and emancipating the Jews led to the creation of two new nations. While the liberation of the serfs did not much improve their economic lot, it made them the target of nationalizing priests and intellectuals, who strove to forge them into a nation both by attributing to them unique ethnic characteristics and by insisting on the differences between them and their neighbors. The emerging Ruthenian (later Ukrainian) nation was thus as much centered around a sense of group solidarity as it was on resentment toward those whose marginally better circumstances appeared to derive from the peasants' own misery.[9]

As for the Jews, whatever linked Jewish communities near and far to each other, the "people of Israel" was no modern nation. It became that only in retrospect, in a Jewish nationalist and Zionist discourse that read future aspirations into a distant past in ways not much different from the "awakening" of the peasants. But the emancipation of the Jews in regions such as Galicia profoundly affected both their self-perception and their relations with their neighbors. If the Jews were no longer one of the estates that made up the population, identified since medieval times both by its religion and by its socioeconomic niche, what were they? Jews were not in a hurry to discover that they were a nation, and Zionism took a long time to reach more than a few youngsters in the small towns of Galicia before the First World War.[10] But emancipation enabled Jews to move out of their congested towns and neighborhoods and exacerbated the tensions between them and the rural population. As they leased or bought estates, manor houses, taverns, and manufacturing facilities, they came to be portrayed in the emerging Ruthenian nationalist press as the peasants' misfortune, bringing alcoholism and exploitation to the village and destroying the nation's culture; rootless bloodsuckers and the lackeys of Polish lords, lacking morals, values, and dignity. In this discourse, only the removal of the Jews would allow the development of a proud and healthy Ruthenian nation.[11]

But the masters, awarded autonomous rule in Galicia by the empire despite their minority status in that region, were the Poles. For the Poles, this was their land, part of the *kresy*, or borderlands, of what had once been the vast Polish-Lithuanian Commonwealth. It was there, according to Polish national lore, that Poland had guarded Europe for centuries from the barbarians in the East—the Tatars, the Cossacks, and the Muscovites—and the Ottoman heathens in the south; it was there that it had built castles and palaces, churches and monasteries, cities and towns, bringing culture to the peasants and all the benefits of enlightened and benevolent Polish rule. If the peasants rebelled every once in a while, their savagery and destructive predilections only demonstrated their need for Polish civilization. Indeed, as Polish nationalist discourse in Galicia asserted, the Ruthenians, unlike those who began to speak of themselves as Ukrainians east of Galicia, were in fact potential Poles who simply spoke a different dialect and adopted a somewhat different version of Christianity. They were, in that sense, Poland's little brothers inhabiting Lesser Poland—just as they came to be thought of as Little Russians inhabiting Malorussia for imperial expansionists in Moscow.[12]

As for the Jews, Polish nationalizers never took seriously the notion that they could become Poles. Especially in the *kresy*, Polish aspirations to transform the Ruthenian majority into Poles and thus eliminate the demographic imbalance never considered Jews as part of this endeavor and increasingly viewed them as hampering the nationalization of the region. To be sure, Ruthenian-Ukrainian nationalists, for their part, completely rejected the Polish assertion of brotherhood and increasingly spoke about Poles as colonizers and exploiters. In this manner, by the outbreak of war in 1914, Polish and Ruthenian-Ukrainian nationalists were pitted against each other, even if the Poles hypothetically wanted to absorb the Ruthenians whereas the Ruthenians wanted to kick the Poles out. The two groups agreed on only one thing, namely, that the Jews did not belong to the land, and thus they featured in neither nation's schemes for the future.[13]

Save for the growing, but still very limited number of Jewish estate owners, most Jews did not make claims on particular plots of land or on the land as a homeland. To be sure, they certainly saw themselves as an inherent part of their societies and insisted that they were playing an important, indeed crucial role in its social and economic progress. After all, it was for that purpose that Polish magnates had invited them to the region centuries earlier, enticing them with a raft of economic and legal privileges. In return, the Jews had developed the economy, commerce, manufacturing, and urban life, as they noted in response to the new exclusionary rhetoric of Polish nationalism, even as hundreds of thousands of them also left, mostly to North America, fleeing the poverty of the region along with multitudes of destitute peasants. But that was not the way they were spoken about by their nationalizing neighbors. Whether seen as parasites by others or perceiving themselves as outside the competition over the land between Poles and Ukrainians, the Jews were in a place of their own.[14]

This sense of being elsewhere was also rooted in an internal Jewish discourse that predated nationalism and Zionism by centuries: it was one focused on transition. Within their own universe of history, myth, and lore, the Jews of Eastern Europe had come from Ashkenaz, or Germany, not simply because they were invited there by Polish lords but also because they had been en route, as they had always been through faith and destiny, to Eretz Israel. Traditional Jews could never entirely call the land in which they lived their own, because they were, almost by definition, in exile. This was not a Diaspora that had to end, and the talk of Eretz Israel was not a nationalist one. But they also could not fully strike roots and call any other land their own, since in the long run a religious Jew's destiny and destination was the land of his ancestors. To be sure, assimilated Western Jews in the nineteenth century, quite apart from shedding much of their religious identity, also increasingly abandoned that deeply seated notion of transition and internalized the local national and patriotic discourse. In turn, they not infrequently encountered much resistance to such assimilation, especially, and ironically, following their emancipation and as a direct result of their attempt to integrate fully into their societies. Yet in the small towns of Eastern Europe, not least in Galicia, where large numbers of Jews resided, Jewish tradition remained strong and a sense of temporariness, however long term, persisted: the transitory state of the Jews was, in a sense, what constituted their very identity, since their ultimate resting point, closely associated with redemption, much delayed though it was, had always to remain the Land of Israel.[15]

It was in the years before, during, and after the First World War that the rise of ethnonationalism among the neighboring populations left no room for the Jews. Simultaneously—yet also in response to these sentiments—the rise of Zionism made for a corresponding Jewish ethnonationalism, according to which this newly discovered nation had to put an end to its centuries-long sojourn in the Diaspora and complete its long-delayed journey to its own homeland. The lands in which the Jews had resided were now reconfigured as nothing more than a temporary haven, a stopping place, on the way to the promised land.[16]

What happened in Galicia in the years leading from the aftermath of the First World War to the Holocaust is known. Polish suppression of Ukrainian nationalism and attempts to colonize the region during the interwar years led to increasingly radical Ukrainian organizations; and growing Polish government anti-Semitism was accompanied by increasingly anti-Semitic sentiments among Galician Ukrainian. The Soviet takeover of eastern Poland and the brutal policies of deportation, incarceration, and executions further exacerbated to interethnic tension in the region. When the Germans marched into Galicia in 1941, they turned these local animosities to their advantage, and exploited Ukrainian resentment against the Jews to implement an almost total eradication of the Jewish population in the region. This was followed by massive ethnic cleansing of the Polish population by Ukrainian insurgents acting independently of the Germans, and then by a thorough suppression of the insurgency by the Soviets when they returned to Galicia. By the late 1940s, the region had become almost entirely Ukrainian. Nowadays, most of the inhabitants of West Ukraine have few memories and little knowledge of, or interest in, the region's multiethnic past and the savage policies of genocide and ethnic cleansing that put an end to four centuries of coexistence.[17]

Jews and Others in Israel-Palestine

The project of Zionism was to bring Jews to their own land. Its main engine was the argument that Jews do not belong in the Diaspora. This view was shared by Zionists and anti-Semites but was also built into much earlier Jewish self-perceptions and the perception of Jews by their neighbors. The mechanism that transformed the age-old relationship between Jews and Gentiles was emancipation and assimilation. Emancipation meant that Jews could "leave the ghetto" and mix into their surrounding societies with equal legal rights. Assimilation meant that Jews would follow up (or precede) emancipation by adapting to and emulating their neighbors, shedding their external and internal manifestations of otherness. But the process did not work as many of the Maskilim of the eighteenth and nineteenth centuries had hoped. The Jews wanted to keep a modicum of their Jewish identity, and Christian society suspected that behind the façade of "German" clothes lurked the old *Ostjude*, the traditional eastern Jew, with caftan and beard. Even when Jews spoke and wrote "Christian" languages with the greatest fluency, Gentile critics detected echoes of the Jewish "jargon"; specialists in the art of identifying Jewish traits insisted that what they referred to as Mauscheln—the alleged Jewish manner of speaking that denoted simultaneously Jewish deceit, scheming, and wheeling and dealing—betrayed even the most assimilated and respectable Jewish members of their societies. As Franz Kafka's ape remarked in his speech to the academy, the assimilated often remained neither here nor there; they could not return to the ghetto (or jungle), yet neither could they avoid being admired or derided for how well they emulated real humans, even to the extent that one was threatened by the inability to discern their innate difference.[18]

Vanishing was an issue: for anti-Semites, it meant that while the Jewish essence polluted Christian societies, its carriers might go undetected. For the Jews, with some exceptions, vanishing meant giving up on the entire millennia-long story of Jewish existence. How to preserve the commitment to Jewish continuity became part and parcel of the Jewish Question. There were those who believed that Jews should retain their particularity among the nations; others believed they should establish their own separate community. But would a renewed tie to the soil deprive the Jews of precisely that quality that set them apart from other nations? That was the conundrum of Zionism: "normalizing" Jewish existence might undo the uniqueness of the Jews, while assimilating into "the nations" might make them disappear altogether. Would the Jews be a light unto the nations or, as in God's covenant with Abraham, renew a commitment to blood and soil? What, after all, was the chosen people chosen to do?[19]

Jewish immigration to Palestine was propelled by the growing anti-Jewish violence in Europe. The more violence there was, the larger the numbers that crossed the sea. To be sure, until the 1930s, most emigration was propelled by economic reasons, and most emigres went elsewhere, especially to the United States, which offered greater economic opportunities and a safe haven as a land of immigrants that had never embraced the European idea of the nation-state. Nonetheless, the United States also experienced lengthy periods of nativism, xenophobia, and racism, which emerged in full force and locked the gates of the *Goldene Medina* (the Golden State, as Jews referred to the United States) just as escaping Europe truly became a matter of life and death. Conversely, those who went to Palestine were engaged in an entirely different undertaking. Even before the mass violence and displacements of 1918–21 in Ukraine, the Zionists settling in Palestine both perceived themselves as being pushed out of their European homes and insisted on coming home in Eretz Israel at the same time. By the 1920s, and even more so the 1930s, ever-larger numbers of Jews were arriving in Palestine both because they were compelled to do so by a combination of anti-Jewish legislation and economic impoverishment, and because they had fewer and fewer alternative destinations.[20]

As they streamed into the land by the tens of thousands, these immigrants, who combined to varying degrees the status of expellees, refugees, and Zionist *"olim"* ("ascenders," as Zionism and the state of Israel have always referred to Jews immigrating to Palestine/Israel) put increasing demographic pressure on the native Arab population. Not all the Jews who arrived in Palestine at that time were devout Zionists, and many of them would have preferred to remain where they had come from or to go elsewhere. But those options had been closed off, and arguably many of those arriving, especially from Eastern Europe, had already felt themselves strangers in their homeland before they left and felt they were traveling to their homeland before they set eyes on it. These Zionists, then, would be in their own land for the first time. And yet, just as in the lands they had left, in Palestine they were hardly alone, indeed not even the majority, but rather surrounded by a population that responded with increasing resentment and rage to their encroachments on land and resources. In a sense, the move from regions such as Galicia to Palestine had changed nothing. The Jews were still a minority, and their neighbors still did not want them, certainly not in such numbers and with such profound economic impact.[21]

But the Jewish immigrants did not see things this way. For them, everything had changed. Their centuries-long journey had come to an end, and now they were finally home. That this home was populated by another group could either be ignored or be contended with later. But whichever way one looked at the land's indigenous population, for most of these immigrants the presence of Arab neighbors had no impact on their fundamental self-understanding that, in complete contrast to the nature of their relationship to the Diaspora, they were in their own land by historical and moral right, the same right claimed by their Christian neighbors for the lands in Europe out of which they had been pushed.[22]

It was, however, the crucial moment between the end of the Holocaust and the aftermath of the 1948 War that fully determined the relationship of the Zionists to the land, even as it simultaneously transformed them from a population of displaced remnants into one of brutal displacement. This moment is, to my mind, at the heart of all that has happened since, and sheds much light on all that had happened before, going back to the first dribbles of immigration in the 1880s. The Jews had come to Eretz Israel as one alternative to growing hardship in the East European and Ukrainian-Russian diaspora and as a response to exclusionary ethnonationalism throughout Europe; but in the wake of the Holocaust, the hundreds of thousands of displaced persons, deprived of their former homes, families, and culture, with no place to return to and no clear idea of where to go, constituted the very essence of what displacement meant. They had been shown time and again that they did not belong in the lands where they had dwelled; indeed, most of their family members had by then been turned into ashes or buried in mass graves throughout the lands in which they had lived for centuries. Nor were they wanted where they were now, in transition camps intended to facilitate their travel from one place to another but certainly not to allow them to stay where they were. For years they had been pushed and shoved, uprooted and hunted, humiliated and robbed of both their property and their dignity; and yet they still had no place to go.[23]

It would not be correct to say that this utter displacement of Jews from everything they had belonged to made them wish to do the same to others; but by all accounts, it rendered many of them indifferent and callous and at times vengeful toward the Arab population they encountered in Palestine. That vague notion that they had been, in a certain sense, a transitory, alien population, Orientals passing through Europe's forests on their way elsewhere, had been translated into a harsh, brutal reality. They did not belong, and they were not wanted. Jews returning to small towns in Eastern Europe, if only in the hopes of finding other surviving relatives, were told in no uncertain terms that they would do better to leave if their lives were dearer to them than their property. Following the July 1946 pogrom in Kielce, those who had not previously gotten the message packed their bags and continued on their journey. But that single pogrom, which stands for all the other acts of violence against surviving Jews throughout Eastern Europe, soon had an equivalent, one that we rarely think about in the same context. Less than two years later, in April 1948, Jewish militias perpetrated a massacre in the village of Deir Yassin, which stands for numerous other cases of violence and intimidation by the military that set off a mass flight of Palestinians, who similarly got the message that they were no longer wanted in an emerging Israeli state newly flexing its muscles.[24]

It is this relationship between displacement and belonging that needs to be explored more thoroughly when thinking about the decade of 1939–49. This is not an exercise in facile comparison, which can work in favor of either one side or the other. It is an attempt to understand the complex links to place and the tragedy and legitimizing power of displacement. The Jews who came to Palestine had been, as they saw it, displaced twice. One displacement had caused the Diaspora; the second displacement uprooted them from the Diaspora and brought them back home. The encounter with the local Palestinian population had some similarities with their experiences in Europe. But in the minds of the immigrants, the relations were largely reversed. The land, after all, was theirs, and the people living on it could not possibly be anything more than a transitory population that had come from elsewhere and could just as easily continue on its journey to another site. Or, as some fancied, taking a page from Polish nationalist fantasies about Ruthenians, the indigenous inhabitants were in fact the remnants of the original Jewish population who had not gone to the Diaspora and over time converted to Islam or Christianity and began speaking Arabic.[25]

This is not to say that even before the First World War, and up to the 1948 War, there were no voices that warned against setting one group against another, perceived the attachment of the Arab population to the land, and noticed the growth of local nationalism and seething resentment against the Jews, as was repeatedly manifested in the anti-Jewish riots of 1921 and 1929, and in the 1936 Arab uprising against British rule. But by and large, the discourse within the Yishuv was not about the injustice of displacing the local population but instead squarely focused on the historical justice of returning to one's own land. Simultaneously, the sense of justice denied to the Jews only grew during the 1930s, as those seeking to flee Europe were increasingly denied shelter throughout the world, and British policies, responding to the Arab uprising, sought to limit immigration to Palestine. And once the news began filtering in about the mass murder of European Jewry, the sense of injustice toward the Jews overshadowed any remaining sympathy for the local Arab population and the pressure its leadership put on the British to curtail Jewish immigration. Palestinian leader Mufti Haj Amin al-Husayni's flirtation with Adolf Hitler certainly also played into this sentiment.[26]

One might add two other historical moments that are often left out of this discussion yet contributed to a sense of both imminent danger and national catastrophe. First, the successes of Erwin Rommel's Panzer Corps in Africa temporarily brought the potential of Nazi-led extermination of the Zionist enterprise in Palestine home to the population, exposing the vulnerability of those who had seen themselves as having overcome the condition of the Diaspora. Indeed, as we now know, Nazi Germany was preparing a special task force to carry out genocide in Palestine; it was only thanks to the British Eighth Army's victory in El Alamein in November 1942 that this plan was reluctantly shelved. Second, we should recall that thousands of young men from the Yishuv volunteered to serve in the Jewish Brigade of the British Army and were the first representatives of Jewish Palestine to encounter the survivors of the Holocaust in all their misery. These young men from Palestine often sought revenge for crimes committed by the Germans that they had not and could not have prevented and whose perpetrators were out of their reach. They also wanted to prove to themselves and to others that they would "no longer go like sheep to the slaughter." They returned to Palestine just months before the 1948 War broke out.[27]

The violence of 1948 has often been portrayed, as is the case with many other national wars and, to an even larger extent, ethnic conflicts, from polar perspectives; it is almost as if the two sides are describing completely different events. For Jewish Israelis this was a bitter war of independence (or liberation); for the Palestinians it was the Nakba, the catastrophe, referring to the mass expulsion of the Arab population and the destruction of its villages. But these events are linked not only because the fighting encouraged and facilitated the realization of the Zionist dream of creating a Jewish majority in Palestine but also because population displacement—violent expulsion—was part of the collective Jewish memory of anti-Jewish violence. To be sure, there was already talk within the Yishuv leadership about population transfer in the 1930s, and the "model" of the 1923 Greek-Turkish exchange was positively invoked. But something much deeper was at work once the fighting began in November 1947, as Jewish losses mounted and a sense of impending doom seized an anxious population, allowing the demons of Jewish history and the trauma of the Holocaust to take over.[28]

A few, such as the writer Yizhar Smilansky (under the pen name S. Yizhar), were troubled by the sight of Hebrew soldiers—as they were called at the time in order to suggest the link between Zionism's "new Jews" and biblical Hebrew warriors—expelling Arabs, invoking echoes of German expulsions of Jews, although such ruminations apparently never rose in his mind—and certainly not in his public utterances—to the level of criticizing the violent creation of the state as a whole. The poet Avot Yeshurun wrote more explicitly about the links between the violence against the Jews and that perpetrated by them, but his complex and multilingual verses remained inaccessible to most readers.[29] By and large, this nexus played not an inhibiting but an enabling role (as it does to this day): the powerful psychological–ideological engine behind the Jewish expulsion of the Palestinians was the perceived justification granted to the displaced to displace others, the right of the uprooted to uproot, the ruthless urge of the forgotten and abandoned to create for themselves a space under the sun, at any price. The brutality and heavy bloodshed of the fighting made it all the easier, so to speak, as is often the case. It had become—as even many of the young men and women who had supported a binational state until then now asserted—a war of existence. It was also to a certain extent a war of revenge for acts committed by others, elsewhere, at other times; displaced vengeance, we might say, but one with long-term consequences and an inevitable boomerang effect.[30]

For as the cunning of history would have it, once the displaced had displaced others, they became pawns of the fate they had imposed on themselves, recreating another version of that inescapable trap from which they had hoped to liberate themselves. Now that the land was theirs, and they were the majority, their previously indisputable right to it increasingly came into question. For what of the people they had evicted? What gave them permission to drive out an entire people and then act as if it had never existed? The Palestinians refused to accept the logic of eviction, refused to assimilate into other Arab nations, refused to forget their homes and their lands. And the Jews, who had come back to their land and called it their home, discovered that here too the land would never be fully and entirely theirs, so long as millions of people, those who had been pushed out and all their progeny, remained refugees from a land that had once been their own.

This condition can lead to denials and obfuscations. There is no doubt that both groups tend to deny, minimize, or reverse blame for the other's displacement as a psychological compensatory mechanism. Among Palestinians one may still find various forms of Holocaust denial, which is particularly galling and provocative for a Jewish population that has been deeply imbued with a nationalized Holocaust "consciousness." By the same token, despite the mountains of evidence accumulated over the years to refute such claims, not a few Jewish Israelis still harken back to the old claims that in 1948 the Palestinians left of their own accord or were instructed to leave by Arab leaders who promised them to return as victors.

Yet the sense of not being finally and assuredly at home also leads to doubts and dilemmas. That displaced population sitting in your midst, across your borders, never giving up, never forgiving, becomes part of your own condition, your own state of being and mind. Displacement is at the root of the very thing itself—Jewish displacement, Arab displacement, they gnaw at each other constantly, for ultimately, it seems, no one came home, no one is at home, every inch of soil is disputed, conquered, occupied, settled, and covered up; and as people are moved from here to there, as communities surround themselves with walls and fences and barbed wire, or enclose their neighbors within walls and fences and barbed wire, home is nowhere to be found, and uncertainty, doubt, and fear are ubiquitous. That decade of 1939–49 will not loosen its grip on Jews and Palestinians alike, the two tragedies rubbing against each other, never allowing either one to settle down, to live in peace. The land is patient. It has seen people come and go, the conquerors and the vanquished, the settlers and the raiders, the builders and the destroyers. But the people are seething, constrained and uncomfortable in their spaces, violent and fearful. They are not at home. Perhaps the only way to put an end to displacement is no longer to push out but to bring in, not to demarcate but to dismantle the barriers, to recognize that this land can be a home only when it is finally all its peoples' homeland.

CHAPTER 10
MY TWISTED PATH TO AUSCHWITZ, AND BACK

I grew up in a country where the Holocaust was ubiquitous. There were many survivors on the street, mostly wearing long sleeves that they did not roll up even in the summer heat. Sometimes they would raise their arms to pick up an item from the shelf of the grocery store or to point at something on the blackboard, and a blue tattooed number would emerge on their forearms. Occasionally they went to the beach and took off their shirts, and we children wanted both to look at these numbers and to look away, because we were curious and mortified at the same time.

Then there were those we never encountered in the grocery store, or in the classroom, or on the beach, but who always hovered in the background, ghosts that populated whispered conversations and photo albums, whose names were the cause of tears and outbursts of memories in languages we did not know. They were always there, but not in the way of deceased relatives who could be recalled with regret and nostalgia, with love and longing. Because the manner of their disappearance, the unnatural age at which they were snatched away, the very fact that they were dead while those who remembered yet rarely spoke about them had somehow survived were all a cause of shame and distress, of a sentiment deeper than sorrow, akin, perhaps, to the lingering effects of having watched a child run over by a bus, an event you could not prevent but wish you had, by grabbing the child's hand in time, or stepping in front of the bus, falling under its wheels instead of that child, or even with it, just so that its death would not be so unimaginably lonely and endlessly, eternally sad.

For children of my generation, born right after everything had already happened, the Holocaust was all around us and yet never actually there. And then, when we were still children or young teens, came the Eichmann trial, and the detailed depictions of all those gruesome deaths were broadcast on the radio every evening as families sat down for supper on their balconies, to catch the evening breeze, the fathers in their sweaty undershirts, the mothers laying out salad and cottage cheese and vegetables and hardboiled eggs and subsidized standard bread and lukewarm water with sweetener, as the sun dropped like a red ball into the sea between flat, tarred roofs, dotted with hot water boilers and solar panels. Those disembodied voices, emanating from radios throughout the neighborhood, speaking heavily accented Hebrew, monotonously detailing mass shootings and beatings, packed rail cars and selections, medical experiments, hangings, gassings, those reports we could not grasp, rising from the nether regions of hell, became part of the mental landscape of our childhood.

Genocide, the Holocaust, and Israel-Palestine

Mine was a generation that for many years—to paraphrase Primo Levi—could not look at the face of the gorgon.[1] We were too close to the Holocaust to be able to think of it as a historical event; but we were also too distant from it to be able to communicate with all those around us who had come from "there." For the generation of our parents, the Holocaust was part of their biography. For our children, it was sufficiently in the past to become a legitimate topic of conversation, rumination, perhaps even research. But for many of my generation there was something embarrassing, even detestable about the entire thing: those terrifying figures with the numbers tattooed on their forearms, those vacant gazes of broken men and women on the bus, those endless, solemn commemorations in the sun-drenched school yard, those vacuous speeches by politicians and the never-ending bluster about never again going like sheep to the slaughter, and our own mute and inarticulate terror that any moment a horde of Nazis could suddenly show up on our street and kill everyone as they did then. Everything was too fresh: both the memories and the corpses.[2]

Members of my generation chose different ways to come to terms with this invisible yet overwhelming burden of a past increasingly known yet never expressed as anything more than a lesson and a moral. My own path led me to an interest in history. But since I could not conceive of the Holocaust as history, I sought to understand the context in which it occurred—that prewar and wartime Europe that my family left just before the disaster, so distant from the dusty little town of Tel Aviv on the coast of the Mediterranean where I grew up. And since I was raised in a country where wars and other forms of armed conflict were almost as recurrent as the scorching wind and clouds of sand that blow into the land from the Sahara every fall and spring—sending people to seek shelter in darkened rooms behind closed shutters—I was drawn to Europe's wars and the destruction they wrought on the continent in the first half of the twentieth century.

This led me quite naturally to Germany, created through war by a military equaled by none, from tiny Prussia to the great German Reich, whose army marched from the English Channel to the gates of Moscow, from the suburbs of Leningrad to within reach of Baku, before being crushed by its multiple foes. After spending four years in the military myself, I began wondering why soldiers do what they do and what it is that makes young, fresh-faced, and optimistic lads go out to the field of battle to kill and be killed, and so I read studies of combat motivation, memoirs by generals, and accounts of modern warfare's capacity to destroy lands and peoples. Coming out of the service, all I wanted was to read and learn much more; yet none of it seemed to have anything to do with the Holocaust.

Not long after I began my undergraduate studies at Tel Aviv University, I was called on reserve service. One night I was riding in an army vehicle along a patrol route near the junction of the Syrian and Lebanese borders with a much older reservist, a child Holocaust survivor from Romania. A working-class man with rudimentary education, he was curious about my studies at the university. I said I was studying history and was especially interested in what had motivated German troops to keep fighting so bitterly even after it became clear that they had lost the war. In response, the man asked me whether I knew anyone who was studying the Holocaust. That's not my field, I said, but there are some students who are interested in it. And what do you do with a degree in history, he asked. Well, if you earn a PhD, I said, you might be able to find a job at the university. The man appeared somewhat bewildered. Strange, he said, I never thought one could make a career out of the Holocaust.

What this child Holocaust survivor said to me on that cold, pitch-dark night somewhere in the far north of Israel almost five decades ago had a much greater impact on me than he could have possibly imagined. No, I certainly did not want to make a career out of the Holocaust, I said to myself at the time. I went on to write a dissertation on precisely the topic I had outlined, almost improvised, when speaking to the elderly reservist from Romania in 1978. Over those years, the more I read German generals' accounts of the Second World War, the less I believed them. And the more I contemplated my own experience in the army and the reflections of friends and comrades about why they had fought as fiercely as they had and why they were eventually so deeply disillusioned—and disillusionment was the prevailing state of mind in post-1973 Israel—the more skeptical I became of the then influential theories of American sociologists about German soldiers' motivation in battle.[3] Writing about belief without ever having had faith, I thought, is as difficult as writing about soldiering and being under fire without ever having experienced it.

But I also discovered that German soldiers were motivated—as soldiers invariably are—by a mix of positive and negative images. On the positive side, they saw themselves, their leaders, and their nation as deserving domination over others by dint of their superiority. On the negative side, they saw others as dangerous and treacherous, and as threatening to degrade their own superior qualities and to undermine their noble goal of rule and domination. Those who stood in their way were working hand in hand with the devil. And among those working against them, the Jews featured as the most inferior and insidious, yet at the same time also as the most dangerous: ridiculous, weak, degenerate, frightened, passive in their dying, and entirely expendable in their absence, they somehow also carried within them the seeds of one's own destruction, to the extent that contact with them, even as one was exterminating them, could be fatal.

And so, as I was studying the motivation, indoctrination, and crimes of the German army in the Soviet Union, I ended up also moving slowly toward the heart of the matter, the genocidal core of the Nazi undertaking. But in the 1980s, German history and the history of the Holocaust were largely seen as separate fields of inquiry. Indeed, even the argument I made in my dissertation and first two monographs, namely, that German soldiers were motivated in large part by a version of Nazi ideology that made them not only fight fanatically but also act with murderous brutality against their so-called Judeo-Bolshevik enemies, was not especially welcomed by German or military historians at the time, let alone the general public. And while academe has gradually accepted the notion of the German army's deep ideological and political complicity in Nazi crimes, resistance to the implications of this insight, that is, the fact that individual soldiers were also complicit, and that such complicity meant, among other things, involvement in the Holocaust, remains strong, as was clearly seen in the uproar against the exhibition on the crimes of the Wehrmacht in 1999.[4] Popular military historians of the Second World War still dislike this notion, perhaps because it takes the glory and the "pity" out of the war, making for a less compelling story, where one side is disproportionately more evil than the other, thereby depriving the final end of a more edifying sense of tragedy, since we can no longer pity the defeated enemy but, in fact, rejoice that he is finally smitten. For Germans, of course, it is still difficult to accept that not just those very distant relatives who might have served in the SS and the Gestapo were involved in crimes but also possibly their closer kin, until recently considered proud or at least decent Wehrmacht soldiers who fought bravely for their country even as the Nazis were committing crimes behind their backs, and then fell heroically or survived wretchedly as victims of Hitler's reckless policies.

In 1979, when I was studying German at the Goethe Institute in Murnau, Bavaria, I befriended my German teacher, Herr Hülsen, who had fought and lost a leg on the Eastern Front as a member of the 18th Panzer Division, a formation I subsequently researched and wrote on. My teacher, to be sure, never spoke about war crimes, nor did the chronicle of his formation, which he kindly gifted me, stray from providing a straightforward military history of the division's battles, stressing that these brave and tough Panzer troops "never wanted to go there." Similarly, in the few passages of the textbook we used in that German language school—funded by the German Academic Exchange Service—that mentioned the war, only one line referred to the "persecution of the Jews" by the Nazi regime. At the top of the page was a photo not of Germany's victims but rather of the bombed-out city of Cologne, its famed cathedral towering over miles of flattened houses. A couple of years later, as a student at Oxford, I read Martin Broszat's book, *The Hitler State*, which was then seen as a fundamental functionalist interpretation of the workings of the Third Reich. It took me many more years to realize that this book, too, contained merely one paragraph on the Holocaust. By then I was also discovering that the many books on the Second World War I had read as a teenager and student said virtually nothing about the genocide of the Jews, let alone the army's participation in it, and that such terms as extermination, Holocaust, Shoah, and mass murder featured nowhere in their indices, whereas Jews were only occasionally mentioned, often fleetingly, as was also the case, to cite one cinematic classic—often wrongly thought to be about the Holocaust—in Alain Resnais's 1956 *Night and Fog*.

In December 1987, just eight years after my encounter with Herr Hülsen, I was teaching as an assistant professor of history at Tel Aviv University, when the first Intifada—the Palestinian uprising in the occupied West Bank—broke out. I had returned to Israel four years earlier, having completed my DPhil at Oxford and eager to reunite with my friends and family. My first book on what I called the "barbarization of warfare" on the Eastern Front of the Second World War, which followed several important studies by German scholars on the topic, was published in 1985.[5] It differed from previous works in that it provided a history "from below," focusing on the men at the front rather than the generals and politicians in the rear. As a young reserve officer, I could expect to be called up to crush the uprising. The defense minister at the time, retired General Yitzhak Rabin, called on the troops in the occupied territories facing stone-throwing Palestinian youths to "break their bones," which young Israeli soldiers all too often took quite literally.

My Twisted Path to Auschwitz, and Back

There were a number of protests against this brutality. One postcard, which opponents of this policy were expected to sign and send to Rabin, described the case of a Palestinian boy who was hauled into a military police jeep and then thrown to the ground while the vehicle was moving, which caused his death. Enraged by this story, I used the empty space on the postcard to tell Rabin that I had recently written about the barbarization of the German army and that under his leadership the Israel Defense Forces (IDF) were in danger of undergoing their own process of brutalization.

I had no expectation of receiving a response from Rabin. But a couple of weeks later a letter from the Defense Ministry arrived in the mail. It contained only one line: "How dare you compare the IDF to the Wehrmacht?" Below that line was Rabin's own signature.[6] I had clearly touched a nerve. Rabin, it will be recalled, subsequently served as prime minister during the Oslo Accords and was assassinated in 1995 by a Jewish terrorist. The assassin had been influenced by an incitement campaign against Rabin led by Benjamin Netanyahu, in which Rabin was portrayed as a Nazi officer, a campaign that eventually propelled Netanyahu to his own premiership. But by then I was no longer living in Israel. I vividly recall watching a report of Rabin's assassination in the wake of a peace rally, with my six-month-old daughter on my lap; I was crying, not because of my love for Rabin but because I knew at that point that the oppression of the occupation he had led as minister of defense and the efforts he then made as prime minister to put a peaceful end to it had culminated in a tragedy for which Israeli Jews and Palestinians would pay the price for generations to come.

I had left Israel before being called up. This was partly coincidence and partly intentional. I had no inclination to break Palestinian bones. I also did not particularly want to spend time in jail for refusing orders, especially after the birth of my first child, in March 1988. My salary was so meager that I could not afford to go to any academic conferences, and I was spending long hours translating trashy novels into Hebrew just to make ends meet. Hence, when I was offered a three-year fellowship at Harvard's Society of Fellows, there was very little to deliberate; it felt like manna from heaven. An extended period of time away from the noise and the rage, the heat, and the rocks, from scraping together pennies and spending sweaty nights on the porch typing on a primitive computer—what was there to think about? For the first time in my life, I was told that everything would be taken care of—an office, a computer, housing, meals, health insurance—just so long as I would do what I had always wanted to do: read, research, and write. It was literally incredible.

I spent the next three years doing just that. I also discovered that I could have a career in the United States, and never returned to Tel Aviv University. It was the distance, the serenity, the quiet, that opened me up and began removing the barriers I had never known existed. One such barrier, which ended up consuming much of my subsequent career, was the Holocaust. As a historian, before leaving Israel, what had troubled me most about people's attitudes toward the Holocaust was its frequent invocation, on the one hand, and the general ignorance of its history, on the other. People did not truly bother to learn what had happened there, but nonetheless drew very firm conclusions from what they believed it meant. While this was also part of a more general cultural trait in Israel—where strong opinion often remains immune to facts and listening to others—in the case of the Holocaust this attitude resulted more directly both from its overwhelming yet largely silent presence, and from the intimate familial links so many had to those who either perished there or had somehow survived. Trained in Britain within a firmly empirical tradition, according to which one had to maintain a critical distance from the object of inquiry and rely heavily on documentary archival evidence, I believed that, at least while in Israel, I would never be able to write on the Holocaust, nor, it seemed to me, ever wish to do so.

That does not mean that either I or other members of my generation managed to retain this distance from the events that had taken place just before we were born. In my case, as in that of several other friends and colleagues, this awareness invaded our consciousness not as historical knowledge but in the form of fiction and imagination. Hence, during my last two years of teaching in Israel I published two short novels that sought to explore this treacherous terrain between fantasies of the Holocaust and the traumas of the wars we had experienced. Based on my personal recollections both as a soldier in the IDF and as a researcher in Germany, these early novels were part of a larger literary trend of not only transition to a new generation of Hebrew-language writers, but also, within my own age group, transition from an awareness of being the first generation of Israelis to one of being a second generation to the Holocaust, and the complex relationship between the two.[7]

Yet upon arriving in the United States, following several attempts that led nowhere, I decided to abandon fiction-writing altogether. In part this had to do with my realization that if I were to survive and thrive in the much more professional American academic environment, I needed to focus on scholarship. But it is also possible that I was increasingly dawn into a field of inquiry that subsumed all my intellectual energies even before I was entirely willing to admit that to myself. Shortly after publishing my second monograph in 1991,[8] I was asked to write a review essay on several recent books about the Holocaust. Until that time I had not written anything directly on that topic, viewing myself solely as a German and social–military historian. While my books dealt with crimes committed by the Wehrmacht, which naturally included Jewish victims as well, their focus was on the murder of Red Army soldiers and Soviet citizens, the vast majority of whom were not Jews. And while the German war machine had certainly facilitated the implementation of the final solution, it was not, for the most part, directly involved in that particular and most extreme form of German crimes, which after the fact came to be designated as genocide. But because the journal that requested this essay was a prestigious scholarly venue, and because the books it proposed for review appeared interesting, I took up the challenge and, indeed, asked to include several additional books that had come out at the time.[9]

Only when I began writing the essay did I realize that while I had spent years suppressing my interest in—nay, fascination with—the Holocaust, I had in fact been reading and thinking about it since my youth. This was an important insight, revealing to me that even the most empirical and rational historian is also constantly working with and influenced by a set of unconscious layers of knowledge and perceptions. Specifically,

My Twisted Path to Auschwitz, and Back

I now grasped that at the core of my own scholarly intellectual endeavors, whether in academic writing or in fiction, I had always sought to understand the relationship between the human motivation to perpetrate violence and its parallel yet contradictory urge to reassert individual and collective humaneness.

The 1990s were the heyday of the "new military history," writing on the Holocaust, and a preoccupation with history and memory. Toward the end of this period a new trend of comparative genocide developed, which built on and competed with the scholarship on the Holocaust. Yet the more I became engaged with these larger questions regarding the cultural, social, military, political, and ideological context of mass murder in the twentieth century, the more I began to feel that I was losing touch with the immediate documentation of events and increasingly veering toward theoretical assertions and generalizations; even more urgently, I felt that the human individuals subjected to these larger trends, the protagonists of these events, were coming out of focus and gradually disappearing.

I recall in particular a 1992 conference in London on the origins of the final solution, in which many of the most distinguished scholars of the Holocaust at the time debated at length various interpretations of when and under what circumstances the decision on the mass murder of the Jews was made. I came out of that conference feeling morally deflated because, while intellectually these debates were intriguing, my sense was that they had entirely omitted the "end product" of that decision, the endless individual horror of mass murder. Not only were the perpetrators often missing from many of these generally "functionalist" interpretations of the time, even the victims were largely nowhere to be found.[10]

Throughout my years in the United States, I also spent lengthy periods in Israel, keeping abreast of academic and intellectual developments there. I came to realize that whereas the "international" scholarship on the Holocaust, particularly in Europe and the United States, was increasingly drawn to the larger questions of context, origins, and interpretations, Israeli scholarship, although it was influenced and at times awed by these international trends, remained largely focused on the Jewish aspect of the Holocaust and resistant to contextualization and comparison.[11]

This was, of course, increasingly related to the growing politicization of the Holocaust in Israel, which transitioned from eliciting silence and embarrassment in the 1950s to providing an opportunity for national assertion and self-justification since the 1980s. Prime Minister David Ben-Gurion had orchestrated the Eichmann trial in the early 1960s (after initially resisting it) as an opportunity to teach young Israelis about the core reason for the creation of the state; Prime Minister Menahem Begin opined in 1982 that Yasser Arafat was hiding in Beirut like Adolf Hitler in his Berlin bunker; and under Prime Minister Benjamin Netanyahu, the ceremonial visits to Yad Vashem by all foreign heads of state coming to Israel were geared to underscore that the Jewish state would do "all it takes" to prevent another Holocaust, that "the world" was eternally guilty of silence or collaboration, and that any criticism of Israeli policies of occupation and oppression was akin to anti-Semitism and a desire to destroy the Jewish people. In contemporary Israel the Holocaust has become a cardinal component of identity and politics.[12]

Israeli historians of the Holocaust are generally not part of this radical political discourse. But for them, and for their students, the Holocaust is Jewish history; non-Jews are often relevant only insofar as they played a role in its perpetration, whether as collaborators, rescuers, or passive bystanders.[13] Traveling frequently from the United States to Israel, I increasingly found both the emerging "international" view of the Holocaust and the Israeli Judeocentric perspective insufficient. In a sense, both marginalized or ghettoized the actual events of mass murder as they occurred and were experienced by thousands of communities, especially in Eastern Europe, where most of the Jews had lived and were murdered.

In other words, whereas moving to the United States had, for the first time, made it possible for me to research, write, and teach about the Holocaust, it was my sustained link to Israel and my ability to feel comfortable—though never entirely at home—in both academic and intellectual environments that alerted me to what I saw as the limits and deficits of both approaches, and enabled me to maintain a critical distance from both. It was precisely at that time, in the mid-1990s, just after the fall of communism and two ensuing genocides—in Bosnia and Rwanda, where people often slaughtered their own neighbors—that I began conceptualizing a different approach to studying the Holocaust. What I sought was to analyze the genocide of the Jews as part of a much larger pattern of communal violence and mass murder, while also contextualizing the local slaughter of a single community within the larger history of interethnic relations, rather than only as an instance of the encounter between external perpetrators and local Jews.

For those engaged in the larger questions surrounding the decision on the final solution or the bureaucracy of modern genocide, such a local study, I believed, would potentially illustrate the manner in which policies of genocide were worked out "below"—namely, how even the most bureaucratic and sophisticated genocidal apparatus ultimately came to be engaged in bloody, one-on-one slaughter. For those focused on the Holocaust as a Jewish event, this local perspective might show that in thousands of towns similar to the one that I spent the next twenty years researching, there were numerous non-Jewish neighbors who were neither victims of the Nazi genocide nor simply bystanders, but rather active social agents in their communities, whose engagement ranged from full collaboration with the perpetrators to the rescue of Jewish friends, colleagues, and strangers. Moreover, this "view from below" could demonstrate that, in fact, the notion of the shtetl as a purely Jewish town had always been a mere figment of Jewish lore and fiction: that all the towns where Jews had lived and were murdered were multiethnic communities in which Jews and Christians of various ethnicities had lived side-by-side for centuries, mostly peacefully albeit never harmoniously.

My local study of the Holocaust taught me a great deal about the intimacy of genocide, the complex interaction between Jewish victims, Gentile neighbors, and German perpetrators, and the links between the violence of the German occupation and that of the preceding and subsequent Soviet rule. I found that during that extended period violence and brutality became so commonplace and ubiquitous that they constituted a part of people's daily routine, even as the roles of victim and perpetrator were reversed more than once and bystanders largely disappeared from view. Finally, I became aware that this history had more or less vanished from the local scene in which these events had occurred and had been given at best short shrift by historians.

This in turn led me to understand that in reconstructing local genocide, one cannot begin at the moment of the killing but must go back in time to understand the complex web of relations that culminated in massacre. This is true for the Holocaust as it is for many other genocides. We need to reconstruct the shared lives of our protagonists before they began killing and dying if we are to understand what it was that triggered the bloodshed. That is, we need to look for motivation as part of the historical context, in the culture, norms, traditions, and beliefs, as well as ideologies, of the individuals involved. To be sure, the Holocaust, even in such remote towns as Buczacz, is also, perhaps primarily, a German story. The Germans came, saw, and murdered. But without local participation, including killing, identifying, denouncing, and rescuing, this would have been a very different story.

While researching that town, I traveled a great deal to West Ukraine, and was repeatedly struck by the visible, yet vanishing, remains of a previous Jewish civilization that had been wiped out by the Nazis and their collaborators. There were skeletal shells of synagogues, filled with wild vegetation or garbage; there were cemeteries, from which the most usable tombstones had been removed, while the weeds growing around the remaining stumps served as fodder for grazing cows and goats led by local Ukrainian boys and girls; there were unmarked mass graves, at times eclipsed by memorials to Ukrainian martyrs and freedom fighters; and there was a glaring absence of any direct reference to the Jews who had previously inhabited these towns, or to the manner of their murder.

In 2007 I published a book about the erasure of Jewish memory from Galicia and the post-communist West Ukrainian politics of memory.[14] But in the back of my mind there was another erased memory, one that had not surfaced in my consciousness since my childhood. As I wondered what the current Ukrainian inhabitants of former Jewish homes thought about those remaining symbols of a culture and a civilization that had once existed in their midst, I was reminded of my own childhood in 1950s and 1960s Tel Aviv. I recalled playing at a site we called Jamusin (al-Jammasin al-Gharbi) in north Tel Aviv, and later, after moving to Ramat Aviv—just north of the Yarkon River, adjacent to and now mostly occupied by Tel Aviv University—playing cops and robbers on a hill we knew as Sheikh Munis (al-Shaykh Muwannis). Both were sites of "abandoned" Palestinian villages. There was a Muslim cemetery there, and sabra fences that surrounded the homes from which the inhabitants had been driven out, making a sharp contrast with the trees and lawns of the new Jewish neighborhood below. The cemetery is mostly gone by now, its tombstones removed to make room for a new student dormitory complex; what little remains of it is overlooked by a somewhat sinister building housing the Israeli General Security Service, the Shabak.[15]

All this made me think increasingly about that other black hole of my generation's childhood and upbringing. The Holocaust and the Diaspora have resurfaced, of course, even if often in a politicized and mobilized (or as often described today, weaponized) Zionist version. But that other black hole—the removal of the Palestinian population to make room for us—is still absorbing those flickers of light that occasionally flare up in an attempt not merely to expose what had once been but also to facilitate new thinking on what can still be.

It was this barely self-evident link, between my study of the erasure of Jewish existence and memory in Eastern Europe and the surfacing consciousness of the erasure of Palestinian existence and memory in Israel, that ironically facilitated my own partial return from the Diaspora. "What you see from there, you can't see from here," in the words of a well-known Israeli song. But once you have seen it, once that long journey across the ocean has opened your eyes, refreshed your memory, dispelled the fog of obfuscation and ideology, you can either remain a distant, albeit perhaps critical and keen observer, or you can, perhaps must, engage with the reality that had always been there and was never acknowledged with anything more than, at best, a shrug.

Historians know perhaps better than others that history never repeats itself and that what was can never be again: we can study the past—indeed, we must—but we cannot reverse it. In the Diaspora you must accept that once you have left, you will never return, however many times you come back. But that very transition is part of a process of learning and understanding. As a historian, you are always striving to visit that other country that is the past, knowing that you can only stay there temporarily, cannot tamper with its rules and regulations, and must always reemerge in your own time and place. And yet, once you have left the present and delved into the past, you will never fully return, however often you may come back. You live in the twilight of time, rooted in neither the past nor the present, neither the home you left nor the home you make. And from that vantage point, precarious and unstable though it may be, you may gain glimpses of those flashes of light that time and oblivion are constantly threatening to snuff out. Perhaps it is also time to return to fiction.[16]

CHAPTER 11
BUILDING THE FUTURE BY TELLING THE PAST

Origins and Oblivion

In his vast posthumous biography of Buczacz—his hometown and, as he depicted it, the symbol of East European Jewry—the Hebrew writer and Nobel Prize laureate Shmuel Yosef Agnon spins a lengthy tale of the town's mythical origins: "When was our city founded, and who was its founder?" he asks. "Long have all the chroniclers labored to find this out in vain. But some few facts have been revealed to us," continues Agnon, possibly tongue-in-cheek, since he was famous for his fine sense of irony, "and I am herewith setting down a faithful record of all I know." As he relates it, "there was once a band of Jews who were moved by their own pure hearts to go up to the Land of Israel, together with their wives and their sons and their daughters." But they did not know the way, only that they should head to the east, and "as they proceeded, people became scarce, vineyards and fields vanished, and all the roads led through forests that never seemed to end." Finally, they had to stop for the Jewish High Holidays. And while they camped, a fierce East European winter arrived, and they had no choice but to remain there.

Then one day "they found themselves surrounded by strange people," with "huge and fearsome dogs at their heels and great trumpets to their lips." As it turned out, these were local noblemen who were out hunting. Responding to one of the lords' queries, the Jews "told him their whole story," and "in such detail that the noblemen were struck by their cleverness and eloquence. So enchanted were they," writes Agnon, that "they urged the Jews to live with them, at least until the end of winter." And once the Jews agreed, the "noblemen who had taken the Jews into their homes enjoyed prosperity in whatever they did," and asked the Jews to stay, telling them, "the whole land is yours; make your home wherever you like. If you want to engage in commerce in the land, better yet, for no one here knows anything about commerce." The Jews debated the matter among themselves, agreeing that "to leave where they were and to go to the Land of Israel was out of the question; for by now, they had acquired property in the land and built houses and were in favor with the nobility." And so, "after much discussion, they agreed unanimously to establish a permanent house of prayer." Soon, "the local nobleman built himself a stone house," and later "he built a castle up on the mountain facing the Strypa river," and "that is how Buczacz began." The Jews "dwelled for many generations in security and tranquility, except for years of war and revolution … until the Enemy came and eradicated them all."[1]

The story told by Agnon is more than a legend; it is, in many ways, the distilled version of what generations of Jews living in the vast territories of what was once the Polish-Lithuanian Commonwealth—stretching from the German lands and the Carpathian Mountains to east of the Dnieper, and from the Baltic almost all the way to the Black Sea—had told themselves about where they had come from and where they were heading. Polin, as the Jews called Poland, was interpreted as the Hebrew words "poh lin," or "here we shall dwell," or "stay overnight." There is an inner logic to this tale, for it both establishes origins and indicates the goal. Just as the Jews had founded Jewish Buczacz, or rather the Jewish civilization of Eastern Europe, so too, after their destruction, their remnants were to be naturally gathered by God in the Land of Israel, their eternal object of pilgrimage and their final resting place.[2]

Agnon's 1939 novel, *A Guest for the Night*, as we saw in Chapter 8, is based on the author's last visit to Buczacz in 1930. The protagonist is now a guest in his own hometown, and while in reality this visit, which occurred twenty-two years after Agnon left Buczacz at age twenty-one, lasted only a week, in the novel it stretches for an entire year. Neither Agnon nor his protagonist just stay overnight, but nevertheless neither of them returns. The title, of course, alludes to the entire conceptual edifice of temporality: the unresolvable conflict between home and temporary abode. How can one think of the landscape of one's youth as a site that one had merely passed through, in the same way that a refugee child born en route from the ancestral home to a new place of refuge might imagine the sights its eyes perceived when they first opened? And how does one reimagine a place of refuge as a homeland, even if its sights are foreign and exotic, its smells, sounds, people, and language strange and unfamiliar? Can one in fact leave one's homeland, hometown, or just one's home, and ever come home to another place and be at home there?

Agnon, who made his home for a while in Jaffa, and then, after a long sojourn in Germany, finally settled down in Jerusalem for the rest of his life, did not write about the origins of Jerusalem, or of the land of Israel, and definitely not of Jaffa.[3] The tale of origins was about Buczacz, the real hometown; and yet, a hometown imagined as a transitory space, a stop for the night on the way to Eretz Israel that lasted four centuries and ended up in the massacre of its entire Jewish population. He writes:

> This is the chronicle of the city of Buczacz, which I have written in my pain and anguish so that our descendants should know that our city was full of Torah, wisdom, love, piety, life, grace, kindness and charity from the time of its founding until the arrival of the blighted abomination and their befouled and deranged accomplices who wrought destruction upon it.[4]

This is how Agnon opens his "biography" of Buczacz and how, some seven hundred pages later, he closes it, recalling the day he heard of the destruction of his hometown. Living in Jerusalem, the holy city, which was his destination, and where indeed he had made his home, he is beset by endless sorrow for the universe, the town, and the home he had lost, and feels completely alone and cut off from his roots. He tries to remember the words of a poem whispered to him in a vision by the apparition of the great eleventh-century Andalusian poet, Rabbi Solomon Ibn Gabirol, "each line of which began with one of the letters of the name of my town." He thinks:

> Were it not for remembering the poem, I would have been like all my townsfolk, who were lost, who had died at the hand of despicable people, those who trampled my people until they were no longer a nation. It was because of the power of the poem that my soul went out of me. And if my town has been wiped out of the world, it remains alive in the poem that the poet wrote as a sign of my city.

Yet the words are lost:

> To whom shall I now turn who can tell me the words of the song? To the old cantor who knew all the hymns of the holy poets? I alone remain to shed their tears. The old cantor rests in the shadow of the holy poets, who recite their hymns in the Great Synagogue of our city ... But here—here there is only a song of mourning, lamentation, and wailing, for the city and its dead.[5]

Agnon filled that void of forgetting with his vast collection of stories about Buczacz. In the wake of the destruction, as the modern State of Israel was being built over the remnants of Palestinian civilization, Agnon engaged in another act of construction. Asked by the critic Baruch Kurzweil about his new literary endeavor, Agnon replied: "I am building a city."[6]

The city he built, a literary edifice that has taken long to be recognized as a masterpiece and is still unknown to many Hebrew readers familiar with Agnon's prewar works, is not merely a monument to the Jewish civilization of Eastern Europe encapsulated in his hometown and destroyed by the Nazis, it is also an extraordinary mélange of historical fact and fiction, fantasy and imagination, deep research and erudition and keen psychological insight. One central insight is that while Buczacz, as representative of the Jewish Diaspora in Eastern Europe, was the heart of Jewish existence, at the same time its own heart was elsewhere. It was there in Poland that it was formed, yet part of its very being was a profound sense of not-quite-being in place. The Jews—who did not in fact build the city of Buczacz—come as guests of the noblemen on their way elsewhere, and are delayed merely by practical matters, which keep them there for close to half a millennium.[7]

But when they eventually come to where they were going, even though they are not welcome guests and are as foreign to that new landscape as they were to the old, they know that they have come home. Yet that home is inhabited by others, just as the home they left behind is taken over by others. The indigenous populations of the lands of the forests, the Poles and the Ukrainians, had always seen the Jews as guests and, with the rise of nationalism, as increasingly less welcome guests. Now, as the Jews come to their home, they declare the indigenous population of that land foreign to it, and themselves, the newcomers, as its rightful owners. As a people that had spent much of its historical existence in a condition of imagined transition, they can imagine the Arab population too as transitory, in the land but not of it, no matter how long it had actually lived there. Its origins, like those of the Jews, lie elsewhere, and it is to that other place that they belong.[8]

Yet, for the generation of such men as Agnon, the heart of Jewish civilization remained behind in that world destroyed by the enemy; it remained there, on the margins of his consciousness, like the words of the poem that bring the city back to life but which he cannot remember. As for the generations that come after, those born into the new land, their literal homeland, they have no memory at all of that other world, and by their sheer birth and faith are normalized as the indigenous population of the land. Having forgotten not only the words of the poem but its very existence and all that it symbolized, they are bereft of the civilization that made their own existence a hope and a dream. They do not know that they are the last link in a long chain and imagine themselves as newly made, as the originators of it all. They reside in their own myth of creation oblivious to the origins of their very existence. They thus claim a right to a place based on a history of faith and tradition of which they know nothing; all that is left to them is their indigeneity, which is by definition newer and more tenuous that that of those they had displaced. Hence it must be backed up with fire and sword.[9]

Agnon's own creation myth of Buczacz is, of course, largely divorced from the historical record, and he must have been as aware of that as anyone who has studied this complex interethnic world subjected to many rulers and regimes. The city, in brief, was not founded by Jews. But in another sense Buczacz, and innumerable cities like it, did become a city because of the Jews, and ceased to be one when they were murdered. The violence that made for the destruction of those cities was just as deeply embedded in assertions of origins as were the fantastic tales of pristine beginnings. The Jews were hardly alone in seeing themselves as the originators of it all. In this imaginary genealogy of origins, the nationalized peasants lay claim to being the indigenous population; the Poles, who literally owned the city, imagined themselves as carrying out a grand civilizing mission; and the Jews confidently saw themselves as those who made it all happen, the commercial, managerial, financial engine that made medieval castles and estates into cities and constituted the bourgeoisie that put an end to the feudalism of nobles and serfs. But if the Ukrainians said the town was theirs because they were there first, and the Poles said it was theirs because they had built it, the Jews conceded that they had not only wandered in from elsewhere but were also, in fact, on their way to another destination. Hence they did not belong in their town, even though they were the majority of its citizens.[10]

Agnon left Buczacz in 1908 and settled down in Jaffa. David Ben-Gurion, the founding father of modern Israel, had come to Jaffa two years earlier, but since to his taste it was too dirty and too full of Arabs, he spent his first night in Eretz Israel in the Jewish settlement of Petah Tikva; thirty years later he wrote in his diary that Jaffa, the city he had always detested, should be torn down.[11] Agnon, for his part, wrote some of his early stories in Jaffa and described it with much more compassion and eventual nostalgia. Unlike his fellow townsfolk, who served as grist to his literary mill for many years thereafter, he had continued on that mythical journey to the East and reached their purported destination. But like Ben-Gurion, for Agnon the Land of Israel was a place of origins in the sense that it was naturally and indisputably his to settle in. He eventually built himself a house in Jerusalem and lived in that city for the rest of his life. He was never troubled by the relationship to that land. In this mythical tale of origins, which he never told, he had come home and was part and parcel of the great return of the Jewish people to its homeland. In his writing, however, the soul and spirit of Jewish civilization was elsewhere: in Buczacz, Podolia, Galicia, that land in which the Jews had stopped for a rest on the way to their place of origins and where they remained until they were murdered. For Agnon, the extinction of East European Jewry was the assassination of the essence of Jewish existence.

The Jaffa in which Agnon lived in his early years and the Jerusalem in which he spent the rest of his life were cities filled with Arabs. But for Agnon, with his European clothes and Galician mannerism, his coming home to Palestine, to the land of the birth of the Jewish people, had nothing to do with the presence of hundreds of thousands of Palestinian townspeople and villagers. The claim of origins here did not need a mythical tale spun by an author—it was in the Bible and the myriad texts and prayers, poems, and lamentations that followed it. It was, essentially, ours. But as that home was built, as modern tenements went up and cities sprouted, that other population was pushed out ever more to the margins of awareness and existence. The Jews in Palestine imagined themselves as the majority even though they were a minority, just as the Jews of Buczacz were seen as a minority even though they were the majority. Long before Agnon began building his city—the Buczacz whose Jews had been murdered—other concrete cities were displacing the Arab population that surrounded him in Israel. Within the span of a few years, Jews were no longer the majority or substantial minority in Eastern Europe's cities; indeed, in most cases they were entirely gone. And almost simultaneously in historical time, the Jews of Palestine were transformed from a minority into a majority: their own population tripled thanks to mass emigration of survivors from Europe and refugees from the Middle East and North Africa, and the Arab population was reduced by three-quarters with the expulsion of 750,000 Palestinians in 1948.[12]

Yet traces of that other tale of origins remained, visible to anyone who wished to look, in abandoned villages, untended groves, cactus fences, and neglected cemeteries. These material, tactile origins of the land challenged the Jewish story of return home, the home that was said to be indisputably the origin of it all, the very beginning of everything, entirely and absolutely theirs, by covenant with God and through the sword of Joshua. These troubling reminders of another story, of other origins, had to be removed. And so they were demolished, four hundred villages, pulled down, planted over, and erased from maps and memory.[13] And in Buczacz, in 2001, the last remaining Jewish house, *beit hamidrash* in which Agnon used to pray as he looked out to Fedor Hill, where in 1943 half of the Jewish community was murdered and buried in mass graves, was also demolished and replaced by a modern shopping mall. There is now a street in Buczacz called Vulitsa Agnona, where a new bust of the famous writer stands. The plaque boasts that this little provincial town had produced a Nobel Prize laureate, but it never mentions that he was

Jewish and wrote in Hebrew. In this story of origins, Agnon has become Ukrainian, just as Bruno Schultz, the great writer and artist of nearby Drohobycz, was claimed decades after his murder to be a Polish writer by the Poles, an inhabitant of West Ukraine by Ukrainians, and a Jewish victim of the Holocaust by Yad Vashem.[14]

To each his origins and oblivion; and yet, even as the cold wind howls over the mass graves and through the skeletons of synagogues in Ukraine, and as the sun burns down upon the scars left by Israeli bulldozers and demolition crews, the scattered sabra fences and broken terraces, the tales and myths, the memories and remnants of the past refuse to go away, each claiming their right to have once existed, to be remembered and respected. For all these tales of origins appear to have always had deep within them the seeds of their own ruin and erasure:

> I belong there. I have memories. I was born as everyone is born.
> I have a mother, a house with many windows, brothers, friends, and a prison cell
> With a chilly window! I have a wave snatched by seagulls, a panorama of my own.
> I have a saturated meadow. In the deep horizon of my word, I have a moon,
> A bird's sustenance, and an immortal olive tree.
> I have lived on the land long before swords turned man into prey.
> I belong there. When heaven mourns for her mother, I return heaven to her mother.
> And I cry so that a returning cloud might carry my tears.
> To break the rules, I have learned all the words needed for a trial by blood.
> I have learned and dismantled all the words in order to draw from them a *single word*: Home.[15]
>
> Mahmoud Darwish, *I Belong There*

Erasure and Memory

Is it possible to build a new world without uncovering the crimes and misdemeanors of the past, by drafting a future-oriented agenda geared as much to erasing the past as to constructing the future? Repressed pasts rarely go away; eventually they will resurface in an altered form but with no less ferocity. This is why workable futures must be anchored in their origins instead of detaching themselves from them, however difficult the confrontation with events leading to the present may be. Suffice it to think of the complex and often tragic history of Eastern Europe and Russia, to recognize the price that was paid by building the world of tomorrow—now so hopelessly lodged in the past—on the ruins of yesterday—now the focus of so much, often misdirected, nostalgia. As I write this, the misuse of a past that has never been properly worked though is employed to justify Russia's brutal invasion of Ukraine, with the Kremlin claiming to be refighting the Great Patriotic War against Nazism. The glorification of that war in the former Soviet Union and now the Russian Federation was never accompanied by a coming to terms with the crimes of Stalinism. In Ukraine, which has made important steps on the path to democracy and civil society, an inability to come to terms with the complicity of Ukrainian nationalists in the crimes of Nazism has left it more vulnerable to specious Russian claims of the need to denazify a state led by a Jewish president.

There are always those who believe that by entirely eradicating the past they can look forward without ever looking back. This may be another way of saying that history is always written by the victors. But this aphorism is neither always true nor does it tell us much about the nature of victory. For we can also say that the road to Hades is paved with forgetting, and that civilizations become sterile not because they glance back at their path out of hell but because they refuse to do so.

Since the turn of the last century, the vast swath of territory stretching from the Baltic to the Balkans has been the site of an extraordinary exercise in destruction and reconstruction. Within the context of such "population policies" entire peoples were murdered, deported, ethnically cleansed, and resettled. The borders of nations were made and remade; cultures have vanished; languages have disappeared; identity has been defined and redefined.[16]

Following the collapse of the Soviet Union and the toppling of communism in Eastern Europe, both the new and the old nations of the region have been engaged in creating a new future, distinct from the socialist future they have left behind. As they have striven to join the European Union—whose very identity is based on a renunciation of its constituent members' nationalist legacies—they have also engaged with their own national roots, long suppressed by communism. They have been preoccupied not only with assigning the revolutionary rhetoric of the past to the dustbin of history but also with erasing recollections of recent affiliations and complicity.

But at the same time, these new/old nations must do what all nations have done: define their national identity and anchor it in history, the midwife of modern nationalism. Ironically, then, the entry of the newly independent East European states into the new European Union of states that have overtly given up many attributes of their national identity entails first asserting such identity and only then agreeing to subject it to the larger category of a united of Europe, a process which, as we have seen, for instance, in the cases of Hungary and Poland, can hardly be said to have worked smoothly.[17]

Indeed, this is a difficult exercise, complicated by the fact that it is largely based on an invented past, from which much of its complexity—some would also say richness, but, in any case, diversity—has been expunged. It is erased in word and representation, rewritten history, and new rhetoric, but it was also initially physically obliterated by means of genocide, ethnic cleansing, and deportations. Thus the entry into a supposed multicultural and diverse European community was dependent—or was made dependent—upon massive forgetting of one's own past diversity as multiethnic and multireligious societies and cultures.[18]

To some extent it can be argued that this is a necessary process on the way to normalizing one's relationship with the past, with one's neighbors, and with a projected or recreated future. But the question is, to what extent can populations be reeducated into tolerance, acceptance of other cultures, traditions, religions, faiths, or even physical appearance and manners of dress, speech, and conduct, if they set out with a highly impoverished and distorted view of their own past, that is, if they do not confront both their own history of diversity and their complicity in its eradication. Let us remember, for instance, that only two-thirds of interwar Poland's population were ethnic Poles, and 10 percent were Jews; that most towns in present-day West Ukraine and Belarus were inhabited primarily by Jews and Poles; that Vilnius was a city in which Polish and Yiddish were spoken and Lithuanian hardly known; that much of the intelligentsia of Prague and Czernowitz (Chernivtsi) spoke German and was either Jewish or ethnic German.[19]

As I traveled in the former Eastern Galicia in the first two decades of the present century, I was repeatedly struck by the extent to which the new Ukrainian nationalism in this region was basing itself on the erasure of its own multicultural or multiethnic past, creating thereby a culturally impoverished and historically distorted society amid the ruins of what had existed there before. I was also increasingly aware of some of the consequences of such an undertaking from my own native land of Israel, where I was born as a result of the departure of my mother's family from Galicia in the mid-1930s, and where the remnants of a former Arab Palestinian culture and life had been thoroughly erased. To be sure, we can no longer turn back the clock. But we can also not expect to build a healthy culture and society on the basis of unacknowledged erasure. Just as the states of Eastern Europe must come to terms with the richness of a past that was purged and destroyed, so too Israel will never become a normal society without acknowledging the wrongs it perpetrated on the Palestinians. Societies that erase the past do not neglect history; on the contrary, they are obsessed with it. But they tend to be obsessed with a history of conflict, bloodshed, and subjugation, where they are the victims—and heroes—and the others are the perpetrators and villains. It is a history that justifies erasure rather than fills in the gaps. States can reach political compromises, sign treaties, and even provide restitution.[20] But without incorporating into their own culture and identity their whole, full, rich past, replete with catastrophe and mayhem just as much as with creativity and diversity, any exercise in democratization and liberalization is likely to be hampered by xenophobia, racism, and authoritarianism.

Let us then set out on two brief journeys to sites where remembrance of their past inhabitants, removed through murder and ethnic cleansing, can contribute to historical reconciliation and cultural enrichment. Whereas repressing this past also impoverishes the present, recalling those who had once inhabited these sites, respecting their culture, and acknowledging their loss and suffering may instill a deeper and more complex historical awareness in the current residents.

Buczacz—My Mother's Hometown

We come to Buczacz, situated by the Strypa River, a tributary of the Dniester, about a hundred miles southeast of Lviv (Lwów, Lvov, Lemberg), by way of the smaller neighboring town of Potok Złoty (Zolotyi Potik), where my mother spent the first year of her life.[21] In June 2004, when I visited the Jewish cemetery in Potok Złoty, it was serving, as it has for many decades, as a meadow for the local goats. Some of its extraordinary tombstones were still standing, decorated with intricate carvings dating back several centuries. Others were piled up and ready to be carted off. Photographs shared with me in the intervening period reflect a similar condition. Some of the tombstones had been used to repair the staircase leading into the only standing part of the once grand and now ruined palace of the Polish noble Potocki clan that had owned the city, as well as for the steps and banister of a dilapidated prewar villa, now serving as the "Municipal Veterans Clinic." In the grove by the clinic a displaced tombstone was left on the ground, carved with the words: "The important virgin, Miss Leah, daughter of Israel, may her soul be gathered into the bundle of life."

I asked an old woman I saw at the cemetery whether she remembered my mother's family, but although she nodded vigorously, she could provide no more information. The yard of the simple farmhouse across from the derelict palace was another site of vicarious memories. Eight decades earlier my great-grandfather had been an estate manager for Count Potocki, and for all I knew it was precisely in that courtyard that my mother had lived before her parents moved to Buczacz. Had it not been for the upheavals that followed, I too might have been born there.

From Potok Złoty we drive along the Strypa river valley on a winding dirt road to Buczacz. This must be the same path that my great-grandfather traveled on by wagon when he went to the larger town's market to buy or sell goods. It is a very quiet and peaceful afternoon. Only the sound of the car's wheels rolling on the gravel disturbs the silence. The Strypa keeps flowing slowly to the Dniester, just as it did all those decades ago.

Present-day Buczacz, like all other towns in this region of West Ukraine, is ethnically almost completely homogeneous. Its memory of the past parallels its national and religious identity. While a few older inhabitants still remember the events of the war and can even recall some individual victims of the Holocaust, there is no collective memory of either the presence or the elimination of non-Ukrainians. Visitors to Buczacz will find no official indication of this city's rich Jewish past. The Great Synagogue, which can still be seen standing in a German aerial photograph taken in April 1944, is no more. There is no indication in town as to where it had once stood, but its location can be established from documents, recollections, old photographs, and maps. The site now serves as an open market.

For many years it remained unclear what had become of the massive structure, built in the local tradition of fortress synagogues, whose walls at the base are said to have been about 5 meters thick. Some people in town reported that its stones had been used to build the ungainly Soviet cinema that still stand nearby. But in March 2006 Oresta Synenka, a local resident of Buczacz, whose family moved to the city in 1945, related in an interview that her father had been employed in Buczacz as the foreman of a construction brigade until 1950. According to Synenka, the synagogue was part of an entire block of houses that had been heavily damaged—apparently in the last bout of fighting over the city in the late spring and summer of 1944—and the workers had to decide which houses to repair and which to demolish. "There was no sense in repairing the synagogue," she said, "so they demolished it. The work was done by 1950."[22]

The study house (Beit Hamidrash) adjacent to the Great Synagogue remained standing very close to the main city square and marketplace as late as 2001. It was then torn down, despite the protests of some Israeli tourists who happened to have been there at the time and took photographs of the bulldozer demolishing the structure. The study house is mentioned in many of the stories and novels written by the town's most illustrious son, Agnon. The Jewish cemetery on the Baszty Hill overlooking the town still contains many tombstones, including those of Agnon's father and mother. Over the years, the more recent tombstones have been periodically cleaned up and photographed by volunteers from the United States and Israel. Another largely overgrown part of the cemetery, located on the slope leading down to the city, contains stones dating back to 1587.[23]

Since the town municipality has put up no signs indicating the location of the cemetery, visitors must come equipped with prior knowledge of its whereabouts and history. In 2006 a small memorial was finally installed in an isolated spot over the mass grave behind the cemetery. Again, no sign leads to this shabbily constructed and only slightly raised slab of stone, which has since been damaged and is often covered with thick, thorny bushes. It took until 2017 and 2018 for an Israeli volunteer group and the European Jewish Cemeteries Initiative (ESJF) to thoroughly clear the cemetery, map and record the tombstones, and surround it with fence for the first time since the destruction of its Jewish community.[24]

The handsome Gymnasium building in the town, built in the late nineteenth century in the Habsburg style, does carry a commemorative plaque. But this plaque is dedicated to the Ukrainian students arrested by the Soviet authorities there, making no mention of the numerous Jewish and Polish students deported or murdered during the Nazi occupation. The gymnasium is now named after Volodymyr Hnatiuk, an important figure in the revival of Ukrainian culture, who was born in Buczacz County in 1871 and worked closely with the writer Ivan Franko.[25] Although Simon Wiesenthal, who died at the ripe age of ninety-seven in 2005, and became internationally known as the "Nazi hunter," was born in Buczacz and attended the gymnasium in the 1920s, no mention is made of him there.[26]

Fedor Hill, where several unmarked mass graves contain the bodies of thousands of the town's former Jewish residents, is within easy walking distance from the main square. But without a local guide it would be extremely difficult to locate the site of the graves even if visitors had any prior knowledge of these events. As a few old photographs illustrate and survivors' testimonies record, a memorial was put up there immediately after the town's liberation, but it has long vanished, likely removed by the Soviet authorities. There is no indication in Buczacz of what had transpired on the hill, and no signposts leading one to the lone memorial at the site, a simple tombstone-sized edifice erected to commemorate the victims of the first killing of the Jewish intelligentsia. The inscription, written in Ukrainian, reads simply: "Here rest 450 people slain by the German executioners on August 27, 1941." The Star of David on the stone indicates the identity of these otherwise unnamed victims. Put up shortly after the liberation, this stone lay broken into two parts on the forest floor for most of the communist period. It was put up again in the 1990s thanks to Roman Antoshkiv, who was serving then in the town municipality and found the broken memorial, and the Jewish (but not Buczacz native) principal of the agricultural school on Fedor Hill, who provided cement and a tractor for this purpose.[27]

There is one impressive memorial on Fedor Hill—a large cross planted on a round mound of earth that can be seen from afar—but it is dedicated to the men of the Ukrainian Insurgent Army (UPA), many of whom had first helped the Germans murder the Jews and then engaged in the ethnic cleansing of the Polish population in the region, before finally resisting the returning Red Army.[28] At the bottom of the cross is a plaque that reads: "Glorious heroes who have fallen [in the struggle] for freedom; holy knights, hear this in your graves: We swear here, by your grave, to preserve the freedom of Ukraine." This postindependence memorial stands in competition to an older monument, erected during the Soviet regime, located elsewhere on the same hill. Featuring an oversized Red Army soldier, the monument is simply inscribed with the words "Eternal Memory to the Fallen Heroes," and the dates 1941–5, clearly indicating that it is about the Great Patriotic War of the Soviet Union against Nazi Germany and bears no links to—indeed refutes the legitimacy of—the Ukrainian struggle against the Soviets. One can safely assume that the cross attached to the side of the monument was added only after 1991.

Buczacz also contains now a museum for the UPA, situated in the former offices of the NKVD (the Soviet Secret Police) and put together in the early 1990s by the abovementioned same Oresta Synenka, who had worked there voluntarily as part of her self-appointed task of preserving the memory of Ukraine's local freedom fighters and victims of the NKVD, one of whom was her husband. Finally, another monument has been erected in the yard of St. Nicolas Greek Catholic Church, situated on a hill overlooking the town center. It is a simple wooden cross commemorating the sixtieth anniversary of the Holodomor, the Ukrainian famine of 1933. When I visited the site, there was a bouquet of fresh flowers at the foot of the cross.

For over seven decades after the end of the Second World War, almost every opportunity to commemorate Jewish life and death in Buczacz had been missed. No plaque was attached to the local police station and jail, though parts of it were renovated, to indicate that it had served to hold many of those who were subsequently led up the path to be shot on Fedor Hill. No plaque was put up at the Christian cemetery to commemorate the heroism of Mańko Szwierszczak, the undertaker who hid four Jews for almost two years in the cemetery.[29] The train station, from which some five thousand Jews were sent to Bełżec, carries no sign commemorating this horror. The railroad tunnel, blown up by the retreating Soviets in 1941, rebuilt by Jewish slave labor under the Nazis, and still used by freight trains to this day, bears no indication identifying these workers, most of whom were eventually shot. The site of the Jewish hospital, the most modern in the region before the Second World War, is now an empty lot without any mark of its past glory or the ghastly manner in which its Jewish patients were murdered by the Germans.[30]

During my early visits to Buczacz in the 2000s, the only site in town where a former Jewish presence was publicly, if indirectly, acknowledged was the humble museum in the main square. Here several glass cases containing books by Agnon, mostly donated by visiting Israeli tourists in 2001, made a somewhat ghostly appearance, in that no context was provided for the presence of this yarmulke-wearing, Hebrew language author in what is otherwise an almost purely Ukrainian town. However, the belated revelation of this former resident's celebrity stimulated the municipality to rename the street on which he had lived at the beginning of the twentieth century. An elaborate marble plaque that was put up at 5 Vulitsa Agnona in 2003 to commemorate the author's residence—a somewhat derelict tenement at that point—was apparently stolen soon thereafter. It was replaced by simpler, wood frame sign, which read: "In this house lived in 1888–1907 the writer, Nobel Prize laureate (1966) Shmuel Yosef Agnon (Czaczkes), July 17, 1888–February 17, 1970." Written only in Ukrainian, the plaque made no mention of the author's Jewish identity or the language in which he wrote.[31]

But in recent years a local initiative by Buczacz native Mariana Maksymiak has brought more attention to Agnon's works and legacy both in Buczacz and nationally in Ukraine. In 2016 a bust of Agnon was placed on a column in a small, redesigned square next to his family's former residence. The building itself now contains a new Agnon Literary Center, which has since hosted a number of Ukrainian writers, who commit to reading his novel *A Guest for the Night* as part of their week-long residence in the town (paralleling Agnon's stay there in 1930), and to produce stories inspired by his book and their own presence in Buczacz almost a century later. As of this writing, the current war in Ukraine has disrupted this impressive effort, which had also reached out to Israel and included a shared event at the Agnon House Museum and Center in Jerusalem. But it has already demonstrated the potential for forging new ties between the past and the present, and between Ukrainian and Jewish writers and intellectuals.[32]

That being said, Buczacz has also been undergoing a different kind of memory renaissance, which has included the construction of a prominent monument for Stepan Bandera, the leader of the OUN-B (the more radical faction of the Organization of Ukrainian Nationalists), on a hill overlooking Buczacz. Known popularly as the *Banderivtsy* (*Banderowcy* in Polish), Bandera's followers actively participated in the murder of innumerable Jews in Eastern Galicia. The funds for this edifice were collected by public subscription among the residents of the town, despite its depressed economy. This was part of a larger nationalist undertaking in Buczacz, which in turn reflects similar trends throughout West Ukraine.[33] In January 2006 the town celebrated the ninety-seventh anniversary of Bandera's birth with solemn patriotic speeches and a performance by the women's choir. The event took place at a building that had previously housed the Polish gymnastics and cultural association Sokół (Falcon) but had been made available before the war also for Jewish and Ukrainian groups. The plaque on this fanciful structure, built in 1905, as well as the city's Internet announcement of the event, blandly describe the building as the "District Culture House," making no reference to its past role in bringing together the different groups that had once inhabited the city.[34]

My maternal grandfather received a certificate of immigration to Palestine on March 12, 1935. My mother, her two brothers, and their parents reached the port of Jaffa in December that year. From a comfortable bourgeois existence, they were reduced to the status of blue-collar workers. My grandmother, who had been educated at a gymnasium in Prague when the family fled the Russians in the First World War, and spoke fluent German as well as Yiddish, Hebrew, Polish, and some Ukrainian, worked for years packing oranges an hour's walk away from their home in Petah Tikva. My grandfather worked as a laborer until he was felled by a heart attack. My mother was the first in her family to have a college degree. But the rest of the extended family—except for two great-uncles who also left in the 1930s—disappeared without a trace. No one knows how they were murdered or where their bodies lie. I am the only member of my family to have ever returned to Buczacz. By then my mother had passed away. I was glad that we never accomplished our plan to go there together. She had fond memories of her childhood there and took them to her grave without seeing the merciless erasure of the postwar years.[35]

In June 2004, as I was leaving Buczacz, the sky cleared and the sun lit the main square with its still handsome, though dilapidated, town hall, with a soft afternoon glow. The massive stone statue of Ukraine's national poet, Taras Shevchenko, looked out toward the bridge over the Strypa, the Basilian Monastery, and the Fedor Hill in the distance. This was the path the Jews of the city had followed on their way to execution in public view of all other residents. I was standing more or less where the synagogue had once stood, when a funeral procession began winding its way down from the monastery to the marketplace. A coffin was being carried on the back of a truck. In front of the procession marched two men carrying flags: the blue and yellow national flag of Ukraine, and the black and red flag of the UPA. Ukrainian Buczacz, I thought, had come into its own.

Al-Shaykh Muwannis—Site of My Childhood

On June 10, 1954, former Israeli prime minister, David Ben-Gurion, addressed a crowd of eight thousand Israeli youths at the site of the Palestinian village of Shaykh Muwannis, just north of Tel Aviv, urging them to commit themselves to a pioneering style of life.[36] I was born two months earlier in Kibbutz Ein Hahoresh, a socialist commune located about thirty miles north of that site. As a baby, I lived in the "children's home"; older children were expected to address their parents by their names. The nuclear family was seen as an obstacle to achieving the ideal of a community of equals, whose members would work as hard as they could and receive as much as they needed. The most famous member of our kibbutz was Abba Kovner, who on the night of December 31, 1941, had called upon the Jewish youth of Vilna (Wilno, Vilnius) to resist the German occupiers rather than "be led like sheep to the slaughter."[37] Kovner became even better known to the Israeli public thanks to his testimony at the Adolf Eichmann trial in Jerusalem in 1961. Even as children we knew that we would never be sheep.[38]

My mother did not want her children to call her by name. By the early 1960s we were living in Ramat Aviv, a new neighborhood north of Tel Aviv, built to accommodate immigrants from Eastern Europe, soon to be joined by Jews expelled from Poland following the anti-Semitic campaign of Władysław Gomułka's communist regime.[39] Just east of our neighborhood was the hill that had once been the site of Shaykh Muwannis. By then, however, it was populated by Jews from North Africa, mostly from Morocco, who began leaving their homes in increasing numbers in response to anti-Jewish violence triggered by the establishment of the State of Israel and the expulsion of the Palestinians. We, the "Polacks," had our share of fights with the "Moroccans" on the hill, who lived in dilapidated stone houses that did not resemble the modern housing of the new neighborhood, mostly two- and four-story tenements surrounded by lawns and trees. One building stood out in the village, the "Sheikh's House," as we called it—a large, impressive structure even in its state of progressive decay. Occasionally we would make our way to what was left of the tall cactus fences that surrounded the village, snapping the juicy fruit from the thorny bushes with empty food cans tied to long sticks. The vague notion that this had once been the home of Palestinian Arabs never made the slightest impression on us, nor was it discussed at home or in school. That past was definitely in the past, and we had enough difficulties making sure that we had a future.[40]

Years later, after completing my D.Phil. in Britain, I taught for several years at Tel Aviv University. By then the university, which was born two years after me, had spread from its original site and stretched over much of what had been Shaykh Muwannis, whose poor, postindependence Jewish residents had been meanwhile mostly relocated.[41] Tel Aviv University was considered to be a stronghold of the political left. But in 1991, two years after I left for the United States, the old "Sheikh's House" was transformed into a prestigious restaurant and event center frequented by many of the university's employees. The history of what came to be called the Green House, which also served as the faculty club, was outlined in a newly designed Hebrew-language website in 2007:

> The University Club ... is located in the "Green House," which is within the bounds of Tel Aviv University. The house is a unique architectural asset left over from the village of Sheikh Munis ... In the first half of the nineteenth century the village grew and expanded, and alongside its simple stone houses, large mansions made of chiseled stones were built. Toward the end of World War I, British forces arrived at the edge of the village, which was under Turkish control. The village fell into British hands in a surprise night attack on December 2, 1917.
>
> The transition to Mandatory rule brought progress to the entire region of Tel Aviv, Jaffa, and also to the village of Sheikh Munis. The green house stood out from the distance thanks to its color and the magnificent arcade that decorated its front. At this point the two top floors served as living quarters and the first floor served for commerce and workshops. As of 1924 conditions in the village changed, some of its lands were sold and negotiations began to buy more lands. In March 1948 an encampment of *Lehi* [a militant Jewish underground known by the British as the Stern Gang] was situated in the village ... At this spot all of *Lehi*'s fighters were

assembled to hear the order of the day announcing their entry into the ranks of the IDF.[42]

Following the establishment of the State (June 1948) Sheikh Munis housed members of the Air Force and *Mahal* [Foreign volunteers]. As of 1949 the village accommodated immigrants ... war refugees ... [and] soldiers who returned from fighting ... and lacked housing ... With the development of the university, the Green House came to accommodate the faculty club ...

The planners of the house strove to preserve its characteristic architectural elements, combined with contemporary design. The house stands out on the campus for its beauty and uniqueness.

The website that carried this account, however, has meanwhile been removed. The faculty club's updated site still vaguely describes the house as "a unique architectural asset," now stating that it "was ruined over the years until a new initiative was born to replace it with a new house in the spirit of the house that had stood there in the past." The architects, we are told, "strove to maintain the oriental style of the local Arabic architecture of the nineteenth century, combined with contemporary planning."[43] An embedded link provides some more information about "architecture on campus," including an item titled "the Green House—a link to the past." Here we read that the planners of the campus "believed that it is especially important to refer to the past by way of creating an architectural link between the site and the period. The Green House was built with architectural cues reminiscent of the ancient [sic] Arabic village—Sheikh Munis."[44] The management of the Green House now has its own version of its pedigree, informing us that "the Green House, built in 1800, remained standing on the ruins of the village Munis," and that the current edifice "preserves the authentic characteristics of the building and enhances them with exotic European construction, making for a modern and unique classic."[45]

But what actually happened to the village of Shaykh Muwannis? The contemporary Israeli verbiage about the Green House neglects the most salient and disturbing aspects of the story, celebrating instead its "oriental" and "exotic," as well as "modern" redesign and reconstruction, without dwelling for an instant on the original destruction of the "ancient" village and the displacement of its population. Other sources provide the information that was unknown and unavailable to me when I was growing up in the shadow of the village, and has since been obfuscated by vague references to the building's "characteristic architectural elements." But few, if any, of those who gather for delectable meals or festive events at the Green House wish to know the history of the village that once stood on a hill overlooking the Mediterranean to the west and the mountains of Judea and Samaria to the east.

The Green House is said to have first been documented by an Australian painter at the time of the British campaign against Ottoman forces in al-Shaykh Muwannis in 1917. During the interwar British mandate in Palestine the village saw a great deal of development, including land registration, house and road construction, and irrigation. The Green House was also enlarged. This process was linked to the massive increase of the Jewish population in the area following the Balfour Declaration of 1917, and favorable British regulations regarding Jewish immigration, which only changed in response to the Arab Revolt of 1936–9.[46] In the years 1931–45 the population of Shaykh Muwannis grew from 1,154 to 1,930 inhabitants. An elementary school for boys was established in the village in 1932, enrolling 232 students by 1945; and a girls' school was established in 1943, whose enrollment reached thirty-four students two years later.[47]

On November 29, 1947, the United Nations General Assembly voted to partition Mandate Palestine into a Jewish State and a Palestinian State (thirty-three in favor, thirteen against, ten abstentions). The Jewish leadership accepted the partition, but the leadership of the Arabs in Palestine rejected it, not least because the plan would have brought large numbers of Palestinians, such as the inhabitants of Shaykh Muwannis, under Jewish rule, or led to their transfer to the Palestinian state. Instead, the Palestinians unleashed a series of mostly unorganized hostile actions against the Jews. As the British progressively lost control over the situation, they announced their departure from the country by May 15, 1948. Much of the Jewish and Arab population was geographically mixed, a condition that intensified the brutality of the conflict. In the early months of the conflict the Jewish population, which numbered only 650,000, was largely on the defensive, coming under especially heavy pressure in February and March 1948, as Arab fighters blockaded the main roads. But in April and May the Haganah (the main Jewish underground military organization) went on the offensive; the paramilitary Palestinian forces were routed, and thousands of Palestinian civilians fled or were expelled from their towns and villages. On May 14, 1948, the Jewish leadership proclaimed the establishment of the State of Israel, and the following day, as the British officially left, the new state was attacked by Arab armies from Egypt, Iraq, Jordan, Lebanon, and Syria. The bitter and bloody fighting continued until January 1949 and ended with the victory of the newly established IDF.[48]

In 1949, the Palestinian population totaled an estimated 1,380,000 people, of whom at least 730,000 were refugees. By the end of the second decade of the twenty-first century, several more generations had been added to the original refugees. Palestinians have one of the fastest natural growth rates in the world. According to the United Nations Relief and Works Agency (UNRWA), in 2019 their number stood at 5.6 million, with other organizations estimating as many as seven million Palestinian refugees around the world.[49]

The most authoritative study of the events of 1948, by the Israeli historian Benny Morris, has concluded that while there was never any overtly official overall plan by the Jewish leadership to expel the Palestinian population, in practice this became the policy in most, although not all, cases. The consensus among the Jewish political and military leaders, as well as the Jewish population more generally, was that the fewer Arabs left within the borders of the young and fragile Jewish State, the easier it would be to consolidate and secure it. And as the Arabs became increasingly reluctant to leave of their own free will, the measures of expulsion by Israeli military commanders grew progressively harsher. Once the war ended, Israeli disinclination to consider any return of refugees, and the decision of the surrounding Arab states to make the refugees into a powerful political and propagandistic weapon against Israel, determined that this problem would remain one of the main issues on the political agenda of the world to this day.⁵⁰

The case of al-Shaykh Muwannis needs to be seen within this context. Shaykh Muwannis overlooked the main airport of the state in the making, Sdeh Dov, and the Reading power plant; it was also suspected of harboring armed residents who might pose a potential threat to the surrounding Jewish communities. At the beginning of March 1948, the Haganah General Staff received reports that Arab volunteers with large quantities of arms had entered Shaykh Muwannis, though other sources contradicted this information. Indeed, subsequent events demonstrated that there were probably no armed men in any number in the village at the time. On March 7, the Haganah's Alexandroni Brigade blocked all access roads to the village. Five days later, five village elders were kidnapped, apparently by members of the dissident Jewish underground *Etzel* (known as the Irgun by the British) or of the more radical underground group *Lehi*.⁵¹ Meanwhile, local Arab residents complained about looting, random shootings, and acts of humiliation and intimidation by Jewish forces in and around the village.

According to the historian Haim Fireberg, written testimonies indicate that the Haganah did not intend to expel the residents of al-Shaykh Muwannis, but merely to isolate the village and prevent its residents from linking up with other Arab forces. Indeed, a senior officer in the Haganah's Kiryati Brigade is quoted in the formation's operations log on March 17, 1948, as expressing the hope that it would be possible to ensure calm in the area by means of cooperation between the "moderate" circles in Shaykh Muwannis and "Jews who are well-acquainted with the village and its residents." But on March 20, 1948, soldiers of the Alexandroni Brigade encircled Shaykh Muwannis and seized houses on the outskirts of the village. Within twenty-four hours the more than three thousand inhabitants of the village fled their homes, leaving much of their property behind. The Green House, which belonged to the village chief (*mukhtar*), Ibrahim Abu Kahil, was still filled with packed boxes and other items waiting to be packed, when soldiers of the Kiryati Brigade set up their headquarters there.

The Haganah troops, together with officials from the municipality of Tel Aviv, then registered the Palestinian property. Historian Uriya Shavit and journalist Jalal Bana argue that "the chief of the General Security Service, Zvi Averbuch, was concerned that the village would become the object of looting by Jewish forces," and therefore "recommended the 'speedy entry of [Jewish] refugees' from the outlying areas of Tel Aviv into Sheikh Munis. The village," they write, thus "became the home of destitute Jewish refugees, who clung to the land and the homes they received. Within a year, some three thousand Jews were settled in two hundred of the village's abandoned homes."⁵²

This is a somewhat gentler version of events than the one presented by many Palestinians. Shavit and Bana conclude that "the direct cause of the flight from Sheikh Munis is not entirely clear," and speculate that "the residents were fearful of the Haganah's 'true' intentions," or that "Jewish 'friends' intimated to them that it would be best for them if they left," or that "leaders of the Arab forces in Jaffa called on them to leave the village, based on the mistaken assumption that this would induce the British to intervene in the area of north Tel Aviv."[53] A Palestinian Internet site notes that "either in December 1947 or January 1948 the leaders of al-Shaykh Muwannis" and other Arab villages in the vicinity "met with Haganah representative [sic] in the house of Avraham Shapira in Petah Tikva and expressed desire for peace. Despite the commitment of these villages not to harbor any Arab Liberation Armies or local Arab Militia, they were all completely ethnically cleansed. In late March, al-Shaykh Muwannis inhabitants were intimidate[d] into fleeing after the kidnapping of village leaders."[54]

This is, in fact, also the version of events offered by Morris. Thus, he writes that the Arabs in the central sector of the country—where Shaykh Muwannis is also located—refused to launch attacks on the Jews despite appeals from the commanders of the paramilitary Arab forces. Indeed, he cites the leaders of al-Shaykh Muwannis and other nearby villages declaring to Shapira in late 1947 or early 1948 that "if they could not keep out the irregulars unaided, they would call on the Haganah." These initiatives by local Arab leaders were reciprocated by Jewish officials who visited their villages and asked them to accept the protection of Jewish forces and to remain in their homes.[55] Nevertheless, as the hostilities intensified, mutual suspicions and lack of trust also grew. What seems to have been the main cause for the tragedy of al-Shaykh Muwannis was the kidnapping, presumably by *Lehi*, of the five village elders in late March. Morris quotes an intelligence source of the IDF reporting less than three months later that it was this kidnapping that brought about the exodus of the population, because the inhabitants had "learned that it was not sufficient to reach an agreement with the Haganah and that there were 'other Jews' [i.e., dissidents] whom one should fear perhaps more than the Haganah, which had no control over them."[56]

Morris flatly rejects the notion that was popular in Israel for many decades, one that I was taught in school and that much of my generation had internalized as a rationalization of an event that neither we nor our teachers were willing to concede, according to which the Palestinians left of their own accord, encouraged to do so by their own leadership, with the expectation of returning soon thereafter behind the victorious Arab armies. In fact, as he conclusively demonstrates, the local Arab leadership was strongly opposed to the exodus. On March 30, 1948, the Jaffa newspaper *Al Sarikh* wrote:

> The inhabitants of the large village of Shaykh Muwannis and of several other Arab villages in the neighbourhood of Tel Aviv have brought a terrible disgrace upon us all by quitting their villages bag and baggage. We cannot help comparing this disgraceful exodus with the firm stand of the Haganah in all localities in Arab territory ... Everyone knows that the Haganah gladly enters the battle while we always flee from it.[57]

The Jewish leadership was also well aware of what was happening, and while its ambivalence about expelling Arabs remained, apart from a few exceptions it had no intention of halting the fleeing Palestinians or, even less so, of allowing them to return. Golda Myerson (Meir), at the time director of the Jewish Agency's Political Department, reported on May 6, 1948, on her visit to Arab Haifa a few days after it was conquered:

> It is a dreadful thing to see the dead city. Next to the port I found children, women, the old, waiting for a way to leave. I entered the houses, there were houses where the coffee and pita bread were left on the table, and I could not avoid [thinking] that this, indeed, had been the picture in many Jewish towns [i.e., in Europe during World War II or previous pogroms].[58]

Myerson, who was born in Kyiv in 1898, wrote in her autobiography that one of her earliest memories was of her father boarding up the front door in response to rumors of an imminent pogrom.[59] Clearly this issue was on her mind when a few days later she told the (Labor) Mapai Party Central Committee that the Jews could not treat villagers who had fled because they did not want to fight the Yishuv, "such as [those of] Sheikh Muwannis," in the same manner as hostile villagers. Then she added:

> What do we do with the villages ... abandoned by friends? Are we prepared to preserve these villages in order that their inhabitants might return, or do we want to wipe out every trace that there had been a village on the site?[60]

Myerson obviously had compunctions. But even in the same speech, she made room for what would eventually become the policy of erasure:

> I am not among those extremists—and there are such, and I applaud them, who want to do everything that can be done in order to bring back the Arabs. I say I am not willing to make extraordinary arrangements to bring back Arabs.[61]

She then went on to say that the question remained as to how the Yishuv should behave toward those who had stayed behind. Ill treatment could prompt those who had remained to leave and discourage those who had left from returning—"and we would [then] be rid of the lot of them." She then called for a comprehensive discussion of the "Arab Question" in the Central Committee. But no such discussion ever took place.[62]

By June 16, the position of the Israeli government had hardened. On that day, Ben-Gurion told the Cabinet that he opposed allowing the Arabs to return to Jaffa or to any other site. The views expressed in this forceful speech, as Morris puts it, "were to serve as the basis of the consensus that emerged" in the Israeli leadership:

> I believe we should prevent their return ... We must settle Jaffa, Jaffa will become a Jewish city ... To allow the return of the Arabs to Jaffa would be ... foolish. [If the Arabs are allowed to return] and the war is renewed, our chances of ending the war as we wish to end it will be reduced ... Meanwhile, we must prevent at all costs their return ... I will be for them not returning also after the war.[63]

In 1948–9 about four hundred Arab villages and towns were depopulated and soon thereafter they were fully or partially destroyed and made uninhabitable. Most of the destruction was not due to fighting but part of an intentional policy of plunder and erasure.[64] Al-Shaykh Muwannis, next to which I spent much of my own childhood, was one of those villages. The fate of the refugees of these towns and villages may not be resolved by returning them to sites that no longer exist. What was done cannot be undone. But their fate remains at the core of the conflict, and without recognizing, acknowledging, and taking responsibility for the past, the only future that awaits the coming generations of Palestinians and Israelis is one of continuing conflict, bloodshed, distortion of the past, and lack of any prospects of reconciliation and peace.

***

There is no need to make any direct analogies between Buczacz and al-Shaykh Muwannis. In the former, the Jews were murdered by the Germans and their local collaborators, even as a few were saved by their Polish and Ukrainian neighbors. In the latter, the Palestinians were intimidated, threatened, and forced into fleeing from their homes and became refugees, a status which remains the fate of millions of their brethren and their offspring. The first case is genocide; the second is ethnic cleansing in time of war, a war in which the Arab leadership in fact hoped to eradicate the small Jewish population in Palestine and the newly declared State of Israel. But the attempted erasure of memory and its few remaining physical traces, the callous and ruthless rewriting of history, and the aspiration to build a prosperous and hopeful future on the basis of a distorted past—of constructing new edifices over the half-buried corpses of forgotten victims, or of redesigning the relics of requisitioned property without even a hint of their original owners' identity and fate—are a perilous undertaking. This is not because history can be reversed and its victims ever sufficiently compensated, which is impossible and perhaps not even desirable. It is because building the future on an erased past ensures that its memory will never be fully buried, the bones will keep resurfacing, and the animosity, fear, and prejudice that had fueled the destruction in the first place will keep simmering, awaiting new opportunities to burst forth and wreak the revenge of the forgotten.

Retelling the Past

One alternative path is to tell this story of catastrophe and erasure as a personal political history. By this I mean not only, but certainly also, my own coming to terms with my identity as a Jewish Israeli. More importantly, what I have in mind is the story of my generation of Jewish and Palestinian Israeli citizens, born between the late 1940s and the early 1960s, that is, the first generation of citizens of a newly created state. What seems to me of particular interest is this generation's link to the place, and it is in this sense that I speak of a personal political history rather than any party-based political affiliation. And what greatly complicates this story is the fact that while the new Jewish Israeli citizens were expected to normalize the state's existence by the very fact of their birth in it, so that, in a purely biological sense, they became indigenous to it, the existence of the new Arab Israeli citizens of the same state, who had mostly been indigenous to the land for generations, was denormalized, as they became an ethnic minority on their own land—often with only limited civil rights. Since this generation is more or less the same age as the state itself, its personal story is in a certain sense the personal story of the state: a state whose most important personal characteristic is its alleged ability to "normalize Jewish existence" and by the same token its capacity to "denormalize" the native Arab population that remained on the land after the mass expulsion of the Palestinian majority in 1948.

Ultimately, then, beyond the conventional, albeit highly contentious and competing political narratives, we still need to explore how Israeli Jews and Arabs born into the state have understood, articulated, and felt their link to their homeland—*homeland* in the simple sense of the land in which they were born as the first citizens of a newly born state, and homeland in the abstract sense of the home of their respective nations. This question, although it is clearly at the heart of the Israeli-Palestinian conflict, has never been addressed in this manner. Indeed, the very idea of a collective subjective history, particularly one that is split into at least two cardinal personas, is challenging, in that it requires narrating a generation's link to a place through the personal tales of its protagonists. Yet the benefit of such an undertaking may well be that at its core it seeks neither contention nor argumentation, but rather empathetic understanding, without which history is nothing more than "one damn thing after another," a "dogma" about reconstructing the past against which the great historian Arnold Toynbee famously warned.[65]

My own scholarly journey took me to Israel-Palestine from Eastern Europe, and to Eastern Europe from Germany. This was also the path charted by Shmuel Yosef Agnon in his creation myth of Buczacz, his and my mother's hometown. Yet Agnon himself, of course, did not come from Germany but was born in Buczacz; and he did not stay in Buczacz but rather went to live for four years in Ottoman Jaffa, from which he moved to Germany, where he stayed for twelve years spanning the First World War, the Balfour Declaration, and the beginning of the consolidation of a Jewish "national home" in what was, by the time he returned and settled down in Jerusalem, British Mandatory Palestine.[66]

I too did not personally cross these geographies in the chronological order suggested above but rather did so by way of following the focuses of my research. Born just six years after the establishment of the State of Israel, I am the only native son of Kibbutz Ein Hahoresh in my family, although I have no recollections of my very early childhood there. My parents are now buried side by side in the kibbutz cemetery, an intimate place with many familiar names, the kind of site that some people still refer to as "a piece of old Eretz Israel." Yet I am not the first "Sabra" in my family. My father, who subsequently insisted that he was not the "mythological Sabra," was born in Petah Tikva (Mulabbis, Mlabbes, Um-Labbes), shortly after his parents arrived in Palestine from the poverty-stricken shtetl of Pyzdry, near the western Polish city of Kalisz. That was the same Petah Tikva where Ben Gurion preferred to stay instead of Arabic Jaffa when he arrived in Palestine two decades before my father's birth. In August 1939, on the occasion of his bar mitzvah, my father received a greeting card from his grandfather in Poland; that was the last that anyone heard of the family there.[67]

But my mother came from Buczacz, Agnon's town, in 1935, with her parents and two younger brothers. Years later, when he traveled to London after receiving the 1966 Nobel Prize in Literature, Agnon was hosted by my father, who was then cultural attaché to Her Majesty's government. When my mother mentioned to him that she too came from Buczacz, he responded dismissively: "Nowadays everyone wants to be from Buczacz." That was certainly not the case when my mother's family also settled down in Petah Tikva, where she met my father. Both families were poor, and my father, whether because he wanted to escape his home, or because he wanted to fight the Nazis, forged his birth certificate to make him appear old enough for military service and joined the Jewish Brigade of the British Army. I doubt that he killed any Germans during his service in Italy, but he never forgot his encounter with the survivors of the Holocaust.[68]

By 1948, after one semester at the Hebrew University, both my parents were in uniform, my mother in besieged Jerusalem and my father in the convoys trying to break through. She suffered malnutrition and lost a child; he was twice pronounced dead, erroneously. They lost many friends in the students' companies that had been scratched together when the fighting broke out. I have no doubt that in that war my father did kill others as the commander of a machine-gun squad; and I know that later in life he was haunted by the crimes he saw fellow soldiers commit, and he described a few such instances in his writing.[69] I don't think my mother killed anyone, but despite her small stature, she proudly carried a Mauser K98, known in Israel as a Czehi, one of the captured German Army rifles that were shipped off to Israel from Czechoslovakia as part of an arms deal. I still used one for sniper training in 1973; a little swastika was engraved on its steel breech.

My parents went back to the Hebrew University after the war, although they could no longer study at Mount Scopus since the Jordanian Legion had occupied the eastern part of the city where the campus was located. When they completed their studies, they went to the kibbutz as part of what Israeli socialists called at the time *hagshamah* (realization), intended to transform individuals into active contributors to the social collective and facilitate the creation of a just society.[70] Some of the children they taught there at the school were orphaned Holocaust survivors. They lasted only five years in the kibbutz, but that time coincided with my birth. I spent the first eighteen months of my life in a children's home; it was the rule in the kibbutz, although I do not think my mother liked this arrangement. Six decades later, at my father's funeral in the kibbutz in December 2016, an elderly woman approached me. "You may not remember me," she said, "but I was your nanny when you were a baby." She remembered me as being cute, of course, and showed me a photograph from that time to prove it.

I went to Germany for the first time in 1979. I was twenty-four, almost exactly the same age as Agnon when he went there in 1912, but it was a very different country. For me, this was the beginning of a long journey, at whose core was a question that has remained with me to this day: What motivates young men, men not unlike myself at the time, to take part in mass crimes, such as those perpetrated by German troops on an unprecedented scale in the Second World War? I too had been a soldier and an officer. I don't think I ever killed anyone, although I fired in the direction of Syrian soldiers from too great a distance to be able to tell whether any were hit. I had been shot at and shelled, but the only serious injuries I sustained as a soldier happened in an entirely avoidable army training accident. Still, after four years in uniform, I knew something about being a young soldier. My driving question was, of course, directed just as much at myself and my generation as well as at the soldiers of 1948, such as my father, who were of the same age group as the younger cohorts of the German troops I subsequently studied. What makes young men—there were also women, but far fewer—commit atrocities? How do they perceive their actions and later remember them?

Coming to Germany was a challenge. There were still many elderly men with missing limbs on the streets and in the bars; I could overhear them speaking about their wartime experiences at the local pub. After I published my first book on the barbarization of warfare on the Eastern Front they would come and sit at the front rows of the lecture halls when I gave talks in Germany.[71] Some of them would insist, "Nothing like that ever happened in my unit. We were decent soldiers." Others would respond, "Maybe not in your unit, but certainly in mine." That was the mid-1980s. It took another decade for the so-called *Wehrmachtsausstellung* (Wehrmacht Exhibition) on the crimes of the German Army in the East to begin making the rounds in the Federal Republic and Austria, garnering close to a million visitors over four years.[72] There were the same confrontations between those who denied the evidence and those who were appalled by it. A German member of parliament cried in public at the thought that her father might have been a war criminal simply by serving the fatherland.

By then Germans were quite ready to recognize that the Holocaust was a German crime committed by rather than simply in the name of the German people. But the extermination of the Jews, it was said, was perpetrated only by a few thousand Germans, mostly the Gestapo, SS, and other dregs of society. The armed forces were a different matter altogether: some twenty million Germans had gone through the ranks. Was it possible that the Wehrmacht was a criminal organization?[73] This assertion was and remains controversial in Germany—and, in fact, elsewhere. But if German soldiers were not to blame, who killed all those millions? Surely not just the sparsely staffed security services that allegedly committed crimes behind the backs of the decent fighting units.

People told themselves, and their families, different stories. Soldiers came back from the war with memories they did not divulge; the photos they had sent to their loved ones of wartime atrocities were stored away in attics and never seen again; the amateur movies they made were kept in drawers that were never opened. There were also letters, diaries, oral accounts, and, of course, those pub conversations among old comrades and family chats around the breakfast table that sounded very different from what people said publicly. Political correctness enabled Germany to develop a democratic culture; it also taught people to lie, hide, and obfuscate.[74] As we are learning now again, it is a double-edged sword. Once people are allowed to say what they think, their words quickly turn into action; but when they keep their thoughts to themselves, the repressed rage and resentment eventually boil over in unexpected ways. Men who had served in the Wehrmacht rarely talked to those who had not served about the war; when a few of them finally did talk as old men, they often remembered those years as the best time of their lives, when they were young, healthy, optimistic, and omnipotent. The crimes were not their doing or their fault, they argued; and in any case, they had only reacted to even worse crimes by the enemy, which were, moreover, committed first. No one was innocent, and in war terrible things happen. But they had been decent soldiers, believed in what they were doing, and were eventually deceived and betrayed, they said.

I had been a founding member of Peace Now, before Anwar Sadat's visit to Israel in 1977; a decade later, when the first intifada broke out, I protested to Minister of Defense Yitzhak Rabin that under his leadership the IDF could undergo a process of brutalization akin to that of the Wehrmacht. And while my words infuriated him, in retrospect I wonder whether they did not also rankle him into thinking that such comparisons were not entirely vacuous; he had commanded elite forces in 1948, and knew full well, as did my father, how easily young men with guns can be made or choose of their own volition to do terrible things. But now the IDF was a far mightier organization, and Palestinians had only rocks.[75]

It was then, too, that the Israeli historian Yehuda Elkana, who had been my professor at the university, published a searing article, warning that when we drum into young Israelis that the Holocaust should never happen again, we provide them with a license to see all threats as existential and to view all opponents as potential Nazis: and the only good Nazi, of course, is a dead Nazi. But this time it was the Jews who were armed to the teeth while the "Nazis" were Palestinian teenagers with slingshots.[76] Elkana, who had survived the Holocaust as a child, could get away with issuing this warning. But he could not prevent Israeli society from sliding down the slippery slope. Certainly my own curious exchange with Rabin could not. And as we know, the slope became much steeper after Rabin was gunned down.

In some ways, the question I had asked myself when I first went to Germany had been answered. What makes young men kill and murder? They are taught to believe that they are facing a dangerous enemy, one who had victimized them in the past and would do so again if given the chance. The Jews, so the Nazi argument went, had betrayed Germany in 1918, stabbing the Imperial Army in the back, unseating the emperor, and bringing about the corrupt, degenerate, and Jew-ridden Weimar Republic. They had also taken over the Soviet Union and were pulling the strings of the plutocrats in London and Washington. Now it was their time to pay. If the Jews incited another world war, warned Adolf Hitler in 1939, they would be exterminated. And so they were. In this view, young German men did not see Jewish human beings but demonic figures that must be crushed out of existence. In genocide, one dehumanizes enemies before killing them; that makes the killing of another person easier and provides murder with moral sanction. In Heinrich Himmler's words, precisely by being able to exterminate men, women, and children, his SS men had proven themselves to be decent, for they were strong enough to fulfill this unpleasant but world-historical task for the benefit of Aryan generations to come.[77]

But what did that look like in practice? Was there no recognition of the victims' humanity even when the killing did not occur in extermination camps but face-to-face? After all, vast numbers of Jews were not transported in trains across Europe, but killed where they lived, in full view of their friends, colleagues, and neighbors, by a single bullet to the back of the head, if they were lucky. This was not mechanical killing and not anonymous genocide. How was this possible? What made men act in such a way, at times after they had first gotten to know their victims personally? And what about all those so-called bystanders, the men, women, and children, who were looking on? What did they do, think, and remember?

And so I went east, from Germany to Eastern Europe, and chose one town out of hundreds in which such killing had happened. I soon realized that the encounter between the perpetrator and the victim I had sought to understand was complicated by the fact that so many other people were involved, people who had lived side by side for generations, whose entire culture was rooted in four centuries of coexistence, yet without whose complicity the killing would have been much harder to accomplish.[78] In observing the social dynamic of local genocide, it turned out that everyone was engaged in one way or another. Some moved into freshly abandoned apartments; others carried away down blankets and pillows, pots and pans; others still demolished the floors in search for hidden gold. Some hid Jews out of kindness; others took all their money and then denounced them; others still axed those they had sheltered just to get hold of their gold or furs, their cow or their horse. Whether they behaved cruelly or kindly, callously or indifferently, these people often knew each other by name; it was all quite familiar and intimate.

Nor were the Germans engaged in anonymous murder, since before they killed the Jews, they had spent months in the town getting to know them, as the Jews came in and out of their homes, babysitting the children, cleaning their apartments, shopping and cooking for them, making them shoes and suits, fixing their teeth and tending to their health. By the time the killing began, they knew each other by name. Finally, once the Jews were mostly gone, and as German rule in the region began to disintegrate, Ukrainian nationalists unleashed a brutal campaign of ethnic cleansing against their Polish neighbors, massacring and burning down entire villages, including mixed Polish-Ukrainian communities and even families, a wave of violence that subsided only after the return of the Red Army.

There were many reasons for the extreme violence that characterized this period. But in the present context, what is especially important to understand is that over an extended period of time each group, Jews, Poles, and Ukrainians, had created its own narrative about its place in the region, its relations with the other groups, and its past and destiny. Narrating one's story did not necessarily entail animosity toward others, as we can see from Agnon's mythology of Buczacz. But once nationalism gave birth to the idea that the place belonged exclusively to one's own group, it became no longer possible to live with the stories of others: such competing narratives had to be eradicated along with their carriers, for without its story a group no longer had the historical validation and moral right to be what it was and to live where it lived. Crucially, too, especially since the rise of nationalism, each group saw itself as the victim of others, particularly of its neighbors, whose successes it often viewed as the cause of its own misfortunes. Thus the interwoven fabric of narratives that had made up the social whole frayed and disintegrated. In truth, despite the nationalizers' claims, before the First World War it had often been difficult to distinguish between Poles and Ukrainians, whereas Jews were seen as a necessary if not always likable component of society. But as the walls between the groups grew ever higher, the stories they told about themselves became increasingly irreconcilable. Eventually, their internal exclusionary logic was sealed in blood.

These different narratives about such regions as Galicia are almost as irreconcilable today as they were at the time, although the conflict on the ground has receded into the distant past. But if we want to understand what had made it so vicious, we must reconstruct it as it had been told and seen by all those concerned. For this reason, I tried to evoke the individual voices of the town's people so as to reveal the multiple nuances, complexities, and contradictions contained in each of these narratives. My goal was not so much to point out what was accurate and what was false, although such narratives are always filled with distortions and denials, as well as empathy, compassion, and love. Rather, I sought to reconstruct the very perceptions that motivated people to act as they did at the time and that still mold present-day memory and historiography. People's voices tell a history that is always missing from official documentation, namely, how individuals experienced events rather than how officials translated them into bureaucratic reports. First-person accounts are by their very nature subjective, and they may contain much that is biased or inaccurate. But that does not make them any less true for the historical actors at the time; in that sense, these stories constitute an essential component of the historical record just as much as the official documents conventionally used by historians.[79]

Following this decades-long detour, I have now resumed my journey, retracing Agnon's and my mother's footsteps as they traveled from their hometown to Palestine.[80] My own homecoming is as incomplete as any other: I return to a home as familiar as the landscape of my childhood and as foreign as Ithaca is to Odysseus at the end of his travels. Indeed, it is precisely this notion of an impossible yet inevitable return that guides my path from Buczacz to Israel: the return to a land where I was born and raised, a land that my ancestors had confidently claimed to be their own even as they landed on its shores at the end of long journeys from sites that had been their homes for generations, the return to a land colonized and radically transformed, yet to which attachment, deeply rooted in conflicting and seemingly irreconcilable narratives, is both intense and filled with contradictions. Just as in the case of Buczacz, understanding the link to place in Israel-Palestine by groups that otherwise appear to have nothing in common but their rivalry, demands the kind of empathy generated by personal accounts. From my own personal perspective, the connection between Buczacz and Israel is encapsulated in Agnon's, my mother's, and my own journey there, making for a biographical, emotional, and chronological link that cannot be broken or denied. In other words, the kind of first-person history I have in mind is intensely personal both for its author and for the protagonists, Jews and Arabs alike, telling their own individual tales of belonging, longing, and loss.

In comparing Jewish Zionist accounts of the return to the Land of Israel since the late nineteenth century to the increasingly vibrant and rich literature on pre-1948 Arab society in Palestine, the Nakba, exile, and Palestinian nationalism, one cannot avoid a distinct sense of reading about two entirely separate universes. This was precisely how I felt when reading about Buczacz from the point of view, for instance, of Agnon, who told its story as a Jewish town, and from that of Sadok Barącz, that nineteenth-century Roman Catholic Armenian monk, who wrote its history as a Polish outpost of civilization on the edge of Turkish, Tatar, and Cossack barbarism.[81] These two tales are as impossible to reconcile as those of Jews depicting their settlement of the Land of Israel and those of Arabs writing about the Jewish colonization of Palestine. Moral righteousness, historical justice, fate and destiny, and, most of all, suffering and victimhood proliferate on both sides to such a degree that one would expect there never to be room for dialogue.

And yet, as it turns out, dialogue is not only necessary and possible; it is, in fact, spontaneous and natural. That does not mean that it lacks a violent potential. The intimacy of recognition and violence, familiarity and hostility, so transparent in such cases as Eastern Europe (or Rwanda, Bosnia, and numerous other sites of communal violence, ethnic cleansing, and genocide), is part and parcel of the Israel-Palestine conundrum. But it is also such because the stories people tell, irreconcilable as they are, concern the same place and follow a similar emotional and narrative trajectory. At their core, they are about an impossible and unbreakable link. This does not mean that they can be either merged or reconciled; indeed, the core of their existence is differentiation from the other. But by removing ourselves from the dispute, yet at the same time not detaching ourselves from the passions it evokes, we should be able to interchangeably empathize with one story or the other. Here the author's personal story should make room for the personal narratives of others, suspending one's own tale but never relinquishing the sensibility of subjectivity. The point then is not to confront one narrative with another but to tell them side by side, episode by episode, and person by person, thereby facilitating identification with their human core. This should not merely entail recognition that "we have our stories, and they have theirs." Rather, it should enable us to see the world through the eyes of others, to imagine ourselves in their shoes, even as we cannot accept or fully integrate the narrative context within which their experiences transpired: because most of these individual stories, like all human stories, are about people not unlike ourselves and about the quest for a home that we all share.[82]

This, then, is what I mean by a "personal political history" of Israel and Palestine, as told by members of its first generation, which is my own. Such a history, yet to be written, will excavate how this generation formed a link to a place that had come into existence as a political entity just before it was born, and just after the multiple catastrophes of the Second World War, the Holocaust, and the Nakba. For everything that generation had taken for granted, could just as easily have never happened, and what appeared at the time as natural and self-evident, indeed, as the unfolding of a historical logic, was mere coincidence, or luck, or the result of a concerted effort that might have failed. And yet, once the state was established, it acted and was perceived as if it was inevitable, thereby creating a consciousness, a state of being, among all those exposed to it that could not be ignored or denied, even though it had a radically different impact on its citizens depending on where they stood and how they were viewed by it.

Genocide, the Holocaust, and Israel-Palestine

There is a profound asymmetry to this tale, which must be integrated into its telling, if such a future personal political history is indeed to include voices of those on both sides of the divide. It is the asymmetry in the conditions of Jews and Palestinians. Its components are easily identified: Palestinians were the majority indigenous population in the land until 1948, while the vast majority of Jews arrived from Europe, and later the Middle East and North Africa, as settlers. The war of 1948, seen by Jews as the "War of Independence" and by Palestinians as the Nakba, or catastrophe, led to the expulsion of over two-thirds of the Palestinians from what became the State of Israel, and transformed those who remained there into a minority. Finally, the vastly superior strength of the Jewish state is exerted not only against this minority of Arab citizens but is also overwhelmingly greater than that of the rest of the Palestinian Diaspora. Whereas the Palestinians never gained a state and mostly lost their land, the Jews established a state and erased hundreds of emptied villages. For the Zionists, the State of Israel was an "answer" to the Holocaust; for Palestinians that very "answer" implied a negation of their existence as a nation, a mass expulsion, and an ongoing repression and existence as a stateless people. All this must be recognized openly and clearly.[83]

For precisely this reason, if we are to envision a personal political history of Israeli Jews and Palestinians, this asymmetry must be at the narrative core of telling vastly different yet always related stories of attachment to the land, its peoples and cultures, sights and nature, histories and myths. For the more nationally oriented or rigorously empirical, those disdainful of oral history and personal perspectives, such a first-person history may appear suspect. But just as testimony has come to play an increasingly important role in the reconstruction of the history of the Holocaust, as I have tried to show in this volume, so too it is high time for the individual voice to be heard over the tumult of the collective in telling the story of Israel and Palestine. For both Palestinians and Jews, ultimately it is their personal stories, beyond political rhetoric and ideology, that make for and reflect their link to the land.[84]

The State of Israel was only six years old when I came into the world. It was in its youth when my generation were teenagers; expanding and flexing its strength and capacities when we were young men and women; and growing less agile, heavier, more affluent, and less innocent as we moved into ever more advanced stages of middle age. We, Jews and Arabs, experienced it in many different ways, but it was our unavoidable defining circumstance; it provided schoolteachers and policemen, judges and politicians, the media and the military. It also created the framework for the deep divides in understanding—of what was taken for granted and what was entirely unthinkable.

As a young Jewish Israeli, I took the very connection to the land as a given: I spoke Hebrew, was a citizen, and internalized a view of the land as having been always somehow my own, long before the establishment of the state. I also viewed Jewish life outside of Israel as a distant, somewhat unpleasant, collective but in no way personal memory, an abnormality corrected in the nick of time by Zionism, as exemplified by my own birth into a state of my own in my own land. My first encounter with anti-Semitism came when I was living as a twelve-year-old in London. I was taught to see certain aspects of that land as they really were and others as they had been or should still be. I lived next to "abandoned" Palestinian villages, and never once thought as a child what the ruins of the houses or the sabra (*sabr*) fences of tall cactuses implied.[85] My classmates and I relished the sweet prickly fruits they produced, despite the tiny thorns that would prick out tongues and lips. We were "Sabras," and these were our forbidden fruits, yet we had no idea what stories they could tell. The overgrown Muslim cemetery nearby was more forbidding, as all cemeteries are to children. But it was all the more daunting because it was different and alien, and no one ever explained why it was there. After all, we were the natural inhabitants of the place, even though it had become ours only a few years before we were born.

It is this naturalness, this sense of what belongs and what does not, the tactile relationship to land, and the internalized imagery that transformed Israeli Jews into literally the first native generation, which still needs to be explored in telling this tale. At the same time, the very same historical process had transformed the Palestinians who remained in the new state into a minority in their own land, a contradiction in terms of Muslim and Christian Arabs in a Jewish State, not quite normal and yet, despite all denials and obfuscations, known as the indigenous inhabitants of the land, those who had always, so to speak, been there. Their far more numerous expelled brethren became the first generation of exile; they, those who remained, were the first Arab citizens of a Jewish, ethnonational state, which never quite knew what to do with them and never really accepted them. Instead, the Jewish state initially subjected the majority of its Arab citizens to almost two decades of military rule and has since then systematically discriminated against them, with the clear intention of marginalizing this population and at times barely concealing the desire to induce it to leave the country altogether.

I had not previously thought of myself as "the first man," in the sense of Albert Camus's reflections on his childhood in Algeria, which, for not entirely different reasons, remained unpublished until long after his tragic death in 1960, since at a time when the war in France's annexed territory was raging, recalling it as his homeland hardly fit the rhetoric of decolonization adopted by most of his fellow intellectuals.[86] The first man, in the sense that I ascribe to it here, is the first born into a new state and thus the first to take it for granted. He, or she is the first in the sense of being not a Zionist, since Zionism is an ideology and not a state of being, but the product of Zionism, a native, an indigenous inhabitant who cannot conceive of himself, or herself, as an alien, a foreigner, and a colonizer: in other words, one becomes an involuntary symbol of the success of an ideology and an improbable movement that created within merely a few decades an entirely new nation, even as vast parts of that very same nation, conceived very differently by another new nation and its murderous regime, were annihilated. And that, too, is part of this tale. Because, while my mother and her parents and two younger brothers came from Buczacz in 1935, thereby enabling my own eventual birth into the state that she and my father had fought, and many of their friends had died for, the rest of my extended family was murdered; and while I know by now more than any living soul about the genocide in my mother's hometown, I still know practically nothing about how my own family was butchered and perhaps should be grateful for having never found out.[87]

But mine is also the generation of Palestinians born in the wake of the catastrophe, at times still in their own villages and towns, but often as "internal refugees" in other villages and towns to which they were displaced. They were born after an entire people had been removed from its land, born as remnants but hardly as liberated survivors, since their childhood and youth were spent under Israeli military rule, and the iron fist of the Israeli authorities razed the emptied villages that had been their parents' native, natural, self-evident environment. This was a generation born into material and psychological devastation all the more profound because for so long it was pushed into the margins, stranded within a state that denied what had happened to its people, villages, communities, and families. It was a generation reduced to the status of second-class citizens, not only because of a whole slate of discriminatory laws, rules, and practices but also because that generation's culture was publicly denigrated, its language relegated to minority status, its links to its own homeland denaturalized and cast into doubt, its history defamed and distorted, its schooling limited, and its dignity as a people, a civilization, and a culture thrown to the dust and trampled upon.

Perhaps what is most striking, then, when we contemplate this generational aspect of creating a new normality, is that just as Zionism strove to "normalize" Jewish existence and viewed the Diaspora as an abnormal condition, the State of Israel denormalized Arab existence in its own land; indeed, it made its very raison d'être the denial of Palestinian indigeneity. And thus a young generation of Palestinians was born into a condition entirely unlike that of their parents, uprooted from their land even though they remained in it. In such sites as Ein Hod, once the Arabic village of Ein Hawd, an Israeli "artist colony" was created, where I spent some happy weeks with my sister and parents as a child, enjoying the "Oriental" structures in which we lived and the bucolic settings of the Carmel Mount. The "colony" was both alien and our own—the Orient was what we were and what we had taken over; we were coming into our own and we were being naturalized as sunbaked, athletic, confident new Jews. That the village had once been populated by Arabs was not unknown and yet was somehow irrelevant, something that happened before we were born, and we had naturalized the place by our very existence. We were the prickly and sweet fruits of Zionism's triumph. The Arabs were over the hilltop, crouching in their wretched villages, humiliated, perhaps plotting to kill us: alien, shadowy apparitions that came to be linked in the mind not to the original inhabitants of the land but to all those others that had always plotted to extinguish Jewish existence but would now never be able to accomplish their goal because we were in our own land and armed to the teeth.

Can one write such a story of a generation, of Jews and Arabs living side-by-side and, as it were, on separate planets? In the last few years, there has been a spate of new research on Jews and Arabs in Israel-Palestine.[88] But the history I have in mind concerns the formation of an internalized understanding of a link to a place. Some of the greatest domestic critics (a small minority) of Israeli state policies vis-à-vis the Palestinians, people described as "extreme leftists" in the current political rhetoric, belong to my generation. I remember us calling out to Prime Minister Golda Meir when she visited my high school, Tikhon Hadash, in 1972: "What about the Palestinian people?" And

I recall her answer, speaking in her distinctive American accent as an immigrant from Milwaukee born in Kyiv: "There is no Palestinian people. I am a Palestinian; I lived in Mandatory Palestine and have the ID to prove it." The following year, in the war that should not have happened, some of those who had called out were killed or maimed. And yet many of these same friends, now in their late sixties and more critical of Israeli government policies than ever before, cannot conceive of living anywhere but in Israel, and feel at home, to the extent that it is possible anywhere in our world, as well as completely alienated in an intimate, deeply personal manner, only there, and are foreigners everywhere else.

Albert Camus had written on being at home in a land that was, by that time, engaged in a savage war of decolonization. He had been a member of the *Résistance*; his father was killed in the First World War shortly after he had set foot for the first time on French soil. Yet Camus's sense of homeland, of childhood smells and tastes and sounds, was not to be found in Paris but in his hometown of Dréan in French Algeria. His book would not have been understood for what it was at the time of his death in 1960. It could be read with compassion and admiration only when it was published thirty-five years later, when all of that had become history, albeit a history that keeps returning with the growing xenophobia that has been gripping Europe in recent years. Yet essentially what he wrote then still remains deeply controversial: for how can we conceive of two opposing powerful links to the same land?

Poles still wax sentimental about the *kresy*, that eastern borderland that had been their zone of expansion and symbolizes a moment of greatness that can only be experienced nostalgically, as one travels through regions dotted with decaying castles and manor houses of days gone by. Members of my generation in Germany will tell stories, when prompted in intimate surroundings, about the lost lands of their ancestors in the east, from which millions of Germans were expelled in the wake of the Second World War. But in Israel-Palestine, despite the expulsion of the lion's share of the Palestinian population and the massive effort by the Jewish state to normalize its existence by erasing all traces of what had been before, the remaining Palestinians have clung to their land, reclaimed their identify, and stubbornly proclaim their hold on the soil and the stones, the hills and the groves. They are a constant irritant to the nationalizing Jewish state, unremittingly challenging its very claim to be the natural, eternal, and exclusive indigenous owner of the land.

Resolving this century-long conundrum by condemning the other side as illegitimate, alien, violent, fanatical, and contemptible may very well lead to one more attempt to radically change the status quo, resulting in yet another generation that will perceive a newly created state of affairs as normal and what had been before as no longer relevant. I recall a Ukrainian intellectual saying to me in the mid-1990s that there was little reason for melancholy at the site of the few material remnants of the once proud Jewish communities of Eastern Galicia, now West Ukraine. After all, she said, this is what happened to many other civilizations, such as ancient Greece and Rome, which left only ruins behind. To be sure, my own grandparents had come from Galicia; but for my interlocutor, the absence of Jews had been normalized.[89]

There are, as we know, those who would like to accomplish normalization through annihilation in Israel-Palestine too. But for many more on both sides, normality does not include the other, whether they are seen as alien, Nazi-like anti-Semites, or as foreign settler colonizers operating at the behest of the West. Yet there is another kind of normalization that includes accepting our neighbors' internalized view of the world: understanding, for instance, that for a generation such as my own, living in that place, despite all the catastrophes that led to our being there, was experienced as part of our making and that no other existence (and I exclude myself, since once one leaves, one never entirely comes back home) is normal. That seeing the world through another's eyes does not mean accepting all the ills and evils of history, and does not preclude rebelling against injustice and oppression, loss and mourning. But it does imply that one's own success must not always come at the price of another's failure, and that one's sense of victimization does not necessitate victimizing others in return. Indeed, it implies that a sense of victimhood and suffering, just as much as that of belonging and ownership, can be shared by those who have experienced the former and cannot give up the latter, precisely because of the pain, personal and collective, they have endured for so long.[90]

In the political sphere, which is not the subject of this chapter or book, yet deserves consideration elsewhere, what is called for is a process of decolonization, whereby Jewish Israelis will not only have to leave occupied lands—or be accepted as legal residents of a Palestinian state—but must also be liberated from the occupier mentality deeply lodged in their psyche; and Palestinians will be liberated not only from Israeli oppression but also from the mentality of the colonized and the oppressed. But my own vision entails a first-person history of a generation, the personal political history of Israel, and Palestine, as told by Jews and Palestinians. It is the story of their complex, conflicted, often contradictory, at times impatient or rageful, certainly evolving, but always profound sense of belonging to the land where they were born, a land that has been rapidly changing, yet remains the same, where past catastrophes have receded into history, yet overshadow the present more than ever before. For ultimately, I believe that if we listen to each other, we may actually learn something about ourselves. And that may be the first step toward a new politics.

NOTES

Introduction

1 "The Catechism Debate," http://newfascismsyllabus.com/news-and-announcements/the-catechism-debate/; O. Bartov, "Historikerstreit 0.0," in *Historiker Streiten*, ed. S. Neiman and M. Wildt (Berlin, 2022). See also A. D. Moses, *The Problems of Genocide* (New York, 2021) and O. Bartov, "Blind Spots of Genocide," *JMEH* 19, no. 4 (2021): 395–9.
2 B. Engelking and J. Grabowski, eds., *Night without End*, trans. A. Brzostowska, J. Giebułtowski, J. Grabowski, E. Olender-Dmowska, and T. Frydel (Bloomington, IN, 2022), orig. pub. in 2018 in Poland as *Dalej jest noc*.
3 See, e.g., "Polish Appeals Court Overturns Ruling against Holocaust Historians," *The Guardian*, August 16, 2021, www.theguardian.com/world/2021/aug/16/polish-appeals-court-overturns-ruling-against-holocaust-historians.
4 See Chapter 6.
5 See further in O. Bartov, *Tales from the Borderlands* (New Haven, CT, 2022).
6 See especially Chapter 10.
7 O. Bartov and E. D. Weitz, eds., *Shatterzone of Empires* (Bloomington, IN, 2013).

Chapter 1

1 R. Lemkin, *Axis Rule in Occupied Europe*, 2nd ed. (Clark, NJ, 2008 [1944]), esp. 79–95, and introductions by W. A. Schabas and S. Power, vii–xvi and xvii–xxiii, respectively; D.-L. Frieze, ed., *Totally Unofficial* (New Haven, CT, 2013), esp. 112–79.
2 See, e.g., W. A. Schabas, "The 'Odious Scourge,'" *GSP* 1, no. 2 (2006): 93–106.
3 See further in O. Bartov, "Genocide and the Holocaust," in *Lessons and Legacies XI*, ed. H. Earl and K. A. Schleunes (Evanston, IL, 2014), 11–12.
4 O. Bartov, *The Eastern Front 1941–45* (London, 1985); O. Bartov, *Hitler's Army* (New York, 1991).
5 O. Bartov, *Murder in Our Midst* (New York, 1996), 53.
6 J.-M. Chaumont, *La concurrence des victimes* (Paris, 1997); P. Novick, *The Holocaust in American Life* (Boston, MA, 1999); T. Segev, *The Seventh Million*, trans. H. Watzman (New York, 1993).
7 O. Bartov, "Defining Enemies, Making Victims," *AHR* 103, no. 3 (June 1998): 811–12.
8 O. Bartov, *Mirrors of Destruction* (New York, 2000), 5–6.
9 Bartov and Weitz, *Shatterzone of Empires*; O. Bartov, *Erased* (Princeton, NJ, 2007); J.-P. Himka and J. B. Michlic, eds., *Bringing the Dark Past to Light* (Lincoln, NE, 2013).
10 As articulated in Z. Bauman, *Modernity and the Holocaust* (Ithaca, NY, 1989).
11 Subsequently published as Bartov and Weitz, *Shatterzone of Empires*.
12 O. Bartov, *Anatomy of a Genocide* (New York, 2018), and Chapter 3.
13 As in R. Hilberg, *The Destruction of the European Jews* (Chicago, 1961).
14 Most prominently S. Friedländer, *Nazi Germany and the Jews*, 2 vols (New York, 1997–2007).

Notes

15 D. Bloxham, *The Final Solution* (New York, 2009).
16 Saul Friedländer uses only diaries. See also A. Garbarini, *Numbered Days* (New Haven, CT, 2006); A. Goldberg, *Trauma in First Person*, trans. A. Greenberg et al. (Bloomington, IN, 2017). For comparative studies see, e.g., E. D. Weitz, *A Century of Genocide* (Princeton, NJ, 2003); B. A. Valentino, *Final Solutions* (Ithaca, NY, 2004); J. Semelin, *Purify and Destroy*, trans. C. Schoch (New York, 2007).
17 Bloxham, *Final Solution*, 318; A. D. Moses, "Empire, Colony, Genocide," in *Empire, Colony, Genocide*, ed. A. D. Moses (New York, 2008), 25.
18 Bartov, "Genocide and the Holocaust," 6.
19 Bloxham, *Final Solution*, 318.
20 Moses, "Empire, Colony, Genocide," 25.
21 A. Dirk Moses, "Revisiting a Founding Assumption of Genocide Studies," *GSP* 6, no. 3 (2011): 296.
22 Bartov, "Genocide and the Holocaust," 20.
23 I. V. Hull, *Absolute Destruction* (Ithaca, NY, 2005); J. Zimmerer, "The First Genocide of the Twentieth Century," in *Lessons and Legacies VIII*, ed. D. L. Bergen (Evanston, IL, 2008), 34–64.
24 Ibid., 35-6, 58-9.
25 G. Aly, *Final Solution*, trans. B. Cooper et al. (New York, 1999); C. R. Browning, *The Origins of the Final Solution* (Lincoln, NB, 2004); O. Bartov, *Germany's War and the Holocaust* (Ithaca, NY, 2003), 79–98; W. Lower, *Nazi Empire-Building and the Holocaust in Ukraine* (Chapel Hill, NC, 2005).
26 Moses, "Founding Assumption," 296.
27 M. Mazower, *Hitler's Empire* (New York, 2009), 8.
28 Ibid., 585, citing A. Césaire, *Discourse on Colonialism*, trans. J. Pinkham (New York, 2000), 36.
29 Mazower, *Hitler's Empire*, 586–7.
30 Ibid., 414–15.
31 A. D. Moses, "The Holocaust and World History," in *The Holocaust and Historical Methodology*, ed. D. Stone (New York, 2012), 274, echoing Martin Broszat's assertion that Jews have a "mythical form" of Holocaust remembrance, whereas German historians are "operating only in scientific terms." M. Broszat and S. Friedländer, "A Controversy about the Historicization of National Socialism," in *Reworking the Past*, ed. P. Baldwin (Boston, MA, 1990), 106. More recently, Moses has applied the language of political theology to what he calls the high priests of the "German Catechism" of the Holocaust. See "The Catechism Debate."
32 Moses, "The Holocaust and World History," 275.
33 Ibid., 281.
34 See, e.g., J. Herf, *The Jewish Enemy* (Cambridge, MA, 2006); P. Longerich, *Holocaust* (New York, 2010); D. Cesarani, *Final Solution* (New York, 2016).
35 Moses, "The Holocaust and World History," 285–6.
36 See, e.g., U. Herbert, *Best* (Bremen, 1997); M. Wildt, *An Uncompromising Generation*, trans. T. Lampert (Madison, WI, 2009); C. Ingrao, *Believe and Destroy*, trans. A. Brown (Cambridge, 2013).
37 D. Bloxham, "Holocaust Studies and Genocide Studies," in *Genocide Matters*, ed. J. Apsel et al. (New York, 2013), 63.
38 Ibid. For an analysis of the final solution within a wider context of Nazi and European violence, see C. Gerlach, *The Extermination of the European Jews* (Cambridge, UK, 2016).
39 See also J. Zeller et al., eds., *Völkermord in Deutsch-Südwestafrika* (Berlin, 2003); G. Prunier, *The Rwanda Crisis* (New York, 1995).
40 Bartov, "Genocide and the Holocaust," 21.
41 On early effort to do so after the Holocaust, see Laura Jockusch, *Collect and Record!* (New York: Oxford University Press, 2012).

Chapter 2

1. Bartov, *Erased*.
2. U. D. Adam, *Judenpolitik im Dritten Reich* (Düsseldorf, 1972); K. A. Schleunes, *The Twisted Road to Auschwitz*, 2nd ed. (Urbana, IL, 1970); Hilberg, *The Destruction of the European Jews*.
3. I. Trunk, *Judenrat* (Lincoln, NE, 1996); Y. Gutman and A. Saf, eds., *The Nazi Concentration Camps*, trans. D. Cohen and others (Jerusalem, 1984).
4. Reitlinger, *The Final Solution*; Hilberg, *The Destruction of the European Jews*; M. Gilbert, *The Holocaust* (New York, 1985); D. J. Goldhagen, *Hitler's Willing Executioners* (New York, 1996); Friedländer, *Nazi Germany and the Jews*; Longerich, *Holocaust*; Browning, *Origins of the Final Solution*.
5. E. Mendelsohn, *The Jews of East Central Europe between the World Wars* (Bloomington, IN, 1983); Y. Gutman et al., eds., *The Jews of Poland between Two World Wars* (Hanover, NH, 1989); A. Polonsky, ed., *My Brother's Keeper?* (London, 1990); M. Opalski and I. Bartal, *Poles and Jews* (Hanover, NH, 1992); J. D. Zimmerman, ed., *Contested Memories* (New Brunswick, NJ, 2003); H. Dreifuss, *We Polish Jews?* (Jerusalem, 2009 [Hebrew]); J. Grabowski, *Hunt for the Jews* (Bloomington, IN, 2013); Engelking and Grabowski, *Night without End*.
6. M. Broszat, "Hitler and the Genesis of the 'Final Solution,'" in *Aspects of the Third Reich*, ed. H. W. Koch (London, 1985), 390–429; H. Mommsen, "The Realization of the Unthinkable," in H. Mommsen, *From Weimar to Auschwitz*, trans. P. O'Connor (Princeton, NJ, 1991), 224–53; C. R. Browning, *Ordinary Men* (New York, 1992); Browning, *The Path to Genocide* (New York, 1992); Wildt, *An Uncompromising Generation*.
7. G. Aly, *Hitler's Beneficiaries*, trans. J. Chase (New York, 2006); M. Dean et al., eds., *Robbery and Restitution* (New York, 2007); C. Goschler et al., eds., *Raub und Restitution* (Frankfurt, 2003); C. Goschler et al., eds., *"Arisierung" und Restitution* (Göttingen, 2002). See also G. Feldman et al., eds., *Networks of Persecution* (New York, 2005) and A. Tooze, *The Wages of Destruction* (New York, 2006), 461–85, 513–31.
8. D. Nirenberg, *Anti-Judaism* (New York, 2013); W. I. Brustein, *Roots of Hate* (New York, 2003); J. Weiss, *The Politics of Hate* (Chicago, 2003); W. Bergmann et al., eds., *Exclusionary Violence* (Ann Arbor, MI, 2002); J. Carrol, *Constantine's Sword* (Boston, MA, 2001); A. S. Lindemann, *Anti-Semitism Before the Holocaust* (New York, 2000); K. P. Fischer, *The History of an Obsession* (New York, 1998); P. Schäfer, *Judeophobia* (Cambridge, MA, 1997); R. S. Wistrich, *Antisemitism* (New York, 1994); S. L. Gilman et al., eds., *Anti-Semitism in Times of Crisis* (New York, 1991); G. I. Langmuir, *History, Religion, and Antisemitism* (Berkeley, CA, 1990).
9. Compare, e.g., Y. Gutman, *The Jews of Warsaw, 1939–1943* (Bloomington, IN, 1989), and Y. Gutman et al., *Unequal Victims*, trans. T. Gorelick et al. (New York, 1986), with G. S. Paulsson, *Secret City* (New Haven, CT, 2002) and R. C. Lukas, *The Forgotten Holocaust* (Lexington, KY, 1986). Compare also M. Wierzbicki, *Polacy i Żydzi w zaborze sowieckim* (Warsaw, 2001) with J. T. Gross, *Revolution from Abroad*, expanded ed. (Princeton, NJ, 2002), 241–88.
10. J. T. Gross, *Fear* (Princeton, NJ, 2006); E. Hoffman, *After Such Knowledge* (New York, 2004); J. Michlic, *Poland's Threatening Other* (Lincoln, NE, 2006); D. Blatman, "Polish Jewry, the Six-Day War, and the Crisis of 1968," in *The Six-Day War and World Jewry*, ed. E. Lederhendler (Bethesda, MD, 2000), 291–310; D. Stola, "Fighting against the Shadows," in *Antisemitism and Its Opponents in Modern Poland*, ed. R. Blobaum (Ithaca, NY, 2005), 284–300. See also J. T. Gross, *Neighbors* (Princeton, NJ, 2001); A. Bikont, *The Crime and the Silence*, trans. A. Valles (New York, 2015); J. Tokarska-Bakir, *Pod klątwa* (Warsaw, 2018). On Eastern Europe as the victim of totalitarianism and war, see T. Snyder, *Bloodlands* (New York, 2010), and critique in O. Bartov, "Featured Review," *SR* 70, no. 2 (2011): 424–8.
11. L. Wolff, *Inventing Eastern Europe* (Stanford, CA, 1994).

Notes

12. For some Western publications on the debate over Gross's *Neighbors*, see J. B. Michlic et al., eds., *The Neighbors Respond* (Princeton, NJ, 2004); M. Shore, "Conversing with Ghosts," *Kritika* 6, no. 2 (2005): 1–20; J. Connelly, "Poles and Jews in the Second World War," *CEH* 2, no. 4 (2002): 641–58, and Bikont, *The Crime and the Silence*.
13. T. Mason, "Intention and Explanation" (orig. pub. 1981), in T. Mason, *Nazism, Fascism, and the Working Class*, ed. J. Caplan (Cambridge, UK, 1995), 212–30.
14. E.g., Philip Friedman, Yehuda Bauer, Yisrael Gutman, Raul Hilberg, and Saul Friedländer. But last two had limited familiarity with East European languages and historiographies.
15. B. Cohen, *Israeli Holocaust Research* (London, 2012); D. Michman, "Is There an 'Israeli School' in Holocaust Research?" *Zion* 74 (2009): 219–44 (Hebrew). Israeli historian and Israeli minister of education in 1951–5, Ben Zion Dinur, played a leading role in formulating the law establishing Yad Vashem in 1953. See his book, *Remember* (Jerusalem, 1958 [Hebrew]), 18–19; R. Stauber, *The Holocaust in Israeli Public Debate in the 1950s*, trans. E. Yuval (London, 2007), 60–5, and Segev, *The Seventh Million*, 421–45.
16. For the debate over Hilberg's views on Jewish complicity, his book's rejection by Yad Vashem, and the debate over H. Arendt, *Eichmann in Jerusalem* (New York, 1963), see Bartov, *Mirrors of Destruction*, 129–32.
17. N. Berg, *Der Holocaust und die westdeutschen Historiker* (Göttingen, 2003); Baldwin, *Reworking the Past*, 77–134.
18. See, e.g., Y. Gutman, ed., *Major Changes within the Jewish People in the Wake of the Holocaust* (Jerusalem, 1996 [Hebrew]). Further in Bartov, *Germany's War and the Holocaust*, 99–121.
19. See the "European Parliament resolution on remembrance of the Holocaust, anti-semitism and racism," January 27, 2005, www.europarl.europa.eu/doceo/document/TA-6-2005-0018_EN.html.
20. See, e.g., E. Barkan et al., eds., *Shared History—Divided Memory* (Göttingen, 2007), and compare W. W. Hagen, "Before the 'Final Solution,'" *JMH* 68, no. 2 (1996): 351–81, Connelly, "Poles and Jews in the Second World War," and Gross, *Fear*, chaps. 3–4, with M. J. Chodakiewicz, "Affinity and Revulsion," in *Spanish Carlism and Polish Nationalism*, ed. Chodakiewicz et al. (Charlottesville, VA, 2003), 51–6 and Chodakiewicz, *After the Holocaust* (New York, 2003), 159–76.
21. See, e.g., T. W. Ryback, *The Last Survivor* (New York, 1999), and J. L. Baker et al., *The Book of Jedwabne* (Jerusalem, 1980 [Hebrew]). See also P. Machcewicz et al., *Wokół Jedwabnego*, 2 vols. (Warsaw, 2002). Further on local complicity, see Pohl, *Nationalsozialistische Judenverfolgung in Ostgalizien, 1941–1944* (Munich, 1996); T. Sandkühler, *"Endlösung" in Galizien* (Bonn, 1996); B. Chiari, *Alltag hinter der Front* (Düsseldorf, 1998); M. Dean, *Collaboration in the Holocaust, 1941–44* (New York, 2000).
22. R. Hilberg, *Perpetrators Victims Bystanders: The Jewish Catastrophe, 1933–1945* (New York, 1992).
23. O. Bartov et al., eds., *Crimes of War* (New York, 2002); H. Heer et al., eds., *War of Extermination* (New York, 2000); Hamburg Institute for Social Research, ed., *The German Army and Genocide*, trans. S. Abbott et al. (New York, 1999).
24. B. Boll, "Złoczów, July 1941," in Bartov, *Crimes of War*, 61–99; D. Bechtel, "De Jedwabne à Zolotchiv," in *CEC 5: La destruction de confines*, ed. D. Bechtel et al. (Paris, 2005), 69–92. For a revisionist view, see B. Musial, *Konterrevolutionäre Elemente sind zu erschießen* (Berlin, 2000). The most recent study is A. Zapalec, "Złoczów County," in Engelking, *Night without End*, 235–94. See also K. C. Berkhoff, *Harvest of Despair* (Cambridge, MA, 2004); R. Brandon and W. Lower, eds., *The Shoah in Ukraine* (Bloomington, IN, 2008); W. Lower, *The Ravine* (Boston, MA, 2021).
25. C. Delbo, *None of Us Will Return*, trans. J. Githens (New York, 1968 [1965]); P. Levi, *The Reawakening (La tregua)*, trans. S. Woolf (New York, 1995 [1963]).

26 See, e.g., Pohl, *Nationalsozialistische Judenverfolgung*, 144-7; Sandkühler, *"Endlösung" in Galizien*, 150-2; E. Freundlich, *Die Ermordung einer Stadt namens Stanislau* (Vienna, 1986), 154-64; A. Liebesman, *With the Jews of Stanisławów in the Holocaust* (Tel Aviv, 1980 [Hebrew]), 22-31; Bartov, *Anatomy of a Genocide*, 232-64.
27 Julija Mykhailivna Trembach, written by her daughter, Roma Nestorivna Kryvenchuk, collected by Mykola Kozak, translated by Sofia Grachova, speaking of Buczacz in Eastern Galicia, now West Ukraine, in 2003.
28 Maria Mykhailivna Khvostenko (née Dovhanchuk), interviewed by Mykola Kozak, translated by Sofia Grachova, speaking of Buczacz in 2003.
29 Ibid.
30 See, e.g., Eliasz Chalfen (Elijahu Chalfon), *YVA*, M1/E 1559 (Polish), and 03/8553 (Hebrew), October 21, 1947.
31 Ibid.
32 See note 7, and F. Bajohr, *"Aryanisation" in Hamburg*, trans. G. Wilkes (New York, 2002); Bajohr, *Parvenüs und Profiteure* (Frankfurt, 2001).
33 C. Goschler, *Wiedergutmachung* (Munich, 1992); L. Herbst et al., eds., *Wiedergutmachung in der Bundesrepublik Deutschland* (Munich, 1989); C. Pross, *Paying for the Past*, trans. B. Cooper (Baltimore, MD, 1998); M. J. Bazyler, *Holocaust Justice* (New York, 2003).
34 Gross, *Revolution from Abroad*, 187-224; B.-C. Pinchuk, *Shtetl Jews under Soviet Rule* (Oxford, 1990); B. Milch, *Can Heaven Be Void?* trans. and ed. S. Milch-Avigal et al. (Jerusalem, 1999 [Hebrew]), 37-48. For memoirs, taped testimonies, and interviews from Buczacz, see P. Anderman, *The Will to Life* (Tel Aviv, 2004 [Hebrew]), 24-9; A. Appleman-Jurman, *Alicia* (New York, 1988), 5-12; R. Zuroff (Tabak), *SFV*, August 31, 1995; G. Gross, *SFV*, June 17, 1996; E. Grintal (Nachtigal), *SFV*, September 21, 1997 (Hebrew); S. Tischler, *YVA*, 03/10229, VT-1585, June 26, 1997 (Hebrew); interview with W. Halkiewicz by F. Grelka, April 27, 2004; J. Anczarski, *Kronikarskie zapisy z lat cierpień i grozy w Małopolsce Wschodniej 1939-1946* (Kraków, 1998), 15-176 (original document in *HI, AW*, II/1224); W. Janda, *AW*, II/1561.
35 Generally, see L. Dobroszycki et al., eds., *The Holocaust in the Soviet Union* (Armonk, NY, 1993); Y. Arad, *History of the Holocaust* (Jerusalem, 2004 [Hebrew]).
36 On the idea that eliminating Jews would facilitate the emergence of an ethnic Polish middle class, see J. Tomaszewski, "The Role of Jews in Polish Commerce, 1918-1939," in Gutman, *The Jews of Poland*, 141-57; Mendelsohn, *The Jews of East Central Europe*, 11-83; G. Aly et al., *Architects of Annihilation*, trans. A. G. Blunden (Princeton, NJ, 2002).
37 R. E. Gruber, *Virtually Jewish* (Berkeley, 2002). On looting mass graves of Jews, see J. T. Gross, *Golden Harvest* (New York, 2021).
38 I. Bobyk, *The City of Butchach and Its Region* (London, 1972 [Ukrainian]), 475-7.
39 I. Gelbart, *YVA*, 033/640.
40 Ibid.
41 I. Duda, *Buchach* (Lviv, 1985 [Ukrainian]).
42 T. Pavlyshyn, "The Holocaust in Buczacz," *Nova Doba* 48 (December 1, 2000 [Ukrainian]).
43 Ibid.
44 Ibid.
45 D. Engel, *In the Shadow of Auschwitz* (Chapel Hill, NC, 1987), and Engel, *Facing a Holocaust* (Chapel Hill, NC, 1993).
46 Pavlyshyn, "The Holocaust in Buczacz."
47 Ibid.
48 See also M. S. Mandel, *In the Aftermath of Genocide* (Durham, NC, 2003); A. Astro, ed., "Discourses of Jewish Identity in Twentieth Century France," in *YFS* 85 (New Haven, CT, 1994); E. Benbassa, *The Jews of France*, trans. M. B. DeBevoise (Princeton, NJ, 1999), 178-99; P.

Notes

E. Hyman, *The Jews of Modern France* (Berkeley, CA, 1998), 193-214; H. S. Hughes, *Prisoners of Hope* (Cambridge, MA, 1983).

49 H. Fireberg et al., eds., *Being Jewish in 21st-Century Germany* (Berlin, 2015); M. Brenner, *After the Holocaust*, trans. B. Harshav (Princeton, NJ, 1997); Y. M. Bodemann, ed., *Jews, Germans, Memory* (Ann Arbor, MI, 1996); J. Borneman and J. M. Peck, *Sojourners* (Lincoln, NE, 1995). But see also J. Reinharz et al., eds., *Inside the Antisemitic Mind* (Waltham, MA, 2017).

50 See note 10, and K. Gebert, "Revival? Rebirth? Renaissance? What Has Happened to Polish Jews over the Last Four Decades?" *NJ* 31, no. 1 (2020): 65-75; J. Michlic, "'The Open Church' and 'the Closed Church' and the Discourse on Jews in Poland between 1989 and 2000," *CPCS* 37, no. 4 (2004): 461-79; S. Ury, "Who, What, When, Where, and Why Is Polish Jewry?" *JSS* 6, no. 3 (2000): 205-28; R. F. Scharf, *Poland, What Have I to Do with Thee*, 2nd ed. (Kraków, 1999); E. Forgács et al., eds., *Contemporary Jewish Writing in Hungary* (Lincoln, NE, 2003). For current Jewish population estimates in Poland, see *World Jewish Congress*, www.worldjewishcongress.org/en/about/communities/PL and Institute for Jewish Policy Research, www.jpr.org.uk/country?id=244.

51 See Gerlach, *Extermination of the European Jews*; P. Hayes, *Why?* (New York, 2017).

52 But see Browning, *Remembering Survival* (New York: W. W. Norton & Co., 2019) and S. Spector, *The Holocaust of Volhynian Jews, 1941-1944*, trans. J. Michalowicz (Jerusalem, 1990 [1986]).

53 See, e.g., H. Dreifuss, *Warsaw Ghetto—The End* (Jerusalem, 2017 [Hebrew]). G. J. Horwitz, *Ghettostadt* (Cambridge, MA, 2008) is innovative.

54 See, e.g., J. S. Milligan, "'What Is an Archive?' in the History of Modern France," in *Archive Stories*, ed. A. Burton (New York, 2005), 159-83.

55 See, e.g., R. Hilberg, *The Destruction of the European Jews*, 3 vols., 3rd ed. (New Haven, CT, 2003), 3: 1080-1104.

56 L. Douglas, *The Memory of Judgment* (New Haven, CT, 2001); H. Yablonka, *The State of Israel vs. Adolf Eichmann*, trans. O. Cummings et al. (New York, 2004); S. Meinl et al., eds., *Im Labyrinth der Schuld* (Frankfurt, 2003); D. Pendas, *The Frankfurt Auschwitz Trial, 1963-1965* (Cambridge, UK, 2006); R. Wittmann, *Beyond Justice* (Cambridge, MA, 2005).

57 Goldhagen, *Hitler's Willing Executioners*; Browning, *Ordinary Men*.

58 Douglas, *Memory of Judgment*, 65-80. See also M. R. Marrus, ed., *The Nuremberg War Crimes Trial, 1945-46* (Boston, MA, 1997).

59 An overview in F. Bauer et al., eds., *Justiz und NS-Verbrechen* (hereafter *J.u.NS-V*), multiple vols. (Amsterdam, 1968-). A bitter Jewish perspective in A. Gutfreund, *Our Holocaust*, trans. J. Cohen (New Milford, CT, 2006). See more in Chapter 6.

60 Further in Bartov, *The "Jew" in Cinema*, 78-92. Hannah Arendt famously covered the trial for the *New Yorker Magazine* and subsequently published her influential, but deeply flawed account, *Eichmann in Jerusalem*, in 1963.

61 I would argue that the Eichmann Trial was far more instrumental in this regard than the 1967 Six-Day War. See on this Novick, *The Holocaust in American Life*. Further in O. Bartov, "The Holocaust as Leitmotif of the Twentieth Century," in *Lessons and Legacies VII*, ed. D. Herzog (Evanston, IL, 2006), 3-25.

62 P. Weiss, *The Investigation*, trans. U. Grosbard et al. (New York, 1966 [1965]). See also D. Herzog, *Sex after Fascism* (Princeton, NJ, 2005).

63 In this context, see B. Schlink, *The Reader*, trans. C. B. Janeway (New York, 1997).

64 J. Wulf, *Das Dritte Reich und seine Vollstrecker* (Berlin-Grunewald, 1961).

65 M. Broszat, *Nationalsozialistische Polenpolitik, 1939-1945* (Stuttgart, 1961).

66 N. Berg, "Die Lebenslüge vom Pathos der Nüchternheit," *SZ* (July 17, 2002); Berg, *Der Holocaust und die westdeutschen Historiker*, 337-70, 447-65, 594-615; Baldwin, *Reworking the Past*, 77-134.

Notes

67 See further in Bartov, *Mirrors of Destruction*, 129–30.
68 M. Broszat, *The Hitler State*, trans. J. W. Hiden (London, 1981 [1969]). See also O. Bartov, "A Man without Qualities," *TNR* (March 12, 2001): 34–40.
69 Hilberg, *The Politics of Memory* (Chicago, 1996), 154–7; Browning, *Origins of the Final Solution*.
70 See Jewish Historical Institute, www.jhi.pl/en/about-the-institute; Early Holocaust Testimony, https://early-testimony.ehri-project.eu/exhibits/show/history-of-collections/jhi-warsaw.
71 Yad Vashem, www.yadvashem.org/.
72 Fortunoff Video Archive for Holocaust Testimonies, www.library.yale.edu/testimonies/.
73 D. P. Boder, *I Did Not Interview the Dead* (Urbana, IL, 1949); D. P. Boder, "Topical Autobiographies of Displaced People Recorded Verbatim in Displaced Persons Camps, with a Psychological and Anthropological Analysis" (Chicago, 1950–7 [microform]); D. L. Niewyk, *Fresh Wounds* (Chapel Hill, NC, 1998); Voices of the Holocaust, https://voices.iit.edu/.
74 S. Miltenberger et al., eds., *Archiv der Erinnerung*, 2 vols. (Potsdam, 1998).
75 USC Shoah Foundation, https://sfi.usc.edu/.
76 Mandel Center, USHMM, www.ushmm.org/research/center/.
77 Archiwum Wschodnie, karta.org.pl/aktualnosci/archiwum-wschodnie; Hoover Institution, www.hoover.org/library-archives/collections/poland-during-world-war-ii.
78 Z. Kovba, *Humanity in the Abyss of Hell* (Kyiv, 1998 [Ukrainian]); B. Zabarko, ed., *"Nur wir haben überlebt,"* trans. M. Hegge et al. (Lutherstadt Wittenberg, 2004).
79 R. Szporluk, *Russia, Ukraine, and the Breakup of the Soviet Union* (Stanford, CA, 2000), 109–50.
80 See, e.g., *Pinkas Hakehillot, Poland*, vol. 2: *Eastern Galicia*, ed. D. Dąbrowska et al. (Jerusalem, 1980 [Hebrew]); Y. Cohen, ed., *Sefer Buczacz* (Tel Aviv, 1956 [Hebrew and Yiddish]); W. Szklarz, ed., *Głos Buczaczan* (Wrocław, 1991).
81 J. Czaplicka, ed., *Lviv* (Cambridge, MA, 2000); S. Redlich, *Together and Apart in Brzeżany* (Bloomington, IN, 2002); K. Brown, *A Biography of No Place* (Cambridge, MA, 2004); W. W. Hagen, "The Moral Economy of Popular Violence," in Blobaum, *Antisemitism and Its Opponents*, 124–47; R. Brubaker et al., *Nationalist Politics and Everyday Ethnicity in a Transylvanian Town* (Princeton, NJ, 2006); F. Golczewski, "Shades of Grey," in Brandon and Lower, *The Shoah in Ukraine*, 114–55; H. Case, *Between States* (Stanford, CA, 2009); T. Amar, *The Paradox of Ukrainian Lviv* (Ithaca, NY, 2015); T. R. Weeks, *Vilnius between Nations, 1795–2000* (DeKalb, IL, 2015); Bartov, *Anatomy of a Genocide*; Engelking, *Night without End*.
82 See, e.g., educational programs at the USC Shoah Foundation and the Los Angeles Museum of Tolerance.
83 W. S. Allen, *The Nazi Seizure of Power* (Chicago, 1965).
84 In a different context, this is the assertion of Brown University's Slavery and Justice report: www.brown.edu/Research/Slavery_Justice/.
85 P. Nora, ed., *Les Lieux de mémoire*, 3 vols. (Paris, 1984–92).

Chapter 3

1 Gross, *Neighbors*; Grabowski, *Hunt for the Jews*; A. Żbikowski, "Pogroms in Northeastern Poland," in Barkan, *Shared History*, 315–54; B. Engelking, "Murdering and Denouncing Jews in the Polish Countryside, 1942–1945," and A. Żbikowski, "'Night Guard,'" *EEPS* 25, no. 3 (2011): 433–56, 512–29; Bartov, *Anatomy of a Genocide*.
2 For various interpretations of perpetrator motivation, see Goldhagen, *Hitler's Willing Executioners*; Browning, *Ordinary Men*; R. J. Lifton, *The Nazi Doctors* (New York, 1986);

Waller, *Becoming Evil* (New York, 2002). See the chilling portrayal of camp commandant Franz Stangl in G. Sereny, *Into That Darkness* (New York, 1974).

3 D. Laor, *S. Y. Agnon* (Tel Aviv, 1998 [Hebrew]), 13–48.
4 Overviews in Pohl, *Nationalsozialistische* Judenverfolgung; Sandkühler, *"Endlösung" in Galizien*. According to the former Ukrainian mayor of Buczacz under the German occupation, the town numbered 8,000 Jews, 3,600 Ukrainians, and 3,500 Poles in summer 1941. He also cites a postwar letter from Jewish survivor Isidor Gelbart estimating a Jewish population of 8,000 in 1939 and stating that in the early period of Nazi rule, the number of Jews in Buczacz "grew considerably" because it was considered safer than other sites. Bobyk, *The City of Butchach*, 475–9.
5 For a definition of a *shtetl* based on the share of Jews in a town's population, see Y. Bauer, *The Death of the Shtetl* (New Haven, CT, 2009), 3–4.
6 In 1870 the 6,077 Jews of Buczacz constituted 67.9 percent of the total population of 8,959. M. Bałaban, "Buchach (Buczacz)," in *Jewish Encyclopedia*, ed. L. Katznelson et al. (St. Petersburg, 1906–13 [Russian]), vol. 5, 135. In 1914 Buczacz numbered 3,500 Poles, 2,000 Ukrainians, and 7,500 (57.7 percent) Jews. M. Orłowicz et al., eds., *Ilustrowany Przewodnik po Galicyi* (Lwów, 1914), 141.
7 In 1890 Eastern Galicia had a population of 3.1 million—19 percent Roman Catholics, 66 percent Greek Catholics, 14 percent Jews; Jews comprised 47 percent of the urban population, but only 7.26 percent of villagers. Between 1849 and 1910 the population of Galicia (Eastern and Western) as a whole rose from 5 to 8 million: 45 percent Poles, 43 percent Ukrainians, and 11 percent Jews. P. R. Magocsi, *A History of Ukraine* (Seattle, 1996), 424; Jit, *Stosunki narodowościowe w Galicyi wschodniej* (Kraków, 1894), 15–16, 38–39, 75–7.
8 See, e.g., Longerich, *Holocaust*.
9 See Bartov, *Erased*; Bartov, *Anatomy of a Genocide*; Bartov, *Tales from the Borderlands*; M. Hirsch and L. Spitzer, *Ghosts of Home* (Berkeley, CA, 2010); D. Mendelsohn, *The Lost* (New York, 2006).
10 R. Brubaker, "Aftermaths of Empire and the Unmixing of Peoples," in R. Brubaker, *Nationalism Reframed* (New York, 1996), 148–78; M. Carynnyk, "Foes of Our Rebirth," *NP* 39, no. 3 (2011): 315–52; Aly, *Architects of Annihilation*.
11 Samantha Power, *"A Problem from Hell": America and the Age of Genocide* (New York, 2002).
12 L. Wolff, *The Idea of Galicia* (Stanford, CA, 2010).
13 J.-P. Himka, "The Lviv Pogrom of 1941," *CSP* 53, nos. 2–4 (2011): 209–43; K. Struve, "Tremors in the Shatterzone of Empires," in Bartov and Weitz, *Shatterzone of Empires*, 463–84.
14 Bartov, *Anatomy of a Genocide*. See also Bartov, *Tales from the Borderlands*, and O. Bartov, ed., *Voices on War and Genocide* (New York, 2021). The town's memorial book is Cohen, *Sefer Buczacz*.
15 N. N. Hanover, *The Book of the Deep Mire* (Tel Aviv, 1944–5 [Hebrew, 1653]), trans. A. J. Mesch as *Abyss of Despair* (*Yeven Metzulah*), reprint ed. (New Brunswick, NJ, 1983). See also J. Raba, *Between Remembrance and Denial* (New York, 1995).
16 *Das Reisejournal des Ulrich von Werdum (1670–1677)*, ed. S. Kramer (Frankfurt am Main, 1990), 210–11.
17 F.-P. Dalairac, *Les Anecdotes de Pologne ou Mémoires secrets du Règne de Jean Sobieski* (Paris, 1699), 230, cited in S. Barącz, *Pamiątki Buczackie* (Lwów, 1882), 12.
18 Dalairac, *Les anecdotes*, 228, cited in Barącz, *Pamiątki Buczackie*, 12.
19 Z. Krasiński, *Nie-Boska komedyja* (Paris, 1862), 98; Polski *Słownik Biograficzny* 28 (Kraków, 1984–5), 113–14; C. Miłosz, *The History of Polish Literature*, 2nd ed. (Berkeley, CA, 1983), 143–7; S. Grodziski, *Wzdłuż Wisły, Dniestru i Zbrucza* (Kraków, 1998), 136–7; A. Żarnowski, *Kresy Wschodnie II Rzeczypospolitej* (Kraków, 1992), 8. Wolff, *The Idea of Galicia*, 145.
20 Barącz, *Pamiątki Buczackie*.

21 S. Y. Agnon, *Ir u-melo'ah* (Tel Aviv, 1973 [Hebrew]), partially translated as *A City in Its Fullness*, ed. A. Mintz et al., eds., multiple translators (New Milford, CT, 2016).
22 N. Sinkoff, *Out of the Shtetl* (Providence, RI, 2004); M. Wodziński, *Haskalah and Hasidism in the Kingdom of Poland* (Portland, OR, 2005).
23 Cohen, *Sefer Buczacz*, 212–24; P. S. Wandycz, "The Poles in the Habsburg Monarchy," in *Nationbuilding and the Politics of Nationalism*, ed. A. S. Markovits, et al. (Cambridge, MA, 1982), 75–81; J.-P. Himka, *Galician Villagers and the Ukrainian National Movement in the Nineteenth Century* (New York, 1988); K. Struve, *Bauern und Nation in Galizien* (Göttingen, 2005).
24 A. Siewiński, "Memories of Buczacz and Jazłowiec during the Great War, 1914–1920," in Bartov, *Voices on War and Genocide*, 21–137. The original is at the BJ, manuscript division, BJ 7367.
25 A. Lev, "The Devastation of Galician Jewry in the Bloody World War," trans. from Yiddish by B. Aizenberg, in *Jewish Chronicle*, vol. 3, ed. L. M. Klyachko et al. (Leningrad, 1924 [Russian]), 174.
26 S. An-Ski, *The Destruction of the Jews in Poland, Galicia, and Bukovina*, trans. from Yiddish by S. L. Zitron, 2 vols. (Berlin, 1929/Tel Aviv, 1936? [Hebrew]), vol. 2, pt. 4, 406, partially translated by J. Neugroschel as *The Enemy at His Pleasure* (New York, 2002). See also *1915 Diary of S. An-sky*, trans. P. Zavadiker (Bloomington, IN, 2016); G. Safran, *Wandering Soul* (Cambridge, MA, 2010), 225–57.
27 For photos of wartime Buczacz in 1914–18, see at AT-OeSt/KA, BS I WK Fronten Galizien. In summer 1918, a total of 569 destroyed houses were listed: TsDIAL, fond 146, op. 48, spr. 31–2.
28 See, e.g., I. Krypiakevych et al., *History of the Ukrainian Army* (Lviv, 1936 [Ukrainian]), 502–12; W. Hupert, *Zajęcie Małopolski Wschodniej i Wołynia w roku 1919* (Lwów-Warsaw, 1928), 42–3, 96–105.
29 See, e.g., Parliamentary Commission for the Investigation of Ukrainian Raids against Polish Civilians, testimonies from Buczacz: AAN/MSZ/Eastern Division, 5341a, 227, 233–4.
30 For British reports on Eastern Galicia in 1920–4, see TNA, FO 688/2/3, 229–30; FO 688/2/3, 295–303; FO 688/9/2/, 553–56; FO 688/15/12, 679–88. See also I. Petruševych, "L'Ukraine Occidentale," 1921, PAAA, Pol. 1, R 81428; Hagen, "The Moral Economy of Popular Violence."
31 See, e.g., P. Shandruk, ed., *The Ukrainian-Russian War of 1920 in Documents* (Warsaw, 1933 [Ukrainian]), 114–17, 120–51, 216–37; N. K. Kolesnik et al., eds., *The Civil War in Ukraine, 1918–1920* (Kyiv, 1967 [Russian]), 336–9.
32 F. Bruder, *"Den ukrainischen Staat erkämpfen oder sterben!"* (Berlin, 2007); J.-P. Himka, *Ukrainian Nationalists and the Holocaust* (Stuttgart, 2021).
33 Hagen, "Before the 'Final Solution'"; S. Rudnicki, "Anti-Jewish Legislation in Interwar Poland," in Blobaum, *Antisemitism and Its Opponents*, 148–70; H. Michael, *Zwischen Davidstern und Roter Fahne* (Berlin-Brandenburg, 2007), 85–122.
34 Mendelsohn, *The Jews of East Central Europe*, 68–83; M. Mishkinsky, "The Communist Party of Poland and the Jews," and A. Brumberg, "The Bund and the Polish Socialist Party in the late 1930s," both in *The Jews of Poland between the Two World Wars*, ed. Y. Gutman et al. (Hanover, NH, 1989), 56–74 and 75–94; C. S. Heller, *On the Edge of Destruction* (Detroit, MI, 1994), 249–93.
35 See, e.g., "Ekscesy ukraińskie w Trościance," Buczacz, June 12, 1934, DATO, fond 231, op. 1, spr. 2264, 14–16; Starosta Buczacki, Nr. 9/33/Taj. "Żydowskie życie polityczne," Buczacz, January 29, 1933; "K.P.Z.U. w Buczaczu—informacje," Buczacz, June 24, 1935, DATO, fond 231, op. 1, spr. 2325.
36 See, e.g., *Księga Adresowa Małopolski, Rocznik 1935/1936*, 12–13.
37 T. Segev, *Simon Wiesenthal* (New York, 2010), 29–43; S. D. Kassow, *Who Will Write Our History?* (Bloomington, IN, 2007), 17–26; Cohen, *Sefer Buczacz*, 225–8.

Notes

38   S. Y. Agnon, *Ore'ah natah lalun*, rev. ed. (Tel Aviv, 1998 [1939]), trans. M. Louvish as *A Guest for the Night* (Madison, WI, 1968).
39   Bartov, *Anatomy of a Genocide*, 101-2.
40   See records of Soviet trial (1956-7) of Volodymyr Kaznovskyi, commander of Ukrainian police in Buczacz, with names and records of other police officers and their prewar political engagement: HAD SBU, Ternopil, spr. 30466, vols. 1-2; 26874; 14050-P; 736; 3713; 14340; 9859-P; 8540-P; 8973-P; 14320-P; and Soviet "Extraordinary State Commission" report, USHMM RG- 22-002M, Reel # 17 (Ternopil region). See also Himka, *Ukrainian Nationalists and the Holocaust*; G. N. Finder and A. V. Prusin, "Collaboration in Eastern Galicia," *EEJA* 34, no. 2 (2004): 95-118.
41   Gross, *Revolution from Abroad*; Musial, "*Konterrevolutionäre Elemente.*" Berkhoff, *Harvest of Despair*, 14, cites Soviet documents indicating a total of 8,789 Ukrainian, Polish, and Jewish prisoners killed by the NKVD in Ukraine.
42   G. Rossoliński-Liebe, "Debating, Obfuscating and Disciplining the Holocaust," *EEJA* 42, no. 3 (2012): 203, estimates over 13,000 Jewish victims; D. Pohl, "Anti-Jewish Pogroms in Western Ukraine," in Barkan, *Shared History*, 306, estimates up to 35,000 killed. See also K. Struve, "The Explosion of Violence," in Bartov and Weitz, *Shatterzone of Empires*, 463-84; J.-P. Himka, *Ukrainians, Jews and the Holocaust: Divergent Memories* (Saskatoon, 2009).
43   For Moshe Wizinger's account of events in Buczacz during the early days of the German occupation, see Chapter 4. Similarly in G. Gross 1996 and Gelbart 1948. The German army entered Buczacz on July 5, 1941. The next day it reported: "A Ukrainian militia took over local police duties until the arrival of German troops." See BArch RH20-17/32, 5.7.41, 6.7.41; RH26-101/8, 5.7.41; RH24-52/3, KTB, Heft 2, 40-2, 55; RH20-17/38, 6.7.41, 12.7.41; RH26 257/8, KTB Nr. 5, 20.5.41-12.12.41. On the self-proclaimed Ukrainian "Sich" (militia) Buczacz, see Bartov, *Anatomy of a Genocide*, 158-69, 179-82.
44   Yitzhak Bauer, interviewed by me in 2003 in Hebrew, recalled his anti-Semitic Polish teacher in the 1930s. But Appleman-Jurman, *Alicia*, and M. Rosner, *I am a Witness* (Winnipeg, 1990), report being protected by Poles during the German occupation. Bruder, "*Den ukrainischen Staat erkämpfen oder sterben!*," 168, cites a March 1943 OUN-UPA report complaining that "The Poles very eagerly help the Jews and hide them ... because they view the Jews as their natural allies in the struggle against the Ukrainians."
45   See, e.g., Z. Pollak (Zonka Berkowicz), SFV, August 23, 1995.
46   Bartov, *Anatomy of a Genocide*, 169-79. Further in Chapter 5.
47   Bauer 2003 and Chapter 5.
48   Testimonies in Cohen, *Sefer Buczacz*, 233-302; Bartov, *Anatomy of a Genocide*, 232-64. For a West German court's summary of the events, see *J.u.NS-V*, 18: 658-83.
49   Ibid., 657; BArch, MfS, ZB 827, Akte 2, and GLA Karlsruhe 309 Zug. 2001_42/881: Eisel Werner (last commander of Czortków Sipo outpost), R.u.S. Fragebogen, September 1, 1944.
50   See note 32. See also T. Snyder, "The Causes of Ukrainian-Polish Ethnic Cleansing 1943," *P&P* 179, no. 1 (2003): 198-234; G. Motyka et al., *Antypolska akcja OUN-UPA 1943-1944* (Warsaw, 2002); P. A. Rudling, "The OUN, the UPA and the Holocaust," *REES*, no. 2107 (Pittsburgh, 2011); J.-P. Himka, "Debates in Ukraine over Nationalist Involvement in the Holocaust, 2004-2008," *NP* 39, no. 3 (2011): 353-70.
51   G. Motyka, *Ukraińska partyzantka 1942-1960* (Warsaw, 2006); J. Burds, *The Early Cold War in Soviet West Ukraine, 1944-1948* (Pittsburgh, PA, 2001).
52   See, e.g., Longerich, *Holocaust*; Friedländer, *Nazi Germany and the Jews*; Gerlach, *Extermination of the European Jews*; Pohl, *Nationalsozialistische Judenverfolgung*; Sandkühler, "*Endlösung" in Galizien*.

Notes

53   J. Dietsch, *Making Sense of Suffering* (Lund, Sweden, 2006); W. Jilge, "The Politics of History and the Second World War in Post-Communist Ukraine (1986/1991–2004/2005)," in *Divided Historical Cultures?* ed. W. Jilge et al., *JGO* 54, no. 1 (2006): 51–82.
54   Chalfen 1947.
55   Grintal 1997.
56   See notes 32, 50, 51. See also T. Snyder, *The Reconstruction of Nations* (New Haven, CT, 2003), 165–78. M. J. Melnyk, *To Battle* (Solihull, UK, 2002), dedicated to the Waffen-SS "Galicia" Division, contains no mention of anti-Jewish violence.
57   A. Klonicki-Klonymus, *The Diary of Adam's Father* (Jerusalem, 1969 [Hebrew]), 47.
58   *Przeżycia i rozporządzenie Joachima Mincere,* probably written in 1943, YVA.
59   Y. Katz, SFV, December 11, 1995 (Hebrew).
60   E. Spielberg-Flitman, SFV, March 14, 1995.
61   M. Szpigiel, USHMM, reel 37, 301/3492, March 10, 1948.
62   Trembach 2003. Compare literary descriptions of a Galician marketplace by I. Franko, *Fateful Crossroads,* trans. R. Franko (Winnipeg, 2006 [1900]), 178–9, and Agnon, *Ir u-melo'ah,* 269.
63   Khvostenko 2003.
64   Bartov, *Voices on War and Genocide,* 209–10, 217.
65   Returning to Buczacz after the liberation, nine-year-old Aliza Rosenwasser (Gripel) found that the neighbors had "dismantled the floor" in her home in search for hidden valuable. The unmarked mass grave on Fedor Hill could be found only because that section of the forest remained "entirely bare"; apparently "the soil was too rich" with corpses to allow any vegetation. YVA 03/10402, VT-1612, July 17, 1997, transcript, 55. Returning to Buczacz four months after its liberation, fourteen-year-old Bronia Kahane stayed with the few Jews still living there in a single house behind locked doors, "because we're afraid during the night they shouldn't kill us"; she never visited her family's house "because they said don't you dare go back because they're going to kill you." SFV, August 8, 1995.
66   Gross, *Fear*; Gross, *Golden Harvest*; Himka & Michlic, *Bringing the Dark Past to Light*.
67   See, e.g., TsDIAL, fond R-1, op. 1, spr. 101, 284, 561, 871, situation reports of the Regional Committee of the Communist Party in Ternopol (Ternopil), September 3–November 3, 1944. See also Bartov, *Anatomy of a Genocide,* 284–8.
68   Zuroff 1995.
69   See, e.g., Duda, *Buchach*.
70   Sklarz, "Głos Buczaczan"; Bobyk, *Butchach*; Cohen, *Sefer Buczacz*. Mayor Bobyk's interwar Polish police file describes him as a "presumed member of UVO." DATO, fond 274, op. 4, spr. 78, p. 13. The Ukrainian Military Organization (UVO), founded in 1920, was the predecessor of the OUN.

Chapter 4

1   Engel, *Facing a Holocaust,* 1–14, calls for an objective, value-free use of documents.
2   Pohl, *Nationalsozialistische Judenverfolgung,* 17–21; Sandkühler, *"Endlösung" in Galizien,* 15–19; R. Hilberg, *Sources of Holocaust Research: An Analysis* (Chicago, 2001), 141–2, 155–9, 161–2; Friedländer, *Nazi Germany and the Jews,* vol. 2: xxiv–xxvi.
3   This is ultimately also the case in Friedländer, *Nazi Germany and the Jews*. See discussions in Garbarini, *Numbered Days,* Goldberg, *Trauma in First Person,* and S. Gigliotti, *The Train Journey* (New York, 2009).
4   A. Wieviorka, *The Era of the Witness,* trans. J. Stark (Ithaca, NY, 2006).

Notes

5   See, e.g., L. L. Langer, *Holocaust Testimonies* (New Haven, CT, 1991); C. Caruth, ed., *Trauma* (Baltimore, MD, 1995); S. Felman and D. Laub, *Testimony* (New York, 1992); K. Jacobson, *Embattled Selves* (New York, 1994); E. Sicher, ed., *Breaking Crystal* (Urbana, IL, 1998). An early exception is T. Des Pres, *The Survivor* (New York, 1976).
6   See, e.g., M. Goren, *Silent Cries from the Black Forest* (Rehovot, 2009 [Hebrew]); E. Yones, *Smoke in the Sand* (Jerusalem, 2001 [Hebrew]).
7   Trembach 2003.
8   Ibid.; Khvostenko 2003; Pavlyshyn, "The Holocaust in Buczacz."
9   A. H. Resnik (Herzog), interview with the author, September 11, 2002.
10 R. Gertner, interview with the author, July 31, 2002.
11 Bauer 2003.
12 J. Saunders, interview with the author, July 30, 2002.
13 R. Barton (Bertisz), interview with the author, July 5, 2002.
14 J. Heiss, interviews with the author, December 2002, and July 5, 2003.
15 Undated account by Yitzhak Shalev (Izio Wachtel) provided by his son, Ziki Slav, on February 25, 2007.
16 S. Aberdam (Freiberg), SFV, April 28, 1998 (Hebrew).
17 F. Kupitz (Feldman), SFV, April 25, 1994.
18 F. Kupitz, interview with the author, October 10, 2002.
19 Kupitz 1994.
20 Ibid.
21 R. Brecher, YVA 033, 765, E/32-3, 1945; ŻIH 301/4911, May 20, 1945.
22 Kupitz 1994.
23 A. Appleman-Jurman, SFV, January 29, 1996.
24 See apologetic accounts of Kaznovskyi's career in Y. Hasai, "Under a Police Uniform Beats the Heart of a Ukrainian Patriot," *Nova Doba*, no. 16 (8065), April 23, 2004 (Ukrainian), and M. Kheifetz, *Ukrainian Silhouettes* (Kharkiv, 2000 [Ukrainian]). See also Kaznovskyi's trial, Chapter 4, n. 40).
25 Chalfen 1947.
26 Katz 1995.
27 Joe (Yekhezkiel, Jechezkiel, Olszy) Perl, SFV, October 14, 1996.
28 Spielberg-Flitman 1995.
29 Szpigiel 1948.
30 I. Szwarc, ŻIH 301/327, USHMM RG-15.084 Acc.1997 A.0125 1945, Reel 5, 1945.
31 Zuroff 1995.
32 See, e.g., Langer, *Holocaust Testimonies*, and Wieviorka, *The Era of the Witness*.
33 R. Moses, ed., *Persistent Shadows of the Holocaust* (Madison, CT, 1993); D. Bar-On, *Legacy of Silence* (Cambridge, MA, 1989); D. Bar-On, *Fear and Hope* (Cambridge, MA, 1995).
34 S. Prüfer, USHMM, reel 49, from ZIH 301/4581, probably given in 1945–6.
35 Trembach 2003.
36 E. Skamene (Kleiner), SFV, February 3, 1998.
37 G. Weksler, USHMM, RG-15.084 Acc.1997 A.0125, Reel 19, 1865, ŻIH 301/1865, 1946.
38 B. Kahane, SFV, August 8, 1995.
39 A. Golobov (Bernfeld), YVA 03, 10241, VT 033C/5361, April 29, 1997 (Hebrew).
40 H. Weitz, SFV, November 4, 1998.
41 Pollak 1995.
42 C. Sznajder (Huss), ŻIH 301/5699, January 25, 1960.
43 S. (Rosen, USHMM, reel 20, *1935*, ŻIH 301/1935, August 6, 1946.
44 S. Rosen, YVA 03/2055, M-49/1935, December 20, 1960.

45 H. Rosen, SFV, November 10, 1997. See also M. Paldiel, *The Path of the Righteous* (Hoboken, NJ, 1993), 191–3, with a photo of Świerszczak.
46 S. Rosen 1960; S. Rosen and Z. Anderman interview with the author, March 12, 2002.
47 S. Rosen 1960; H. Rosen 1997.
48 See "Righteous Among the Nations Honored by Yad Vashem by 1 January 2020," www.yadvashem.org/yv/pdf-drupal/poland.pdf, under "Swierszczak, Manko & Marynka."
49 Bartov, *Voices on War and Genocide*, 334, 338, 343, 361–2; 421.
50 Bauer 2003.
51 BArch B 162/5182, January 10, 1968, 6212–14.
52 Gross 1996.
53 Bartov, *Voices on War and Genocide*, 292–3, 300–3, 317, 321, 331.
54 Pollak 1995.
55 Rosen 1960.
56 Ibid.; Bartov, *Anatomy of a Genocide*, 229–30.
57 Rosen and Anderman 2002.
58 See also accounts by Y. Shikhor (Szwarc) and E. Bazan (Worman) in Cohen, *Sefer Buczacz*, 246, 288, and Szwarc's original 1945 testimony, commenting on "the Jewish policeman Janek Anderman"; Bartov, *Anatomy of a Genocide*, 176–8, 253, 347n, 348n, 360n; Z. Gerber, SFV, November 28, 1996 (Russian); Wizinger in Bartov, *Voices on War and Genocide*, 332; Bauer 1968.

Chapter 5

1 Pendas, *The Frankfurt Auschwitz Trial*; Wittmann, *Beyond Justice*.
2 Hilberg, *The Destruction of the European Jews* (2003), 3: 1301–21.
3 R. Gutman et al., eds., *Crimes of War* (New York, 1999), 107–8, 153–7. Further in Marrus, *The Nuremberg War Crimes Trial*; Douglas, *Memory of Judgment*; P. Sands, *East West Street* (New York, 2016).
4 Pendas, *The Frankfurt Auschwitz Trial*, 8–15; Wittmann, *Beyond Justice*, 17–37.
5 Wittmann, *Beyond Justice*, 44.
6 Pendas, *The Frankfurt Auschwitz Trial*, 53–5; Wittmann, *Beyond Justice*, 45. This is one problem with the evidence used in Browning, *Ordinary Men*.
7 Wittmann, *Beyond Justice*, 37.
8 F. Buscher, "'I know I also Share the Guilt,'" *YVS* 34 (2006): 249–92; A. Rückerl, *The Investigation of Nazi Crimes, 1945–1978*, trans. D. Rutter (Hamden, CT, 1980).
9 Wittmann, *Beyond Justice*, 46.
10 Ibid., 271–4; Pendas, *The Frankfurt Auschwitz Trial*, 56–79.
11 M. Roseman, *The Wannsee Conference and the Final Solution* (New York, 2002); P. Burrin, *Hitler and the Jews*, trans. P. Southgate (New York, 1994); Browning, *Origins of the Final Solution*; N. Wachsmann, *A History of the Nazi Concentration Camps* (New York, 2015); Y. Arad, *Belzec, Sobibor, Treblinka* (Bloomington, IN, 1987); Pohl, *Nationalsozialistische Judenverfolgung*; Spector, *The Holocaust of Volhynian Jews*; Aly, "*Final Solution*"; Browning, *Ordinary Men*; Sereny, *Into That Darkness*.
12 Redlich, *Together and Apart in Brzeżany*; Gross, *Neighbors*; Y. Bauer, *The Death of the Shtetl* (New Haven, 2009); Bartov, *Anatomy of a Genocide*.
13 In this context, see B. Schlink, *The Reader*, trans. C. B. Janeway (New York, 1997), and Bartov, "Germany as Victim," *NGC* 80 (2000): 29–40.

Notes

14 On this see also O. Bartov, "The Wehrmacht Exhibition Controversy," in *The Crimes of War*, ed. Bartov et al. (New York, 2002), 41–60.
15 For German women's testimonies about the private lives of the occupiers and their accomplices, see Bartov, *Anatomy of a Genocide*, 213–29.
16 Gross, *Revolution from Abroad*; Pinchuk, *Shtetl Jews under Soviet Rule*; Bauer, *The Death of the Shtetl*; A. V. Prusin, *The Lands Between* (New York, 2010); Snyder, *Bloodlands*.
17 Pohl, *Nationalsozialistische Judenverfolgung*; Sandkühler, *"Endlösung" in Galizien*; T. Friedman, ed., *Report by SS-General Fritz Katzmann on the Killing of the Half Million Jews of Eastern Galicia* (Haifa, 1993); *J.u.NS-V*, 18: 659–60.
18 Bartov, *Anatomy of a Genocide*, 158–231.
19 This account is based on *J.u.NS-V*, 18: 658–9; Pohl, *Nationalsozialistische Judenverfolgung*, 255, 419; Sandkühler, *"Endlösung" in Galizien*, 251, 254–5, 442.
20 This account is based on *J.u.NS-V*, 18: 655–8; Pohl, *Nationalsozialistische Judenverfolgung*, 226, 393, 416; Sandkühler, *"Endlösung" in Galizien*, 146, 250–3, 269.
21 This account is based on *J.u.NS-V*, 16: 728–33; Pohl, *Nationalsozialistische Judenverfolgung*, 169, 340, 392, 421; Sandkühler, *"Endlösung" in Galizien*, 141–8, 194, 254–6.
22 A. Angrick, "Annihilation and Labor," in Brandon and Lower, *The Shoah in Ukraine*, 190–223.
23 *J.u.NS-V*, 18: 677–9, 682; Sandkühler, *"Endlösung" in Galizien*, 442.
24 *J.u.NS-V*, 18: 656–7.
25 Ibid., 657, 660.
26 Ibid., 660–2.
27 Ibid., 662.
28 *J.u.NS-V*, 18: 662–5.
29 *J.u.NS-V*, 16: 733.
30 Ibid., 734–40.
31 Ibid., 742–3. The court similarly found Dr. Schorr's testimony at Köllner's trial in 1962 entirely reliable, since it was given "in a calm and precise manner" and "even provided evidence favoring the defendant." Ibid., 669–70; ŻIH 301/4682; USHMM RG-15.084M Reel 51.
32 *J.u.NS-V*, 16: 744.
33 Ibid., 747–8.
34 Ibid., 748–9.
35 Ibid., 750–1.
36 Ibid., 751–2.
37 Ibid., 752–3.
38 Ibid.
39 Ibid., 753–4.
40 Ibid., 754–6. See also S. Wolkowicz, *Das Grab bei Zloczow* (Berlin, 1996).
41 *J.u.NS-V*, 16: 756–7.
42 *J.u.NS-V*, 18: 665–6.
43 Ibid., 666–70.
44 Ibid., 676.
45 Ibid.
46 Ibid., 680.
47 Ibid.
48 Ibid.
49 Ibid., 682.
50 *J.u.NS-V*, 16: 763–4.
51 Ibid., 764.
52 Ibid.
53 Ibid., 764–5.

Notes

54 Ibid., 765.
55 See many examples cited in Goldhagen, *Hitler's Willing Executioners*, and Browning, *Ordinary Men*, and esp. now E. B. Westermann, *Drunk on Genocide* (Ithaca, NY, 2021).
56 Heinrich Himmler and Adolf Eichmann both reportedly became physically ill when observing mass executions. Generally, see P. Longerich, *Heinrich Himmler* (Munich, 2008) and D. Cesarani, *Becoming Eichmann* (Cambridge, MA, 2006).
57 See Marrus, *The Nuremberg War Crimes Trial*; H. Earl, *The Nuremberg SS-Einsatzgruppen Trial, 1945–1958* (Cambridge, UK, 2009).
58 *J.u.NS-V*, 16: 765–6.
59 Ibid., 766–7.
60 Ibid., 767.
61 Ibid., 767–8.
62 On this, see Bartov, *Hitler's Army*.

Chapter 6

1 For the Turkish Penal Code as amended in 2008, see N. Koposov, *Memory Laws, Memory Wars* (New York, 2018), 111–12. See also J. Tate, "Turkey's Article 301," *GJICL* 37, no. 1 (2008): 181–217; B. Algan, "The Brand New Version of Article 301 of Turkish Penal Code and the Future of Freedom of Expression Cases in Turkey," *GLJ* 9, no. 12 (2008): 2237–52.
2 See Koposov, *Memory Laws*; and Himka and Michlic, *Bringing the Dark Past to Light*.
3 "Law of Ukraine №376–V 'On Holodomor of 1932–33 in Ukraine'" (Ukrainian): zakon.rada.gov.ua/laws/show/376-16?zahyst=4%2FUMfPEGznhhAMY.Zi691C5hHI4ags80msh8Ie6#Text. See also Koposov, *Memory Laws*, 189.
4 The 169th session of the 17th Knesset, November 14, 2007: Special Session in Honor of the President of Ukraine, Viktor Yushchenko (Hebrew): knesset.gov.il/tql/knesset_new/knesset17/HTML_28_03_2012_04-57-19-PM/20071114@06243107@018.html.
5 "Russian envoy says Israeli bill on Ukraine's Stalin-era deaths a 'wrong step'" (February 7, 2018), www.reuters.com/article/us-israel-russia-ukraine/russian-envoy-says-israeli-bill-on-ukraines-stalin-era-deaths-a-wrong-step-idUSKBN1FR1YW.
6 See J. Veidlinger, *In the Midst of Civilized Europe* (New York, 2021); E. Bemporad, *Legacy of Blood* (New York, 2021); Bartov, *Tales from the Borderlands*, 36–58.
7 K. Struve, *Deutsche Herrschaft, ukrainischer Nationalismus, antijüdische Gewalt* (Berlin, 2015); Himka, *Ukrainians, Jews and the Holocaust*; Himka, *Ukrainian Nationalists and the Holocaust*; Bartov, *Anatomy of a Genocide*, 158–264.
8 D. R. Marples, *Heroes and Villains* (Budapest, 2007); P. A. Rudling, "'The Honor They So Clearly Deserve,'" *JSMS* 26, no. 2 (2013): 114–37; P. A. Rudling, "The Cult of Roman Shukhevych in Ukraine," *Fascism* 5, no. 1 (2016): 26–65; Rudling, "The OUN, the UPA and the Holocaust"; Himka, "Debates in Ukraine Over Nationalist Involvement in the Holocaust"; Rossoliński-Liebe, "Debating, Obfuscating and Disciplining the Holocaust"; Carynnyk, "Foes of Our Rebirth."
9 Bartov, *Anatomy of a Genocide*, 265–302; G. Motyka, "Der Krieg im östlichen Galizien," *Karta* 30 (2000): 36–7; Snyder, "The Causes of Ukrainian-Polish Ethnic Cleansing"; M. Terles, *Ethnic Cleansing of Poles in Volhynia and Eastern Galicia, 1942–1946* (Toronto, 1993).
10 G. N. Arad, "Israel and the Shoah," *NGC* 90 (2003): 5–26; Stauber, *The Holocaust in Israeli Public Debate*; Y. Klar et al., "The 'Never Again' State of Israel," *JSI* 69, no. 1 (2013): 125–43. See also B. Bashir and A. Goldberg, "Deliberating the Holocaust and the Nakba," *JGR*

16, no. 1 (2014): 77–99; B. Bashir and A. Goldberg, eds., *The Holocaust and the Nakba* (New York, 2018).
11 See, e.g., L. Levy, "'You just Can't Compare,'" in *Israel-Palestine*, ed. O. Bartov (New York, 2021), 58–77; S. Stav, "Nakba and Holocaust," *JSS* 18, no. 3 (2012): 85–98.
12 See, e.g., Shore, "Conversing with Ghosts"; P. Śpiewak, *Żydokomuna* (Warsaw, 2012); A. Żbikowski, *U genezy Jedwabnego* (Warsaw, 2006); Michlic, *The Neighbors Respond*; Wierzbicki, *Polacy i Żydzi w zaborze sowieckim*; J. T. Gross, *Upiorna dekada* (Kraków, 1998).
13 "Act of 18 December 1998 on the Institute of National Remembrance—Commission for the Prosecution of Crimes against the Polish Nation (Journal of Laws, 19 December 1998)," www.memoriaabierta.org.ar/materiales/pdf/act_poland_1998_inr.pdf. See also Koposov, *Memory Laws*, 161.
14 Ibid., 161–2.
15 "Full text of Poland's controversial Holocaust legislation," *TOI*, February 1, 2018, www.timesofisrael.com/full-text-of-polands-controversial-holocaust-legislation/.
16 See, e.g., T. John, "Poland Just Passed a Holocaust Bill That Is Causing Outrage," *Time*, February 1, 2018, time.com/5128341/poland-holocaust-law/; M. Santora, "Poland's 'Death Camp' Law Tears at Shared Bonds of Suffering with Jews," *NYT*, February 6, 2018, www.nytimes.com/2018/02/06/world/europe/poland-death-camp-law.html; B. Katz, "Poland's President Signs Highly Controversial Holocaust Bill into Law," *Smithsonian Magazine*, February 7, 2018, www.smithsonianmag.com/smart-news/poland-grants-initial-approval-controversial-death-camp-bill-180967975/; N. Koposov, "Memory Laws and Nationalist Lies," *Project Syndicate*, March 7, 2018, www.project-syndicate.org/commentary/poland-holocaust-law-nationalist-tool-by-nikolay-koposov-2018-03; A. Valles, "Scrubbing Poland's Complicated Past," *NYREV*, March 23, 2018, www.nybooks.com/daily/2018/03/23/scrubbing-polands-complicated-past/.
17 See note 13.
18 Grabowski, *Hunt for the Jews*; Dreifuss, *We Polish Jews*; Gross, *Fear*; Michlic, *Poland's Threatening Other*; N. Aleksiun, "Jewish responses to Antisemitism in Poland, 1944–1947," in Zimmerman, *Contested Memories*, 247–61; D. Engel, "Patterns of Anti-Jewish Violence in Poland, 1944–1946," *YVS* 26 (1998): 43–85; Golczewski, "Der Jedwabne-Diskurs," *JGO* 50, no. 3 (2002): 412–37.
19 A. Cherviatsova, "Memory Wars," *Verfassungsblog*, February 9, 2018, verfassungsblog.de/memory-wars-the-polish-ukrainian-battle-about-history/.
20 Ibid. See also Koposov, *Memory Laws*, 201–3. The law introduced no specific sanctions for such acts.
21 Cherviatsova, "Memory Wars"; Koposov, *Memory Laws*, 205.
22 See, e.g., R. Lyman, "Polish Parliament Approves Law Curtailing Courts' Independence," *NYT*, July 21, 2017, www.nytimes.com/2017/07/21/world/europe/poland-courts-independence.html; C. Davies, "Polish MPs Pass Judicial Bills Amid Accusations of Threat to Democracy," *The Guardian*, December 8, 2017, www.theguardian.com/world/2017/dec/08/polish-mps-pass-supreme-court-bill-criticised-as-grave-threat.
23 See "Polin: Museum of the History of Polish Jews," www.polin.pl/en.
24 O. Bartov, "The Truth and Nothing But," in *New Directions in the History of the Jews in the Polish Lands*, ed. A. Polonsky et al. (Brighton, MA, 2018), 111–18.
25 D. Stola, director of POLIN Museum, and P. Wiślicki, chairman of the Board of the Association of the Jewish Historical Institute of Poland, "Statement of POLIN Museum concerning a proposed amendment to the Act on the Institute of National Remembrance," January 29, 2018, www.polin.pl/en/news/2018/01/29/statement-of-the-director-of-polin-museum-concerning-a-proposed; E. Hoffman, "Hearing Poland's Ghosts," *NYREV*, March

22, 2018, www.nybooks.com/articles/2018/03/22/hearing-polands-ghosts/. In February 2019 Stola's contract as director of the POLIN Museum expired and was not renewed.

26 "About the Memorial," www.vvmf.org/About-The-Wall/#facts/, declares that it "is dedicated to honor the courage, sacrifice and devotion to duty and country of all who answered the call to serve during one of the most divisive wars in U.S. history."

27 On the politics of memory in Ukraine, see, e.g., C. Mick, *Lemberg, Lwów, L'viv, 1914–1947* (West Lafayette, IN, 2016); Bartov, *Erased*.

28 Moshe Shamir's iconic novel, *With His Own Hands* (Merhavyah, 1951 [Hebrew]), opens with the line, "Elik was born from the sea," thus establishing the identity of the so-called "mythological Sabra." See also O. Almog, *The Sabra*, trans. H. Watzman (Berkeley, 2000); Y. Dror, "From 'Negation of the Diaspora' to 'Jewish Consciousness,'" *ISF* 18, no. 2 (2003): 58–82; G.Katz, "Negation of the Diaspora from an Israeli Perspective," in *Handbook of Israel*, ed. E. Ben-Rafael et al. (Berlin, 2016), 2: 1116–1333.

29 On Nathan Alterman's 1954 poem, "The Day of Remembrance—and the Rebels," expressing early criticism of the "sheep to the slaughter" accusation, see C. Malul, "When the Separation between 'Holocaust Victims' and 'Ghetto Fighters' Collapsed," blog.nli.org.il/eichmann_trial/. See also A. Confino, "Miracles and Snow in Palestine and Israel," *IS* 17, no. 2 (2012): 25–61; A. Confino, "The Warm Sand of the Coast of Tantura," *H&M* 27, no. 1 (2015): 43–82.

30 The main exceptions at the time were the novella by S. Yizhar, *Khirbet Khizeh*, trans. N. de Lange et al. (Jerusalem, 2008 [1949]), and the poem by Avot Yeshurun, "Passover on Caves," published in 1952. See also A. Eshel et al., eds., "History and Responsibility," special issue, *JSS* 18, no. 3 (2012): 1–224; H. Hever, *Hebrew Literature and the 1948 War* (Leiden, 2019).

31 Central District 57/3/ Military Prosecutor, Defendants Major Malinki et al., Verdict XVII 90 (1958): 211–14 (Hebrew). See also L. Y. Bilsky, *Transformative Justice* (Ann Arbor, MI, 2004), 170; A. Parush, "Critique of the 'Black Flag' Test," in *Kafr Qasim*, ed. R. Rosenthal (Tel Aviv, 2000 [Hebrew]), 131–77; K. Weidberg, "Justice Dr. Benjamin Halevy" (seminar paper, Law School, Haifa University, 2009 [Hebrew]), 27–36.

32 See, e.g., Y. Kilnger, "The Most Moral Army in the World," June 18, 2006 (Hebrew), 2jk.org/praxis/?p=570; A. Burg, "The half-most moral army in the world," April 5, 2016 (Hebrew), www.haaretz.co.il/opinions/.premium-1.2904314?=&ts=_1528508023351.

33 Weidberg, "Benjamin Halevy," 32. For similarities with the case of the My Lai Massacre during the Vietnam War in 1968, see C. J. Levesque, "The Truth Behind My Lai," *NYT*, March 16, 2018, www.nytimes.com/2018/03/16/opinion/the-truth-behind-my-lai.html; S. M. Hersh, "The Scene of the Crime," *New Yorker*, March 23, 2015, www.newyorker.com/magazine/2015/03/30/the-scene-of-the-crime. And see the US Manual for Courts-Martial's definition of lawful and illegals orders, Article 90, 2 (a) (1), jsc.defense.gov/Portals/99/Documents/MCM2016.pdf?ver=2016-12-08-181411-957.

34 The interim report of the IDF and the Israeli Foreign Ministry issued on June 14, 2015, mentions 2,125 Palestinians killed during the operation, of whom 761 were "uninvolved civilians," including "369 children under the age of 15 … 284 women … and 108 men …." See "Annex—Palestinian Fatality Figures in the 2014 Gaza Conflict," mfa.gov.il/ProtectiveEdge/Documents/PalestinianFatalities.pdf. On material damage, see, J. Ashkenas et al., "Assessing the Damage and Destruction in Gaza," *New York Times*, August 15, 2014, www.nytimes.com/interactive/2014/08/03/world/middleeast/assessing-the-damage-and-destruction-in-gaza.html?_r=0.

35 A June 14, 2015, report by the Israeli Foreign Ministry on the 2014 Gaza conflict blames Hamas for crimes against humanity, while insisting that the IDF went out of its way to avoid civilian casualties or damage to structures: mfa.gov.il/ProtectiveEdge/Pages/default.aspx and "Israel's Investigation of Alleged Violations of the Law of Armed Conflict," mfa.gov.il/ProtectiveEdge/Documents/IsraelInvestigations.pdf. See also D. Shulman, "Israel without

Notes

Illusions," *NYREV*, November 17, 2009, www.nybooks.com/daily/2009/11/17/israel-with out-illusions-what-goldstone-got-right/.
36 See, e.g., Segev, *The Seventh Million*, 255–322; Weidberg, "Benjamin Halevy," 14–26.
37 Segev, *Seventh Million*, 323–86; Weidberg, "Benjamin Halevy," 22–6; Yablonka, *The State of Israel vs. Adolf Eichmann*.
38 Cited in Bartov, *The "Jew" in Cinema*, 87, 91–2.
39 See, e.g., D. Bar, "Holocaust and Heroism in the Process of Establishing Yad Vashem (1942–1970)," *Dapim* 30, no. 3 (2016): 166–90; J. C. Blutinger, "Yad Vashem and the State of Holocaust Education in Israeli Schools in the 1960s," *JSS* 21, no. 1 (2015): 123–50; A. Goldberg, "The 'Jewish Narrative' in the Yad Vashem Global Holocaust Museum," *JGR* 14, no. 2 (2012): 187–213.
40 Further on this in Bartov, *Erased*. See also Chapter 10.
41 See, e.g., A. Liebich and O. Myshlovska, "Bandera," *NP* 24, no. 5 (2014): 1–21; W. Jilge, "'Nationalist-Ukrainian Struggle for Liberation,'" *Osteuropa* 58, no. 6 (2008): 167–86; Jilge, "The Politics of History and the Second World War in Post-Communist Ukraine."
42 That is the basic contention of Snyder, *Bloodlands*.
43 See "Records of the Law Book," March 30, 2011, www.nevo.co.il/law_word/law14/law-2286.pdf, p. 686.
44 Appeal by Hagai Elad and Hassan Jabarin, www.acri.org.il/he/wp-content/uploads/2011/05/nakbaletter.pdf.
45 The Association for Civil Rights in Israel, "Abolish the Nakba Law," January 5, 2012, www.acri.org.il/he/11916; Appeal to Supreme Court of Justice, case 3429/11, May 4, 2011, www.acri.org.il/he/wp-content/uploads/2011/05/hit-4.5.11.pdf.
46 Supreme Court of Justice ruling, case 3429/11, January 5, 2012 (Hebrew), p. 17, www.adalah.org/uploads/oldfiles/upfiles/2012/Sup%20Ct%20Nakba%20Law%20Decision%20Hebrew%205.1.2012.pdf.
47 See, e.g., R. Schocken, "The Chilling Effect of the Nakba Law," *Haaretz*, May 16, 2012 (Hebrew), www.haaretz.co.il/opinions/1.1708904.
48 The 1948 War is usually called in Israel the War of Independence. Israel's first prime minister, David Ben-Gurion, coined the name Milhemet Hakomemiyut, which can be translated as the War of Resurrection. Menahem Begin, who became prime minister in 1977, preferred to call it the War of Liberation.
49 But see the remarkable and largely forgotten novel by D. Ben-Amotz, *To Remember, To Forget*, trans. Z. Shapiro (Tel-Aviv, 1979), about this once iconic Israeli public figure's relationship to his Diaspora past.
50 Things are different as far as Russia and Ukraine are concerned, however. See, e.g., O Bartov, "Why Does Russia's Leadership Keep Saying that Ukrainians Are Nazis?" *WSJ*, May 12, 2022, www.wsj.com/articles/why-does-russias-leadership-keep-saying-that-ukrainians-are-nazis-11652361854?st=lg7a5lcq6nznbet&reflink=desktopwebshare_permalink.

Chapter 7

1 H. G. Adler, *Panorama*, trans. P. Filkins (New York, 2011). Originally published in German as *Panorama* (Freiburg i. Br., Ger., 1968).
2 See A. Finkielkraut, *Remembering in Vain*, trans. R. Lapidus et al. (New York, 1992), 31: "Thus civilization discovered (or rediscovered) in 1945 that men are not the means, the instruments, or the representatives of a superior subject—humanity—that is fulfilled through them, but that humanity is their responsibility, that they are its *guardians* … Exposed and vulnerable,

Notes

humanity itself can die ... The notion of crimes against humanity is the legal evidence of this realization."

3   The classic Bildungsroman is J. W. von Goethe's *Wilhelm Meister's Apprenticeship* (1795–6). By *Unbildungsroman*, I do not quite mean *Antibildungsroman* as several literary scholars have defined the term. See, e.g., J. Kociatkiewicz, *Towards the Antibildungsroman* (Frankfurt am Main, Germany, 2008). What I mean is that *Panorama* is a novel about the unmaking, or the un-formation, of the protagonist. Adler depicts an individual who had already been formed by pre-Second World War society and is then stripped of that formation, unformed and deformed, in the camps, and must recreate himself thereafter to survive that un-formation; yet the novel does not deal with that re-formation, ending instead with the faint hope of its possibility.

4   A. Camus, *The First Man*, trans. D. Hapgood (New York, 1995 [1994]).

5   R. Polanski, *Roman* (New York, 1984), 21–47.

6   W. Szpilman, *The Pianist*, trans. A. Bell (New York, 1999); *Pianista: Warszawskie wspomnienia 1939–1945* (Kraków, 2000), originally published in 1946 under the title *Śmierć Miasta*; *The Pianist*, dir. R. Polanski (2002).

7   Bartov, *The Eastern Front*; Bartov, *Hitler's Army*; Bartov, *Petihat Tsir* (Border Patrol) (Tel-Aviv, 1988); Bartov, *Karev Yom* (Surrogate Killers) (Tel Aviv, 1989).

8   See, e.g., Segev, *The Seventh Million*. The overwhelming weight of an unlived past on the second generation is powerfully represented in Asher Tlalim's remarkable 1994 film, *Don't Touch My Holocaust*. See also Bartov, *The "Jew" in Cinema*, 282–311. This is the underlying theme of my recent novel, *The Butterfly and the Axe* (Amsterdam, 2023).

9   This informed my early work on German combat soldiers in the Second World War, cited above, as much as my recent book, *Anatomy of a Genocide*.

10 The diaries were C. Pressburger, ed., *The Diary of Petr Ginz, 1941–1942*, trans. E. Lappin (New York, 2007); A. Klonicki, *The Diary of Adam's Father*, trans. A. Tomaschoff (Jerusalem, 1973). Testimonies were taken from the University of Southern California's Shoah Foundation in Los Angeles, http://sfi.usc.edu/. West German trial records of former Nazis were taken from, among others, *J.u.NS-V*. Memoirs included W. Lotnik, et al., *Nine Lives* (London, 1999); R. Höss, *Death Dealer*, trans. A. Pollinger (New York, 1996); R. Kluger, *Still Alive* (New York, 2001). Historical fiction included J. Littell, *The Kindly Ones*, trans. C. Mandell (New York, 2009); S. Sem-Sandberg, *The Emperor of Lies*, trans. S. Death (London, 2011); E. Morante, *History: A Novel*, trans. W. Weaver (New York, 1977). Films included *Shoah*, directed by C. Lanzmann (1985) and Polanski's *The Pianist*. On the problems of historical fiction on atrocity, see O. Bartov, " 'Sitrah Akhra' (The Other Side)" *YVS* 40, no. 1 (2012): 233–46.

11 Camus, *The First Man*; Delbo, *None of Us Will Return*; Levi, *The Reawakening*; S. Friedländer, *When Memory Comes*, trans. H. R. Lane (New York, 1979 [1978]); G. Perec, *W, or the Memory of Childhood*, trans. D. Bellos (Boston, 1988 [1975]); W. G. Sebald, *Austerlitz*, trans. A. Bell (New York, 2011 [2001]).

12 For an earlier attempt to analyze this genre, see O. Bartov, "Trauma and Absence (pt. 1): France and Germany, 1914–45," in *Time to Kill*, ed. P. Addison et al. (London, 1997), 347–58; O. Bartov, "Trauma and Absence (pt. 2)," in *European Memories of the Second World War*, ed. H. Peitsch et al. (New York, 1999), 258–71.

13 Delbo's entire trilogy was published as *Auschwitz et après* (Paris, 1970–1), and in translation as *Auschwitz and After*, trans. R. C. Lamont (New Haven, CT, 1995).

14 P. Levi, *Se questo è un uomo* (Turin, Italy, 1947), translated originally by S. Woolf as *If This Is a Man* (New York, 1959); a third edition was issued in Turin in 1960, and translated by Woolf as *Survival in Auschwitz* (New York, 1961); along with the publication of *La tregua* (*The Truce*) in Turin 1963, the publisher issued a fourth edition of *Se questo è un uomo* that same year.

Notes

15 Primo Levi, *Hahafugah* (*La tregua*), trans. into Hebrew by A. Paska (Tel Aviv, 1979), 5. The Hebrew title preserves the original Italian meaning.
16 Friedländer, *Nazi Germany and the Jews*.
17 S. Friedländer, *Franz Kafka* (New Haven, CT, 2013).
18 P. Modiano, *La Place de l'Étoile* (Paris, 1968); H. Raczymow, *Writing the Book of Esther*, trans. D. Katz (New York, 1995 [1985]); A. Finkielkraut, *The Imaginary Jew*, trans. K. O'Neill et al. (Lincoln, NE, 1994 [1980]).
19 On this see also W. G. Sebald, *On the Natural History of Destruction*, trans. A. Bell (New York, 2003).
20 See, esp., H. G. Adler, *Theresienstadt 1941–1945*, 2nd expanded ed. (Tübingen, 1960 [1955]); H. G. Adler, *The Jews in Germany* (Notre Dame, IN, 1969 [1960]); H. G. Adler et al., eds., *Auschwitz*, 2nd ed. (Frankfurt am Main, 1979 [1962]); H. G. Adler, *Der verwaltete Mensch* (Tübingen, 1974); H. G. Adler, *Die Freiheit des Menschen* (Tübingen, 1976).
21 See, e.g., Bartov, "Germany as Victim." See also L. L. Wolff, "H. G. Adler and W. G. Sebald," *Monatshefte* 103, no. 2 (2011): 257–75.
22 See, e.g., O. Bartov, "Kitsch and Sadism in Ka-Tzetnik's Other Planet," *JSS* 3, no. 2 (1997): 42–76.
23 P. Levi, *The Drowned and the Saved*, trans. R. Rosenthal (New York, 1988 [1986]), 157.
24 Ibid., 157–8.
25 For a recent work on *Theresienstadt*, see A. Hájková, *The Last Ghetto* (New York, 2020). See also Bartov, "The Holocaust as Leitmotif of the Twentieth Century"; R. Evans, *Lying about Hitler* (New York, 2001).

Chapter 8

1 J.-P. Himka, *Religion and Nationality in Western Ukraine* (Montreal, 1999); P. R. Magocsi, *The Roots of Ukrainian Nationalism* (Toronto, 2002); Struve, *Bauern und Nation in Galizien*.
2 J. Shanes, *Diaspora Nationalism and Jewish Identity in Habsburg Galicia* (New York, 2012), 31–7.
3 Himka, *Galician Villagers*, 158–75; Struve, *Bauern und Nation*, 384–433.
4 Y. Hrytsak, "A Strange Case of Antisemitism," in Bartov and Weitz, *Shatterzone of Empires*, 232–5; I. Franko, *Boa Constrictor and Other Stories*, trans. F. Solansko (Moscow, 1957?).
5 T. Herzl, *Der Judenstaat* (Leipzig, 1896); Hrytsak, "Antisemitism," 233–7; I. Franko, *Zur Judenfrage—Do iudeiskoho pytannia: statti* (Kyiv, 2002); M. Shkandrij, *Jews in Ukrainian Literature* (New Haven, CT, 2009), 69–80.
6 K. E. Franzos, *Der Pojaz* (Frankfurt am Main, 1988), 5–6. Translated by E. Lerdau as *The Clown of Barnow* (New Orleans, 2004).
7 Franzos, *Der Pojaz*, 6–7. See also S. W. Baron, "The Impact of the Revolution of 1848 on Jewish Emancipation," *JSS* 11, no. 3 (1949): 195–248.
8 Franzos, *Der Pojaz*, 8.
9 B. Phillips, "Preface to the American Edition," in *The Jews of Barnow*, trans. M. W. Macdowall (New York, 1883), v–vi.
10 See, e.g., his novella, *Leib Weihnachtskuchen and His Child*, trans. M. Mitchell (Riverside, CA, 2005 [1896]).
11 J. R. Malkin, "Introduction," in *Jews and the Making of Modern German Theatre*, ed. J. R. Malkin et al. (Iowa City, IA, 2010), 10.
12 See his early story, "The Shylock of Barnow" (1873), in *The Jews of Barnow*, 19–71.
13 Franzos, *Der Pojaz*, 312, 354. I have translated from the German original. Dawison is based on the celebrated Warsaw-born actor Bogumil Dawison (or Davidsohn), who went insane

Notes

and died aged fifty-four in 1872. See H. Rosenthal and E. Mels, "Dawison (Davidsohn), Bogumil," *Jewish Encyclopedia* (1906), www.jewishencyclopedia.com/articles/5005-dawison-davidsohn-bogumil.

14 J. Hermand, afterword to Franzos, *Der Pojaz*, 360.
15 Ibid., 371–3. See also P. Pulzer, *The Rise of Political Anti-Semitism in Germany & Austria*, rev. ed. (Cambridge, MA, 1988). In Agnon's last, unfinished novel, his protagonist Manfred Herbst, born and raised in Germany and a lecturer at the Hebrew University, realizes later in life that "even Germany's best bards were not free of that malice, so much so that they lyricized it and made it into a virtue, so that all manner of cruelty to the Jews became acceptable," yet "the Jewish spirit had become enslaved to such an extent to Germany that they did not perceive the hatred of Jews lyricized by these books." S. Y. Agnon, *Shira*, 3rd ed. (Tel Aviv, 1999), 296, and trans. Z. Shapiro (New York, 1989), 295.
16 S. Morris, "introduction," I. Franko, *Winds of Change*, trans. R. Franko (Winnipeg, 2006), 8–9.
17 Franzos, preface to *The Jews of Barnow*, ix–xx. See also K. E. Franzos, *Aus Halb-Asien*, 2nd rev. ed. (Leipzig, 1878). In a letter to Karl Jaspers describing the trial of Adolf Eichmann in Jerusalem, Hannah Arendt described derisively "the oriental mob" outside the court "as if one were in Istanbul or some other half-Asiatic country." Cited in A. Raz-Krakotzkin, "Jewish Peoplehood, 'Jewish Politics,' and Political Responsibility," *CL* 38, no. 1 (2011): 72.
18 G. Kressel, "Professor David Zvi (Heinrich) Müller," in Cohen, *Sefer Buczacz*, 109–11; "David Heinrich Mueller," *OW* 13, no. 2 (February 1913): 162; "Dr. Zvi Heinrich Müller z"l," *Hatsevi* (January 9, 1913): 2.
19 "Dr. Zvi Heinrich Müller," *Hatsevi*, 2.
20 "David Heinrich Mueller," *OW*, 163.
21 Kressel, "Professor David Zvi Müller," 111; D. H. Müller, *Die Propheten in ihrer ursprünglichen Form* (Vienna, 1896); D. H. Müller, *Die Gesetze Hammurabis und ihr Verhältnis zur mosaischen Gesetzgebung sowie zu den XII Tafeln* (Vienna, 1903). Agnon refers to this book in *Shira*, 77 (75 in the translation).
22 "David Heinrich Mueller," *OW*, 164–6, and "Dr. Zvi Heinrich Müller," *Hatsevi*, 2. Müller was recently rediscovered; see G. Sturm, *David Heinrich Müller und die südarabische Expedition der Kaiserlichen Akademie der Wissenschaften 1898/99* (Vienna, 2015).
23 Letter by Müller, April 12, 1893, reprinted in Cohen, *Sefer Buczacz*, 118.
24 D. Laor, "A Meeting in Vienna, May 1908," *Haaretz*, August 8, 2008 (Hebrew), www.haaretz.co.il/literature/1.1341697; S. Y. Agnon, *From Myself to Myself* (Tel Aviv, 2000 [1947, Hebrew]), 18.
25 For Freud's impact on Agnon's writing see, e.g., A. J. Band, *Nostalgia and Nightmare* (Berkeley, CA, 1968); D. Aberbach, *At the Handles of the Lock* (New York, 1984); Y. S. Feldman, "The Latent and the Manifest," *Prooftexts* 7, no. 1 (1987): 29–39; Y. Halevy-Wise, "Reading Agnon's *In the Prime of Her Life* in Light of Freud's *Dora*," *JQR* 98, no. 1 (2008): 29–40.
26 M. Grunwald, "Encounters with Sigmund Freud," in Cohen, *Sefer Buczacz*, 119–22; E. Jones, *The Life and Works of Sigmund Freud*, vol. 1 (New York, 1953), 1–3, 12–13. Freud's father, Jacob, referred to his own father and grandfather as "ha-Rav Shlomo son of ha-Rav Ephraim," although they may not have practiced as rabbis. See B. Goodnick, "Jacob Freud's Dedication to His Son," *JQR* 82, nos. 3–4 (1992): 329–360; M. Krüll, *Freud and His Father*, trans. A. J. Pomerans (New York, 1986); W. J. McGrath, "How Jewish Was Freud?" *NYREV* (December 5, 1991): www.nybooks.com.ezp-prod1.hul.harvard.edu/articles/1991/12/05/how-jewish-was-freud/; R. Kaplan, "Soaring on the Wings of the Wind," *AP* 17, no. 4 (2009): 318–25.
27 M. Freud, *Sigmund Freud* (New York, 1958), 11. See also H. P. Fry, *Freud's War* (Stroud, UK, 2009) and J. B. Heller, "Freud's Mother and Father," *Commentary*, May 1, 1956, www.commentarymagazine.com/articles/freuds-mother-and-father-a-memoir/.

Notes

28 Grunwald, "Encounters with Sigmund Freud," 119–22; I. Singer, "Max Grunwald," *The Jewish Encyclopedia* (1906), www.jewishencyclopedia.com/articles/6911-grunwald-max.
29 Grunwald, "Encounters with Sigmund Freud," 119–22.
30 S. Freud, *Moses and Monotheism*, trans. K. Jones (London, 1939); D. Cohen, *The Escape of Sigmund Freud* (London, 2009), 178, 205–7. See also Y. H. Yerushalmi, *Freud's Moses* (New Haven, CT, 1991).
31 W. Portmann, *Die wilden Schafe* (Münster, 2008), 12–15.
32 M. Nomad, *Dreamers Dynamiters and Demagogues* (New York, 1964).
33 Cohen, *Sefer Buczacz*, 181–2; Portmann, *Die wilden Schafe*, 15–17. BArch B 162/5182, deposition by Yitzhak Bauer, January 10, 1968, pp. 6212–14.
34 *Tydzień Robotnika* (Warsaw, Lemberg Edition) no. 6, February 6, 1938, cited in Portmann, *Die wilden Schafe*, 18–19.
35 Agnon, *Ir u-Melo'ah*, 644–6. See references to socialism in pre-1914 Buczacz in S. Y. Agnon, *Sippur pashut* (1935), in *Al kappot haman'ul* (Tel Aviv, 1998), 58, 71.
36 *Tydzień Robotnika*, in Portmann, *Die wilden Schafe*, 23.
37 Nomad, *Dreamers*, 7.
38 Portman, *Die wilden Schafe*, 11–12, 23–7, 30; "Autobiographical Sketch" in *Max Nomad Papers 1902–1967*, Tamiment Library, New York; Z. Heller, "Mezikhronotai," and N. Menatseah, "Miyemei ne'urai," in Cohen, *Sefer Buczacz*, 158 and 173, respectively.
39 Nomad, *Dreamers*, 8–9.
40 *Służba dworska: Gazeta dla robotników rolnych powiatu buczackiego i innych powiatów podolskich* 1 (June 1905): 1–3, Biblioteka Sejmowa, P. 50730. See also Heller, "Mezikhronotai," 150.
41 Agnon, *Ore'ah natah lalun*, 228–9. See also references to Knabenhut in Agnon, *Sippur pashut*, 58, 71, 200–1.
42 Agnon, *Ore'ah natah lalun*, 234–5.
43 Ibid., 235–41. See also Y. Mosner, "Maine yugent yoren in Buczacz," in *Pinkes Galitsye*, ed. N. Tsuke (Buenos Aires, 1945), 476.
44 Portmann, *Die wilden Schafe*, 55–8, citing M. Nacht, "Anarchistenjagd," *Neues Leben* 23 (June 6, 1903) and 24 (June 13, 1903). Agnon's narrator in *Ore'ah natah lalun*, 236–7, praises Knabenhut for having "learned to speak Yiddish, so that he could speak with his comrades in their language. Which was not the case with most of our [Zionist] leaders, who were too lazy even to learn the Hebrew alphabet."
45 Portmann, *Die wilden Schafe*, 30–4; Nomad, *Dreamers*, 11–14. See also J. Kolasky, ed., *Prophets & Proletarians* (Edmonton, 1990), 212–13.
46 Portmann, *Die wilden Schafe*, 117–18.
47 E. Wilson, introduction to M. Nomad, *Aspects of Revolt* (New York, 1961), vii, xviii, 236–7. Siegfried's pamphlet "The Social General Strike," published under the name Arnold Roller in 1905, is available at Robert Graham's Anarchism Weblog, robertgraham.wordpress.com/2010/09/10/siegfried-nacht-the-social-general-strike-1905/.
48 Menatseah, "Miyemei ne'urrai," 168–9; "Droga życiowa Ostapa Dłuskiego," n.d., Akta Ostapa Dłuskiego, AAN, 450/I-1, p. 1; *Sprawozdanie dyrekcyi C. K. Gimnazyum w Buczaczu za rok szkolny 1901* (Lwów, 1901), 36–9.
49 Laor, *Agnon*, 22; Heller, "Mezikhronotai," 15–18; D. Pohorille, "Pirkei havai," in Cohen, *Sefer Buczacz*, 199–200; letter to author from Dr. Alain Kanfer, Paris, March 22, 2010, with copies of Sara Kanfer's certificate of residence in Buczacz dated 1912, and a Paris police prefect certificate dated May 1915, stating that she was born in Buczacz to Markus and Civje Herman Kanfer and arrived in Paris in August 1912; email to author from Alain Kanfer, June 14, 2010; Portmann, *Die wilden Schafe*, 85, and n. 522; 111, and n. 673; 117–18; E. Prokop-Janiec, "Mojżesz Kanfer a teatr jidysz," in *Teatr żydowski w Krakowie*, ed. J. Michalik and

E. Prokop-Janiec (Kraków, 1995), 125–50; S. Martin, *Jewish Life in Cracow, 1918–1939* (London, 2004), 66, 111–19, 218–33. Irène Kanfer also translated Yiddish and Polish poems for the volume *Le Luth brisé: Première anthologie en français de poèmes du ghetto et des camps* (Paris, 1965).

50 "Droga życiowa," 1. See also "Dłuski Ostap—Langer Adolf (1892–1964)," *Słownik Biograficzny Działaczy Polskiego Ruchu Robotniczego*, ed. F. Tych, 2nd ed., vol. 2 (Warsaw, 1985), 585–6.

51 "Dłuski," *Słownik* and "Droga życiowa," 1–2. See also R. Solchanyk, "The Foundation of the Communist Movement in Eastern Galicia, 1919–1921," *SR* 30, no. 4 (1971): 774–94.

52 S. Królikowski et al., eds., *Proces komunistów we Lwowie (sprawa świętojurska) sprawozdanie stenograficzne* (Warsaw, 1958), 114–28; F. Świetlikowa, *Komunistyczna Partia Robotnicza Polski 1918–1923* (Warsaw, 1968), 279–306; Solchanyk, "Foundation," 788–91; "Relacje tow. Dłuskiego," AAN, 450/I-3, pp. 1–5 (c. 1960); and "Droga życiowa," 2.

53 "Relacje tow. Dłuskiego," 8–12 and "Dłuski," *Słownik*. See also, e.g., O. Dłuski, "Pan Beck oszukuje społeczeństwo polskie" *Correspondance Internationale*, published in Paris, AAN, 450/IV-4 (1937). For Dłuski's interwar Polish police file, see AAN, 450/I-2.

54 O. Ostenrode, "Die Rostowlüge und ihre Folgen: Ein Kapitel aus der Broschüre 'Deutschland ein Schaudermarchen oder der Weg zur Freiheit, mit einem Aufruf an den Leser. Beitrag zur Entlarvung des Hitlerismus," manuscript, January 7, 1943, AAN, 450/VI-1, pp. 4–5.

55 O. Dłuski, "Il n'y a qu'un seul chemin qui mène à la l'indépendance"; "Aux immigrants slaves en France," AAN, 450/II-69, pp. 20–3, 72–6, respectively (undated, likely late 1943 and early 1944).

56 "La Pologne nouvelle et la France en face de l'impérialisme germanique," attributed to "M. André Dluski, Représentant du Comité Polonais de Libération Nationale en France, Centre d'Étude de Politique Étrangère," February 28, 1945, AAN 450/II-71, pp. 9–10. In a questionnaire for admittance into the Central Committee of the Polish Workers' Party dated July 17, 1945, he identified himself as "Andrzej Dłuski (Adolf Langer)," being "of Jewish origins, Polish," and "leader of the Ukrainian resistance movement in France." AAN 450/I-1.

57 Gross, *Fear*, 35; Engel, "Patterns of Anti-Jewish Violence in Poland."

58 Gross, *Fear*, 125; Michlic, *Poland's Threatening Other*, 211.

59 Stola, "Fighting against the Shadows."

60 "Dłuski," *Słownik*; "Droga życiowa," 4; B. Szaynok, "The Role of Antisemitism in Postwar Polish-Jewish Relations," in Blobaum, *Antisemitism and Its Opponents*, 274–5.

61 See, e.g., Dłuski's article for the organ of the World Peace Council in 1955: "Pour une vaste tribune de discussion," AAN, 450/IV-24.

62 O. Dłuski, "Aussprache während der 'Goethefeier in Warschau,'" AAN, 450/III-103, pp. 6–7.

63 Dłuski on Stalin, AAN, 450/IV-21, pp. 1, 9. See also J. Rubenstein et al., eds., *Stalin's Secret Pogrom*, trans. L. E. Wolfson (New Haven, CT, 2001).

64 Dłuski, *Słownik*; "Droga życiowa," 5. See Dłuski's death certificate: AAN, 450/V-1.

65 Agnon, *Ir u-Melo'ah*, 716.

Chapter 9

1 Bartov, *Anatomy of a Genocide*.

2 The revised Hebrew edition of B. Morris, *The Birth of the Palestinian Refugee Problem, 1947–1949* (New York, 1987), trans. A. Magen (Tel Aviv, 1991), had a major impact in Israel. In this volume Morris points out that "until June 1948 the flight of the Arabs was caused ... primarily by Jewish attacks," and that "the Haganah and the Irgun also routinely assembled and expelled the residents who remained in captured villages (mostly the

Notes

elderly, widows, and handicapped)" (384). It was, he writes, "agreed by all those concerned that in this life-or-death struggle it would be militarily better if the fewest possible Arabs were left in the Jewish state" (386). During the war's second part, "the offensives in July and October were accompanied by far more expulsions" and "acts of cruelty toward the Arab civilian population," motivated by "the feeling ... that soon there would be the real prospect that Israel could be entirely cleansed of Arabs," and by "Ben Gurion ... [who] wanted as few Arabs as possible to remain in the state of Israel, and spoke in that spirit to his colleagues and assistants," but "preferred that his generals 'understand' his wish" rather than issuing explicit orders, leading to an additional three hundred thousand Palestinian refugees (390–1). Thus Morris's harsh criticism of Ilan Pappé's *The Ethnic Cleansing of Palestine* (Oxford, 2006) in "The Liar as Hero," *TNR*, March 16, 2011, 1–11, 17, https://newrepublic.com/article/85344/ilan-pappe-sloppy-dishonest-historian, is not about the actual mass expulsion but merely over the existence of a prior plan to do so and whether explicit orders were issued.

3   I. Zertal, *From Catastrophe to Power* (Berkeley, CA, 1998); Segev, *The Seventh Million*; D. Porat, *The Blue and the Yellow Stars of David* (Cambridge, MA, 1990); H. Bartov, *Shesh kenafayim le'ehad* (Each had Six Wings) (Tel Aviv, 2014 [1954]); G. Daniel (B. Harshav), "Peter hagadol" (Peter the Great), in *Shirei Gabi Daniel* (Tel Aviv, 1990), 94–100.

4   S. Robinson, *Citizen Strangers* (Stanford, CA, 2013), and R. Zreik, "Notes on the Value of Theory," *LEHR* 2, no. 1, art. 13 (2008): 1–44.

5   For the Declaration of the Establishment of the State of Israel, see the Knesset website, http://main.knesset.gov.il/About/Occasion/Pages/IndDeclaration.aspx.

6   For the Palestinian Declaration of Independence, see https://fmep.org/resource/palestinian-declaration-of-independence/.

7   On December 11, 1948, the UN General Assembly adopted resolution 194, stating that "refugees wishing to return to their homes and live at peace with their neighbours should be permitted to do so at the earliest practicable date, and that compensation should be paid for the property of those choosing not to return and for loss of or damage to property which, under principles of international law or equity, should be made good by the Governments or authorities responsible." See https://www.unrwa.org/content/resolution-194. The issue gained prominence following the formation of the Palestine Liberation Organization (PLO) and especially after the Arab defeat in the 1967 War.

8   M. Zuckermann, *Holocaust in the Sealed Room* (Tel Aviv, 1993 [Hebrew]); Bashir & Goldberg, *The Holocaust and the Nakba*.

9   Markovits, *Nationbuilding and the Politics of Nationalism*; Himka, *Galician Villagers*; Himka, *Religion and Nationality in Western Ukraine*; Magocsi, *The Roots of Ukrainian Nationalism*: Struve, *Bauern und Nation in Galizien*.

10 Shanes, *Diaspora Nationalism*, 1–5, notes that "despite having been fully emancipated since 1867, most Jews in Galicia remained for years largely ... unfamiliar ... with notions of 'assimilation' or 'nationality.'" But by 1914 most Galician Jews agreed that they "in fact constituted one of the nationalities of the Habsburg Empire that deserved national rights," and "increasing numbers of Jews" in Galicia "imagined themselves members of a Jewish national community." See also Bartov, *Anatomy of a Genocide*, 25, 82–7, 96–101.

11 P. J. Potichnyj et al., eds., *Ukrainian-Jewish Relations in Historical Perspective* (Edmonton, 1988); Bartov, *Anatomy of a Genocide*, 6–36, and Chapter 8.

12 A. Zamoyski, *The Polish Way* (New York, 1988); D. Stone, *The Polish-Lithuanian State, 1386–1795* (Seattle, 2001). See the immensely popular Polish novel by H. Sienkiewicz, *With Fire and Sword*, trans. W. S. Kuniczak (New York, 1991), originally published as *Ogniem i mieczem* in 1884.

13. Bartov, *Anatomy of a Genocide*, 33–6. See also T. Snyder, *Sketches from a Secret War* (New Haven, CT, 2005), and Wolff, *The Idea of Galicia*.
14. Bartov, *Anatomy of a Genocide*, 22–9. See also B. D. Weinryb, *The Jews of Poland* (Philadelphia, PA, 1973); G. D. Hundert, *Jews in Poland-Lithuania in the Eighteenth Century* (Berkeley, CA, 2005); and M. J. Rosman, *The Lord's Jews* (Cambridge, MA, 1990).
15. On the Jewish foundation myth of Buczacz, see Chapter 11. See also Bartov, *Tales from the Borderlands*.
16. On the many faces of early Zionism see, e.g., D. Shumsky, "Leon Pinsker and 'Autoemancipation!'" *JSS* 18, no. 1 (2011): 33–62, and A. Dubnov, "'True Art Makes for the Integration of the Race,'" in *New Directions in Anglo-Jewish History*, ed. G. Alderman (Boston, MA, 2010), 101–34.
17. Bartov, *Anatomy of a Genocide*, 82–302; Bartov, *Erased*; Chapter 4. See also E. Melzer, *No Way Out* (Cincinnati, OH, 1997); K. B. Moss, *An Unchosen People* (Cambridge, MA, 2021); J. M. Karlip, *The Tragedy of a Generation* (Cambridge, MA, 2013); S. Rudnicki, "Anti-Jewish Legislation in Interwar Poland," in Blobaum, *Antisemitism and Its Opponents*, 148–70; S. Redlich, "Jewish-Ukrainian Relations in Inter-War Poland as Reflected in Some Ukrainian Publications," *Polin* 11 (1998): 232–46; Rudling, "The OUN, the UPA and the Holocaust"; Struve, "Tremors in the Shatterzone of Empires"; Terles, *Ethnic Cleansing of Poles in Volhynia and Eastern Galicia*; and K. Stadnik, "Ukrainian-Polish Population Transfers, 1944–46," in *Warlands*, ed. P. Gatrell et al. (Basingstoke, UK, 2009), 165–87.
18. U. Tal, *Christians and Jews in Germany* (Ithaca, NY, 1975); S. L. Gilman, *Difference and Pathology* (Ithaca, NY, 1985), 175–90; P. Reitter, *The Anti-Journalist* (Chicago, 2008), 107–36; J. Katz, *Out of the Ghetto* (Cambridge, MA, 1973); F. Kafka, "A Report for an Academy," in *The Metamorphosis, In the Penal Colony, and Other Stories*, trans. J. Neugroschel (New York, 2000), 173–83. For somewhat analogous current fears, see, e.g., J. Anderson and L. Rainie, "Artificial Intelligence and the Future of Humans," *Pew Research Center* (December 10, 2018), https://www.pewresearch.org/internet/2018/12/10/artificial-intelligence-and-the-future-of-humans/.
19. See note 15. See also G. Rubin, "From Federalism to Binationalism," *CEH* 24, no. 3 (2015): 393–414; Raz-Krakotzkin, "Jewish Peoplehood, 'Jewish Politics,' and Political Responsibility"; E. Chowers, "Time in Zionism," *PT* 26, no. 5 (1998): 652–85; E. Friesel, "Zionism and Jewish Nationalism," *JIH* 25, no. 2 (2006): 285–312; Y. Weiss, "Central European Ethnonationalism and Zionist Binationalism," *JSS* 11, no. 1 (2004): 93–117.
20. Veidlinger, *In the Midst of Civilized Europe*; H. Abramson, *A Prayer for the Government* (Cambridge, MA, 1999); R. Breitman and A. M. Kraut, *American Refugee Policy and European Jewry* (Bloomington, IN, 1987); M. Tolts, "Population and Migration," *YIVO Encyclopedia of Jews in Eastern Europe*, October 12, 2010, www.yivoencyclopedia.org/article.aspx/Population_and_Migration/Migration_since_World_War_I.
21. T. Segev, *One Palestine, Complete*, trans. H. Watzman (New York, 2001). See also M. U. Campos, *Ottoman Brothers* (Stanford, CA, 2011); J. M. Gribetz, *Defining Neighbors* (Princeton, NJ, 2014); R. Ben-Arie and M. Svirsky, *From Shared Life to Co-Resistance in Historic Palestine* (London, 2017); A. Jacobson, *Oriental Neighbors* (Waltham, MA, 2016); and L. R. Halperin, *Babel in Zion* (New Haven, CT, 2015).
22. See, e.g., letters cited in A. Shapira, "Jerusalem in 1948," *JSS* 17, no. 3 (2011): 78–123. See also H. Cohen, *Year Zero of the Arab-Israeli Conflict*, trans. H. Watzman (Waltham, MA, 2015).
23. G. D. Cohen, *In War's Wake* (New York, 2012); A. Grossmann, *Jews, Germans, and Allies* (Princeton, NJ, 2007); Z. W. Mankowitz, *Life between Memory and Hope* (New York, 2002); J. T. Baumel-Schwartz, *Kibbutz Buchenwald* (New Brunswick, NJ, 1997).
24. On Holocaust revenge fantasies, see, e.g., H. Bartov, *The Brigade*, trans. D. S. Segal (Philadelphia, PA, 1967); A. Goldberg, "Three Forms of Post-Genocidal Violence in Beni

Notes

Wircberg's Memoir," in *Talking about Evil*, ed. R. Lazar (London, 2017), 50–67; and Y. Kaniuk, *1948*, trans. A. Berris (New York, 2012 [2010]). See also H. Hever, "The Political Theology of Eretz Israel," in Bartov, *Israel-Palestine*, 23–42. On Kielce, see Gross, *Fear*. On Deir Yassin, see, e.g., D. A. McGowan et al., eds., *Remembering Deir Yassin* (New York, 1998); N. Masalha, "On Recent Hebrew and Israeli Sources for the Palestinian Exodus, 1947–49," *JPS* 18, no. 1 (1988): 121–37; B. Morris, "The Historiography of Deir Yassin," *JIH* 24, no. 1 (2005): 79–107; and U. Milstein, *The Birth of a Palestinian Nation* (Jerusalem, 2012).

25 On David Ben-Gurion and Yitzhak Ben-Zvi's theories of Palestinians as ancient Jews, see Gribetz, *Defining Neighbors*, 123–6. On Polish rhetoric about Ruthenians, see Bartov, *Anatomy of a Genocide*, 26–7, 116–23.

26 In addition to H. Cohen, *Year Zero*, see A. Shapira, *Land and Power*, trans. W. Templer (New York, 1992), and T. Swedenburg, *Memories of Revolt* (Minneapolis, MN, 1995). See also Porat, *Blue and the Yellow Stars*; D. Ofer, *Escaping the Holocaust* (New York, 1990); H. Yablonka, *Survivors of the Holocaust*, trans. O. Cummings (New York, 1999); J. Herf, *Nazi Propaganda for the Arab World* (New Haven, CT, 2009); Ilan Pappé, *The Rise and Fall of a Palestinian Dynasty* (Berkeley, CA, 2011).

27 K.-M. Mallmann and M. Cüppers, *Nazi Palestine*, trans. K. Smith (New York, 2010). See also M. Beckman, *The Jewish Brigade* (Staplehurst, UK, 1998), and H. Blum, *The Brigade* (New York, 2001).

28 See, e.g., D. Tal, "The Forgotten War," *IA* 6, nos. 3–4 (2000): 3–21; M. S. Dajani Daoudi and Z. M. Barakat, "Israelis and Palestinians," *IS* 18, no. 2 (2013): 53–69; and A. Manna', "The Palestinian Nakba and Its Continuous Repercussions," *IS* 18, no. 2 (2013): 86–99. On the pre-1948 Zionist idea of transfer, see B. Morris, *Birth of the Palestinian Refugee Problem Revisited* (New York, 2003), 39–64; J. R. Hammond, "Benny Morris's Untenable Denial of the Ethnic Cleansing of Palestine," *FPJ*, November 14, 2016, www.foreignpolicyjournal.com/2016/11/14/benny-morriss-untenable-denial-of-the-ethnic-cleansing-of-palestine/.

29 I am referring here to S. Yizhar, *Khirbet Khizeh* (1949) and A. Yeshurun, "Pesah 'al kukhim" (Passover on Caves, 1952). See Eshel, "History and Responsibility" and Hever, *Hebrew Literature and the 1948 War*.

30 See, e.g., Bartov, "Kitsch and Sadism in Ka-Tzetnik's Other Planet"; D. Laub, "An Event without a Witness," in Felman and Laub, *Testimony*, 88–92. Holocaust survivor B. Virtzberg's (Wircberg) memoir, *From Death to Battle*, trans. M. Pagis et al. (Jerusalem, 2017), originally published in Hebrew in 1967, shortly before the author's suicide, contains numerous allusions to this linkage.

Chapter 10

1 "We, the survivors, are not true witnesses … we are those who by their prevarications or abilities or good luck did not touch bottom. Those who did so, those who saw the Gorgon, have not returned to tell about it or have returned mute, but they are … the complete witnesses, the ones whose deposition would have a general significance." Levi, *The Drowned and the Saved*, 83–4.

2 For another view of that generation, see H. Yablonka, *Children by the Book* (Rishon LeZion, 2018 [Hebrew]).

3 E. A. Shils and M. Janowitz, "Cohesion and Disintegration in the Wehrmacht in World War II," *POQ* 12 (1948): 280–315.

4 Bartov, "The Wehrmacht Exhibition Controversy"; Hamburg Institute for Social Research, ed., *The German Army and Genocide* (New York, 1999).

Notes

5 Bartov, *The Eastern Front*; M. Messerschmidt, *Die Wehrmacht im NS-Staat* (Hamburg, 1969); C. Streit, *Keine Kameraden* (Stuttgart, 1978); H. Krausnick and H.-H. Wilhelm, *Die Truppe des Weltanschauungskrieges* (Stuttgart, 1981).
6 I responded to Rabin with a lengthier explanation of my research and anxieties, and received a second letter from him, with essentially the same content as the first. Rabin's original letters are still in my possession.
7 Bartov, *Petihat Tsir* and *Karev Yom*.
8 Bartov, *Hitler's Army*.
9 O. Bartov, "An Idiot's Tale," *JMH* 67, no. 1 (1995): 55–82.
10 The papers of this conference, with additional contributions, including my own, adding many other perspectives, were published in D. Cesarani, ed., *The Final Solution* (London, 1994).
11 Y. Bauer, *Rethinking the Holocaust* (New Haven, CT, 2001); D. Michman, *Holocaust Historiography* (London, 2003).
12 Yablonka, *Israel vs. Adolf Eichmann*; Stauber, *The Holocaust in Israeli Public Debate*; I. Lustick, "The Holocaust in Israeli Political Culture," *CJ* 37, no. 1 (2017): 125–70.
13 See, e.g., Dreifuss, *Warsaw Ghetto*.
14 Bartov, *Erased*.
15 See also Chapter 11.
16 Bartov, *The Butterfly and the Axe*.

Chapter 11

1 Agnon, *A City in Its Fullness*, 31–7.
2 For Agnon's earlier, 1916 version of this myth as the tale of East-Central European Jewry in general, see S. Y. Agnon, "Polin," in I. Bartal and A. Polonsky, eds., *Polin* 12 (1999), ix–x.
3 For Agnon's early years in Buczacz, Jaffa, and Germany, see Laor, *Agnon*, 19–168.
4 *A City in Its Fullness*, dedication page.
5 Ibid., 28–9. The editors of the English translation chose to locate this section in the opening part of the book. In the original Hebrew volume, edited posthumously by Agnon's daughter, Emunah Yaron, this passage, which is part of the story "The Sign," closes the volume.
6 A. Mintz, "'I am Building a City,'" Ibid., xx. See also Y. (J.) Saks, "From New York to Jerusalem," *Shabbat: Makor Rishon* (January 11, 2013 [Hebrew]).
7 On Buczacz as a multiethnic city and its bloody end, see Bartov, *Anatomy of a Genocide*.
8 On the Jewish-Polish-Ukrainian relationship see, e.g., Bartal and Polonsky *Polin* 12, and Bartov, *Anatomy of a Genocide*. On the Jewish-Arab encounter in Palestine see, e.g., M. Klein, *Lives in Common*, trans. H. Watzman (New York, 2014); M. Levine et al., eds., *Struggle and Survival in Palestine/Israel* (Berkeley, CA, 2012); Y. Auron, *Israeli Identities*, trans. G. Forman (New York, 2012); H. Lazar, *Out of Palestine* (New York, 2011); M. Benvenisti, *Intimate Enemies* (Berkeley, CA, 1995). On the Jewish-Zionist self-fashioning, see, e.g., B. Neuman, *Land and Desire in Early Zionism*, trans. H. Watzman (Waltham, MA, 2011); A. B. Saposnik, *Becoming Hebrew* (New York, 2008); B. Kimmerling, *The Invention and Decline of Israeliness* (Berkeley, CA, 2005); E. Luz, *Wrestling with an Angel*, trans. M. Swirsky (New Haven, CT, 2003); N. Abu El-Haj, *Facts on the Ground* (Chicago, 2001); Y. Zerubavel, *Recovered Roots* (Chicago, 1995).
9 See, e.g., Almog, *The Sabra*; D. Ohana, *Modernism and Zionism* (New York, 2012).
10 Bartov, *Anatomy of a Genocide*, 115–16, 271, 308, 348.
11 T. Segev, *A State at Any Cost*, trans. H. Watzman (New York, 2019), 59–60, 262, 577.

Notes

12 On the expulsion of the Palestinian, see esp. Morris, *The Birth of the Palestinian Refugee Problem Revisited*. See also N. Masalha, *Politics of Denial* (London, 2003); G. Achcar, *The Arabs and the Holocaust* (New York, 2009); I. Zertal, *Israel's Holocaust and the Politics of Nationhood* (Cambridge, UK, 2005).

13 N. Leshem, *Life after Ruin* (Cambridge, UK, 2017); N. Kadman, *Erased from Space and Consciousness*, trans. D. Reider (Bloomington, IN, 2015); T. Sorek, *Palestinian Commemoration in Israel* (Stanford, CA, 2015); E. Ben-Ze'ev, *Remembering Palestine in 1948* (New York, 2011); A. H. Sa'di et al., eds., *Nakba* (New York, 2007); M. Benvenisti, *Sacred Landscape*, trans. M. Kaufman-Lacusta (Berkeley, CA, 2000).

14 Bartov, *Erased*; B. Paloff, "Who Owns Bruno Schulz?," *BR* (December 2004/January 2005).

15 M. Darwish, *Unfortunately, It Was Paradise*, trans. M. Akash et al. (Berkeley, CA, 2013), 7.

16 Bartov & Weitz, *Shatterzone of Empires*; F. Hirsch, *Empire of Nations* (Ithaca, NY, 2005); T. Martin, *The Affirmative Action Empire* (Ithaca, NY, 2001); A. Roshwald, *Ethnic Nationalism and the Fall of Empires* (New York, 2001); Aly, *Final Solution*; M. S. Quine, *Population Politics in Twentieth-Century Europe* (New York, 1996).

17 P. Panayi, *An Ethnic History of Europe Since 1945* (Harlow, UK, 2000); B. R. Rubin et al., eds., *Post-Soviet Political Order* (New York, 1998); K. Barkey et al., eds., *After Empire* (Boulder, CO, 1997); G. Eley et al., eds., *Becoming National* (New York, 1996).

18 W. Kymlicka, *Politics in the Vernacular* (New York, 2001).

19 Snyder, *The Reconstruction of Nations*; B. Porter, *When Nationalism Began to Hate* (New York, 2000); A. Lichtblau, "Jewries in Galicia and Bukovina, in Lemberg and Czernowitz," in *Jewries at the Frontier*, ed. Sander L. Gilman et al. (Urbana, IL, 1999), 29–66.

20 E. Barkan, *The Guilt of Nations* (New York, 2000).

21 On Potok Złoty, see Dąbrowska, *Pinkas Hakehillot*, 415–16; Bartov, *Erased*.

22 Interview with Oresta Synenka and her husband Ivan Synenkyi by Sofia Grachova and Andryi Pavlyashuk on March 2, 2006, in Buczacz.

23 M. Nosonovsky, *Hebrew Epitaphs and Inscriptions from Ukraine and Former Soviet Union* (Washington, DC, 2006), 25.

24 "The Journey to Buczacz, 2017," The Association of Jewish Galicia and Bukovina (Hebrew); http://jgbherzog.jgaliciabukovina.net/he/node/147; "Buczacz Cemetery," The Association of Jewish Galicia and Bukovina, www.jgaliciabukovina.net/183010/cemetery/buczacz; "400-year-old Jewish cemetery in Ukraine restored," JP, December 11, 2018, www.jpost.com/diaspora/400-year-old-jewish-cemetery-in-ukraine-restored-574065.

25 "Hnatiuk, Volodymyr," Internet Encyclopedia of Ukraine, www.encyclopediaofukraine.com/display.asp?linkpath=pages%5CH%5CN%5CHnatiukVolodymyr.htm.

26 Segev, *Simon Wiesenthal*, 40–9.

27 Interview by the author with Roman Antoshkiv in Buczacz on June 21, 2004. Antoshkiv remembered how the Jews of his nearby village were assembled by the Germans and led away. At the time of the interview, he was being praised in the local press for donating money to construct a monument for OUN leader Stepan Bandera.

28 F. Golczewski, "Die Kollaboration in der Ukraine," in C. Dieckmann et al., eds., *Kooperation und Verbrechen* (Göttingen, 2003), 151–82; D. Pohl, "Ukrainische Hilfskräfte beim Mord an den Juden," in G. Paul, ed., *Die Täter der Shoah* (Göttingen, 2002), 205–34; K. Berkhoff and M. Carynnyk, "The Organization of Ukrainian Nationalists and Its Attitude toward Germans and Jews," *HUS* 23, nos. 3–4 (1999): 149–84; J.-P. Himka, "Ukrainian Collaboration in the Extermination of the Jews during the Second World War," in J. Frankel, ed., *The Fate of the European Jews, 1939–1945* (New York, 1997), 170–89.

29 Paldiel, *The Path of the Righteous*, 191–3; Bartov, *Voices on War and Genocide*, 295, 427 n. 70; Bartov, *Anatomy of a Genocide*, 254, 361 n. 23.

Notes

30 Ibid., 176–7. See also Pohl, *Nationalsozialistische Judenverfolgung*; Sandkühler, *"Endlösung" in Galizien*.
31 See further on Agnon in Chapter 8, and Bartov, *Tales from the Borderlands*. Agnon was actually born on August 8, 1887, and apparently chose the later date for the symbolic value of its Hebrew equivalent.
32 See, e.g., Agnon Literary Center, https://agnoncenter.org/en/main/; "A dialogue between Buchach (Ukraine) and Israel," *Ukrainian Jewish Encounter*, September 9, 2019, https://ukrainianjewishencounter.org/en/a-dialogue-between-buchach-ukraine-and-israel-maryana-maksymiak/; "Buchach-Jerusalem: A Bridge of Inspiration for New Ukrainian Literature," *Ukrainian Jewish Encounter*, November 16, 2018, https://ukrainianjewishencounter.org/en/buchach-jerusalem-a-bridge-of-inspiration-for-new-ukrainian-literature/. N. A. Feduschak, "Returning Agnon to Ukraine," *The Odessa Review*, January 24, 2018, http://odessareview.com/returning-agnon-ukraine/.
33 On development in the first decade after Ukrainian independence, see Bartov, *Erased*. On more recent developments, see, e.g., J. McBride, "Who's Afraid of Ukrainian Nationalism?" *Kritika* 17, no. 23 (2016): 647–63; J. Dekker, "The Politics of Memory," https://heritageandmemorystudies.humanities.uva.nl/index.php/1718-2/research-projects-lviv/stepan-bandera-monument/.
34 The Buchach city website no longer carries this information, accessed on June 26, 2007. The speakers included the director of the Bandera Memorial (Society) Oresta Synenka, mentioned above. The speeches were reportedly "full of heartfelt feelings, reflections on the figure of Stepan Bandera in the history of our Fatherland and the region, and his enormous role in the formation of Ukrainian self-consciousness, national spirit, and the striving for freedom and liberty."
35 On my family's transition from Galicia to Palestine, see Bartov, *Tales from the Borderlands*, chapters 12–14.
36 "On Ben-Gurion's Impressive and Failed Speech to Israeli Youth," in "This Happened … Israeli Historical Blog," August 13, 2016 (Hebrew), http://ze-kara.blogspot.com/2016/08/1954.html. Contemporary news reports remarked that the teenagers assembled at the site showed little interest in the speech.
37 See S. Hochstadt, ed., *Sources of the Holocaust* (New York, 2004), 186–9.
38 See Bartov, *The "Jew" in Cinema*, 326 n. 61, for the testimony and the judges' response. See also Yablonka, *Israel vs. Adolf Eichmann*; Stauber, *The Holocaust in Israeli Public Debate*; Segev, *The Seventh Million*.
39 Blatman, "Polish Jewry, the Six-Day War, and the Crisis of 1968"; D. Blatman, "Polish Antisemitism and 'Judeo-Communism,'" *EEJA* 27, no. 1 (1997): 23–43.
40 See discussion in A. Raz-Krakotzkin, "Historical Consciousness and Historical Responsibility," in *From Vision to Revision*, ed. Y. Weitz (Jerusalem, 1997 [Hebrew]), 97–133.
41 Tel Aviv University was officially established in 1956 near Jaffa; in 1959 it was recognized as a branch of the Hebrew University in Jerusalem; construction of the campus on the lands of al-Shaykh Muwannis began in 1955; the campus was officially inaugurated in 1964 and the university was recognized as an independent institution of higher education in 1969.
42 Lehi (LHI) is the Hebrew acronym for Fighters for the Freedom of Israel. Its first leader, Avraham Stern, was killed by the British in 1942.
43 The Faculty Club, Tel Aviv University, www.tau.ac.il/facultyclub (Hebrew).
44 Architecture on campus: Tel Aviv University, www.tau.ac.il/Campus-architecture.
45 The Green House, www.camilo.co.il/%d7%90%d7%95%d7%93%d7%95%d7%aa/.
46 Hanaa Abueid, *The "Green House" History* (2003): www.palestineremembered.com/Jaffa/al-Shaykh-Muwannis/Story1114.html. More generally on the period see Tom Segev, *One Palestine, Complete*.

Notes

47 "Al-Shaykh Muwannis," PalestineRemembered.com, www.palestineremembered.com/Jaffa/al-Shaykh-Muwannis/.
48 Morris, *The Birth of the Palestinian Refugee Problem Revisited*, 12–14, 34–5. See also I. Pappé, *A History of Modern Palestine* (New York, 2004); A. Shlaim, *The Iron Wall* (New York, 2000); B. Morris, *Righteous Victims* (New York, 1999); M. Tessler, *A History of the Israeli-Palestinian Conflict*, 2nd ed. (Bloomington, IN, 2009); C. D. Smith, *Palestine and the Arab-Israeli Conflict*, 10th ed. (New York, 2020).
49 UNRWA, www.unrwa.org/palestine-refugees; Palestinian refugees and the right of return, American Friends Service Committee, www.afsc.org/resource/palestinian-refugees-and-right-return#:~:text=Today%20there%20are%20more%20than,of%20the%20Palestinian%2DIsraeli%20conflict. See also U. Shavit and J. Bana, "Everything you wanted to know about the right to return but were too afraid to ask," *Haaretz* (July 6, 2001), www.mideastweb.org/refugees3.htm; Morris, *The Birth of the Palestinian Refugee Problem Revisited*, 602–4.
50 Ibid., 588–601.
51 Etzel (IZL) is the Hebrew acronym for National Military Organization.
52 Shavit and Bana, "Everything You Wanted to Know."
53 Ibid.
54 "Al-Shaykh Muwannis," PalestineRemembered.com, www.palestineremembered.com/Jaffa/al-Shaykh-Muwannis/. On Avraham Shapira (1870–1965) and his generation see L. R. Halperin, *The Oldest Guard* (Stanford, CA, 2021).
55 Morris, *The Birth of the Palestinian Refugee Problem Revisited*, 91.
56 Ibid., 127–8.
57 Ibid., 138.
58 Ibid., 310.
59 G. Meir, *My Life* (New York, 1975), 11. See also "Golda Meir," New World Encyclopedia, www.newworldencyclopedia.org/entry/Golda_Meir.
60 Morris, *The Birth of the Palestinian Refugee Problem Revisited*, 310.
61 Ibid.
62 Ibid.
63 Ibid., 318.
64 Ibid., 342–3. See also A. Raz, *The Looting of Arab Property in the War of Independence* (Jerusalem, 2020 [Hebrew]).
65 A. J. Toynbee, *A Study of History*, abridgement of vols. 7–10 by D. C. Somervell (New York, 1987 [1957]), 267.
66 Laor, *Agnon*, 19–168.
67 H. Bartov, *Ani loh hatzabar hamitologi* (I am not the Mythological Sabra) (Tel Aviv, 1995); H. Bartov, *Regel ahat bahutz* (Halfway Out) (Tel Aviv, 1994).
68 H. Bartov, *The Brigade*.
69 H. Bartov, *Mitom ad tom* (From Innocence to End), (Or Yehuda, 2003), 165–6.
70 See, e.g., N. Even, *Teach "Values," Not "Shapes,"* 2nd ed. (Israel, 2016 [Hebrew]), https://bleknet.net/tni/Lehanech_Learachim_Velo_Letzurot.pdf.
71 Bartov, *The Eastern Front*.
72 Bartov et al., introduction to Bartov, *Crimes of War*, ix–xxxiv; Bartov, "The Wehrmacht Exhibition Controversy."
73 Bartov, *Hitler's Army*; O. Bartov, "Reception and Perception," in *The "Goldhagen Effect,"* ed. G. Eley (Ann Arbor, MI, 2000), 33–87; Bartov, *Germany's War and the Holocaust*.
74 O. Bartov, review of *Mein Krieg* (film), dir. H. Eder and T. Kufus, *AHR* 97, no. 4 (October 1992): 1155–7; A. Lichtblau, "Mördervater–Vatermörder?" in *Umkämpfte Erinnerung*, ed. H. Embacher et al. (Salzburg, 1999), 133–56.

75 See, e.g., A. Hass, "Broken Bones and Broken Hopes," *Haaretz*, November 4, 2005, www.haaretz.com/1.4880391.
76 Y. Elkana, "In Praise of Forgetting," *Haaretz*, March 2, 1988 (Hebrew), www.haaretz.co.il/opinions/1.1841380.
77 Bartov, *Mirrors of Destruction*, 108–11.
78 For sources, see Bartov, *Anatomy of a Genocide*, and Chapter 3.
79 For more, see Chapter 4.
80 Further in Bartov, *Tales from the Borderlands*, Chapters 12–14.
81 Barącz, *Pamiątki Buczackie*.
82 See, e.g., M. Golani and A. Manna, *Two Sides of the Coin*, English-Hebrew ed. (Dordrecht, Netherlands, 2011); S. Adwan et al., eds., *Side by Side* (New York, 2012); E. Khoury, *Gate of the Sun*, trans. H. Davies (London, 2006).
83 See, e.g., R. Khalidi, *Palestinian Identity* (New York, 1997); Benvenisti, *Sacred Landscape*; Kadman, *Erased from Space and Consciousness*; Almog, *The Sabra*; Zertal, *Israel's Holocaust and the Politics of Nationhood*; Segev, *The Seventh Million*.
84 On Palestinian oral accounts of the Nakba, see, e.g., Ben-Ze'ev, *Remembering Palestine in 1948*; Sa'di, *Nakba*.
85 See N. Leshem, *Life after Ruin* (Cambridge, UK, 2017), 177.
86 Camus, *The First Man*.
87 But I have tried to imagine it. See Bartov, *The Butterfly and the Axe*.
88 See, e.g., Bartov, *Israel-Palestine*; Bashir, *The Holocaust and the Nakba*; Hever, *Hebrew Literature and the 1948 War*; Auron, *Israeli Identities*; LeVine, *Struggle and Survival in Palestine/Israel*; Lazar, *Out of Palestine*; S. Tamari, *Mountain Against the Sea* (Berkeley, CA, 2009).
89 Bartov, *Erased*; Bartov and Weitz, *Shatterzone of Empires*.
90 See, e.g., Bartov, "Defining Enemies, Making Victims."

SELECT BIBLIOGRAPHY

Almog, Oz. *The Sabra: The Creation of the New Jew*. Translated by Haim Watzman. Berkeley: University of California Press, 2000.
Aly, Götz. *Hitler's Beneficiaries: Plunder, Racial War, and the Nazi Welfare State*. Translated by Jefferson Chase. New York: Metropolitan, 2006.
Aly, Götz. *"Final Solution": Nazi Population Policy and the Murder of the European Jews*. Translated by Belinda Cooper and Alison Brown. New York: Hodder Education, 1999.
Bartov, Omer. *Anatomy of a Genocide: The Life and Death of a Town Called Buczacz*. New York: Simon and Schuster, 2018.
Bartov, Omer. *Erased: Vanishing Traces of Jewish Galicia in Present-Day Ukraine*. Princeton, NJ: Princeton University Press, 2007.
Bartov, Omer. *Tales from the Borderlands: Making and Unmaking the Galician Past*. New Haven, CT: Yale University Press, 2022.
Bartov, Omer and Eric D. Weitz, eds. *Shatterzone of Empires: Coexistence and Violence in the German, Habsburg, Russian, and Ottoman Borderlands*. Bloomington: Indiana University Press, 2013.
Bauman, Zygmunt. *Modernity and the Holocaust*. Ithaca, NY: Cornell University Press, 1989.
Benvenisti, Meron. *Sacred Landscape: The Buried History of the Holy Land since 1948*. Translated by Maxine Kaufman-Lacusta. Berkeley: University of California Press, 2000.
Berkhoff, Karel C. *Harvest of Despair: Life and Death in Ukraine under Nazi Rule*. Cambridge: Belknap Press, 2004.
Bloxham, Donald. *The Final Solution: A Genocide*. New York: Oxford University Press, 2009.
Bloxham, Donald and A. Dirk Moses, eds. *The Oxford Handbook of Genocide Studies*. New York: Oxford University Press, 2010.
Browning, Christopher R. *Remembering Survival: Inside a Nazi Slave-Labor Camp*. New York: W. W. Norton, 2009.
Browning, Christopher R. and Jürgen Matthäus. *The Origins of the Final Solution: The Evolution of Nazi Jewish Policy, September 1939–March 1942*. Lincoln: University of Nebraska Press, 2004.
Douglas, Lawrence. *The Memory of Judgment: Making Law and History in the Trials of the Holocaust*. New Haven, CT: Yale University Press, 2001.
Friedländer, Saul. *Nazi Germany and the Jews*. Vol. 1: *The Years of Persecution, 1933–1939*. New York: Harper Perennial, 1997. Vol. 2: *The Years of Extermination, 1939–1945*. New York: HarperCollins Publishers, 2007.
Frieze, Donna-Lee, ed. *Totally Unofficial: The Autobiography of Raphael Lemkin*. New Haven, CT: Yale University Press, 2013.
Garbarini, Alexandra. *Numbered Days: Diaries and the Holocaust*. New Haven, CT: Yale University Press, 2006.
Gerlach, Christian. *The Extermination of the European Jews*. Cambridge: Cambridge University Press, 2016.
Goldberg, Amos. *Trauma in First Person: Diary Writing during the Holocaust*. Translated by Shmuel Sermoneta-Gertel and Avner Greenberg. Bloomington: Indiana University Press, 2017.

Select Bibliography

Goldberg, Amos and Bashir Bashir, eds. *The Holocaust and the Nakba: A New Grammar of Trauma and History*. New York: Columbia University Press, 2018.

Grabowski, Jan. *Hunt for the Jews: Betrayal and Murder in German-Occupied Poland*. Bloomington: Indiana University Press, 2013.

Grabowski, Jan and Barbara Engelking, eds. *Night without End: The Fate of Jews in German-Occupied Poland*. Translated by Anna Brzostowska, Jerzy Giebułtowski, Jan Grabowski, Elżbieta Olender-Dmowska, and Tomasz Frydel. Bloomington: Indiana University Press, 2022.

Graziosi, Andreas and Frank E. Sysyn, eds. *Genocide: The Power and Problems of a Concept*. Montreal: McGill-Queen's University Press, 2022.

Gross, Jan T. *Fear: Anti-Semitism in Poland after Auschwitz*. Princeton, NJ: Princeton University Press, 2006.

Gross, Jan T. *Neighbors: The Destruction of the Jewish Community in Jedwabne, Poland*. Princeton, NJ: Princeton University Press, 2001.

Hilberg, Raul. *The Destruction of the European Jews*. 3rd ed. 3 vols. New Haven, CT: Yale University Press, 2003.

Khalidi, Rashid. *Palestinian Identity: The Construction of Modern National Consciousness*. New York: Columbia University Press, 1998.

Kiernan, Ben. *Blood and Soil: Genocide, Conquest, Cultivation, and History, 1400-2005*. New Haven, CT: Yale University Press, 2007.

Kuper, Leo. *Genocide: Its Political Use in the Twentieth Century*. New Haven, CT: Yale University Press, 1981.

Lemkin, Raphael. *Axis Rule in Occupied Europe: Laws of Occupation, Analysis of Government, Proposals for Redress*. 2nd ed. Clark, NJ: The Lawbook Exchange, 2008. Originally published in 1944.

Longerich, Peter. *Holocaust: The Nazi Persecution and Murder of the Jews*. New York: Oxford University Press, 2010.

Mazower, Mark. *Hitler's Empire: How the Nazis Ruled Europe*. New York: Penguin Books, 2008.

Morris, Benny. *The Birth of the Palestinian Refugee Problem Revisited*. 2nd ed. New York: Cambridge University Press, 2004.

Moses, A. Dirk. *The Problems of Genocide: Permanent Security and the Language of Transgression*. New York: Cambridge University Press, 2021.

Naimark, Norman M. *Fires of Hatred: Ethnic Cleansing in Twentieth Century Europe*. Cambridge, MA: Harvard University Press, 2001.

Novick, Peter. *The Holocaust in American Life*. Boston, MA: Houghton Mifflin, 1999.

Pappé, Ilan. *The Ethnic Cleansing of Palestine*. London: One World Publications, 2006.

Power, Samantha. *"A Problem from Hell": America and the Age of Genocide*. New York: Harper Perennial, 2002.

Redlich, Shimon. *Together and Apart in Brzeżany: Poles, Jews and Ukrainians, 1919-1945*. Bloomington: Indiana University Press, 2002.

Segev, Tom. *One Palestine, Complete: Jews and Arabs under the British Mandate*. Translated by Haim Watzman. New York, 2001.

Segev, Tom. *The Seventh Million: The Israelis and the Holocaust*. Translated by Haim Watzman. New York: Hill and Wang, 1993.

Weitz, Eric D. *A Century of Genocide: Utopias of Race and Nation*. Princeton, NJ: Princeton University Press, 2003.

Zertal, Idith. *Israel's Holocaust and the Politics of Nationhood*. Translated by Chaya Galai. Cambridge: Cambridge University Press, 2005.

INDEX

Aberdam (Freiberg), S. 67
Abyss of Despair, The (Hanover) 50
Adler, H. G. 5–6, 91, 123–35
Agnon, S. Y. 6, 47, 51–2, 138–40, 144–5, 173–8, 182, 184, 193–4, 197–9
akcja shootings 30
Aktion 67, 71
Aktionen 75
Aleichem, S. 48
Alfortville 146
Algeria 127
Allan, W. S. 42
anarchism 142, 144
Anatomy of a Genocide (Bartov) 42, 59
Anderman, Z. 77
Anschluss 140
Ansky, S. 52
anti-Jewish violence 1; *see also* Holocaust; Jews
anti-Semitism 12, 14–15, 84, 106, 114, 138–9, 142, 144, 147, 169
    Eastern Europe 22
    Poland 24
Appleman-Jurman, A. 68
Arafat, Y. 169
Archive of Memory 40
Aryanization of Jewish property 90
Aspects of Revolt (Nomad) 145
assembly-line killing 93
Auerbach, L. 89
Austerlitz (Sebald) 126
Australia 41, 77, 187
Austrian Social Democracy 143

Baku 164
Baltic states, the 28
Bandera, S. 54–5
Banderivtsy (Banderowcy) 184
Barącz, S. 51
Baron Hirsch School 145
Barton, R. 66
Baruch, K. 76
Baszty (Jewish cemetery) Hill 53
Bauer, Y. 66, 74–5
Bavaria 88, 128, 166
Begin, M. 169
Beinisch, D. 118
Beirut 169

beit hamidrash 177
Belarus 28, 180
Belgium 41
Bełżec extermination camp 48, 72, 75, 86, 90, 141, 183
Ben-Gurion, D. 169, 176–7, 185, 191, 193
Berg, N. 39
Bergen Belsen concentration camp 123
Berlin 40, 47, 138, 144, 169
betrayal 66–7, 70
Bible 177
bifurcated Holocaust scholarship 22–5
Blum, B. 92
Bobyk, I. 33–6
Boder, D. 40
Bolshevik Party 147
Bolsheviks 27
Borszczów 91
Bosnia 42, 170, 199
Brecher, R. 67
Britain 15, 41, 59, 168, 186
Broszat, M. 39–40, 166
Browning, C. 40
brutalization of Wehrmacht soldiers 12
Buchenwald 87
Buczacz 4, 6–7, 33–4, 54, 180–5
    Al-Shaykh Muwannis 185–92
    anti-Jewish violence 53
    Christian population 74
    destruction 50–1
    eighteenth century 51
    extermination action 91
    Fedor (Fedir) Hill 182–3
    Great Synagogue, The 181–2
    Gymnasium building 182
    Holocaust 48
    intelligentsia members 86
    Jewish cemetery 182
    Jewish–Christian interaction 51
    Jews 48–50, 173–6
    judenfrei 86
    local genocide 49
    mass killings 86
    mass shootings 53
    memory renaissance 184
    museum, UPA 183
    mythical origins 173–4

Index

nationalism 51
premodern 51
Russian occupation 51–2
Soviets, the 52–3
Ukrainian atrocities 52
violence, external and fraternal 49–50
Vulitsa Agnona 177
Zionism 52
Bund Deutscher Mädel (BDM) 115

Camus, A. 126–7, 129, 201, 203
Canada 41
Catechism Debate, 2021 1
Césaire, A. 17
Chagall, M. 48
Chalfen (Chalfon), E. 55, 68
City in Its Fullness, A (Agnon) 142, 147
Clown of Barnow, The (Franzos) 137–8
Cologne police force 87
colonial genocides 3, 15–16, 18; *see also* genocide
colonialism 3, 11, 14–17
commemoration 2, 5, 21–2, 26, 37, 49, 59, 63, 106, 111–19, 132–3, 164, 182–4
communal genocide 3, 28–32, 48, 66, 77–9
communal violence 13, 20, 42, 170, 199
communism 3
  fall of 26, 32, 35
Crimea 107
crime of crimes 19
crimes
  "base motives" 84
  deportations 86
  judgments 95–101
  Köllner, K. 90–1
  life imprisonment 97, 99
  murderer, definition 84
  Nazi and Soviet 108–9
  Peckmann, H. 89
  perpetrators 86–9
  superior orders 84–5
  Thomanek, P. 91–5
  town/site 85–6
  Ukrainian nationalists 109–10
Ćwitowa (Tsvitova) 34
Czechoslovakia 88, 98, 100, 102, 194
Czernowitz (Chernivtsi) 34, 137, 180
Czortków 4, 30, 48, 53, 67, 86–92, 94–6, 101–2, 136
Czortków labor camp 89, 91–2

Dalairac, F. -P. 51
de-communization package, Ukraine 110
dehumanization 47, 123
Delbo, C. 126–7, 129

denials
  criminalization 112
  prohibiting 113
  shelilat hagalut 112
  Warsaw Ghetto Uprising 113
denunciations 31, 65–6, 70, 78
deportations 28, 36, 58, 79, 83, 86, 90–1, 110, 115, 156, 179
Der Judenstaat (Herzl) 136
Diamant, G. 92
displacement (population policies) 6, 61
  Arabs 161
  and belonging 159
  Israel-Palestine 151–61
Dnieper 174
Dniester River 75, 180
Drohobycz 178
Drowned and the Saved, The (Levi) 130
Duda, A. 108
Duda, I. 34
Dutkiewicz, M. 73
Dybbuk, The (Ansky) 52

Eastern Europe 3–4, 7, 16
  anti-Semitism 22
  bifurcated scholarship 22–5
  communal massacre 28–32
  communism, fall of 26, 32, 35
  communist dictatorship 24
  genocide, economy of 32–6
  interethnic relations 24–5, 37, 41
  Jedwabne debate 27
  Jewish life and death 21
  Jews and others 153–6
  as *lieu de mémoire* 42–3
  testimony and history 36–42
  Wehrmacht debate 27
Eastern Galicia 4, 41, 48, 53–4, 65, 70, 116, 135, 145–6, 180, 184, 203
Ebenstein, J. 76–7
Eichmann, A. 38, 75, 114–15, 144
Eichmann Trial, the 38, 114, 163, 169
Elkana, Y. 196
elusive justice 101–3
empathetic detachment 130
empathy 2, 12, 27, 38, 48, 56, 66, 119, 125, 130–2, 138, 193, 198–9
Engelberg, B. 76
Engelking, B. 1
erasure and memory 178–80
Eretz Israel 152, 155, 157–8, 174, 176, 193
ethnic cleansing 28, 41, 43, 53–4, 61, 79, 85, 107–8, 110, 119, 151, 156, 179–80, 183, 192, 197, 199
European genocide 14, 19
European Jewish Cemeteries Initiative (ESJF) 182

Federal Republic of Germany (FRG) 83–4
Fedor (Fedir) Hill 30, 53, 73, 93, 177, 182–3
Finkielkraut, A. 128
First Man, The (Camus) 126–7
first-person histories 2–3, 5, 7
First Person History in Times of Crisis: Witnessing, Memory, Fiction 126
First World War 6, 12–13, 15, 32, 42, 48–53, 105, 123, 127, 135, 140, 143–4, 154, 156, 159, 185, 193, 198, 203
Folkenfolk, L. 93
Fortunoff Video Archive, Yale University 40
France 14, 16, 26, 36, 41, 59, 127, 146, 201
Frank, H. 87–8
Frankfurt Auschwitz Trial 38, 83
Franko, I. 6, 136–8, 182
Franzos, K. E. 6, 136–8, 141
Freud, M. 140
Freud, S. 6, 139–40
Friedländer, S. 39, 126–9
Frolov, L. 106

Gabirol, R. S. I. 175
Galicia 4, 19, 41, 50, 74, 86, 88, 158
Galizien Distrikt 48
Gaza operation 114
Gelbart, I. 33–4
gendarmes 30, 48, 75, 93
génocidaires 20
genocidal ideology 99
genocide 1–2, 11
   colonial 16
   comparative 169
   contextualization of 25
   Eastern Europe 21–43
   economy of 32–6
   and Holocaust, relationship 11–20
   of Jews in Europe 15
   legitimizing 105–7
   material benefits of 23
   perpetrators 5
   personal accounts 62–3, 78
   phenomenon 11
   trials 4
   Volhynia 110
   and war crimes 12
Genocide Convention of 1948 11
genocide of the Herero 16
German (Germany) 7, 17, 19, 22–3, 25–6, 28, 32, 34, 39, 52, 59, 67, 74, 85, 88–9, 98, 102, 114, 116, 128, 139–40, 155, 160, 164, 166, 168, 174, 183, 193–7, 203
   catechism 1
   colonialism 16
   criminal code 5

genocide in Europe 14–15
Gertner, R. 66
Gesamtgeschichte 129
Gesamtkunstwerk 129
ghettoization 3
Goethe Institute 166
Golobov, A. 72
Gomułka, W. 24, 147
Grabowski, J. 1
Great Synagogue, The 181–2
Grintal (Nachtigal), E. 55
Gross, G. 75
Gross, J. 26–7, 42, 109
Grunwald, M. 140
Guest for the Night, A (Agnon) 143–4, 174

Habsburg Empire, the 135
Hagen, W. 39
Hagen court 98–9, 102
hagshamah 194
Halevy, B. 113–15
Halpern, J. 91
Hammurabi's Code 140
Hanover, N. 50
Harvard's Society of Fellows 167
Haskalah 138–9
Hatsevi 138–9
Hebrew Bible 139–40
Hebrew University 194
Heiss, J. 67
Hemdat (Agnon) 139
Herschkowicz, S. 91
Hertmann, B. 92
Herzl, T. 136
Hilberg, R. 39–40
Himmler, H. 102, 196
Hirschkorn, J. 91
Historikerstreit 1
History, uppercase *H* and lowercase *h* 125–6
Hitler, A. 17, 19, 98, 146, 169
Hitler State, The (Broszat) 166
Hnatiuk, V. 182
Holocaust 1–2, 16
   anti-Semitic rationalization 35
   bifurcated scholarship 22–5
   communal massacres 14
   crimes 89–101
   denial 107, 116, 161
   extermination camps 14
   historical and geographical specificity 3
   historiography of 22–3, 27
   Israeli historians 170
   Jedwabne debate 27
   Jewish state renewal, Eretz Israel 152
   morality tales 13

Index

and Nakba 2–3, 6
perpetrators 86–9
politicization 2
recollections of 70
scholars 18
site 85–6
Uprising, the 113, 146, 166
Wehrmacht debate 27
Holodomor, the (as genocide) 105–6
Horowitz, G. 91
Hülsen 166

imperialism 14
incarceration 3, 23, 127, 156
industrial killing 12, 47, 66, 83
Investigation, The 38
Iraq 111, 188
Israel 2, 5, 41, 47, 59, 70, 75, 92, 94–5
 foundational denials 112–15
 legitimizing genocide 105–7
 Ukrainian-Polish-Israeli triangle 5, 112, 119
Israel Defense Forces (IDF) 114, 167
Israel-Palestine
 conflict 2–3
 displacement 151–61
 Jews and others 156–61
Italy 36, 92, 194
Itzik, D. 106

Jaffa 139, 174, 176–7, 185–6, 189–91, 193
Jagielnica 94
Jammasin al-Gharbi, al-(Jamusin) 171
Jedwabne debate 27
Jerusalem 7, 25, 38, 40, 73, 107, 114, 174, 177, 184–5, 193–4
Jewish Theological Institute, Vienna 139
Jews
 Borszczów execution 96
 of Buczacz, murder 4
 compassion for 35
 of Czortków 95
 Eastern Europe 21–43, 153–6
 image, Franko's fiction 136
 Israel-Palestine 156–61
 and local Gentiles relationship 23, 25
 murdering, during Nazi Germany 1–2, 4, 6
 in Second World War 2
 vanishing 157
Jezierzany camp 95
Josef, F. 136
Judaism 137, 140
judenfrei 86
Judenrat 75–7
Judenrein 55
Judensachbearbeiter 87, 90, 97

Judeo-Bolshevism 12, 108
Jury State Court of Hagen 98

Kafka, F. 128, 157
Kahane, B. 72
Kalisz 193
Kamionki camp 99, 101
Kanfer, A. 145
Kanfer, M. 145
Kasztner, R. I. 114
Kasztner trial of 1955 114
Katz, Y. 56, 68
Katzmann, F. 86, 89–90, 92–3, 98–9
Kazakhstan 58
Kaznovskyi, V. 74
Khmelnytsky, B. 50
Khvostenko, M. M. 57
Kielce 24
King Edward VII 144
Kitaj, E. 91
Klein, N. 92
Klonicki, A. 56
Knesset 106, 118
Köllner, K. 87–8, 90–1, 95–6, 100, 102
Koposov, N. 108
Kornelimünster 115
Kraków (Cracow) 24, 33, 88, 145
Kramer, B. 93
Kramer, J. 123
Krasiński, Z. 51
Kratter, B. 92
Kristallnacht pogrom 90
Kropotkin, P. 144
Krüger, F. -W. 88
Kupitz (Feldman), F. 67
Kurzweil, B. 175

labor camp 53, 55, 68–9, 73, 76–7, 86, 88–9, 91–4, 99, 124
Langer, A. (Dłuski, O; Ostenrode, O.) 6, 145–7
Langer, J. 145
Latin America 41
Leipzig 87
Lemberg 87–8, 90, 92, 98, 137
Lemkin, R. 11
Lenin 145
Leningrad 164
Le premier homme (Camus) 127
Lev, A. 51
Levi, P. 126–7, 129–31
lieu de mémoire 42–3
Lineal, M. 93
London Charter 84
Longuet, E. 146
Lozynsky, M. 144

Index

Lublin 88
Lwów (Lemberg, Lviv, Lvov) 145

Maksymiak, M. 184
Malorussia 154
Marx, K. 146
maskilim 51
mass murder 1–4, 12, 20, 22–3, 27, 32, 43, 47, 49, 54–5, 57, 71, 85, 99, 106–7, 151, 159, 166, 169–70
Mauscheln 157
Mäuschen 90
Mazower, M. 17
Meir, G. 202
memory laws 1, 3, 5, 105–19
   commemoration 116
   criminalization of denial 112–13
   Diaspora experience, the 116
   foundational denials, Israel 112–15
   legitimizing genocide 105–7
   Nakba law 117–18
   Poland and Ukraine 107–11
   Ukrainian-Polish-Israeli triangle 5, 112, 119
Merchant of Venice, The 137
Mielnica 89
Milošević, S. 49
Mincer, J. 56
modern violence 12–13, 20
Modiano, P. 128
Moravia 140
Morgenstern, H. 91
Moscow 144, 154, 164
Moses, A. D. 1
Moses and Monotheism (Freud) 141
Mosler, A. 6, 142–3, 145–6; *see also* Schützling, A.
Müller, D. H. 6, 138–40, 147
Munich accords of 1938 88
murder 1–4
murderer
   definition 84
   ideologically committed 99
   punishment 97
Murnau 166

Nacht, F. 141
Nacht (Naft), S. 6, 142–5
Nacht (Nomad), M. 6, 138–40, 145, 147
Nagórzanka 91
Nagórzanka labor camp 73, 94
Nakba (expulsion of Palestinians) 2–3, 6, 152, 160
Nakba law 117–18
Naor, M. 118
national consciousness 135, 137
National Socialism 16, 96–7, 100–1
National Socialist dictatorship 97, 101

National Socialist ideology 96, 98
Nazi Germany and the Jews (Friedländer) 128
Nazism 17
   anti-Bolshevik reconfiguration 17
   genocidal project 19
   genocide of the Jews 1–2, 4, 6, 12
   imaginaire 19
Neighbors (Gross) 26, 42, 109
Neinan, F. 93
Netanyahu, B. 167
Netherlands, the 41
New Zealand 41
Night and Fog (Resnais) 166
Night without End (Engelking and Grabowski) 1
None of Us Will Return (Delbo) 126
Nuremberg International Military Tribunal 37–8, 84, 99

Obama, B. 109
Ordnungsdienst (Jewish police) 48, 57
Organization of Ukrainian Nationalists (OUN) 52–3, 116
Ostjude 156
Ost und West 138
Ottoman Empire 154

Palestinian Declaration of Independence, 1988 152
Palestinian nationalism 199
Palestinians
   mass flight and expulsion (Nakba) 2–3, 6, 152, 160
   organizations 18
   Zionists 157–8
Panorama (Adler) 5, 123–33
Panzer troops 166
Paris 19, 144–6, 203
Pavlyshyn, T. 35
Peace Now 196
Peckmann, H. 86–7, 89, 102–3
Perec, G. 126–8
Perl, J. 68
perpetrators 47, 86–9
Petah Tikva 193
Petershofen 88
Petrykevych, V. 57
Pianist, The 125
Poland 5, 22, 24–6, 28, 33, 36, 39, 47, 50, 52, 54, 58, 65, 87, 92, 95, 106–12, 116, 119, 145–7, 154, 156, 174–5, 179–80, 186, 193
   memory laws 107–11
   Polish-Jewish coexistence 111
Polanski, R. 125, 129
Polish-Lithuanian Commonwealth 174
Pollak (Berkowicz), Z. 72–3, 76–7
Potocki, M. 51

243

Index

Potok Złoty 180–1
Prague 5, 71, 92, 123, 128–30, 135, 180, 185
Protective Edge 114
Prufer, S. 71
Prussia 164

Rabin, Y. 196
racial superiority 97
Raczymow, H. 128
radical Islamism 18
Ramat Aviv 171
Reawakening, The (Levi) 126
Red Army 34, 53–8, 71, 77, 86, 146, 168, 183, 197
Redlich, S. 42
rescue and resistance 70–7
Resnais, A. 166
Resnik (Herzog), A. 66
1848 revolution 135
Ringelblum, E. 52
Romania 19, 28, 164–5
Rosen, S. 73, 77
Russia 28, 41, 52, 59, 102, 106, 178
Rwanda 42, 170, 199

Saarbrücken court 102
Saarland 88
Sadat, A. 196
Saunders, J. 66
Scandinavia 41
Schorr, I. 92
Schultz, B. 178
Schützling, A. 143; *see also* Mosler, A.
Schwarz, A. 92
Schwebel, R. 91
scientific racism 14
Sebald, W. G. 126–30
Seifer, B. 76–7
Seldmann, J. 89
Seräth, O. 92
sexual abuse 67
Shabak, the 171
shatterzone of empires 6
Shaykh Muwannis, al- (Sheikh Munis) 171, 185–91
shelilat hagalut 112
Shoah Foundation 41
shtetl 48
Siberia 33
Siewiński, A. 51
Sipo outpost (Sicherheitspolizei Aussenstelle), Czortków 48, 53, 86–7, 89–90, 92, 102
Skamene, E. 71–2
Smilansky, Y. 160
social justice 142
South Africa 41

Spencer, H. 144
Spielberg, S. 41
Spielberg-Flitman, E. 56, 68–9
Stalin, J. 106, 146–7
Stanisławów 72, 141
Steiger, R. 71–2
Steigmann, N. 94
Strypa River 30, 75, 173, 180–1
sumud 117
Survival in Auschwitz (If This is a Man) (Levi) 126, 130
Świerszczak, M. 73–4
Switzerland 144
Synenka, O. 181
Synenkyi, I. 35–6
Sznajder (Huss), C. 73
Szpigiel, M. 56, 69
Szpilman, W. 125, 129
Szwarc, I. (Shikhor, Y.) 69
Śzwierszczak, M. 183

Taganrog 88
Tel Aviv 171
Tel Aviv University 164, 167, 171
testimonies
 benefit 61–2
 clarity and emotional impact 63
 collaboration, betrayal, and denunciation 65–70
 conventional documentation 62
 eyewitness 61
 historians and recorded accounts 65
 as historical evidence 62
 limitations 64
 personal accounts 62–3
 reliability 62–3
 rescue and resistance 70–7
 of trauma 64
 witness 95
Third Reich, the 39, 84, 96, 108–9, 115, 166
Thomanek, P. 88–9, 91–5, 97, 99–101
Thoroughfare (Durchgangsstraße [DG]) IV 88
Together and Apart in Brzeżany (Redlich) 42
Trembach, J. M. 57
trials
 "base motives" 84
 crimes 89–95
 elusive justice and historical truth 101–3
 judgments 95–101
 law 83–5
 life imprisonment 97, 99
 objective grounds 89
 perpetrators 86–9
 subjective grounds 89
Trotsky, L. 145
Truce, The (Levi) 127

Index

true memory, event 133–4
Tyśmienica (Tysmenitz, Tysmenytsya) 140

Ukraine 5, 27–8, 36, 41
    Holodomor 105
    legitimizing genocide 105–7
Ukrainian Insurgent Army (UPA) 54–5, 116, 183
Unbildungsroman
    distancing mechanisms 124
    First Man, The (Camus) 126–7
    History, uppercase *H* and lowercase *h* 125–6
    human catastrophe, world wars 129
    Le premier homme (Camus) 127
    Nazi Germany and the Jews (Friedländer) 128
    Panorama (Adler) 123–33
    panoramic detachment 125
    Survival in Auschwitz (Levi) 130
    Truce, The (Levi) 127
    true memory, event 133–4
United Nations' Genocide Convention 84
United States, the 41, 59, 70, 111, 143–5, 153, 157, 167–70, 182, 186
Uprising, the 113, 146, 166
US Holocaust Memorial Museum (USHMM) 40–1

victimization 12, 24, 79, 108, 111–12, 204
Vienna University 137–9, 141, 145
Vietnam 111
Volhynia 110
von Goethe, W. 147
von Werdum, U. 50
Vulitsa Agnona 177

W, or the Memory of Childhood (Perec) 126
Wachtel, I. (Shalev, Y.) 67
Waffen-SS *Totenkopf* 88
Wagner, R. 129
Waisman, M. 91
war crimes 12–13, 108–9, 114, 166

War of 1948 115, 200
Warsaw 39
Warsaw Ghetto 39, 52, 113, 146
Warsaw Ghetto uprising 113, 146
Wehrmacht debate 27
Wehrmachtsausstellung 195
Wehrmacht soldiers 12–13
Weiss, P. 38
Weissmann, A. 93
Weitz, H. 72
Weksler, G. 72
Western colonialism and hegemony 3
Western Russia 28
West Ukraine 21, 33, 41, 47, 106–7, 116, 156, 171, 178, 180–1, 184, 203; *see also* Buczacz
When Memory Comes (Friedlander) 126
Wiesenthal, S. 52, 182
Wilson, E. 145
Wizinger, M. 73–6
Wolf, S. 92
Wołkowicz, S. 94
Wrocław (Breslau) 41
Wulf, J. 39

Yad Vashem 25, 39–40, 73–4, 106–7, 115, 169, 178
Yarkon River 171
Yugoslavia 49
Yushchenko, V. 105–6

Zimmerer, J. 16
Zionism 6–7, 18, 25, 112, 142–3, 156, 201
    Buczacz 52
    colonization of Palestine 18
    conundrum of 157
    occupation policies of Palestinian lands 14
Złoczów (Zolochiv) 27
Zuroff (Tabak), R. 58, 69–70
żydokomuna 58, 108, 116